# Privatizing Public Lands

# ENVIRONMENTAL ETHICS AND SCIENCE POLICY SERIES

Kristin Shrader-Frechette, General Editor

*Acceptable Evidence:*
*Science and Values in Risk Management*
Edited by Deborah Mayo and Rachelle D. Hollander

*Experts in Uncertainty:*
*Opinion and Subjective Probability in Science*
Roger M. Cooke

*Regulating Toxic Substances:*
*A Philosophy of Science and the Law*
Carl F. Cranor

*Privatizing Public Lands*
Scott Lehmann

# PRIVATIZING PUBLIC LANDS

Scott Lehmann

New York   Oxford
OXFORD UNIVERSITY PRESS
1995

## Oxford University Press

Oxford   New York
Athens   Auckland   Bangkok   Bombay
Calcutta   Cape Town   Dar es Salaam   Delhi
Florence   Hong Kong   Istanbul   Karachi
Kuala Lumpur   Madras   Madrid   Melbourne
Mexico City   Nairobi   Paris   Singapore
Taipei   Tokyo   Toronto

and associated companies in
Berlin   Ibadan

Copyright © 1995 by Oxford University Press, Inc.

Published by Oxford University Press, Inc.,
200 Madison Avenue, New York, New York 10016

Oxford is a registered trademark of Oxford University Press

Library of Congress Cataloging-in-Publication Data
Lehmann, Scott.
Privatizing public lands / Scott Lehmann.
p.   cm. — (Environmental ethics and science policy series)
Includes index.
ISBN 0-19-508972-3
1. Public lands—United States—Management.   2. Privatization—
United States.   I. Title.   II. Series: Environmental ethics and
science policy.
HD216.L44   1995
333.1'6—dc20        94-12012

9 8 7 6 5 4 3 2 1

Printed in the United States of America
on acid-free paper

*To my parents, who took me there*

# Preface

> It rests with the philosophers to change people's ideas and ideals. The entrepreneur serves the consumers as they are today, however wicked and ignorant.
>
> Ludwig von Mises, *Human Action*

When people learn of my research on public lands and the privatization proposal, they generally respond with some variant of "Oh, I thought you were in philosophy" or "And what does that have to do with philosophy?" Their challenge can be met quickly, if superficially, by pointing out that recommendations, such as "Public lands should be privatized," are inescapably normative and therefore fall into the domain of ethics. Moreover, philosophers have always delighted in questioning customary ways of thinking, exposing obscurities in our concepts, and pursuing arguments to their foundations. Since most of the arguments for privatization come out of economics, it is economic concepts and arguments that receive most of this unwelcome attention here.

My own interest in privatization and, more generally, in the normative aspects of economics derives from long-standing environmental concerns. Nearly thirty years ago I joined the Sierra Club, which was then fighting proposals to build a couple of dams on the Colorado River within the Grand Canyon. I got involved in the debate at a letter-to-congressman level and was surprised to find that a good deal of it ran in economic terms. I suppose I was both uneducated and naive, but I recall having some trouble seeing what benefit–cost ratios, discount rates, electricity demand projections, and so forth had to do with what I felt when I viewed the canyon at sunrise, or hiked into its immensity, or watched the stars emerge in a narrow strip of sky over a remote beach. Only much later did I find out that some economists think you can attach a monetary value to such experiences—in terms of willingness-to-pay travel costs to the Grand Canyon, say—and also that some people are apparently quite unmoved by such things: former Interior Secretary James Watt once said of a Grand Canyon raft trip that by the third day he was praying for helicopters to come and take him out.

I soon found that there was nothing extraordinary about the Grand Canyon dam controversy, that in fact all environmental issues tend to get debated in economic terms. Maybe I should have stopped to wonder about this, but instead I just joined in, using appeals to economic considerations when they suited my purpose and trying to make trouble for the other fellow's appeals when they didn't. I was ready to remind legislators of the economic value of the agricultural sector in supporting a proposed agricultural land preservation program in Connecticut. I was ready to argue against extending Interstate 84 from Hartford to Providence by doing back-of-the-envelope calculations showing how slowly traffic would have to move on existing highways to justify construction of the expressway on a value-of-travel-time-saved basis. However, I was never entirely comfortable with this. For one thing, I really knew nothing about economics—I'd somehow managed to get a Ph.D. without the slightest academic exposure to economics. For another, it seemed a misrepresentation of my real concerns, a mere expedient.

Somewhere along the way I began taking a more critical interest in my own commitments. I started worrying about what justified my convictions about the importance of clean air, open space, wilderness, etc. On reflection, it seemed to me that it couldn't be any *rights* or *interests* that the environment has. I doubted that one could make sense of the idea that, unlike most humans and perhaps some animals, the environment had any rights or interests. Furthermore, it wasn't clear to me how ascribing rights or interests would help anyway, since environmental disputes seem to arise because interests and rights conflict. How would throwing *more* interests and rights into the fray help sort things out?

Still, even if only human—and perhaps animal—interests in the environment count, these interests seem to differ, from one individual to another and even within a single individual, and there remains the problem of resolving conflicts in the best way. I prefer Mineral King valley in California's Sierra Nevada in its present more-or-less wild state; others regret that Disney Enterprises didn't get the chance to develop a gigantic ski resort there. I like trees, but I also like them dead: I burn wood to heat my house, I own furniture made from huge trees. How should such conflicts be resolved?

Now some economists, I discovered, have ideas about this and are not shy about making recommendations. Their suggestions generally boil down to this: let each person resolve her internal conflicts as best she can—who, after all, is better situated to do this than the individual herself?—and then let the market resolve interpersonal conflict over resource use. The privatization proposal is of this kind, for a market would be created in the resources of public lands by the simple expedient of privatizing them.

The federal government owns quite a lot of real estate—hundreds of millions of acres, in fact—as National Parks, military bases, National Forests, National Wildlife Refuges, grazing districts, and so forth. A good deal of it is of little economic consequence: the feds own it because nobody wanted it, at least on their terms. But much of it is valuable for timber, pasture, mineral and energy deposits, and recreation.

Use of these lands and their resources is regulated by various government agencies acting under various statutes. As you can imagine, there has been a lot of conflict over how public lands should be used. Utah's Glen Canyon was a spectacular gorge; it was also a spectacular damsite. The Cabinet Mountains in Montana are a promising place to drill for oil and gas, but the associated blasting may drive away the endangered grizzly bears that live there. Should wild horses be removed from arid lands in Nevada so that more cows can be grazed there? Should a high-level nuclear waste repository be constructed just outside Canyonlands National Park? Should certain roadless areas in National Forests be roaded and logged, or should they be removed from the timber inventory by being placed in the Wilderness Preservation System?

Disputes of this sort are common and may be bitter. When one is resolved, another takes its place. Resolutions are frequently compromises that don't entirely satisfy anyone. The system requires a large bureaucracy to run. Lobbyists and bureaucrats may have quite a bit to say about how things turn out. So it is natural to wonder if there isn't a better way to allocate these resources. Enter the free-marketeer with the disarming proposal that the federal government simply sell them off to private interests.

What would this accomplish? According to proponents, resources would be utilized more efficiently. They would, by the unaided and natural operation of the market, be put to more highly valued uses, i.e., to uses people are willing to pay more for. In the case of old-growth forest in the Pacific Northwest, that could be wilderness or lumber, depending on consumer preference; and similarly for dams vs. wild rivers, cattle vs. wild horses, etc. Furthermore, these critics suggest, conflict over resource-use would diminish. If you want to do something with your property, well, that's your business. If I want to make it my business, then, at least in theory, I may do so only by making it worth your while.

When I first learned of the privatization proposal back in 1983, I thought it was quite crazy. I also thought it was interesting. What exactly was the argument for allocation by the market? Why was such allocation supposed to be superior to that achieved by political processes, broadly conceived? Were there some things that should be allocated by the market and others that should not, and if so, what distinguishes them? Could the privatization proposal be criticized by appeal to standard problems for the market: transaction costs, equity, externalities, public goods? Or was a more radical critique required, one which might undercut appeals to the market more generally?

Then again, maybe the proposal wasn't crazy after all. Maybe I just thought it was because I didn't like what I imagined would be its consequences for the environment and for us. I think the folks at Disney Enterprises were probably right in figuring they could make a lot of money out of developing Mineral King into a ski resort; could they possibly be outbid by the Sierra Club? Not likely, I thought. But why should what I like or don't like count for so much? After all, the skiers have their likes and dislikes, too. Isn't my preference for the use of Mineral King on a par with theirs? Am I saying we'll *all* be better off *whether we know it or not*, if a ski resort is not built? If so, why—and does that justify disregarding their wishes? If not, what is the justification for saying "No" to Disney?

Such questions drew me into this study. Some of them are peculiar to the privatization proposal, but many are of more general interest, or could be so framed. It is therefore my hope that this book will be of value, not only to those who are interested in public land policy, but also to those who are interested in policy analysis more generally. The issues I consider here lie at the intersection of public land policy, economics, and ethics. Few readers will be at home in each of these fields, so I have included some background material, mostly in Chapters 2, 4, and 6.

My initial research on privatization was done in 1984–85, when I was a Visiting Fellow at the Center for the Study of Values and Social Policy at the University of Colorado in Boulder. Fragments of my Working Paper "Privatizing public lands" (© 1985 Center for Values and Social Policy) have, with the Center's permission, been incorporated into this book. I learned more about economics when John Troyer and I taught a seminar on philosophy and economics at the University of Connecticut in 1987. I believe that Robert Simmons of the Environmental Protection Agency first suggested that I write a book on the privatization proposal. However, it would still be unwritten but for the kind interest and persistent encouragement of Kristin Shrader-Frechette. John Christman gave me valuable comments on an earlier draft; the sound advice of anonymous readers for the press has further improved the manuscript. I am grateful to my colleagues at the University of Connecticut for their support of a project which is not "real philosophy" and to my wife and daughter for not being too jealous of all the time I spent on it.

Finally, I thank the copyright owners for permission to make what may be more than "fair use" of material from the following sources:

Ludwig von Mises, *Human action*, © 1966 Contemporary Books, Inc., Chicago, IL.
"This land is your land," words and music by Woodie Guthrie, TRO—© Copyright 1956 (renewed), 1958 (renewed) and 1970 Ludlow Music, Inc., New York, NY.
Sterling Brubaker, ed., *Rethinking the federal lands*, © 1984 Resources for the Future, Washington, DC.
Richard A. Posner, *Economic analysis of law*, © 1972 Little, Brown and Company, Boston, MA.
Ronald Coase, "The problem of social cost," © 1966 The University of Chicago, Chicago, IL.
*Manhattan report on economic policy*, © 1982 Manhattan Institute for Policy Research, New York, NY.
Marion Clawson and Jack L. Knetsch, *The economics of outdoor recreation*, © 1966 Resources for the Future, Washington, DC.

Richard L. Stroup and John A. Baden, *Natural resources: bureaucratic myths and environmental management*, © 1983 Pacific Research Institute for Public Policy, San Francisco, CA.

William Niskanen, *Bureaucracy and representative government*, © 1971 William A. Niskanen.

*Storrs, Connecticut* S.L.
*March 1994*

# Contents

1. Introduction, 3

2. Federal Lands, Past and Present, 31

3. The Case for Privatization, 56

4. Productivity Standards, 81

5. The Productivity of Privatization, 109

6. Rationalizing Economic Values, 132

7. The Ethics of Privatization, 156

8. Self-interest and Collective Management, 179

9. Marketization, 201

    Index, 229

# Privatizing Public Lands

This land is your land, this land is my land,
From California to the New York island;
From the redwood forest to the Gulf Stream waters
This land was made for you and me.

As I was walking that ribbon of highway,
I saw above me that endless skyway:
I saw below me that golden valley:
This land was made for you and me.

I've roamed and rambled and I followed my footsteps
To the sparkling sands of her diamond deserts;
And all around me a voice was sounding:
This land was made for you and me.

When the sun came shining, and I was strolling,
And the wheat fields waving and the dust clouds rolling;
As the fog was lifting a voice was chanting:
This land was made for you and me.

As I went walking, I saw a sign there,
And on the sign it said "No Trespassing."
But on the other side it didn't say nothing,
That side was made for you and me. ©

Woody Guthrie[1]

# 1

# Introduction

I doubt that Woody Guthrie had public lands specifically in mind when he wrote "This land is your land."[2] But I am sure he'd be pleased that each American citizen, through the agency of the federal government, is part owner of some six hundred million odd acres, roughly one quarter of the nation's land.[3] To be sure, a good deal of it would strike most of us as uninviting and not at all "made for you and me." Guthrie couldn't have been thinking of the Great Basin when he wrote of "the sparkling sands of her diamond deserts." Even so, his words do fit the public lands. There we may be uplifted by natural wonders such as the Grand Canyon and what's left of the "redwood forest." There we are free to roam and ramble, for the signs read not "Private Property—No Trespassing" but "Please close the gate." There, far horizons and the "endless skyway" can release us for a time from the narrowness of our lives.

The federal estate is also rich in resources of a more conventional and coveted sort: timber, minerals, coal, oil, livestock forage, damsites, etc. Of course, sharing title with a couple hundred million other people would not give you or me much to say about how these lands and resources are used, even if they were managed by public referendum and not, as they are, by federal agencies. Except for weapons test sites and other military reservations, the public generally has free access to federal lands, but that does not mean that we may do whatever we like there. Private use is regulated in various ways. Rights to graze livestock, strip-mine coal, cut sawtimber, gather firewood, drill for oil, develop a ski resort, backpack into certain areas, excavate a prehistoric site, and so forth, are controlled by permit or lease, and some areas are closed to activities that some of us would dearly love to pursue.

Extensive public lands and resources, whose use is governed by regulations rather than the wishes of those willing to pay most to satisfy their desires, may seem anomalous in a country ideologically committed to individual freedom, private property, and the free market. "Why," as Robert Nelson puts it, "should land be an exception to the American consensus against government ownership?"[4] Some critics, in fact, see federal land and resource management as "socialism,"[5] afflicted with the usual problems of central economic planning. Arguing that we'd be far better off if "this land" were "your land" and "my land" in a stronger sense, they urge that federal lands be privatized. This proposal and its rationale are the subject of this book. In this introductory chapter, I shall provide some historical background, elaborate on why the idea is worth close examination, and indicate how I shall proceed with my inquiry.


## FEDERAL LANDS AND FEDERAL POWER

There are, of course, historical explanations for our huge federal landholdings and for the fact that they are generally not managed as a profit-maximizing firm would manage its assets. The federal government initially had no intention of retaining lands acquired through conquest, purchase, or agreement. Instead, it sold or gave them away to meet various obligations (e.g., debts incurred by the Revolutionary War) or to promote various objectives (e.g., railroads to serve the West). Eventually, for a variety of reasons—scandal and fraud in the disposal of federal land, fears of a "timber famine" excited by the ravages of cut-and-run lumbering practices, fortunes made from lands released for a pittance, the realization that the navy was buying oil at the same time that oil lands were being given away—the government came to have second thoughts and responded by reserving certain lands and resources from disposal. The remaining "public domain" continued to be open for entry under various disposal statutes until 1976,[6] by which time virtually all the land anyone wanted on the government's terms had been taken anyway.

Accordingly, the federal lands now fall roughly into two classes: (1) lands reserved or acquired for specific purposes and administered by specialized agencies—primarily, the National Parks, National Wildlife Refuges, and National Forests, administered by, respectively, the National Park Service (NPS), the Fish and Wildlife Service (FWS), and the Forest Service (USFS); and (2) the old public domain—the lands nobody wanted on terms Congress would agree to—administered by the Bureau of Land Management (BLM).

Whatever its historical rationale, federal land is a source or focus of tensions. Since most of it is in the West, the federal government owns a good deal of the West—82% of Nevada, for example.[7] The traditional mainstays of the region's economy—agriculture, mining, and timber—depend on federal resources and thus on federal resource policies, and Westerners sometimes feel that their way of life is leased from an absentee landlord. Statutes governing the use of federal lands are made in Washington, not in the capitals of western states, and increasingly reflect the interests and influence of those who are not ranchers, miners, or loggers. Even if statutes are relatively stable, their interpretation may not be: USFS and BLM lands are to be managed according to the principles of "multiple use and sustained yield,"[8] and decisions about how much weight to give uses such as recreation may reflect the demands of "outsiders."

The federal presence is threatening in other ways as well. To protect themselves from charges of malfeasance, federal managers often act by the book. For example, the BLM, which administers the General Mining Law of 1872, has declared mining claims "abandoned" because papers required to be filed "prior to December 31" were filed *on* December 31.[9] Much of the West is arid, and federal water projects have made its development possible. Unfortunately, few of them can be justified as national economic investments,[10] at least by tests acceptable to the Office of Management and Budget. Like any dependent, the West feels vulnerable, and a "hit list" of water projects drawn up by President Jimmy Carter was particularly upsetting. National security considerations have threatened to bring Westerners unwelcome neighbors. The Carter Administration proposed to use a couple hundred thousand acres of federal land in Nevada and Utah to construct a mobile basing system for 200 MX missiles. It also responded to the energy crisis by pushing for a crash synthetic fuels development program fed by huge federal coal and oil shale deposits; western governors, foreseeing unpleasant social and environmental consequences—strip-mines, boom towns, water-hungry conversion processes—charged that the West was being made a "national sacrifice area" for energy independence.[11]

The federal government is a sovereign power, not a mere proprietor.[12] It may condemn private property for public purposes, and has done so to liquidate private inholdings in National Parks.[13] Its lands and resources are not subject to state and local property taxes.[14] While federal policy is generally formulated to minimize conflict with state and local law, the federal goverment is free to chart a different course, secure in the knowledge that the (federal) courts will almost certainly resolve conflicts in its favor.

Thus, federal resource policy generally prevails over state and local land-use regulations. A lease to explore and develop oil and gas resources on federal land gives you a right to do what local zoning regulations might not permit if you *owned* the land.[15] Federal energy leases to tracts on the outer continental shelf (OCS) may be sold and developed regardless of state offshore drilling policy, coastal-zone management regulations, etc.; preferring "energy security" over "new federalism," the Reagan Administration promoted OCS leasing over the objections of states like California and Massachusetts.[16]

The states' broad authority to manage wildlife[17] is also limited by federal power. Private apple growers beset by hungry deer may not be permitted to shoot them, but the federal government can manage deer to protect its forests.[18] State predator control programs may reach onto private lands, but not into the National Parks, which stockmen sometimes complain are a safe haven for predators. Congress has asserted what amounts to a property right in the wild horses and burros that live on federal land;[19] ranchers who lease federal land for grazing consider them pests, consuming forage that would otherwise be allocated to their livestock. Species listed by the FWS as "endangered" may not be "taken," where "'take' means to harass, harm, pursue, hunt, shoot, wound, kill, trap, capture, or collect,"[20] presumably on non-federal as well as federal land.

Finally, under the 1977 Amendments to the Clean Air Act, many

National Parks and Wilderness Areas are Class I air quality areas, subject to "prevention of significant deterioration."[21] The Environmental Protection Agency (EPA) is charged with regulating emissions so as to maintain air quality, including visibility, over them. More generally, Congress's constitutional power "to dispose of and make all needful Rules and Regulations respecting the Territory or other Property belonging to the United States"[22] may permit regulating activity on adjacent non-federal lands, such as private inholdings in National Parks.

Sovereignty aside, the federal government wields enormous proprietary power as a very large and rich landowner. Locally, the USFS can put loggers and the communities that depend on them out of business simply by revising downward its annual allowable cut in a National Forest.[23] Since the National Forests contain half of the nation's softwood timber inventory, federal timber policies have national implications. Due largely to pressure from environmentalists, federal timber sales fell from 11.5 billion board feet (BF) in 1987 to 4.8 billion BF in 1992,[24] and many economists believe this decline is largely responsible for doubling the price of plywood and framing lumber over the same period. Furthermore, lumber prices affect not only individual mortgages for new homes, but the housing-cost portion of the consumer price index, an indicator that enters into wage negotiations, retirement formulae, and macroeconomic policy.[25]

In 1991, federal energy leases contributed about 17% of the nation's domestic crude oil production, 31% of its natural gas, and 26% of its coal.[26] Since activity is confined to geologically promising locations, local economic effects can be greater than these figures suggest. Since 1980, Congress has been wrestling with the issue of whether to lease the coastal plain of the Arctic National Wildlife Refuge for oil exploration and development, or to preserve its wilderness character.[27] Oil companies think the chances of finding a lot of oil there are good enough to justify spending a lot of money looking for it, and the state of Alaska is eager to have that money circulating in its depressed economy.

Although ranching is no longer a significant sector of the national economy, it is locally important and often dependent on federal forage. The USFS and BLM can effectively shut down ranching operations by reducing the number of stock permitted to graze parcels of BLM and National Forest land.[28] Or they can trade federal grazing land for private land elsewhere,[29] leaving the rancher in the position of the farmer whose rented cropland has just been sold to a suburban developer.

Federal land can also be reclassified so as to alter its permitted uses. "Wilderness" designation limits recreational opportunities for jeepers, trail bikers, and snowmobilers, since Wilderness Areas are closed to motor vehicles.[30] These people are likely to agree with a national coalition of motorized recreation groups that "Wilderness designation is not good for recreation."[31] Creation of a new National Park or Monument closes the area to hunting,[32] and lack of motorized access can, in effect, do the same for Wilderness Areas. This has led the National Rifle Association to go on record against "any further expansion of the National Wilderness System and National Park System."[33]


## THE SAGEBRUSH REBELLION AND BEYOND

In the late 1970s friction between federal management and local interests sparked a revolt of sorts—the Sagebrush Rebellion—by a loose coalition of western politicians and economic interests. The rallying position of these "Sagebrush Rebels" was the transfer of BLM land, the old public domain, to the states. It was rationalized by academic legal arguments,[34] some of which embellished legislative proposals.[35] Some mining, grazing, and timber interests, anticipating more favorable treatment from western statehouses than they were getting from the federal government, endorsed the land transfer. Environmentalists made the same assessment and opposed it. With the ascension of the Reagan Administration, the rebellion subsided. Interior Secretary James Watt's message to the rebels was essentially: "Cool it! In this administration, you can have everything you want from federal lands without a change in ownership."[36]

Among the fears that environmentalists expressed about the proposed transfer of federal land to the states was that the land would not remain public, that the states would in turn simply transfer title to private interests.[37] So it may be startling to learn that there are some who claim to be environmentalists and urge precisely that: public lands should be privatized. These self-styled "radical environmentalists,"[38] while sympathizing with the Sagebrush Rebels, argue that transferring certain federal lands to the states would not eliminate but merely relocate the real problem, which, in their view, is the collective ownership and management of resources.[39]

The environmental values of public lands, they insist, would be more secure if these lands were private. "Surely," they suggest to environmentalists, "*you* could do a better job of protecting National Forest Wilderness than the USFS does. Well, under our proposal, you'd do just that: these Wilderness Areas would be transferred to environmental organizations like the National Audubon Society.[40] And with privatization, even lands you don't own would be better managed. Consider those dams the Bureau of Wreck[41] puts up in places like Glen Canyon: nobody who had to borrow real money would do that.[42] Consider those Bureau of Livestock and Mining[43] 'land treatments' you dislike so much—chaining mile upon mile of piñon-juniper habitat and prehistoric Indian sites: ranchers who invested in such range improvements would be selected out by the market—it just doesn't pay in terms of forage produced.[44] Consider those USFS timber sales in fragile environments: much of that timber wouldn't be cut at all under private management, since the cost of getting it out is too great;[45] even where timber was cut, private owners would be more careful to avoid environmental damage, since that would diminish the market value of their land."[46]

So far, such appeals have been largely ignored by environmentalists. In fact, relatively few who take an interest in public land policy—whether they be environmentalists, land managers, independent policy analysts, land users, or legislators—have taken up the banner of privatization. On the contrary, most have dismissed this proposal as fantasy or heresy, or both, and its political reception has been chilly. In the heady early days of the Reagan Administration, advocates of privatizing federal lands were invited to Washington to serve on the President's Council of Economic Advisors (Steve Hanke, William Niskanen) and to direct the Department of the Interior's Office of Policy Analysis (Richard Stroup). At the time, President Reagan was interested in reducing the national debt and proposed selling off "surplus" federal property to do so. But the Reagan Administration's proposed Asset Management Program was dead on arrival in Congress. Questions, naturally, were raised about what this program portended. Richard Stroup found himself in the ironic position of having to disassociate it from his personal agenda; it was, he said, "a small, careful program involving land sales following extensive planning and public involvement" that had little to do with the privatization proposals advanced by "academics" like himself.[47] As is usual in Washington, these outsiders soon wearied of fighting the system and left for more congenial positions in conservative think-tanks and university economics departments. The privatization proposal largely disappeared from public view with them.[48]

Nevertheless, I think there are good reasons for spending my time and yours in a critical study of it. First, we have certainly not heard the last of the idea. Phillip Foss reminds us that in this country "[t]he losers in any particular policy dispute are not executed; they live on to fight another day."[49] More important, there are pressures here, both internal and external to federal land management, that may advance that day and insure the privatization proposal a more sympathetic hearing when it arrives. It would, I believe, be wise to give the issue some thought in advance. Second, even if the privatization proposal "is, for the moment, comatose," as Frank Gregg puts it,[50] the same cannot be said of some of the ideas behind it. In particular, the notion that resources are best allocated by a free market increasingly influences debate on federal land policy. A critical examination of the privatization proposal should help us to recognize such ideas in their various guises and to assess them before we have to live with their effects. Third, like other radical proposals, this one challenges us to reconsider ordinary ways of thinking and to ask if it is not, as Descartes suggests, "more custom and example that persuade us than any certain knowledge."[51] At least occasionally, people ought to be wakened from their "dogmatic slumbers"[52] and asked to consider what can be said for their commitments. The privatization proposal invites this sort of reflection, whether we regard it as heresy or gospel. I shall elaborate on these reasons in the next five sections.

## REDUCING CONFLICT

At present, there is little political interest in privatization, and the federal land-management regime looks about as secure as the Soviet regime did when Mikhail Gorbachev assumed power in 1985. But the comparison reminds us that even the unthinkable does occur, and divestiture is hardly unthinkable. During our first century as an independent nation it was government policy, and a hundred years of backing away from it have not killed the idea. Like the American chestnut, it keeps sending up sprouts. They will be nourished by scarcity, among other things.

Thomas Hobbes's claim that "the setting forth of public land . . . tendeth to the dissolution of government, and to the condition of mere nature, and war"[53] seems typically extravagant, but there is no doubt that public land management is a contentious business. More and more people want to use federal lands and resources, in ways that are difficult to reconcile, and it is natural to wonder if "letting the market decide" wouldn't be a better and far less costly method of allocating those scarce resources than fighting it out in Congress, in management agencies, and in the courts. To help illustrate this point, let's briefly consider a dispute, picked more or less at random, over water use.

Water on federal lands is generally not owned by the federal government. Congress made western water the property of the western states,[54] and they have settled conflicts over water use by some version of the *prior appropriation* doctrine: my putting $X$ units of unappropriated water to some "beneficial" use establishes my right to this use of $X$ units of water thereafter in perpetuity. However, federal land policy affects the allocation of water in two ways. First, in the arid West, federal irrigation projects—reservoirs to store runoff, canals to channel it to agricultural land—have often enabled individuals to initiate a beneficial use of, and therewith a right to, water. Second, some dedications of federal lands to particular purposes (e.g., Indian reservations) have been held to involve an implied appropriation of unappropriated water sufficient, if available, to serve those purposes.[55]

Unfortunately, there isn't sufficient water to meet all the obligations the federal government has created for itself in the West. The Truckee and Carson rivers used to carry snow melt from the Sierra Nevada into lakes and marshes in northwestern Nevada. But in 1902 the federal government decided to help reclaim the desert for agriculture, and the Truckee Canal now diverts water from the Truckee River into Lahontan Reservoir on the Carson River, from which it is released to irrigate pasture and cropland in the Lahontan Valley. The impact of these diversions on wetlands has been severe: over 120,000 acres have dried up, and the remnants are in trouble. The level of Pyramid Lake, through which the now much-diminished Truckee River flows, has dropped some eighty feet, endangering the cui-ui, an ancient species of fish that lives nowhere else and is culturally important to the Paiutes who live on the Pyramid Lake Reservation: shoals exposed at the river's inlet bar them from their upriver spawning grounds. Winnemucca Lake, which depended on overflow from Pyramid Lake, has vanished; designated a National Wildlife Refuge in 1936, it was completely dry two years later and the useless designation was revoked. Stillwater National Wildlife Refuge in the Carson Sink, an important desert stop for waterfowl on the Pacific flyway, is threatened. The water that formerly reached it now evaporates from irrigated fields or enters its marshes as drainwater loaded with toxic minerals leached from the soil, causing massive fish kills and grotesque deformities in waterfowl.[56]

The endangered fish in Pyramid Lake can perhaps be saved by diverting less water from the Truckee River; but less water diverted *from* Pyramid Lake means less water *to* Stillwater, unless water is also reallocated from irrigation to the refuge.[57] And moving water around isn't as easy as adjusting a sluice gate since current use reflects rights to water. All the water nature was likely to supply was apportioned between individuals, irrigation districts, and the Pyramid Lake Indian Reservation in 1944, after some thirty years of litigation;[58] none was set aside for fish or fowl. Legislation in 1990 authorized federal purchases of water from Lahontan Valley farmers to maintain 15,000 acres of wetlands at Stillwater,[59] but two years later drought had shrunk its marshes to 200 acres.[60] The cui-ui, which have been around for 17 million years, are given only an even chance of surviving the next two hundred.[61]

In cases like this it's tempting to wish government out of the resource allocation business entirely. Why not just make water a pure commodity and let various interests buy as much of it as they're willing to pay for? If Native Americans on the Pyramid Lake Reservation are too poor to buy water, then give them money and let them decide whether they want to use it to buy some for the cui-ui. Let the Audubon Society raise money from private donors to provide marshwater for the birds at Stillwater. Make Lahonton Valley farmers pay the full cost of their water delivery systems and bid against others for the use of scarce water, and then we'll see if it really makes sense to grow low-value, thirsty crops like alfalfa in the Nevada desert.

Privatization would hardly solve all the problems here. Since the natural supply of water varies annually and seasonally, it can't simply be divvied up in terms of perpetual rights to some definite amount per unit time. The complex body of law that now parcels out western water to private users provides a good living for hundreds of water lawyers. But privatization would remove a source of conflicting claims to water, claims undisciplined by a budget constraint. In general, privatization advocates view government power and resources as a source of problems. Various interests make demands on government resources, physical or financial, through a political process that does not require them to "put up or shut up" and thus, in the view of these critics, invites irresponsibility. Such conflicting demands are, of course, reconciled: budgets are adopted, and limited resources are allocated to various uses, but the required compromises are costly to attain and maintain. Furthermore, they frequently make little economic sense. This problem can be made to disappear only by making government disappear, hardly a realistic solution. But, advocates of privatization argue, it can be reduced by minimizing the resources controlled by government, for example, by privatizing federal lands.

## INCREMENTAL PRIVATIZATION

Whatever their intellectual appeal, arguments of this sort generally aren't sufficient to effect change. If public lands are to be privatized, enough of the right people must think it to be in their interest. Analysts like Nelson argue that the privatization movement of the early Reagan years, such as it was, failed because most federal land users feared they would lose by the proposed change.[62] The *de facto* rights they now have to use federal lands would, under this proposal, disappear, to be replaced by *de jure* titles vested in who knows whom. A smarter approach, Nelson suggests, would have been to convert these *de facto* rights into transferable *de jure* rights. Indeed, he imagines that this might come about quite naturally, albeit slowly and incrementally, as users who fear being displaced by rivals seek to secure from political erosion the gains they have made.[63] More generally, Gregg notes that federal lands "contain resources of increasing value to a growing population. Competition for the use of these resources will continue to lead advocates for various uses or control of management decisions or revenues to seek advantage in ownership."[64]

Incremental privatization is a goal of the so-called "County Movement," a successor to the Sagebrush Rebellion. The ranchers who initiated it want federal grazing permits recognized as private property,[65] so that the USFS or BLM may revoke or modify them only by compensating owners for lost revenue. Their strategy has been to encourage county governments to enact land-use plans supportive of a ranching, logging, and mining "culture" and to direct federal land managers to respect them. The interim land-use plan of Catron County, New Mexico, for example, stipulates that "[a]ll natural resource decisions shall be guided by the principles of protecting private property rights, protecting local custom and culture, maintaining traditional economic structures through self-determination, and opening new economic opportunities through reliance on free markets" and that "[f]ederal and state agencies shall comply with the county land use plan."[66] The rationale for the strategy is language in various statutes requiring that federal land-use plans respect important cultural values and be coordinated with those of state and local governments.[67]

The idea that the federal government is bound by decisions of county commissioners is unlikely to impress federal judges, who take seriously the supremacy clause of the U.S. Constitution.[68] But the intended audience for these county plans is probably the USFS and the BLM, their field personnel, and Congress, from which the County Movement hopes to secure policy changes favorable to its interests. Catron County, in fact, has offered to replace the USFS as manager of Gila National Forest rangeland within its boundaries.[69] There, as is typical in the West, grazing fees do not cover federal range-management costs. Ranchers worry about calls to end such "subsidies" by raising fees; they fear it will drive them out of business. They believe that the county can manage the land under contract at lower cost than the USFS, reasoning that reducing the perceived subsidy will secure their grazing rights from the threat of increased fees. No doubt they also reason that county range managers will be less inclined to regulate grazing to protect environmental values, regardless of what any contract says.

Incremental privatization is also on the agenda of the Wise Use movement, a loose coalition of groups formed to counter the influence of environmentalists on federal land policies. One of its goals is congressional enactment of "measures which recognize that private parties legitimately own possessory rights to timber contracts, mining claims, water rights, grazing permits and other claims."[70] A grazing permit, for example, is to be recognized as a private property right, freely transferable and alienable only with its holder's consent.[71] The contracts of National Park concessionaires are not to be abrogated.[72] A National Commodity Use System of federal land designations is to be created to "protect commodity uses forever" by limiting other activities to those consistent with the dominant commodity use.[73]

The Wise Use people are essentially asking for what they regard as theirs. Environmentalists, they think, have done no less: they have their Wilderness Areas and are greedy for more. David Hook of the United Four Wheel Drive Associations, for example, writes of an approaching recreation "crisis" on public lands as "the vast majority of public land users are being locked off of more and more of their National and State Forests and BLM lands" through the efforts of "selfish elites."[74] Now, few environmentalists would agree that federally designated "Wilderness" is *theirs* in any conventional sense, and fewer still would want their interest in it recognized as a property right. But this could change if they perceived such interests to be threatened. The Wise Use movement wants a much smaller Wilderness System;[75] suppose it prospers and succeeds in getting certain Wilderness designations revoked? Would environmentalists then be loath to claim a proprietary interest in what was left?

It hardly occurs to environmentalists to question federal ownership of land, although they do of course object to many management policies. Is this only because they have been relatively successful in getting federal managers to pay attention to their concerns, often at the expense of other user-groups such as ranchers and miners? Is it inconceivable that other interest groups might shoulder them aside in the future? They might do well to reflect on Marion Clawson's observation that "the wilderness groups currently place their faith in their political strength, as did the ranchers of a generation ago."[76]

## EXTERNAL PRESSURES

When a system generates conflict, it is natural, though perhaps naive, to think that there must be a better system. Those who notice that their interests in public lands would be protected if they were somehow converted into private rights may think that privatization will get us there. The contentious nature of public resource allocation is an internal source of pressure for change; but external factors will also help privatization advocates make their case. Socialism is discredited and under attack throughout the former Soviet empire. We will be invited to notice socialist structures within our own economy and to emulate our comrades to the East in dismantling them, and what, it will be suggested, could be a more obvious place to start than federal lands? Dissatisfaction with government in general, and the federal government in particular, appears to be increasing. There will be calls to limit the damage by putting the government out of business where it has no clear business being, and what, it will be suggested, could be a clearer example than the curious case of federal lands? Congress appears to be incapable of balancing the federal budget. Selling off unproductive assets may come to seem a relatively painless way to reduce the deficit, and what, it will be suggested, could be more unproductive than valuable real estate that soaks up billions of dollars in administrative costs?

Large-scale privatization is now underway in eastern Europe and the former Soviet Union. There we see governments extricating themselves (or being removed) from the business of growing crops. Yet here in the United States we have the USFS, a branch of the Department of Agriculture, very much in the business of growing trees for pulp, plywood, dimensional lumber, and other forest products, with, in the view of many critics, the same inefficiency we associate with collectivized agriculture. The USFS routinely sells timber at a loss, invests in reforestation at what amounts to a negative rate of return, and pursues its own version of Nikita Khrushchev's virgin lands program by extending logging operations into marginally productive roadless areas.[77]

Political change at home has also improved prospects for privatizing public lands. The Reagan Administration made it respectable to ask whether various services are really the responsibility of government and, if so, whether government should provide them or merely pay for them.[78] Indeed, President Clinton's Federal Highway Adminstrator has gone so far as to suggest that portions of the interstate highway system be operated as toll roads by private for-profit firms.[79] Privatizing public land is a special case of privatization in general, and it is likely that questioning governmental responsibilities and experimenting with contracting-out in other areas will eventually lead to changes in federal land policy. In fact, the USFS has proposed that the private sector run campgrounds in the National Forests on a profit-making basis, indicating that it would no longer resist "amenities" such as electricity, playgrounds, and swimming pools needed to attract paying customers.[80]

In addition, economic pressures are likely to help renew interest in divestiture. The President's Commission on Privatization suggests that "the most important force favoring a prominent future for privatization is the rapid pace with which a single world economy is developing and the intense competitive pressures thereby being created on each nation to rationalize its economic system."[81] What the commission means by "privatization" is primarily deregulation. But to the extent that federal land policy subsidizes marginal operations, imposes extra costs on competitive enterprises, or absorbs tax revenues, it is a candidate for "rationalization by deregulation." In the commission's view, the best way to "deregulate" federal land policy is to privatize federal lands.[82]

A more immediate concern is government red ink: a national debt of about $4 trillion in 1994, increasing by annual deficits of $200 billion and more. Faced with such politically unattractive options as further shrinking the military, restructuring entitlement programs, or raising taxes, who can be sure that Congress will continue to overlook the huge capital assets bound up in federal lands?[83] USFS and BLM lands were estimated to be worth about $500 billion in 1983, about half the national debt at the time.[84] After a decade of enormous deficits, their relative value has fallen to nearer a quarter of the debt. But we are still talking about a lot of money, and it is not out of the question that a comprehensive debt-reduction plan, should we ever settle on such a thing, will include liquidating some assets. If, as Nelson suggests, those who now enjoy the use of federal lands must in one way or another be paid off in order to privatize them, divestiture is not likely to contribute much to debt reduction. But such truths are probably too subtle to have much impact on public debate. In the past, privatization advocates have certainly viewed the "debt crisis" as an opportunity to advance their cause.[85]

Now one might wonder if selling assets to reduce debt really makes sense. After all, few people would sell their furniture simply to reduce the amount of their home mortgage. But perhaps it does make sense if we are not getting all that much out of federal lands. "What," Marion Clawson asks, "do the residents of [metropolitan New York] gain from the nearly $500 million they contribute annually [in taxes] to the management of the national forests, all of which are remote from this metropolis? Would the governor of New York state, the mayor of New York City, other appropriate local officials, and the various activist groups in the metropolis choose to spend this sum of money in this way, had they any real choice in the matter?"[86] If people begin to ask of federal land, "What's in it for us?," it may be that they'll demand a real choice in the matter and exercise it to unload an unproductive asset. The federal government's debt problems are likely to encourage such questions. Even policies that aim at such popular goals as environmental protection are now being questioned: "People want to know, even with the environment, what we are getting for our money."[87]

## MARKETIZATION

Privatization advocates claim that public lands would be better managed if they weren't public. They argue that free markets direct resources to their most productive uses; hence, privatizing federal lands would increase their productivity and free for other uses those resources now allocated to managing them. Many critics of federal land policy share this general outlook but, perhaps for political reasons, advocate not privatization but *marketization*:[88] if federal lands are to be retained, their resources should be allocated *as if* by a market. This close relative of the privatization proposal has had some impact on federal land-management policy and is likely to have more. Debate over the aims of resource policy increasingly revolves around it.[89] If the ideas behind privatization shape policy as well as debate, we will end up, for better or worse, with an approximation to privatization, albeit with nominal public ownership. From this perspective, privatization is a limiting case of policies now receiving serious attention, and we may hope to learn something useful about them by studying it.

The President's Commission on Privatization sees a general decline in enthusiasm for intervening in the market, even to correct for various "market failures."[90] The commission's observation is not disinterested, but it appears to be accurate. Government ownership or regulation were once standard prescriptions for problems of monopoly or externality, but many economists now wonder if such cures aren't worse than the disease. In cases where markets do fail in significant ways, they are apt to suggest that we think first of solving the problem by utilitizing market mechanisms.

For example, instead of controlling industrial air pollution by setting emission standards for various substances or requiring use of best-available emission-control technology, we should decide what total emissions of various pollutants we are willing to tolerate and then create a market in transferable emission allowances (TEAs) of various types and denominations: to release a ton of $SO_2$ into the air, you need a 1-ton $SO_2$-TEA, which you may purchase in the commodities market. This is not an academic proposal: the EPA is now overseeing an experimental program of this sort, to general applause.[91] Or instead of letting anyone fish in federal offshore waters and trying to maintain fisheries by limiting the season—sometimes to just a day or two per year, as in the case of Alaskan halibut—we might decide what annual harvest the fishery can support and then auction or otherwise distribute individual transferable quotas (ITQs): to bring in a ton of halibut, you need a 1-ton halibut ITQ, which you can bid for at auction or buy from someone else. This also is not an academic proposal: regional Fisheries Management Councils are now divvying up such rights among private fishermen.[92]

Writing in the popular press, Joe Klein suggests that "with the collapse of socialism, the environment has become the last refuge of the left. It is the last hope for those offended by commerce, the last stand for central-planning busybodies."[93] Environmentalists are often placed on the left, but they too have become increasingly interested in using market incentives to achieve their goals. The Environmental Defense Fund is largely responsible for the EPA's experiment in pollution-rights trading. In hopes of reducing overgrazing on federal lands, the Sierra Club has declared its support for market pricing of federal grazing permits.[94] More generally, Peter Berle, President of the National Audubon Society, urges the Clinton Administration to "get the prices right;" in his view, "below-cost timber sales, below-market grazing fees, over-subsidizing water for agricultural uses, [and] giving away minerals . . . are policies that waste and misallocate public resources."[95] The Clinton Administration did, in fact, subsequently propose to reform federal land policy by increasing fees for timber, forage, water, minerals, and recreation.[96]

With slight modifications—delete "over-" and the reference to giving minerals away—Berle's remark could have been made by an advocate of privatization. If privatization is not politically feasible, then marketization may be advanced as a second-best solution. If the federal government is to retain its lands, let us at least discipline claims on them by requiring that would-be users bid against one another. Economists have had some success in getting Congress to endorse this idea. For example, the BLM is to insure that "the United States receive fair market value of the use of the public lands unless otherwise provided for by statute."[97] This falls rather short of endorsing marketization, since land management statutes contain a lot of directives that don't seem motivated by, or clearly consistent with, a concern for maximizing the productivity of federal lands and the resources investing in managing them.[98] Nonetheless, directing federal managers to *think* in economic terms (e.g., to prepare Renewable Resource Assessments containing "an evaluation of opportunities for improving their yield of tangible and intangible goods and services, together with estimates of investment costs and direct and indirect returns to the Federal Government"[99]) will presumably move them in the direction of *acting* accordingly. Pressure from environmentalists for market pricing of those goods and services they'd prefer to see less of, selective though it may be, is likely to encourage this trend. While the Clinton Administration's proposals for increasing user fees were withdrawn under pressure from western interests,[100] many observers believe that reform of this sort is inevitable.[101]

## REASSESSING COMMITMENTS

Radical proposals like divestiture invite us to confront and reassess our commitments. The most obvious challenge here is to those who, while perhaps objecting to various federal land-management policies, are nonetheless comfortable with the current system for arriving at them. We should thank advocates of privatization for reminding us that this system is not the only possible one and for challenging us to say what it is about it that justifies allegiance. But we should also scrutinize the case for privatization, asking whether it would, in fact, promote economic rationality and why economic rationality is worth promoting. So let us note some questions that the privatization proposal raises for environmentalists, for those who oppose divestiture but favor marketization, and, finally, for its advocates.

Environmentalists do not trust federal resource managers, but they trust the private sector even less. Is their mistrust misplaced? Perhaps, as privatization advocates claim, the environmental problems of the frontier, to which current public land policy is in part a reaction, were due not to the presence of private property but to its absence, to the fact that federal lands were in effect a commons. Perhaps also these days there's sufficient demand for environmental quality to render it secure in the marketplace. After all, we're richer than our ancestors and can afford it; furthermore, we understand better than they did the economic costs of environmental destruction. Is it crazy to imagine that the environmental values of federal lands would get at least as much respect from private owners as they now do from federal managers? And if not, maybe the rest of us should conclude that these values are not as great as environmentalists would have us believe. Perhaps environmentalists have no right to arrangements they could not achieve and maintain under privatization. Environmentalists do worry about elitism, but perhaps they don't worry enough. What animates the Wise Use movement, in addition to corporate funding, is the feeling that public land policy now reflects "overwhelming domination by large powerful environmental organizations" that represent the interests of "the highly sensitive and elite nature lover" to the exclusion of "the general unaffiliated public."[102]

It is not only the assumptions of environmentalists that the privatization proposal challenges, but also those of critics who argue not for privatizing public lands but for marketizing their management. Why don't these folks have the same agenda as advocates of privatization? Arguments for privatization seem to be applications of more general arguments for the free market: roughly, resources are best allocated to competing uses by individuals freely exchanging private property in a free market. *So why not the best?* Why settle for trying to manage public lands *as if by a market* when we can have the real thing with less cost and effort? Setting politics aside, the standard reply points out that resources are perfectly allocated only in perfect markets and that privatization would lead to imperfect markets; theoretically, then, federal managers can improve on the performance of private owners. But why should we expect this to happen in practice? And what about policies that can't be rationalized as correcting for market failures? Should they be reformed so as to maximize net benefits to consumers, as might be appropriate if the governing vision were a perfectly competitive market, or can they be defended in different terms?

Finally, the privatization proposal invites questions about *its* rationale. The central appeal here is to productivity: public lands should be privatized because resources are utilized more productively when they are privately owned. This argument raises a number of interesting and difficult issues.

1. What is meant by "productivity?" Imagine two different patterns of use, *I* and *II*, for a batch or flow of resources (e.g., let *I* preserve a bit of old-growth forest and *II* convert it into lumber). What does it *mean* to say that *I* utilizes it more productively than *II*? For economists, resources are means to human ends; one use is better than another insofar as it better satisfies our desires. This helps some, but not much. I may be able to say that, all things considered, I prefer *I* over *II* because, on balance, *I* better satisfies *my* desires than *II*. But suppose *you* make the opposite judgment. What are *we* to say about the relative productivity of *I* and *II*? We might decide to say nothing: in cases like this, neither use improves on the other. Since most cases are like this, we are then in the position of being able to say nothing useful about relative productivity in most cases. Alternatively, we might propose that *II* improves on *I* if those who gain from a shift from *I* to *II* are, in aggregate, willing to pay more than what those who lose are, in aggregate, willing to accept to make good their loss. How is such a standard to be applied, and how can we satisfy ourselves that it is coherent?

2. Would the market in federal resources created by privatization really increase their productivity? In idealized economic models, markets direct resources to their most productive uses. But externalities and transaction costs, among other things, may block such allocations in real markets. To what extent can public land policies be regarded as responses to this problem? Theoretically, productivity can be increased in the face of production externalities by merging firms; can the multiple-use principles by which the USFS and BLM are to manage their lands be regarded as effecting such a solution to the externalities that might result from private ownership (e.g., runoff from my mine tailings poisoning your cows)? Is it ridiculous to imagine that democratic institutions might be better than markets at assembling and acting on certain kinds of information? Do the National Parks, for example, represent a purchase that consumers would, in fact, collectively make in a free market, if only it did not cost so much to marshall their dispersed willingness-to-pay? If certain public land-management policies can be regarded as attempts to correct such market failures, can they be so justified? Does multiple use *maximize*, or even *increase*, the net value of joint output?

3. Assuming that it's good to put resources to their most productive use, whatever that means, is that the only good? All standard characterizations of productivity appear to permit *II* to be productively superior to *I* although the fruits of *II* are distributed much less equally than those of *I*. Are resource allocations that are in some sense more equal more desirable? If so, perhaps we should arrange for them, even at some cost to productivity. Can some aspects of federal land management be regarded as serving equality? Few Boston-area residents could afford beachfront property on Cape Cod, and practically nobody could afford enough of it to preserve a sense of solitude and space; yet they can walk wild beaches at Cape Cod National Seashore at no charge. Perhaps their aggregated willingness-to-pay exceeds the astronomical current market-value of this land, so that

federal ownership is, by some measure, productive. If not, does it follow that the National Seashore is not a productive asset and should be liquidated? Willingness-to-pay depends in part on ability to pay; should our opportunities be limited by that, if we can arrange otherwise?

4. What precisely *is* good about greater productivity? All standard accounts of productivity are grounded in individual preference: it is assumed that, if you prefer *II* to *I*, then *II* is better than *I* so far as you are concerned. But what is good about getting what I prefer? Judas presumably preferred 30 pieces of silver to being a disciple of Jesus; was he better for the exchange in *any* way? It appears not to have made him happy. And if it had, wouldn't we think him even *more* foolish and loathsome? Can some public land-management policies perhaps be defended in terms of helping people to be *better* than they might be, if left to pursue what they want in a free market? Can preserving what's left of the "redwood forest" be justified because it's *better* for people to walk through redwood groves than to eat from redwood picnic tables, even though they might collectively be willing to pay more for the latter than the former? Or does such a value judgment reflect only a personal preference for standing timber over dimensional lumber?

5. Is some of what's attractive about more productive allocations of resources a matter of their history, the fact that they typically result from the autonomous actions of individuals in free exchange? Would you frequent a restaurant where, magically, your waiter brought you just what you'd most enjoy — within your budget, of course—without your having to deliberate and choose? If some of our interest in productivity derives from an interest in participation, are we interested only in participating in markets? Can we distinguish our interest in equality from our interest in having something to say about what it is and how it's implemented? Would having a philosopher king do it for us be just as good? Do we care only about the *results* of federal land management, or are we also interested in participating in the processes which lead to them? Can policies that don't make much sense in *other* terms be justified by appeal to those processes?

## ASSESSING THE PRIVATIZATION PROPOSAL

As some of these questions will suggest, I think that privatization promises more in the arguments of its advocates than it would actually deliver. I also believe that what's promised is not really as appealing as it may at first seem. My general strategy in this study will be to develop arguments for privatization to the point where their weaknesses are apparent and then to exploit them to make a case for continued federal ownership.

In Chapter 2, I review the history of federal lands and their current status, indicating what agencies are responsible for what lands under what statutory authority. Readers who do not need this background may skip to Chapter 3, where I present arguments for privatization without much critical comment.

Those who advocate privatizing public lands appeal mainly to productivity. In my view, there is no sense of "productivity" for which it is both clearly true that privatizing public lands would increase their productivity and clearly desirable that productivity be increased. Chapters 4 and 5 concern the productivity of privatization, Chapters 6 and 7 the issues of desirability. In Chapter 4, I examine the notion of productivity in general: when its advocates claim that privatization will increase productivity, what can they mean? In Chapter 5, I consider what they have said to support this thesis and argue that we should be skeptical of it. In Chapter 6, I review general ethical conceptions that seem to provide a "natural habitat" for privatization arguments: the appeal to productivity suggests a rule form of preference utilitarianism (private property maximizes the satisfaction of desires), while less-prominent appeals to individual freedom suggest a more Kantian outlook (private property secures the integrity of persons). In Chapter 7, I consider normative aspects of arguments for privatization against this background.

In the final two chapters, I answer some of the criticism privatization advocates level at the current system and make a case for continued public management, a case that suggests departures from marketization.

I conclude this introduction with a few qualifications and warnings to the reader. First, I have had to develop a good deal of the argument for privatization that I criticize here. Most of the privatization literature is of a semi-popular nature that relies heavily on argument from anecdote, that is, selected environmental atrocities perpetrated by federal land managers are contrasted with showcase examples of responsible private management.[103] Critical normative assumptions are never defended; they are apt to go unnoticed or to be mistaken for empirical claims.[104] Much of the argument, particularly at the level of general principles and commitments, has to be filled in. I hope that my development of the privatization proposal has not been *too* creative. While I have tried to be fair to the intentions of its advocates, it may be that some of the problems I construct are problems only for arguments they would not advance.

Second, a good deal of the discussion in this study occurs at some distance from public lands. Privatization advocates do not answer the question "How should public lands be managed?" by proposing, for our approval, a giant management plan. Rather, they argue that the current system of institutions for allocating particular parcels to particular uses is inferior to a system of private property rights. At issue, then, are the relative merits of rival institutional systems and the standards by which merit is to be judged. The uses to which such systems put, or would put, public lands are relevant only insofar as they inform that debate, and that is less than one might think. Where possible, I use federal land policies for illustration, but they are not the subject of this work, and readers who expect to learn something of immediate value in understanding and resolving conflicts over the use of public lands or in reforming management agencies will be disappointed.

Third, I shall have little to say about privatization as a process. When people advocate privatizing public lands, they have in mind transferring them to the private sector. Typically, the administrative details of such a massive undertaking are left to the imagination. In part, this is because advocates of privatization believe that "[t]he best reason for the private management of natural resources is to promote economic efficiency."[105] If efficiency (i.e., productivity) is the promised land, what difference does it make how we get there? What suggestions are made tend to be directed to calming potential opposition; recall the suggestion that National Forest Wilderness be given to conservation groups. A striking exception to the general preoccupation with ends rather than means is Vernon Smith's scheme for large-scale public land auctions in which the currency is scrip issued to each American citizen.[106] However, I shall leave consideration of this proposal, fascinating as it is, to those who have more faith than I do that it would achieve something worthwhile. Instead, I shall follow most privatization advocates in ignoring problems of how to get from here to there and concentrate instead on what might be said for or against the move.

Fourth, since I am interested in what, if anything, arguments for privatization justify, I shall be vague about what lands are included in the privatization proposal. It is, of course, possible to urge that only, say, BLM lands be privatized. But then one wants to know: why these? Perhaps for political reasons, privatization advocates have avoided talking about privatizing such public lands as the National Parks. But if an exception is to be made for them and other special "national interest" lands, then it should be a principled exception, not an expedient one. At first glance, arguments for allocating resources by markets appear to underwrite a fairly strong version of the proposal: whatever *can* be privatized without excessive cost *ought* to be. This appears to include not just BLM lands but virtually all federal lands—the National Forests, National Parks, Wildlife Refuges, Historic Battlefields, perhaps even military reservations (lease them)—as well as lands owned by state and local governments. Perhaps a closer look at these arguments will modify this conclusion, for example, by revealing serious imperfections in the market that would result from privatizing such lands. If so, we could then ask how much public ownership can be justified by appeal to the notion of correcting for market failures. Like privatization advocates, I'll discuss privatization in terms of federal lands, primarily those managed by the BLM and the USFS. But this emphasis should not be interpreted as suggesting that a principled case can't be made for privatizing other public lands, both federal and non-federal.

## NOTES

1. Woody Guthrie, "This land is your land," Ludlow Music, New York. There are two additional stanzas:

In the shadow of the steeple I saw my people,
By the relief office I seen my people;
As they stood there hungry, I stood there asking
Is this land made for you and me?

Nobody living can ever stop me
As I go walking that freedom highway;
Nobody living can ever make me turn back,
This land was made for you and me.

2. In fact, the song was Guthrie's response to Irving Berlin's "God bless America." In its original version, each stanza ended with "God blessed America for me." The fifth stanza originally came fourth and began

Was a big high wall there that tried to stop me
A sign was painted said: Private Property.

For a photocopy of Guthrie's manuscript, see Joe Klein, *Woody Guthrie: a life* (New York: Knopf, 1980), at 447.

3. The Director of the Bureau of Land Management (BLM), which managed some 269 million acres of federal land in FY1991, concludes his introduction to *Public land statistics 1986* (Washington: BLM, 1987) with "I urge every citizen to take pride in America, because this land is *your* land."

According to *Public land statistics 1991* (Washington: BLM, 1991), Table 4, the federal government owned 662 million of the nation's 2,271 million acres as of FY1989. When transfers to Alaska and its native peoples authorized by the Alaska Statehood Act of 1959, 72 Stat. 339, and the Alaska Native Claims Settlement Act of 1971, 43 U.S.C.A. §§1601–24, are completed, federal holdings will drop to about 630 million acres. In addition, the federal government owns the minerals below about 60 million acres of private surface, having retained the subsurface rights when it disposed of the land. The Coal Lands Act of 1909, 30 U.S.C.A. §81, specified that agricultural patents issued subsequently (e.g., under the Homestead Act of 1862, 12 Stat. 392) should not convey coal. Later land-disposal statutes also contained reservation language; e.g., the Stock-Raising Homestead Act of 1916, 39 Stat. 862, reserved "coal and other minerals." The federal government also asserts control over the resources of the outer continental shelf (OCS) beyond three miles offshore. In *United States* v. *California*, 332 U.S. 19 (1947), the Supreme Court ruled that submerged offshore lands were owned by the United States rather than by the several coastal states. Congress subsequently ceded the 0–3 mile offshore zone to them in the Submerged Lands Act of 1953, 43 U.S.C.A. §§1301–15, but asserted federal control over the OCS beyond three miles in the Outer Continental Shelf Lands Act of 1953, 43 U.S.C.A. §§1331–43.

4. Robert H. Nelson, "The subsidized sagebrush: why the privatization movement failed," *Regulation* 8(4) (1984), 20 at 22.

5. Barney Dowdle, "Why have we retained the federal lands? An alternative hypothesis," in *Rethinking the federal lands*, ed. Sterling Brubaker (Washington: Resources for the Future, 1984), 61–73 at 63.

6. In the Federal Land Policy and Management Act of 1976 (FLPMA), 43 U.S.C.A. §§1701–84 at §1701(a)(1), Congress declared that "it is the policy of the United States that . . . the public lands shall be retained in Federal ownership."

7. For other western states, the percentages are approximately: Utah 64%, Idaho 63%, California 61%, Alaska 59% (after transfers, note 3 *supra*; in FY1989, 68%), Wyoming 49%, Oregon 48%, Arizona 43%, Colorado 34%, New Mexico

33%, Washington 29%, Montana 28%. *Public land statistics 1991*, note 3 *supra*, Table 4. The federal percentage is computed by (1) excluding from federal property Indian lands and reservations legally owned by the federal government but managed in trust for various Native American tribes, totalling some 50 million acres nationwide, and (2) excluding from land within state boundaries both offshore lands and land beneath navigable streams and lakes, the latter ruled to be state property in *Pollard* v. *Hagen*, 44 U.S. (3 How.) 212 (1845).

8. FLPMA, note 6 *supra*, at §1701(a)(7). National Forest Management Act of 1976 (NFMA), 16 U.S.C.A. §§1600–14 at §1601(d)(1).

9. *U.S.* v. *Locke*, 471 U.S. 84 (1985).

10. See, e.g., Charles W. Howe, "Project benefits and costs from national and regional viewpoints: methodological issues and case study of the Colorado — Big Thompson Project," *Natural Resources Journal* 27 (1987), 5–20.

11. For a restrained statement, see Richard D. Lamm, "Out West Worries," *The New York Times*, 12 August 1980, 19.

12. In *Camfield* v. *United States*, 167 U.S. 518 (1897), the Supreme Court held that the federal government has "a power over its property analogous to the police power of the several States." In *Light* v. *United States*, 220 U.S. 523 (1911), the Court barred Fred Light's cows from the USFS's Holy Cross Reserve without a permit. Had the federal government been just a proprietor of the reserve, it would, under prevailing Colorado estray law, have been required to fence its property against such intrusions. See also note 19 *infra*.

13. The federal right of eminent domain is derived by implication from the Fifth Amendment to the Constitution, which directs in part "nor shall private property be taken for public use without just compensation." Condemnations within what is now Voyageurs National Park are mentioned in *Izaac Walton League of America* v. *St. Clair*, 353 F.Supp. 698 (D. Minn., 1973).

14. The constitutional basis is the "supremacy clause" (Article VI, Paragraph 2), which declares the laws of the United States to be "the supreme law of the land." Following *McCulloch* v. *Maryland*, 4 Wheat. 316 (1819), the Supreme Court ruled in *Van Brocklin* v. *Tennessee*, 117 U.S. 151 (1896), that non-federal power to tax federal property was inconsistent with the supremacy clause, since it could be used to vitiate the will of Congress. However, in *Commonwealth Edison Co.* v. *Montana*, 453 U.S. 609 (1981), the Supreme Court upheld Montana's severance tax on federal coal mined under lease, holding it to be a tax on extraction and not on the coal itself.

In what might be considered payment in lieu of taxes, a significant fraction of federal resource revenue goes to counties and states. Thus, counties receive 25% of the receipts from National Forest timber sales within their boundaries, 16 U.S.C.A. §500, and states receive 50% (Alaska, 90%) of the revenue from federal oil and gas leases under the Mineral Leasing Act of 1920, as amended, 30 U.S.C.A. §§181–287 at §191.

15. In *Ventura County* v. *Gulf Oil Corp.*, 601 F.2d 1080 (9th Cir., 1979), the Court of Appeals ruled that Gulf was free to develop its oil and gas leases in Los Padres National Forest, even though Ventura County had zoned the area Open Space, a designation that precluded such activity without a permit. However, in *California Coastal Commission* v. *Granite Rock Company*, 480 U.S. 572 (1987), the Supreme Court ruled that, while states may not block mining operations on federal lands, they may impose reasonable environmental conditions on them.

16. In the matter of OCS leasing, the Reagan Administration merely continued the policies of the Carter Administration. Cf. *Commonwealth of Massachusetts* v.

*Andrus*, 594 F.2d 872 (1st Cir., 1979) and *Massachusetts* v. *Andrus*, 481 F.Supp. 685 (D. Mass., 1979).

17. In *Geer* v. *Connecticut*, 161 U.S. 519 (1896), the Supreme Court ruled that states could regulate the export of game without usurping Congress' constitutional power to "regulate commerce with foreign nations, and among the several states, and with the Indian tribes" (Article I, Section 8, Paragraph 3), because wildlife was state property.

18. In *Hunt* v. *United States*, 278 U.S. 96 (1928), the Supreme Court affirmed the USFS's right to protect the Kaibab National Forest by killing deer over the objections of the State of Arizona (whose predator control policies were doubtless responsible for the threat).

19. Wild, Free-Roaming Horses and Burros Act of 1971, 16 U.S.C.A. §§1331–40. In *Kleppe* v. *New Mexico*, 426 U.S. 529 (1976), the Supreme Court ruled unanimously that Congress had constitutional authority to manage wild horses on public lands, although under New Mexico law these animals could be rounded up and sold at auction for dog food.

20. Endangered Species Act of 1973, 16 U.S.C.A. §§1531–43, at §1532(19) and §1538(a)(1). Listing the northern spotted owl as a "threatened" species (26 June 1990) may endanger logging on some private and state lands in the Northwest, because (1) threatened species may not be taken either, 50 CFR 17.31(a), (2) owls reside in old-growth forest on these lands and apparently cannot adapt to second-growth, and (3) "harass" and "harm" are understood to include "habitat modification or degradation" that kills or injures wildlife, or is likely to do so, "by significantly impairing essential behavioral patterns, including breeding, feeding or sheltering," 50 CFR 17.3. One timber advocate claims that "thousands of acres of state and private lands are frozen from [timber] harvest due to the spotted owl situation." Larry Mason, "Washington—resources, responsibilities" (Forks, WA: Washington Commercial Forest Action Committee, 1992), at 6.

21. 42 U.S.C.A. §§7470–91. These provisions have less force than one might think, since (1) they are supposed to prevent further deterioration of air quality, not improve it, and the air in some parks is already very bad indeed, and (2) a great many sources of pollution usually contribute to deterioration in air quality. See *Air quality in the National Parks: a summary of findings from the NPS Air Quality Research and Monitoring Program* (Denver: NPS Air Quality Division, 1988); "Pollution shrouding national parks," *The New York Times*, 3 December 1989, E19; and Craig N. Owen, "The protection of parklands from air pollution: a look at current policy," *Harvard Environmental Law Review* 13 (1989), 313–422.

22. U.S. Constitution, Article IV, Section 3, Paragraph 2.

23. NFMA, note 8 *supra*, at §1611.

24. Over the same period, National Forest timber harvests declined from 12.7 billion BF to 7.3 billion BF (sawtimber from 9.2 billion BF to 5.3 billion BF). Figures from *Timber sale program annual report: fiscal year 1987 test* (Washington: USFS, 1988), Table 2; and *Timber sale program annual report: FY 1992* (Washington: USFS, 1993), at 21.

25. Marion Clawson, *The federal lands revisited* (Washington: Resources for the Future, 1983), at 84.

26. *Mineral revenues 1991* (Washington: Minerals Management Service, 1992), Table 9.

27. Under provisions of the Alaska National Interest Lands Conservation Act of 1980 (ANILCA), 16 U.S.C.A. §§3101–233, at §§3142–43, it is closed to leasing

pending Interior Department study of the effects of oil and gas leasing on wildlife and congressional action on its recommendations. See Timothy Egan, "The great Alaska debate: can oil and wilderness mix?," *The New York Times Magazine*, 4 August 1991, 20.

28. Such authority has been affirmed in *Perkins* v. *Bergland*, 608 F.2d 803 (9th Cir., 1979).

29. Cf. *LaRue* v. *Udall*, 324 F.2d 428 (D.C. Cir., 1963).

30. Wilderness Act of 1964, 16 U.S.C.A. §§1131–36, at §1133(c). USFS authority to exclude motor vehicles from administratively designated "Primitive Areas" prior to passage of the Wilderness Act was affirmed in *McMichael* v. *United States*, 355 F.2d 283 (9th Cir. 1965).

31. Letter from Blue Ribbon Coalition, Inc., in *The wise-use agenda*, ed. Alan M. Gottlieb (Bellevue, WA: Free Enterprise Press, 1989), 36–43 at 38.

32. *United States* v. *Brown*, 552 F.2d 817 (8th Cir., 1977). For example, a proposal to join Carlsbad Caverns and Guadalupe Mountains National Parks is opposed by local interests because hunting and grazing now allowed on the USFS and BLM land in between these Parks would be prohibited if it were transferred to the NPS. Kathy Kiely and Karen MacPherson, "Texas Congressman stirs up New Mexico," *High Country News*, 31 May 1993, 3.

33. Resolution dated 27 April 1987, reprinted in Gottlieb, note 31 *supra*, 35–36 at 36. Hunting and fishing per se are unaffected by Wilderness designation, but, as Hildamae Voght of the California Outdoor Recreation League remarks: "Oh yes, you could go hunting and fishing, but how far can you carry a deer?" Id., at 136.

34. Acts of Congress by which new states are admitted to the Union typically specify that the new member joins on an "equal footing" with the original states. The federal courts have interpreted this as giving new states equal governmental powers. However, some "sagebrush rebels" have argued that state title to BLM land can be squeezed out of the equal footing doctrine, inasmuch as the original thirteen states retained their colonial titles to unappropriated land within their boundaries when they agreed to form the Union. Cf. briefs prepared in 1977 by the Utah and Arizona Offices of the Attorney General, excerpted in George Cameron Coggins and Charles F. Wilkinson, *Federal public land and resource law* (Mineola, NY: Foundation Press, 1981), at 56–58 and 64–65. If so, federal title to National Parks, National Forests, etc., would be clouded, since such entities were carved out of public land which should already have passed to the states.

One can dream up a constitutional case of sorts against federal lands. The property clause of Article IV, note 22 *supra*, appears immediately after material relating to the admission of new states. Doesn't that suggest that its authors intended that unappropriated territorial land would simply pass to the states created from it? Furthermore, suppose one takes the enumerated powers of Article I, Section 8, to constrain federal power narrowly, to define "the general welfare of the United States" (Paragraph 1) insofar as the federal government is permitted to look after it. Then the rules and regulations of the property clause will be "needful" insofar as they are required to serve some enumerated power or purpose. But very, very little federal property is thus authorized. This line of argument was suggested to me by David E. Engdahl's "State and federal power over federal property," *Arizona Law Review* 18 (1976), 283–394. Engdahl's own view is more moderate: the property clause gives the federal government only the ordinary rights of proprietorship under state jurisdiction. Authority to manage federal lands in a way that preempts state law must, he argues, be derived from the enumerated powers.

35. Laws enacted in Nevada (1979) and Utah (1980) claimed legal title to federal lands within these states. Coggins and Wilkinson, note 34 *supra*, at 58. Senator Orrin Hatch (R-UT) introduced a bill to effect transfer of BLM land to the states, but it went nowhere. 125 *Congressional Record* S11665 (6 August 1979).

36. Two years into his administration, Watt represented ranchers' change of heart this way: "Hey, two years ago we wanted to get rid of all federal lands. Now we want Jim Watt to manage the federal lands because he is a good guy. Don't sell the lands, Jim Watt. You manage them. We can deal with you." Bil Gilbert, "Alone in the Wilderness," *Sports Illustrated*, 3 October 1983, 96–112 at 104.

37. Cf. Russ Shay, "The Sagebrush Rebellion," *Sierra* 65(1) (1980), 29–32.

38. John Baden so described himself at a conference titled "Preserving the earth: the property rights alternative," held at The University of Bridgeport School of Law, CT, 16 April 1983.

39. Richard L. Stroup and John A. Baden, *Natural resources: bureaucratic myths and environmental management* (San Francisco: Pacific Institute for Public Policy Research, 1983), at 99.

40. John Baden and Richard Stroup, "Saving the wilderness," *Reason* 13(3) (1981), 28–36 at 35.

41. That is, the Bureau of Reclamation (BuRec).

42. Vernon L. Smith, "On divestiture and the creation of property rights in public lands," *Cato Journal* 2 (1982), 663–85 at 684.

43. That is, the Bureau of Land Management (BLM).

44. Stroup and Baden, note 39 *supra*, at 48–49.

45. Id., at 45.

46. Id., at 103.

47. Richard Stroup, "Weaknesses in the case for federal retention," in Brubacker, note 5 *supra*, 149–55 at 149.

48. For more detailed history, see Nelson, note 4 *supra*; and C. Brant Short, "Selling the public lands," *Ronald Reagan and the public lands* (College Station, TX: Texas A&M University Press, 1989), Chapter 6.

49. Phillip O. Foss, ed., *Federal land policy* (New York: Greenwood Press, 1987), at xxii.

50. Frank Gregg, "Public land management in the post-privatization era," *Policy Studies Journal* 14 (1985), 305–14 at 305.

51. René Descartes, "Discourse on the method of rightly conducting the reason and seeking for truth in the sciences," in *The philosophical works of Descartes*, Elizabeth S. Haldane and G.R.T. Ross, trans. (Cambridge: Cambridge University Press, 1967), Vol. I at 91 (Part II).

52. Immanuel Kant speaks of Hume's interrupting his "dogmatic slumbers" in his introduction to *Prolegomena to any future metaphysics*, ed. Lewis White Beck (New York: Liberal Arts Press, 1950), at 8.

53. Thomas Hobbes, *Leviathan*, ed. Michael Oakeshott (New York: Collier, 1962), at 187 (Chapter 24).

54. In *California Oregon Power Co.* v. *Beaver Portland Cement Co.*, 295 U.S. 142 (1935), the Supreme Court held that in declaring that "the water of all lakes, rivers, and other sources of water supply upon the public lands and not navigable, shall remain and be held free for the appropriation and use of the public for irrigation, mining, and manufacturing processes, subject to existing rights" in the Desert Lands Act of 1877, 43 U.S.C.A. §§321–39 at §321, Congress separated title to water on public lands from title to the surface, allowing the states to grant the former.

55. *Winters* v. *United States*, 207 U.S. 564 (1908).

56. Rose Strickland, "Stillwater, a wildlife refuge running out of time," *Public lands: Newsletter of the Sierra Club Public Lands Committee* 6(1) (1988), 10–12. See also David L. Harrison, "The water crisis in the western refuge system: an environmental response," in *Crossroads of conservation: 500 years after Columbus*, ed. R. E. McCabe (Washington: Wildlife Management Institute, 1992), 560–70.

57. "The dilemma: save a fish or a wetland," *The New York Times*, 26 April 1988, C1. The issue is briefly discussed under "Stillwater Wildlife Management Area," in *National Wildlife Refuges: continuing problems with incompatible uses call for bold action* (Washington: General Accounting Office, 1989), 71–73 (Appendix 4: Sixteen case studies).

58. William C. Scott, "The continuing saga of Pyramid Lake: Nevada v. California," *Natural Resources Journal* 24 (1984), 1067–82.

59. Truckee–Carson Pyramid Lake Water Rights Settlement Act of 1990, P.L. 101–618, Title II. For discussion, see Bonnie G. Colby, Mark A. McGinnis, and Ken A. Rait, "Mitigating environmental externalities through voluntary and involuntary water reallocation: Nevada's Truckee–Carson River Basin," *Natural Resources Journal* 31 (1991), 757–83.

60. "Bird breeding marshes in Nevada are drying up," *The New York Times*, 20 December 1992, A32.

61. "Ancient fish finds new life in Nevada," *Sacramento Bee*, 3 May 1993, A1.

62. Nelson, note 4 *supra*, at 26.

63. Id., at 41ff. The President's Commission on Privatization also suggests that privatization will come "as interest groups seek to ensure that their past gains from government are maintained, pressuring governments to convert these gains to privately held and salable property rights." David F. Linowes, et al., *Privatization: toward more effective government* (Washington: President's Commission on Privatization, 1988), at 245.

64. Gregg, note 50 *supra*, at 305.

65. The main line of argument is that a water right implies a grazing right where the former (a) antedates a grazing permit and (b) is secured by the appropriation of unappropriated water for the beneficial use of supporting a public-land grazing operation. For analysis, see Barry Sims, "Private rights in public lands?," *The workbook* 18(2) (Albuquerque: Southwest Research and Information Center, 1993), 50–9.

66. Quoted in Kevin Bixby, *A report on the county movement* (Las Cruces, NM: Southwest Environmental Center, 1992), at 17.

67. For example, FLPMA, note 6 *supra*, requires the Secretary of the Interior, in formulating BLM land-use plans, to "give priority to the designation and protection of areas of critical environmental concern," §1712(c)(3), where such areas are those "where special management attention is required . . . to protect and prevent irreparable damage to important historic, cultural, or scenic values, fish and wildlife resources or other natural systems or processes, or to protect life and safety from natural hazards," §1702(a). It also stipulates that such plans "shall be consistent with the State and local plans to the maximum extent [the Secretary] finds consistent with Federal law and the purposes of this Act," §1712(c)(9).

68. Note 14 *supra*.

69. "In cattle-raising west, a county wants to help U.S. manage lands," *The New York Times*, 6 May 1993, A24. For an environmentalist reaction to the County Movement, see Paul Rauber, "Wishful thinking," *Sierra* 79(1) (1994), 39–42.

70. Gottlieb, note 31 *supra*, at 14 (Wise Use Goal 20).

71. See Section 3 of the model National Rangeland Grazing System Act in Gottlieb, note 31 *supra*, 89–95. This proposal contains a provision, Sec. 3(a)(4), that may imply large-scale privatization of federal rangeland: if the value of a rancher's possessory interest (grazing preference, investment in fencing, etc.) is more than half the market value of the land, it is to be transferred to him. For a revealing discussion, see Steve H. Hanke, "The privatization debate: an insider's view," *Cato Journal* 2 (1982), 653–62 at 657ff.

72. Letter from National Park Users Association in Gottlieb, note 31 *supra*, 103–14 at 109.

73. Letter from Center for the Defense of Free Enterprise in Gottlieb, note 31 *supra*, 86–89 at 89.

74. Letter from United Four Wheel Drive Associations of U.S. and Canada in Gottlieb, note 31 *supra*, 124–29 at 125. The proposed Commodity Use System is explicitly modelled on the Wilderness System. Gottlieb, note 31 *supra*, at 87. Sec. 2(c) of the model National Rangeland Grazing System legislation, note 71 *supra*, parodies the language of §1131(c) of the Wilderness Act, note 30 *supra*: "A rangeland grazing area, in contrast with those areas where urban development or nature preservation dominate the landscape, is hereby recognized as an area where the land and its ecological conditions are suited to the grazing of livestock, where grazing is the historic use, where preservationists are visitors who do not remain."

75. Gottlieb, note 31 *supra*, at 14 (Wise Use Goal 22).

76. Marion Clawson, "Major alternatives for future management of the federal lands," in Brubaker, note 5 *supra*, 195–234 at 232.

77. For an economic critique of USFS practices, see Randal O'Toole, *Reforming the Forest Service* (Washington: Island Press, 1988).

78. See "Reagan plan to privatize government is gaining support from Democrats," *The New York Times*, 15 February 1988, A10.

79. "Privatizing urged to improve roads," *The New York Times*, 1 October 1993, A12. Attractive opportunities for private investors here may be rather limited; see Norman H. Wuestefeld, "Toll roads: private sector funding," *TR News* 155 (1993), 2–5.

80. "Aid is asked on recreation in forests," *The New York Times*, 17 February 1988, B5. The USFS's new "Recreation Strategy" is outlined in rather general terms in *The National Forests: America's great outdoors: National recreation stragegy* (Washington: USFS, 1988).

81. Linowes, note 63 *supra*, at 245.

82. Id., at 241ff. ("A failure to privatize: public lands").

83. "Certainly, in view of a $115 billion Federal deficit, the federal government must stop thinking that it must own everything." Senator Steven Symms (R-ID), "The federal estate," in *Private rights and public lands*, ed. Phillip N. Truluck (Washington: Heritage Foundation, 1983), 39–42 at 41.

84. Marion Clawson, "Reassessing public lands policy," in Truluck, note 83 *supra*, 17–28 at 23.

85. William E. Simon, "Gramm-Rudman as a lever," *The New York Times*, 24 January 1986, A27.

86. Clawson, note 25 *supra*, at 146.

87. Richard J. Mahoney, CEO of Monsanto Chemical Corporation, quoted in "New view calls environmental policy misguided," *The New York Times*, 21 March 1993, A1. See also Alvin L. Alm, "The politics of the environment," *Environmental*

*Science and Technology* 26 (1992), 1717. Alm argues that we must set priorities, since "unmet environmental needs are staggering" and "funds will never be sufficient to cope with these problems in a reasonable period of time."

88. The term is due to O'Toole, note 77 *supra*, Chapter 13 ("Marketizing the Forest Service").

89. See, e.g., "How most of the public forests are sold to loggers at a loss," *The New York Times*, 3 November 1991, D2.

90. Linowes, note 63 *supra*, at 237.

91. See Marc S. Reisch, "SO$_2$ emission trading rights: a model for other pollutants," *Chemical and Engineering News*, 6 July 1992, 21–2; and "Sold: the rights to air pollution," *The New York Times*, 30 March 1993, D1. The use of market incentives to manage SO$_2$ emissions is authorized by the 1990 amendments to the Clean Air Act, 104 Stat. 2399, §403. *Time* magazine put the EPA experiment on its list of "the best [environmental developments] of 1992." *Time*, 4 January 1993, 57.

92. "U.S. starts to allot fishing rights in coastal waters to boat owners," *The New York Times*, 22 April 1991, A1. The Fishery Conservation and Management Act of 1976, 16 U.S.C.A. §§1801–82, established the regional councils and charged them with developing and implementing fishery conservation plans; for what such plans may require, see §1853(b).

On ITQs, see Parzival Copes, "A critical review of the individual quota as a device in fisheries management," *Land Economics* 62 (1986), 278–91; and Lyndal Wilson, "ITQs around the world," *Australian Fisheries* 50(10) (1991), 15–18. For discussion of the limitations of the property-rights approach to fisheries by a supporter, see Pamela M. Mace, "Will private owners practice prudent resource management?," *Fisheries* 18(9) (1993), 29–31. For general discussion of fisheries management problems, see Michael P. Sisserwine and Andrew A. Rosenberg, "Marine fisheries at a critical juncture," *Fisheries* 18(10) (1993), 6–14.

93. Joe Klein, "Cleaning up: how to save the Earth the American way," *New York*, 16 April 1990, 57–58 at 58. For more on "free-market environmentalism," see Joe Alper, "Protecting the environment with the power of the market," *Science* 260 (1993), 1884–5.

94. "Policy on grazing on the public lands," *Public lands: Newsletter of the Sierra Club Public Lands Committee* 9(2) (1992), 6. However, the club opposes "any entrance fees for recreational use" of USFS and BLM lands, as well as "fees for the use of Wilderness or trails on federal lands." "Public lands recreational user fee policy," *Brief of actions of the Sierra Club Board of Directors* (November 15–16, 1986), 10 (item 9).

95. Peter A. A. Berle, "The Audubon view: A new era for America's public lands," *Audubon* 95(1) (1993), 6.

96. "Sweeping reversal of U.S. land policy sought by Clinton," *The New York Times*, 24 February 1993, A1.

97. FLPMA, note 6 *supra*, at §1701(a)(9).

98. E.g., multiple-use management specifically requires attention "to the relative values of the resources and not necessarily to the combination of uses that will give the greatest economic return or the greatest unit output." FLPMA, note 6 *supra*, at §1702(c).

99. NFMA, note 8 *supra*, at §1601(a)(2).

100. "Clinton backs off from policy shift on federal lands," *The New York Times*, 31 March 1993, A1. Subsequently, the administration reaffirmed its intention to raise grazing fees. See "Babbitt unveils new grazing proposal," *High Country*

*News*, 23 August 1993, 3. The proposal, 58 FR 43202–6 (for USFS land) and 58 FR 43208–31 (for BLM land), includes fees that "approximate market value," 43204.

101. "Higher grazing fees have ranchers running scared," *The New York Times*, 12 September 1993, C5. For a study suggesting that their apprehension is justified, see David P. Anderson, et al., "Alternative grazing fee formula impacts on representative public land ranches," *Journal of Range Management* 46 (1993), 548–54.

102. Letter from National Park Users Association in Gottlieb, note 31 *supra*, 103–14 at 111. Grassroots fronts for corporate influence on public land and environmental policy are discussed in Thomas A. Lewis, "You can't judge a group by its cover," and Jay R. Hair, "The National Wildlife view: Recognizing an anti-environmental ruse," *National Wildlife* 30(6) (1992), 9 and 30.

103. Cf. Stroup and Baden, note 39 *supra*, at 45–50. The problem with anecdotes is that it is easy to enlist them in any cause. A particularly depressing example of private abuse is depicted in "Images on stone: the prehistoric rock art of the Colorado Plateau," *Plateau* 55(2) (Museum of Northern Arizona, 1984), at 32: painted across an Anasazi pictograph in Nine Mile Canyon, Utah, is "THIS IS PRIVATE PROPERTY NO TRESSPASSING."

104. "Exchange is not a zero-sum game" is alleged to be an "empirical" principle in Stroup and Baden, note 39 *supra*, at 30.

105. John Baden and Dean Lueck, "Bringing private management to public lands: environmental and economic advantages," in *Controversies in environmental policy*, Sheldon Kamieniecki, Robert O'Brien, and Michael Clarke, ed. (Albany: State University of New York Press, 1986), 39–64 at 54.

106. Smith, note 42 *supra*.

# 2

# Federal Lands, Past and Present

> To a large degree, we are caught in our own history, the evidence of which
> is in the many special arrangements that have accumulated around the use
> of the federal lands. Each of them represents a form of payment for the
> present body of federal land policies. We cannot wish them away. They
> will continue to limit what can be done with the federal lands.
>
> Perry R. Hagenstein[1]

How did the federal government end up with title to a quarter of the land
in a nation with a long-standing distrust of government power, a
corresponding faith in individual enterprise, and democratic institutions
designed to make government policies reflect its will? While explanation is
not justification, an account of their evolution can help make some sense of
current federal land policies. In this chapter, I outline the history of federal
lands and the shape of the current management regime, indicating what
agencies are responsible for what lands under what statutory charters.
Readers familiar with these topics will find nothing new here and may wish
to skip to the concluding observations.

## ACQUISITION AND DISPOSAL

The federal government got into the real-estate business early on. Through
a political compromise between the original states, it acquired the old
"western lands" between the Appalachians and the Mississippi. During the
colonial period, England had rather imprecisely divided the land it claimed
in America among its colonies. Charters granted extensive lands beyond the
Appalachians to some colonies, sometimes the same lands to different
colonies. Connecticut and Massachusetts, for example, claimed the same 26
million acres in the old Northwest (north of the Ohio River, west of the
Appalachians). England revoked some of these grants in 1774, but colonies
thereby severed from their western lands regarded the War of Independence
as a means to regain what had been theirs.

States with no historical claims to press wanted to share in what they
considered war booty "wrested from the common enemy by the blood and
treasure of the thirteen states."[2] They proposed that the western lands be
surrendered to the federal government "to be disposed of for the common
good of the United States."[3] Maryland feared that otherwise it would have

to make good on promises of land in exchange for service in the Revolution that the Continental Congress had made to Maryland troops. For the same reason, the national government, such as it was, promoted state cession of western lands: nobody relished the prospect of angry veterans marching on Congress to demand the land they'd been promised. Furthermore, leaders such as Thomas Jefferson wished to retire the war debt quickly, lest the new nation be beholden to the financiers of the Revolution.

Squabbling between the "ins" over claims to the western lands, resistance from the "outs" to recognizing any such claims, lobbying by national leaders, and Indian problems in the west too big for the states to handle on their own eventually led them to compromise on federal ownership. In some ways, not much has changed here in two hundred years. Various interests acquiesce in federal control of hundreds of millions of acres, in part because they cannot agree among themselves on what to do with them and fear they'd fare worse under a non-federal regime. However, in those early years, federal lands were not to be managed but disposed of. People had different ideas about how disposal should proceed, but nobody proposed that the federal government own land, except perhaps for such narrow purposes as military outposts and the nation's capital—another compromise to avoid favoring one state over another. Indeed, when federal land didn't move, Congress's response was generally to loosen the terms: to allow buying on credit,[4] to drop the price,[5] and to increase the amount of land an individual could acquire by homesteading.[6]

To eliminate inexact land descriptions as a source of conflicting claims, the Land Ordinance of 1785[7] prescribed New England's system of township surveys for federal lands. Before disposal, they were to be surveyed into square *townships*, consisting of 36 numbered square *sections*, each a mile long on a side and 640 acres in area. Land could be precisely located and described in terms of the resulting grid. Unfortunately, the simplicity of this system invited simple-minded disposals. Thus, it was easy for Congress to grant new states sections 16 and 36 from each township, to be managed or sold to support education. But these scattered "school lands" are difficult to administer and, when surrounded by federal land, a source of inter-governmental tensions.[8] Furthermore, the ability to rule the land into squares may have encouraged the conceit that it could be ruled in other ways as well. The quarter-sections offered by the Homestead Act of 1862[9] might have been developed into viable family farms in the "humid" regions, but they wouldn't grow anything in most of the arid West, folk-wisdom that "rain follows the plow" notwithstanding.

While land sales and giveaways helped retire Revolutionary War debts and obligations, disposal was never viewed primarily as a source of revenue but rather as an instrument of national policy. Paul Gates has observed that the different visions of the emerging nation associated with Thomas Jefferson and Alexander Hamilton were to pull disposal policies in somewhat different directions. In Jefferson's view, "distribution of the public lands to the landless so they could become independent farmers would . . . assure the preservation of the American republic and avoid the excesses that might arise from a turbulent population that had no stake in the land," whereas Hamilton thought "that land investors and stock companies were essential in drawing people to the West by their investments in roads, mills, and factories and that the government should sell its lands in large blocks to such men, letting them act as middlemen between the government and the settler."[10] With a little imagination, you can see the shadow of Jefferson and Hamilton in controversies over current federal land policies (equity vs. efficiency, regulation vs. laissez faire).

Hamilton's position was reflected in the early Land Act of 1796, which set a price of $2 per acre for minimum blocks of one section under liberal credit terms.[11] Credit was rationalized as enabling cash-poor settlers to obtain productive cropland, but it also encouraged speculation. This was anathema to Jeffersonians—land was withheld from those who needed it to enrich those who didn't—and they worked to eliminate credit sales. To bring land within reach of the landless, they also succeeded in getting its price and the minimum acreage offered reduced.[12] With the Graduation Act of 1854, cash-sale policy was reversed to specify maximum rather than minimum acreage to a single purchaser, and acreage limitations became a standard feature of disposal policy.[13]

However, speculation continued to flourish through the 19th century, in part because some provisions advertised as beneficial to small settlers (credit, low prices) also benefitted speculators, and in part because anti-speculative provisions (residence requirements, acreage limitations) were often abused. Perhaps the tolerance with which fraudulent entries for speculative purposes were viewed owed something to Hamilton's view. After all, the vast tracts assembled and held for speculation were eventually divided and sold to settlers. However, the fact that lots of people—including many who made and implemented disposal policy—made lots of money in land speculation is doubtless sufficient to explain the half-hearted pursuit of remedies to speculation.

Disciples of Jefferson finally got what they wanted in the Homestead Act of 1862:[14] a quarter-section of federal land free of charge to settlers who were willing to put five years of "sweat equity" into it. Unfortunately, the land itself did not cooperate in realizing their vision of 160-acre family farms from sea to sea. Far more acreage was required for dry farming on the Great Plains or grazing operations in the Great Basin. Acreage limitations were raised in later homestead legislation,[15] but many farms and ranches in the West were viable only with access to federal irrigation water or forage on nearby federal land.

## PREEMPTION AND LAND GRANTS

In the 19th century, the federal government acquired by purchase and treaty some 1.6 billion acres of land.[16] Much of it was, of course, not vacant, being already occupied by Indians and, in some areas, by European colonists. Government treatment of Indian claims was what might be expected of military strength in the service of moral weakness. Settlers streaming into lands reserved by treaty for Native Americans forced the government to choose between "them or us," with the predictable result: Indian resistance was crushed, the survivors fleeing further west or forced onto smaller and poorer reservations.

European claimants fared better. Thirty-four million acres of the lands acquired from foreign powers had already been granted to private individuals, or were successfully represented to have been.[17] Spain had a reputation for being particularly lavish, and private claims to huge blocks of valuable land (e.g., the 1.4-million-acre Forbes grant in Florida[18]) were recognized in its former possessions. Some acquired lands had been previously settled by individuals who lacked any color of title. The prevalence of such squatters, who would doubtless have approved John Locke's theory that a man's labor is what makes *his* a bit of what God gave to man in common,[19] forced Congress to grant them preemption rights to buy land before the government sold it out from under them.[20]

Indeed, preexisting practice has often preempted federal land policy. In the General Mining Law of 1872[21] Congress acquiesced to what miners had long been doing without legal sanction: taking what they found on public land. This statute permitted miners to stake claims and to appropriate whatever their labor brought to light; indeed they could appropriate the surface as well by patenting their claim. Unlike homestead legislation, this antique statute has never been repealed: if you can find an unclaimed, valuable[22] deposit of a locatable ("hardrock") mineral[23] and are willing to spend a mere $100 a year for five years working it, you too may acquire a piece of federal land for $5 an acre.[24]

Mining isn't the only current use of federal land and resources to have acquired legal protection as a *fait accompli*. Most western homesteads weren't suitable for crops or big enough to support a livestock operation, and ranchers simply availed themselves of nearby federal lands to pasture their cattle and sheep. This custom was formalized by the Taylor Grazing Act of 1934:[25] most BLM land was divided into grazing districts, within which particular areas (allotments) were assigned to particular ranches in line with historical use. Such formal arrangements, which evolved somewhat earlier for grazing within National Forests, give ranchers something like the property right to federal grazing allotments they would have acquired under a less restrictive and perhaps more sensible disposal policy.

Another example of use blossoming into right is the recent liberalization of the acreage limitation for recipients of water from federal irrigation projects. The Reclamation Act of 1902[26] limited to 160 the number of acres owned by any one person on which such water could be used. But the prohibition on watering "excess lands" was widely ignored in places like California's Imperial Valley, and in 1980 the Supreme Court agreed with landless farm workers that some 800 farms there were getting federal irrigation water illegally.[27] Congress's response was to raise acreage limitations to 960 acres in the Reclamation Reform Act of 1982.[28]

More generally, it is difficult for federal managers to ignore past uses of federal lands and the expectations they have raised, even where legal obligations have not been assumed. Those who have "always" used old mining roads to jeep into the back country of National Forests will resist attempts to close them to protect wildlife or fragile alpine tundra, whether or not they have a mining claim that would give them legal access. Those who have grown up in mill towns dependent on federal timber will resist efforts to place some of it off limits in Wilderness Areas, whether or not they've bought the right to cut it at a federal timber sale.

In all, cash and preemption sales disposed of over 300 million acres of federal land, and entries under the various homesteading acts privatized nearly as much.[29] In addition, Congress gave away land to promote a variety of special purposes. Indeed, it was often persuaded to give land when it was unwilling to give money, an inclination that persists in current federal land-management policies. For example, Congress won't give ranchers cash to keep them in business, but it will sell them federal forage at below-market prices.

Free land was first offered to entice enlistment in the Continental Army. It was given indirectly in the form of warrants or scrip, redeemable for land in portions of the western lands reserved, as "military reservations", from cash sales. Generally, though, it was not revolutionary war veterans who took title to this land: they sold their warrants to land companies. But Congress, having met its obligations, didn't care and continued to offer land for military service until the Spanish-American War. Some 61 million acres of federal land were privatized in this way.[30]

Another 94 million acres went to railroads.[31] To encourage the construction of rail lines to serve the developing nation, railroads were typically granted a right of way plus odd-numbered sections for some miles to either side, land they could then sell to settlers. It was argued that the Treasury would lose nothing by such largesse, since proximity to rail service would make the remaining even-numbered sections twice as valuable. But many of them in fact remained unsold, and the resulting "checkerboard" lands are awkward to manage.

Many special-purpose land grants were made to states, for example, in aid of transportation or institutions such as asylums or hospitals. States were expected to use their grants for the intended purpose and sometimes did. In any case, it was not expected that they would hang onto the land, and generally they didn't; railroads, for example, received millions of additional acres through transportation grants to states. Beginning with Ohio in 1803, states created from federal territory—the so-called "public-land" states—received designated sections from each township to support education.[32] The Morrill Act of 1862[33] granted to each state scrip for federal land in the west (30,000 acres for each representative and senator) to be sold to support "land grant" colleges.

Other grants to states were less specific. In 1841, Congress decided that each public-land state was to have half a million acres for "purposes of internal improvement."[34] The General Swamp Land Act of 1850[35] permitted states to acquire federal swampland, the theory being that it was worthless until drained, a task Congress was happy to pass to the states with the title. Sixty-five million acres of land, a good deal of it quite dry and valuable, thereby passed out of the federal domain.[36]

However, grants to public-land states were also remarkable for what they didn't include. The original states emerged from the Revolution with title to unclaimed Crown lands within their borders, and title to these "public lands" passed to states split off from them (e.g., Maine from Massachusetts in 1820). As the Sagebrush Rebels maintained two centuries later, it may have been generally assumed that states created from federal territory would similarly assume title to unappropriated federal land. But the same forces that gave the federal government land to begin with prevented this. Education grants became more and more liberal, but only at the last, in the case of Alaska (1958), did the federal government surrender a significant share of its in-state lands to a state at statehood.[37]

## RETENTION

Federal land policy began to shift toward retention after about a century of disposal. To a large extent, the present federal estate is the cumulative result of a process of reserving from disposal certain lands and resources, often to protect them from perceived threats. Though some were acquired from states and individuals, most National Parks and Monuments, National Forests, and National Wildlife Refuges were established in this way. Classifying federal land as an Indian reservation, military reservation, Naval Petroleum Reserve, or BLM grazing district also reserved it from disposal. Coal deposits were withheld from homesteaders, who were supposed to be farmers, by reserving the mineral rights to patented lands; coal and other fuel minerals on unpatented land were removed from the scope of the hardrock mining law and made subject to lease. Finally, in 1976, Congress decided that the leftovers would be retained as well, lest something valuable be disposed of inadvertently.

Retention was a reaction to the excesses of disposal—corruption, fraud, waste, injustice—and the realization that the frontier was not limitless, that the nation would have to live with what it had. Congress wearied of having its will thwarted by wholesale abuse of disposal statutes; by retaining federal land, it might regain control of how it was used. Fraudulent entries on federal land were common from the beginning; much of it was simply stolen, frequently to enrich those who seemed rich enough already. Trees came to be regarded as a valuable resource, not merely an impediment to agriculture, a resource threatened by cut-and-run logging practices that not only wasted timber but left the land vulnerable to erosion. Naturalist John

Muir, speaking from a romantic and transcendental tradition against a backdrop of such devastation, helped change attitudes toward nature and wilderness—from the beginning a strange mixture of repulsion and fascination[38]—so that preservation assumed a place on the national agenda.

In short, evils came to be associated with disposal, and retention was promoted as a remedy. However, it was not simply a "fix" for problems associated with disposal; it too was advertised as promoting various national objectives. If the nation had begun with the perceived needs of retiring debt and promoting development and settlement, it had over the course of a hundred years or so acquired other interests that influenced federal land policy. Thus, where forestlands had once been for sale,[39] they would be reserved as National Forests "to improve and protect the forest within the boundaries, or for the purpose of securing favorable conditions of water flows, and to furnish a continuous supply of timber for the use and necessities of citizens of the United States."[40] By the time it closed federal lands to entry under the homesteading statutes, Congress had discovered all sorts of reasons to hang onto what was left: it was to be "managed in a manner that will protect the quality of scientific, scenic, historical, ecological, environmental, air and atmospheric, water resource, and archeological values."[41] If federal land policies are seen as serving various national objectives, i.e., objectives that Congress could be persuaded to pursue, the shift from disposal to retention seems less remarkable.

Just as different objectives produced tensions in disposal policy, different objectives have produced tensions in the management of lands the government retained. To some extent, they have been resolved by zoning: different lands are managed by different agencies under different management charters. But this solution is incomplete. Some agencies oversee activities on lands administered by others; for example, the BLM handles mineral leasing on lands administered by the USFS. Most management charters, such as the multiple-use statutes under which the BLM and USFS operate, contain vague or contradictory language that invites various interests to try for a bigger slice of the pie. Reclassification of land, for example, moving USFS and BLM lands in eastern Nevada to the NPS as "Great Basin National Park," or congressional revision of management charters is always a possibility.

In the remainder of this chapter, I shall outline the current federal land-management system, indicating who is responsible for what, with some further historical detail to account for the retention of particular lands and resources.

## THE FOREST SERVICE

The United States Forest Service (USFS)—officially, "USDA Forest Service"—manages the National Forests, 156 of them, together comprising about 187 million acres.[42] Those in Alaska (22 million acres) and the western states (141 million acres) were largely reserved from disposal by presidential order under authority of the Forest Reserve Amendment of 1891.[43] Those in the East, Midwest, and South (24 million acres) were purchased under authority of the Weeks Forest Purchase Act of 1911 (to protect watershed) and the Clarke–McNary Act of 1924 (to produce timber).[44] As the land management agency of the Department of Agriculture (USDA), the USFS also administers some 4 million acres of National Grasslands on the high plains, purchased from bankrupt dirt farmers for soil conservation under the Bankhead–Jones Act of 1937.[45] In fiscal year (FY) 1992, the agency spent about $3.3 billion; in FY1991, its lands generated about $1.2 billion in revenue, all but about $80 million of it from timber sales.[46]

The idea of national forest reserves antedates the Declaration of Independence, for in the colonial period England had reserved stands of white pine for naval masts. Congress also thought national security would be enhanced by naval forest reserves, but the tracts of oak it purchased or set aside beginning in 1799 were plundered by settlers. It was difficult to police remote tracts of forest land and to interest Congress in making the effort: the nation's vast tracts of virgin forest must have seemed capable of meeting its timber needs indefinitely.

By the late 1870s, when Secretary of the Interior Carl Schurz resurrected the idea of federal forest reserves, it was clear that the forests were not limitless. Timber in New England, New York and Pennsylvania was largely gone, and the loggers had moved on to the Great Lakes and the West. A good deal was being cut from land fraudulently obtained under various disposal statutes, or simply stolen without troubling to acquire the land at all. The ethos prevailing among "timber barons" seems to have been "get it before someone else does." Far from following Locke's proviso to leave "enough, and as good . . . in common for others,"[47] they aimed "to get that of such grade that there may be little or none left as good as that we take."[48] As might be imagined, such an attitude produced appalling waste: loggers generally cut everything, but took only the best logs, leaving the rest (sometimes 80%) to rot.[49] Land was wasted as well; in some areas erosion stripped off the soil after loggers had stripped off the trees.

Unlike some of his predecessors, Schurz took federal ownership of timberlands seriously. He also worried about the unpleasant environmental effects of deforestation, to which George Perkins Marsh had recently drawn attention,[50] and feared that wasteful logging practices might eventually lead to a "timber famine." By reserving timberlands from disposal, the government might secure its property against theft and fraudulent disposal, and regulate logging to conserve timber supplies and protect the land.[51] But Congress rebuffed Schurz, even denying funds for inspectors to discourage theft of timber from the public domain.

In 1891, forest reserves were finally authorized, probably under cover of night, in the form of a hastily drafted amendment attached to the General Revision Act[52] in the last hours of the 51st Congress. Presidents Harrison and Cleveland gave the measure credibility by reserving some 33 million acres, and in 1897 Congress got around to deciding what was to be done with them: they were to be managed to protect watershed and to provide a continuous supply of timber.[53]

It was European-trained forester Gifford Pinchot who gave enduring shape to this directive, the National Forest System, and the agency that administers it. He got his friend Theodore Roosevelt to reserve another 132 million acres and in 1905 had administration of the forest reserves transferred from the disposal-oriented General Land Office of the Department of the Interior to a new agency of the Department of Agriculture, under his direction. As its first Chief Forester, Pinchot built the USFS into an elite and professional management agency with definite ideas about how the National Forests, as the forest reserves were renamed,[54] should be run.

Pinchot had little interest in preservation; forests were for our use, and he could imagine little use for wilderness. In 1907 he instructed his forest rangers that:

> The land itself can be used for all purposes. The main thing is that the land, as well as what grows upon it, must be used for the purpose for which it is most valuable. On it may be built stores, hotels, residences, power plants, mills and many other things. All these are advantages to National Forests, because they help to get the fullest use out of land and its resources. Railroads, wagon roads, trails, canals, flumes, reservoirs, and telephone and power lines may be constructed whenever and wherever they are needed, as long as they do no unnecessary damage to the Forest. Improvements of this kind help to open up the country, and that is what is wanted.[55]

Federal ownership of the National Forests and oversight of private activities in them was needed to "get the fullest use of the land and its resources." Professional resource managers would know better than private interests what the land was "most valuable" for. They could insure that use did no "unnecessary damage to the Forest" by requiring that timber be cut on a sustained-yield basis (i.e., no faster than it grew), that cut-over areas be replanted, and that range not be overgrazed. Where "conflicting interests must be reconciled," they would judge according to "the greatest good for the greatest number over the long run."[56]

After establishing its authority over federal forests, the USFS had considerable success in managing them according to these principles, in part because demands on the National Forests were manageable. Schurz's fear that "the supply of timber in the United States will, in less than twenty years, fall considerably short of our home necessities"[57] proved premature: there was plenty of fraudulently acquired private timber to cut without turning to the National Forests. Recently, however, the USFS has found it increasingly difficult to apply its principles of multiple use and sustained yield in a way that satisfies those who take an interest in the National Forests. Partly, this is because increased demands have made National Forest resources scarce. Since World War II, recreational use has risen to several hundred million visitor-days annually; over the same period, demand for timber outstripped private supplies.[58] Political pressure to log the National Forests rises with world demand for wood products and the nation's trade deficit; selling federal timber helps pay for Japanese automobiles and consumer electronics.[59] New demands also strain the concept of multiple use: contemporary disciples of Muir want roadless areas of the National Forests kept that way as Wilderness, while the USFS continues to follow Pinchot in thinking that preservation isn't *use* and that roading serves a multiplicity of uses. The agency has also made mistakes—or what many perceive to be mistakes—and few now suppose that it has some special insight into how to arrange for "the greatest good for the greatest number in the long run."

The statutory authority under which the USFS now operates gives it considerable latitude in managing the National Forests. According to the Multiple-Use, Sustained-Yield Act of 1960 (MUSYA), "the national forests are established and shall be administered for outdoor recreation, range, timber, watershed, and wildlife and fish purposes."[60] Administration shall be for "multiple use and sustained yield of the several products and services obtained therefrom."[61]

Such legislative content as *multiple use* and *sustained yield* have is supplied by the following definitions:

> (a) "Multiple use" means: The management of all the various renewable surface resources of the national forests so that they are utilized in the combination that will best meet the needs of the American people; making the most judicious use of the land for some or all of these resources or related services over areas large enough to provide sufficient latitude for periodic adjustments in use to conform to changing needs and conditions; that some land will be used for less than all of the resources; and harmonious and coordinated management of the various resources, each with the other, without impairment of the productivity of the land, with consideration being given to the relative values of the various resources, and not necessarily the combination of uses that will give the greatest dollar return or the greatest unit output.
>
> (b) "Sustained yield of the several products and services" means the achievement and maintenance in perpetuity of a high-level annual or regular periodic output of the various renewable resources of the national forests without impairment of the productivity of the land.[62]

Environmentalists charge that the USFS uses the notion of multiple use to justify a multitude of sins against the land; they think of it as "multiple abuse." For example, they complain that because the agency thinks trees should be *used*, it sells timber that can't be harvested without causing serious erosion and other environmental damage—indeed, timber that costs the USFS more to have cut (in terms of sale preparation, roads, replanting, etc.) than it's worth, even without taking environmental costs into account. The forest products industry, on the other hand, dislikes the USFS's interpretation of sustained yield, arguing that the agency's harvest policies produce lower-than-sustainable yields of timber. For example, the National Forest

Management Act of 1976 (NFMA) mandates that timber will be cut to assure a *non-declining even flow* (NDEF) from each National Forest.[63] Since mature trees grow slower than immature trees, more timber could eventually be cut annually from the National Forests if old-growth stands were liquidated quickly. But that is precluded by NDEF.

## THE NATIONAL PARK SERVICE

The National Park Service (NPS) of the Department of the Interior (DOI) administers the National Park System, consisting of National Parks, Monuments, Preserves, Seashores, Historic Parks, Battlefields, etc.— about 76 million acres in all, 53 million of them in Alaska.[64] Most of this land never passed from federal ownership, having been reserved from disposal or carved out of lands reserved from disposal as, say, National Forests. But important additions to the National Park System and to individual National Parks have been made by purchase. In FY1992, the NPS spent about $1.3 billion; in FY1990, nominal park entrance and user fees (e.g., for camping) generated about $55 million in revenue.[65]

Dedication of federal land for parks antedated the forest reserves. Yosemite Valley and the Mariposa Grove of giant sequoias were ceded to California in 1864 for "public use, resort, and recreation."[66] The congressional grant permitted the state to lease portions of the property, presumably for hotels and the like, but directed that lease revenues be expended on "preservation and improvement of the property, or the roads leading thereto."[67] To prevent its exploitation by miners, loggers, and others, the Yellowstone region was reserved in 1872 as "a pleasuring ground for the benefit and enjoyment of the people."[68] Here, Congress was a bit more explicit about management, directing the Secretary of Interior to "provide for the preservation, from injury or spoilation, of all timber, mineral deposits, natural curiosities, or wonders within said park, and their retention in their natural condition."[69] However, no money was appropriated for administration; it was apparently expected that the park would be supported by the proceeds of leasing "small parcels of ground"[70] for visitor accommodations.

Additional congressional reservations followed, for example, Yosemite, Kings Canyon, and Sequoia (1890), Mt. Rainier (1899), Glacier (1910), and Rocky Mountain (1915). In the Antiquities Act of 1906, Congress authorized the President to reserve lands containing "historic landmarks, historic and prehistoric structures, and other objects of historic or scientific interest" as National Monuments.[71] Limiting such reservations to "the smallest area compatible with the proper care and management of the objects to be protected" suggests that Congress contemplated only rather small monuments. But President Roosevelt soon used the act to reserve the Grand Canyon (1908), setting a precedent for later reservations that culminated in President Jimmy Carter's designation of 56 million acres of "national interest" lands in Alaska as National Monuments (1978).[72]

The early parks were administered in an *ad hoc* manner, sometimes by the army, which had to be called in to secure them. People had different ideas about what uses of parklands were compatible with their status as "pleasuring grounds." How about a reservoir for the city of San Francisco in Yosemite's Hetch Hetchy Valley? Pinchot was for it, confident "that the highest possible use which could be made of it would be to supply pure water to a great center of population."[73] Muir was horrified: "Dam Hetch Hetchy! As well dam for water-tanks the people's cathedrals and churches, for no holier temple has ever been consecrated by the heart of man."[74] The Hetch Hetchy controversy moved Congress toward addressing the management of the parks it had been creating. In 1916, three years after authorizing construction of the dam,[75] it decided that "the fundamental purpose" of the parks was "to conserve the scenery and the natural and historic objects and the wild life therein and to provide for the enjoyment of the same in such manner and by such means as will leave them unimpaired for the enjoyment of future generations," and established the NPS to administer them accordingly.[76]

The NPS's charge is hardly unproblematic, but it is a good deal narrower than the multiple-use charter of the USFS. The NPS's first Director, Stephen Mather, insisted that *conservation* precluded mining, logging, grazing, damming, etc., and his leadership helped to shift the burden of proof to those who would open the parks to such activities. He was less troubled by the impacts of recreational development—hotels, roads, etc. After all, the National Parks were to be conserved *for enjoyment*. Besides, in Mather's time relatively few people visited the parks, and he could scarcely have anticipated the enormous number of visitors that affluence and mobility—and his investments in infrastructure—would bring the parks later in the century.

The popularity of the National Parks is politically useful for the NPS: there is a large constituency for better funding, expanding existing parks and creating new ones, etc. But it has also exposed the tension between conservation and enjoyment; many parks simply can't accommodate the number of people who want to visit, at least without impairing the natural features that attract them. So do we insist upon their conservation, providing for whatever kind and quantity of enjoyment is compatible with it, or the other way around? The NPS isn't as interested in road building as the USFS, but it is too interested for some tastes. Roads, especially paved roads, enhance the enjoyment of motorized tourists but often at significant cost to others, to say nothing of their impacts on wildlife and natural features. Those willing (and able) to walk the five miles from road's end to view the confluence of the Green and Colorado rivers in Canyonlands National Park from an unfenced overlook generally do not welcome proposals to extend the road.[77]

## THE FISH AND WILDLIFE SERVICE

The DOI's Fish and Wildlife Service (FWS) manages the National Wildlife Refuge System: over 400 units totaling 85 million acres, 75 million of them in Alaska.[78] As the federal agency charged with conservation of fish and other wildlife, the FWS has other responsibilities besides refuge management: fishery restoration (fish hatcheries, salmon restoration projects, etc.), predator management, protection of endangered species, policing trade in wildlife products (skins, ivory, etc.) and captured animals, etc. In FY1992, its expenditures were about $1.2 billion; in FY1990, nominal entrance fees to the wildlife refuges generated about $2 million in revenue.[79]

Like the forest and park reserves, the refuges were established to protect resources—in this case, wildlife—from depredation. The first federal wildlife refuge, the 3-acre Pelican Island Reservation in Florida, was established by President Roosevelt in 1903 to save herons from fashions in ladies' hats.[80] In 1908 Congress established the National Bison Range[81] in Montana as a refuge for the remnants of the millions of buffalo that had roamed the Great Plains only a few decades before. Subsequently, other refuges were established on an *ad hoc* basis. But in 1929, the Migratory Bird Conservation Act[82] authorized a program for acquiring waterfowl habitat, lest its loss vitiate the Convention for the Protection of Migratory Birds negotiated with Canada in 1916.[83] In 1966, the refuges, wildlife management areas, etc., established under this program and by congressional and administrative action, were pulled together into the National Wildlife Refuge System under the administration of the FWS.[84]

Originally, refuges acquired for migratory birds were to be "inviolate sanctuaries,"[85] but as their purpose was largely to maintain the integrity of flyways for game birds, and their acquisition was funded by hunters through the federal duck stamp program,[86] they were eventually opened to hunting. However, hunting is to be restricted to what is "compatible with the major purposes for which such areas were established,"[87] viz., the "conservation of fish and wildlife."[88] Wildlife Refuges are sometimes described as "dominant use" lands: the dominant use is wildlife conservation, and other uses—hiking, fishing, hunting, grazing, etc.—are permitted to the extent to which they are compatible. But this is somewhat misleading, since mining and mineral leasing laws generally apply to the refuges,[89] and under these laws mining trumps conservation. For example, if Congress opens the Arctic National Wildlife Refuge to mineral leasing,[90] then it will be leased; and what will be conserved is whatever is compatible with oil exploration and development, not vice versa. Moreover, since wildlife doesn't vote or spend money, commercial uses of refuges have a tendency to become dominant.[91]

## THE BUREAU OF LAND MANAGEMENT

The DOI's Bureau of Land Management (BLM) administers the "leftovers" —federal lands neither reserved for particular purposes nor disposed of—

some 267 million acres of them.[92] It also manages 2 million acres of valuable
timberlands in western Oregon: the so-called "O&C" lands repossessed by
the federal government in one of the few actions it took against companies
that violated the terms of its lavish transportation grants.[93] In addition, the
BLM administers the mining and mineral leasing laws on all federal lands,
except for outer-continental shelf (OCS) lands.[94] In FY1991, the BLM spent
about $1.1 billion; in FY1991, its lands generated revenue of about $1.2
billion, chiefly from energy leases (about $1 billion) and O&C timber sales
(about $164 million).[95]

Although the BLM is charged with managing its lands on a multiple-
use, sustained-yield basis, that charge dates only from the Federal Land
Policy and Management Act of 1976 (FLPMA)[96] and the agency's history
is not generally associated with conservation or even with land management.
The BLM was formed in 1946 by the merger of two Interior Department
agencies: the General Land Office (GLO) and the Grazing Service (GS).
The GLO's business since its founding in 1812 was administering the
disposal of federal land. Such as it is, BLM's historical link to resource
management and conservation is via the GS and mineral leasing.

The USFS began regulating grazing in the National Forests in 1905.
Ranchers initially opposed a similar regime on unreserved federal lands.
However, severe overgrazing and disputes between established ranchers
and outsiders who attempted to "horn in" on their territory eventually led
them to support the stabilization promised by the Taylor Grazing Act of
1934.[97] Under its provisions, most unreserved federal land outside Alaska
was withdrawn from entry "pending its final disposal"[98] and placed under
the management of the GS. It was divided into grazing districts, within
which grazing rights were apportioned on the basis of historical use and
proximity to a home ranch.

The USFS had regularly proposed that it be given control of federal
rangelands, and Interior Secretary Harold Ickes imagined that the GS
might develop into a convincing argument against such inter-agency
imperialism. But the new agency was largely co-opted by the ranchers.
Where USFS policy could be informed and implemented by legions of
forest rangers with local knowledge, the GS was forced to rely on the
knowledge of the ranchers. They were delighted to be asked to serve
on Grazing Advisory Boards and to help in determining their grazing
rights, but they balked when the GS attempted to raise grazing fees or
to reduce herd size to prevent overgrazing. With the help of powerful
friends in Congress, they were largely successful in immobilizing the
GS. The decline of ranching relative to other sectors of the regional
economy and the counterpressure of environmental interest groups has
enabled the BLM to assert more authority over its lands. But the bad
experience of the GS has not been forgotten, and the BLM is noticably
less willing than other federal land-management agencies to buck economic
interests.

In managing grazing on its lands, and hardrock mining on federal lands, the BLM is largely a referee enforcing rules made by graziers and miners and sanctioned by Congress. The case of mineral leasing is a bit different. Here the federal government was not so passive but asserted its ownership of certain minerals and required those who would mine or extract them to pay for the privilege. It early drew a distinction between agricultural land and coal land, charging a higher price for the latter.[99] In 1906 President Roosevelt recommended that federal coal lands be leased, not sold; to get the attention of Congress, he withdrew from disposal all land—some 66 million acres—on which "workable coal is known to occur."[100] As a result, subsequent homesteading legislation reserved the mineral rights to the federal government. In 1909 President Taft withdrew from disposal three million acres of oil lands in California and Wyoming, anticipating that the navy would otherwise be buying back oil given away under provisions of the General Mining Law of 1872.[101] Eventually Congress got around to deciding that such "minerals" should be leased. Under the Mineral Leasing Act of 1920,[102] areas believed to contain deposits of "coal, phosphate, sodium, potassium, oil, oil shale, gilsonite, . . . or gas" are to be leased through competitive bidding, interested parties offering "bonus bids" for the right to extract oil, mine coal, etc. Other areas are open to prospecting under a permit system that rewards discovery with a non-competitive lease. In either case, the government receives a production royalty (generally 12.5%).

I've characterized the BLM's lands as "leftovers," and that is generally true: people didn't want them on the government's terms and couldn't figure out how to get around those terms. But it is not true that nobody wants them, and still less true that nobody takes an interest in them. Ranchers, for instance, might be happy to buy some BLM grazing land, if the price were right; since they'd then have to pay property taxes on it, purchase might not make economic sense, but then ranching doesn't make a whole lot of economic sense anyway. Coal, oil, and gas interests may have little interest in surface rights, except insofar as they restrict operations; but they certainly take an interest in leasing policy. Some BLM lands contain significant "cultural resources"—Indian ruins, pictographs, and other artifacts—that draw archaeologists and (alas) pothunters. And there are fascinating natural areas that environmentalists would like to see protected, such as portions of the Mohave Desert and some of the slickrock canyons of southeast Utah.[103]

## PUBLIC PARTICIPATION AND WILDERNESS DESIGNATION

All of these federal land-management agencies—the USFS, NPS, FWS, and BLM—now operate under statutes or regulations written pursuant to them requiring some form of public participation in policy-formation. The BLM and USFS are required to draft resource management plans for each management unit, to invite comments from the public, and to revise their draft plans accordingly—or to be prepared to explain in court why they haven't.[104] All federal agencies are subject to the National Environmenal Policy Act of 1969 (NEPA),[105] which requires that the environmental consequences of major federal actions be assessed in an environmental impact statement (EIS). Although NEPA does not require public hearings, federal courts have been willing to hear challenges to the adequacy of an EIS from interested segments of the public, and agencies have generally submitted a draft EIS for public comment prior to filing a final EIS.

Cynical observers regard public participation as window dressing: agencies do what they want to do—or what their "client" interest groups want them to do—regardless of what the public—or the tiny segment of it that takes an interest in such proceedings—wants. Most participants, however, believe that public participation makes some difference. From an agency perspective, it allows land managers to keep in touch with those who are interested in federal lands, to adjust agency policies and expectations accordingly, and perhaps to use these interests to advance agency goals by playing one interest group off against another.[106] From a broader perspective, there is the hope that public comments may make some real difference in policy, that throwing antagonists together in a public forum will lead to understanding of and respect for other views, and that compromise will ripen into consensus.

Availablity of a "Wilderness" classification for federal lands, precluding what many people think of as "use" entirely, has sharpened issues and debate in recent federal land-use planning. Congress established this designation in the Wilderness Act of 1964 "to assure that an increasing population, accompanied by expanding settlement and growing mechaniz-ation, does not occupy and modify all areas within the United States and its possessions, leaving no lands designated for preservation and protection in their natural condition."[107] The act placed about 5 million acres of National Forest land that the USFS had been administering as "wild," "wilderness," or "canoe" areas in the new Wilderness Preservation System. It also directed the USFS, NPS, and FWS to review certain other areas within their jurisdiction to determine their suitability for inclusion and to make recommendations to Congress accordingly. The act's definition of "wilder-ness" suggests that land suitable for "Wilderness" designation is that "retaining its primeval character and influence, without permanent improvement or human habitation, which . . . generally appears to have been affected primarily by the forces of nature, with the imprint of man's work substantially unnoticeable, . . . [and] has outstanding opportunities for solitude or a primitive and unconfined type of recreation."[108]

Congressional "Wilderness" designation does not shift jurisdiction of federal land from one agency to another, but it does require that it be managed to preserve its "primeval character." Motor vehicles are not allowed in Wilderness Areas; logging is prohibited, though grazing may be allowed. Wilderness Areas have been closed to mineral entry under hardrock and mineral leasing laws since 1984, and the likelihood of strict regulation to protect wilderness values has discouraged work on preexisting claims and leases. Those who have an interest in such activities generally oppose Wilderness designation as "locking up" resources. They are right: putting a piece of land in the Wilderness Preservation System represents a decision not to use it for mining, logging, motorized recreation, downhill skiing, etc., and one that would not be easy to reverse, given the present constituency for wilderness.

Pressure from environmentalists and agency initiative expanded the review of potential Wilderness Areas far beyond what the 1964 act required. In 1967 the USFS initiated a review (RARE I) of all roadless National Forest areas; lawsuits by environmentalists under NEPA led it to start over on a more detailed review (RARE II) ten years later. FLPMA required the BLM to undertake a similar inventory and review of roadless areas.[109] These review processes are slow and contentious; in 1982 the Wilderness System included about 80 million acres, 56 million of them due to the Alaska National Interest Lands Conservation Act of 1980.[110]

Applying the suitability guidelines of the Wilderness Act obviously calls for judgment, and different judgments can be expected from those want as much as possible of the remnants of the New World wilderness preserved and those who have different plans for them. The USFS concluded from RARE II that 15 million of the 62 million acres studied should be designated Wilderness and 11 million acres studied some more.[111] At the end of FY 1986, the USFS was administering 32 million acres of National Forest Wilderness.[112] The agency is now thinking in terms of a 40-million-acre National Forest Wilderness System, whereas conservationists talk about 65–70 million acres.[113] Pursuant to FLPMA, the BLM examined its non-Alaska holdings (174 million acres at the time) and found in 1980 that only 24 million acres warranted further study for Wilderness designation.[114] At the end of FY1991, less than 2 million acres of BLM land outside Alaska had been designated Wilderness.[115] The BLM and conservationists are generally far apart on wilderness. Thus, the Utah Wilderness Coalition proposed that 5.1 million acres of the 22.1 million acres BLM manages in Utah be designated Wilderness, whereas the BLM thought only 3.2 million were worth looking at and 1.9 acres million worth designating.[116]

This concludes my brief review of the history and management of federal lands. I hope it has not been so brief as to suggest that the situation is simpler than it is. Difficult management problems, in most cases conditioned by a complex history of accommodating various interests, confront every management agency. Immense effort is put into resolving them, though few go away entirely satisfied. Under the circumstances, it's natural to wonder if there isn't a better way. Privatization, maybe? Privatization would resolve these problems by relocation. What happens on federal land would no longer be everyone's business. Instead individuals or firms would be managing it as private property, and their management problems would be of no concern to society at large as long as their uses didn't produce significant spillovers.

I begin considering this proposal in Chapter 3. But let me close this one with a couple of historical observations.

First, the idea of privatizing federal lands is bound to strike anyone with a sense of history as a bit archaic. After all, the country has been there already, wearied of it, and has for the past hundred years been moving in the opposite direction. Perhaps, as academic privatization advocates argue, retention was a bad idea, a cure based on misdiagnosis that turned out to be worse than the disease. However that may be, retention is a long-standing trend in which powerful interests have a lot invested. It will take more than academic arguments to reverse it.

Those who look at public land management and see socialism tend to overlook the fact that federal ownership has, from the beginning, been a compromise between competing interests. Nowadays, these interests are largely embodied in private users of public lands—ranchers, mining and timber concerns, recreationists, energy companies, outfitters, etc.—who disagree about the best use of some of them. Federal land-management decisions are generally not the product of central planning or bureaucratic whim. To a large extent, they reflect the outcome of competition between these interests in open political processes. The competitors are likely to view radical proposals like privatization with suspicion. They have put a good deal of effort into developing spheres of influence and will be loath to risk what they have achieved by heeding calls to revolution. Even where management decisions have disappointed particular interests and appear to be irreversible, government ownership is a way of maintaining their claims, a way to stay in the game.

Second, the main reason now advanced for turning back the clock a hundred years—that privatizing public resources will secure their more efficient use—is not at all like those that have guided federal land policy from the beginning. Whether oriented toward disposal or retention, federal land policy has always been advertised as promoting *national* objectives: paying off war debts, securing peace among the states, settling the frontier, promoting democracy and the family farm, linking far-flung regions with railroads, promoting education, securing oil supplies for the navy, preserving the nation's cultural, historical, and natural heritage, etc. Such objectives have little to do with the sort of efficiency modern advocates of disposal have in mind.

Without offending anyone, we may say that resources are efficiently allocated when they are put to their most valuable uses. But while privatization advocates reckon what uses are most valuable by the desires and bankrolls of consumers, federal land policy has been informed by political determinations of what objectives are most worth pursuing: the political process essentially dictates that federal resources shall be used for such and such, whether or not a free market would so allocate them. It may be that our national habit of substituting collective for individual choice in this area is a bad one. But it is also ingrained and will be hard to break.

## NOTES

1. Perry R. Hagenstein, "The federal lands today—uses and limits," in *Rethinking the federal lands*, ed. Sterling Brubaker (Washington: Resources for the Future, 1984), 74–107 at 105.

2. From the Maryland Legislature's instruction to its delegates to the Continental Congress (1778), quoted in Paul W. Gates, *History of public land law development* (Washington: Government Printing Office, 1968), at 50.

3. From policy adopted by the Continental Congress to encourage state cessions (1780), quoted in Gates, note 2 *supra*, at 51.

4. The Land Act of 1796, 1 Stat. 464, allowed sales on credit (5% down, the balance due a year later), and Congress's response to widespread default was to liberalize terms. By 1820, land purchasers owed the federal government $22 million, and Congress lost patience; henceforth it required cash on the barrelhead.

5. The Graduation Act of 1854, 10 Stat. 574, provided for reducing the price of federal land according to the length of time it had remained unsold—all the way down to one bit ($.125) per acre after 30 years.

6. The 160-acre limitation of the Homestead Act of 1862, 12 Stat. 392, was raised to 320 acres in the Enlarged Homestead Act of 1909, 35 Stat. 369, and again to 640 acres in the Stock Raising Homestead Act of 1916, 39 Stat. 862.

7. Henry Steele Commager, ed., *Documents of American history* (Englewood Cliffs, NJ: Prentice-Hall, 1973), at 123.

8. See the "Cotter case," *State of Utah* v. *Andrus*, 486 F.Supp. 995 (D. Utah, 1979). Utah had leased to the Cotter Corporation mineral rights to a school section surrounded by federal land being considered for Wilderness designation. The federal government sued to enjoin construction of an access road across its land, but won only the right to regulate construction to minimize environmental impacts.

9. Note 6 *supra*.

10. Paul W. Gates, "The federal lands—why we retained them," in Brubaker, note 1 *supra*, 35–60 at 36.

11. Note 4 *supra*.

12. The Land Act of 1800, 2 Stat. 73, dropped the minimum to a half-section at $2 per acre; the Land Act of 1804, 2 Stat. 277, to a quarter-section at $2 per acre; the Land Act of 1820, 3 Stat. 566, to an eighth-section at $1.25 per acre.

13. The Graduation Act of 1854, note 5 *supra*, specified that an individual could acquire no more than 320 acres—and this for his own cultivation and residence. For acreage limitations in later homestead legislation, see note 6 *supra*. The Desert Lands Act of 1877, 19 Stat. 377, permitted individuals to acquire up to 320 acres of "desert land" by irrigating it. The Reclamation Act of 1902, 32 Stat. 388, limited to 160 the number of acres any one person could acquire within a federal irrigation district.

14. Note 6 *supra*.

15. Note 6 *supra*.

16. *Public land statistics 1991* (Washington: BLM, 1992), Table 1.

17. Id., Table 2.

18. Gates, note 2 *supra*, at 87.

19. John Locke, *Two treatises of government*, ed. Peter Laslett (New York: Mentor, 1965), at 329 (Book II, Chapter V, §27).

20. At first this was done retrospectively: settlers who could convince land agents they'd improved land could buy it at the legislated price. But in 1841

legislation (5 Stat. 453) that anticipated homesteading, Congress agreed to prospective preemption: a settler could choose 160 acres of unclaimed federal land, file a declaration of intent to improve it for his or her own use, and thereby preempt other claims until purchased at $1.25 per acre. A prohibition (Sec. 13) against holding the land for speculation was widely abused. Until its repeal by the General Revision Act of 1891, 26 Stat. 1095, prospective preemption was also abused by loggers: they would file for preemption, level the forest, and move on without buying the land.

21. 30 U.S.C.A. §§21–42. For a justification of sorts, one might invoke Locke: "the Grass my Horse has bit; the Turfs my Servant has cut; and the Ore I have digg'd in any place where I have a right to them in common with others, become my *Property*, without the assignation or consent of any body. The *labour* that was mine, removing them out of that common state they were in, hath *fixed* my *Property* in them." Locke, note 19 *supra*, at 330 (§28).

22. Cf. *United States* v. *Coleman*, 390 U.S. 599 (1968), for the Supreme Court's view of what constitutes a valuable discovery.

23. Some minerals have been removed from the scope of the 1872 Law; e.g., fuel minerals are leased under provisions of the Mineral Leasing Act of 1920, 30 U.S.C.A. §§181–287, and gravel, sand, etc. is sold under provisions of the Common Varieties Act of 1947, 30 U.S.C.A. §§601–4.

24. 30 U.S.C.A. §29. Mining claims are not always patented. In 1991, $175M in gold was extracted from the Barrick Gold Strike Mine's unpatented claims on federal land near Carlin, Nevada. "Digging for ore still pays; should miners pay, too?", *The New York Times*, 12 February 1992, A1. The Barrick case has helped renew interest in mining-law reform. For a discussion of recent legislative proposals, see John Livermore and Glenn Miller, "How to break the impasse over mining reform," *High Country News*, 4 October 1993, 12–13.

25. 43. U.S.C.A. §§315–15r.

26. Note 13 *supra*.

27. *Bryant* v. *Yellen*, 447 U.S. 352 (1980).

28. 43 U.S.C.A. §390dd specifies a limit of 960 acres for individuals and legal entities benefitting 25 or fewer individuals and 640 acres for larger entities.

29. *Public land statistics 1991*, note 16 *supra*, Table 2.

30. Id.

31. Id.

32. Ohio got one section (no. 16) per township. In 1846, Congress liberalized the school lands formula to two sections per township and finally, in 1894, to four sections. Some states admitted after Ohio are not considered public-land states because they contained no federal land to begin with. They include states (such as West Virginia) formed from the territory of one of the original states, and Texas, which was treated as an independent nation when it petitioned to join the Union.

33. 12 Stat. 503.

34. 5 Stat. 453, Sec. 8.

35. 9 Stat. 519.

36. *Public land statistics 1991*, note 16 *Supra*, Table 2.

37. The Alaska Statehood Act of 1958, 72 Stat. 339, at Sec. 6(a,b,k), allowed the state to select about 103.3 million acres of federal land, on top of the 1.2 million acres it had been granted as a Territory.

38. See, e.g., Roderick Nash, *Wilderness and the American mind* (New Haven: Yale, 1973) and Mark Sagoff, "On preserving the natural environment," *Yale*

*Law Journal* 84 (1974), 205–67 at II ("America's covenant with nature recognized").

39. E.g., under the Timber and Stone Act of 1878, 20 Stat. 46.

40. Forest Service Organic Act of 1897, 16 U.S.C.A. §475.

41. FLPMA, 43 U.S.C.A. §§1701–84, at §1701(a)(8).

42. *Land areas of the National Forest System as of September 30, 1992* (Washington: USFS, 1993), Table 1.

43. 26 Stat. 1095, at Sec. 24. Regional National Forest acreages from *Land areas of the National Forest System*, note 42 *supra*, Table 1.

44. The Weeks Act authorized purchase of "forested, cut-over, or denuded lands within the watersheds of navigable streams as . . . may be necessary to the regulation of the flow of navigable streams." The Clarke–McNary Act added ". . . or for the production of timber." These authorizations are combined in 16 U.S.C.A. §515.

Ironically, some of this National Forest land is now threatened by strip mining, for, to save money, the federal government often acquired only the surface rights. The Surface Mining Control and Reclamation Act of 1977, 30 U.S.C.A. §§1201–328, at §1272(e), does stipulate that "after August 3, 1977, and subject to valid existing rights [VER] no surface coal mining operations except those which exist on August 3, 1977, shall be permitted . . . on any Federal lands within the boundaries of any national forest." But many private interests may hold VER to mine coal within National Forests; see *Belville Mining Company* v. *U.S.*, 763 F.Supp. 1411 (S.D. Ohio, 1991) and 999 F.2d 989 (6th Cir., 1993).

A brief review of the convoluted history of attempts by the Office of Surface Mining (OSM) to define VER can be found in its discussion of the latest proposal, 56 FR 33152 (1991), at 33152–3. This was that "VER would exist when an applicant for a permit to conduct surface coal mining operations has obtained, or has made a good faith effort to obtain, all necessary permits, or the application of the Section 522(e) [= §1272(e)] prohibitions would effect a compensable taking of the property covered by the application." The "takings test" given by the last clause comes close to identifying VER with mineral rights. However, in the Energy Policy Act of 1992, 106 Stat. 2776, at Sec. 2504(b), Congress stipulated that OSM use only the other two tests for a year, to allow time for legislative clarification of VER.

45. 7 U.S.C.A. §1010. National Grassland acreage from *Land areas of the National Forest System*, note 42 *supra*, Table 1.

46. FY1992 expenditures from *Budget of the United States Government, Fiscal Year 1994* (Washington: Office of Management and Budget, 1992), Appendix 61–2. Not all the $3.3 billion was spent on land management; $146 million went to state and private forestry and $175 million to research. In addition, $338 million went to states and counties as their share of receipts. FY1991 receipts from *National forest statement of receipts, FY91* (Washington: Congressional Information Service, 1992), at 18.

47. Locke, note 19 *supra*, at 329 (§27).

48. From an annual report by John Brooks, land agent for a Michigan canal company with a strong interest in timber, quoted in Russell McKee, "Tombstones of a lost forest," *Audubon* 90(2) (1988), 62–73 at 66.

49. Id., at 68.

50. George Perkins Marsh, *Man and nature; or, physical geography as modified by human action* (New York: Scribners, 1864).

51. Cf. excerpts from Schurz's *Annual report of the Secretary of the Interior on*

*the operations of the Department for the fiscal year ended June 30, 1877*, in *The American environment: Readings in the history of conservation*, ed. Roderick Nash (Reading, MA: Addison-Wesley, 1968), 24–28 at 26.

52. Note 20 *supra*.

53. For statutory language, see page 37 *supra*.

54. 34 Stat. 1269 (1907).

55. Gifford Pinchot, *The use of the national forests* (Washington: Forest Service, 1907), at 13.

56. From the Secretary of Agriculture's letter of instruction to Pinchot, on his appointment as Chief Forester of the Forest Service, quoted in Gifford Pinchot, *Breaking new ground* (New York: Harcourt, Brace, 1947) at 261. Pinchot actually wrote these instructions himself: "The letter, it goes without saying, I had brought myself to the Secretary for his signature." Id., at 260.

57. Schurz in Nash, note 51 *supra*, at 26.

58. In FY1990, the USFS estimates that recreationists spent 263 million (12-hour) visitor-days in the National Forests. *Statistical abstract of the United States 1992* (Lanham, MD: Bernan Press, 1992), Table 380. Recreational use of the National Forests has increased at an annual rate of nearly 10% since at least the 1920s. Marion Clawson, *The federal lands revisited* (Washington: Resources for the Future, 1984), at 101. In the twenty years following World War II, annual timber sales from the National Forests increased from about 2 billion BF to 12 billion BF. Id. at 75. After two decades at approximately this level, sales have declined by about 50%, due primarily to environmental restrictions on logging in the Pacific Northwest.

59. From 1970–90 about 10 billion BF of timber was cut from Alaska's Tongass National Forest to supply mills producing pulp and minimally processed logs, largely for export to Japan. These were deficit sales, costing the USFS more to prepare than was realized in revenue. §705(a) of the Alaska National Interest Lands Conservation Act of 1980 (ANILCA), 94 Stat. 2371, mandated a cut of 450 million BF annually in the National Forest, authorizing $40 million per year to pay for it. These provisions were repealed by the Tongass Timber Reform Act of 1990, 104 Stat. 4426. However, the federal government continues to subsidize Tongass timber-sales. See "The $64 million question," *Sierra* 78(4) (1993), 55–7.

Unprocessed logs from Western federal lands may not be (legally) exported (36 CFR 223.161–2; the restriction originated in the FY1974 appropriations bill for DOI and related agencies, PL 93–404, Sec. 301). However, foreign demand for "raw" logs means increased harvests of federal timber. Private forestlands supply logs for export, so the local mills that would otherwise process them lobby Congress and the USFS for greater access to federal stands.

60. MUSYA, 16 U.S.C.A. §§528–31, at §528. Recalling Pinchot's instructions to himself, note 56 *supra*, the 1960 legislation was essentially drafted by the USFS.

61. MUSYA, note 60 *supra*, at §529.

62. Id., at §531.

63. "The Secretary of Agriculture shall limit the sale of timber from each national forest to a quantity equal to or less than a quantity which can be removed from such forest annually in perpetuity on a sustained-yield basis." NFMA, 16 U.S.C.A. §§1600–14, at §1611(a).

64. As of 31 December 1992. *National Park Service: Listing of acreages by region* (Washington: Congressional Information Service, 1993).

65. FY1992 expenditures from *1994 Budget*, note 46 *supra*, Appendix 100. Not all the $1.3 billion was spent on federal lands; about $58 million went to state and

local governments for land purchases and historic preservation. FY1990 receipts from *Federal recreation fee report to Congress, 1990* (Washington: Congressional Information Service, 1991), Table 14.

66. 13 Stat. 325. In 1905, California ceded them back to the United States, which in 1890 had reserved the surrounding area for Yosemite National Park.

67. 13 Stat. 325.

68. 17 Stat. 32.

69. Id.

70. Id.

71. 16 U.S.C.A. §431.

72. 43 FR 57009–131 (Dec. 1, 1978).

73. Letter to President Roosevelt (1907), quoted in Nancy Wood, *Clearcut* (San Francisco: Sierra Club, 1971), at 1.

74. Quoted in Wood, note 73 *supra*, at 1.

75. 38 Stat. 242 (1913).

76. The National Park Service Organic Act of 1916, 16 U.S.C.A. §1.

77. See, e.g., Edward Abbey, "A walk in the park," *Abbey's road* (New York: Dutton, 1979), 107–16.

78. *Refuges 2003: a plan for the future of the National Wildlife Refuge System* (Washington: FWS, 1993), at 1. These figures include a relatively small amount of private land held by lease or easement; about half of the acreage outside of Alaska was acquired, not reserved.

79. FY1992 expenditures from *1994 Budget*, note 46 *supra*, Appendix 99. Perhaps $700 million was spent on land management. FY1990 recreation receipts from *Recreation fee report*, note 65 *supra*, Table XIV. The refuges also generate some royalties from oil and gas leases.

80. Unnumbered Executive Order dated March 13, 1903. His authority seems to have been a history of presidential reservations for non-statutory purposes; at any rate, Congress didn't object. Cf. *United States* v. *Midwest Oil Co.*, 236 U.S. 459 (1915).

81. 16 U.S.C.A. §671.

82. 16 U.S.C.A. §715–15r.

83. TS 628.

84. The National Wildlife Refuge Administration Act of 1966 (NWRAA), 16 U.S.C.A. §§668dd-ee.

85. 45 Stat. 1222 (1929), Sec. 6. Section 10 prohibited taking birds within refuges acquired under the act.

86. Migratory Bird Hunting and Conservation Act of 1934, 16 U.S.C.A. §§718–18h.

87. NWRAA, note 84 *supra*, at §668dd(d)(1)(A).

88. Id., at §668dd(a)(1).

89. Id., at §668dd(c).

90. Under provisions of ANILCA, note 59 *supra*, 16 U.S.C.A. §§3101–233, at §§3142–3, it is closed to leasing pending Interior Department study of the effects of oil and gas leasing on wildlife and congressional action on its recommendations.

91. Defending closure of Sheldon National Wildlife Refuge in Nevada to grazing, its manager remarked, "This place was being run like a commercial cattle ranch." "Refuges feel strain as wildlife and commerce collide," *The New York Times*, 1 December 1991, A38. See also "Refuge wildlife enhancement efforts being hampered by secondary uses," *National Wildlife Refuges: continuing problems with*

*incompatible uses call for bold action* (Washington: General Accounting Office, 1989), Chapter 2.

92. *Public land statistics 1991*, note 16 *supra*, Tables 5 and 6. At the end of FY1991, the federal government still owed Alaska and its native peoples about 31 million acres, the bulk of which will come from BLM holdings (90 million acres, 1991). However, the native selection formula also makes some USFS and FWS lands liable to transfer.

93. Checkerboard grants (20 sections per mile) to the Oregon and California Railroad, 14 Stat. 239 (1866) and 16 Stat. 94 (1869), and a 6-mile corridor to the state of Oregon for the Coos Bay Wagon Road, 15 Stat. 340 (1869), were subject to a "homestead clause" requiring that the granted lands be resold in blocks of not more than 160 acres at not more than $2.50 per acre. Default on these conditions led Congress to revoke the grants—actually only the unsold portions of them—in 1916 and to put the Interior Department in the timber business (39 Stat. 218).

94. Jurisdiction over OCS leasing was transferred from the BLM to the Minerals Management Service in 1982.

95. FY1992 expenditures from *1994 Budget*, note 46 *supra*, Appendix 95–96. While all of the BLM's outlay is related to land management, $126 million of it went to states and counties in lieu of taxes or as their share of lease and sale revenue. Table 63 of *Public Land Statistics 1991*, note 16 *supra*, gives FY1991 receipts of about $217 million for BLM land, but this does not include mineral leasing revenue, now collected by the Minerals Management Service. Table 1 of *Mineral revenues 1991* (Washington: Minerals Management Service, 1992) puts onshore federal mineral-lease revenue at $1.0 billion for FY1990; no agency breakdown is given, but it is likely that nearly all the lease revenue comes from BLM land.

96. Note 41 *supra*. For multiple-use language, see §1701(a)(7), §1712(c)(1), §1732(a).

97. Note 25 *supra*.

98. Id., at §315.

99. In 1864 the President was directed to sell coal lands at $20 per acre instead of the standard $1.25 per acre for agricultural land, 13 Stat. 343.

100. Quoted in Gates, note 2 *supra*, at 726.

101. Note 21 *supra*. The Supreme Court backed him up in *Midwest Oil*, note 80 *supra*.

102. Note 23 *supra*; the list of leasable minerals is from §181.

103. See, e.g., Debbie Sease, "Protecting the California Desert," *Public lands: Newsletter of the Sierra Club Public Lands Committee* 5(2) (1987), 6–8; and Rick Crocker, et al., "The parks that got away . . . and how we get them back," *Southern Utah Wilderness Alliance Newsletter* 5(2) (1988), 1–5.

104. FLPMA, note 41 *supra*, requires "public involvement" in the BLM's development and revision of land-use plans for all its lands, §1712. It also requires regional citizen advisory councils to "furnish advice to the Secretary [of the Interior] with respect to the land use planning, classification, retention, management, and disposal of the public lands within the area for which the advisory council is established," §1739(d).

NFMA, note 63 *supra*, mandates an "opportunity for public involvement" in the preparation of Renewable Resource Assessments (which consider the role of the National Forests in meeting demands for forest products), §1601(c). It is more explicit about "public participation in the development, review, and revision of land management plans" for units of the National Forest System: the Secretary of

Agriculture is to make "the plans or revisions available to the public at convenient locations in the vicinity of the affected unit for a period of at least three months before final adoption, during which period the Secretary shall publicize and hold public meetings or comparable processes at locations that foster public participation in the review of such plans or revisions," §1604(d).

105. 42 U.S.C.A. §§4321–61.

106. Paul J. Culhane, *Public lands politics: interest group influence on the Forest Service and the Bureau of Land Management* (Washington: Resources for the Future, 1981), at 333.

107. Wilderness Act of 1964, 16 U.S.C.A. §§1131–36, at §1131(a).

108. Id., at §1131(c).

109. FLPMA, note 51 *supra*, at §1782.

110. ANILCA, note 59 *supra*. Wilderness System acreage from *Our public lands: an introduction to the agencies and issues* (San Francisco: Sierra Club, 1982), at 9; ANILCA Wilderness acreage from "The 96th Congress—a wrap up," *Sierra* 66(1) (1981), 14–16 at 14.

111. *Our public lands*, note 110 *supra*, at 11.

112. *What the Forest Service does* (Washington: USFS, 1987), at 13.

113. Peter C. Kirby and Robert W. Turnage, "Two visions of the National Forests' future," *Public Lands: Newsletter of the Sierra Club Public Lands Committee* 5(1) (1987), 5–7 at 5.

114. *Our public lands*, note 110 *supra*, at 11. In ANILCA, note 90 *supra*, Congress directed the BLM to study its lands on the North Slope of Alaska for possible Wilderness designation, §3141(b)(2), but prohibited wilderness study of other BLM Alaska lands, §3213(b).

115. *Public land statistics 1991*, note 16 *supra*, Table 40.

116. See "Utah's wilderness review contains major flaws," *Public lands: Newsletter of the Sierra Club Public Lands Committee* 4(3) (1986), 12–13; and Ray Wheeler, "The BLM wilderness inventory," *Southern Utah Wilderness Alliance Newsletter* 9(2) (1992), insert 1–8. For a synopsis of the Utah Wilderness Coalition's proposal, see "Utah BLM wild lands still at risk," *The Utah Wilderness News* (Salt Lake City, Utah Wilderness Coalition, Summer 1992).

# 3

# The Case for Privatization

> Ideally, all resources should be owned, or ownable, by someone, except resources so plentiful that everyone can consume as much of them as he wants without reducing consumption by anyone else. . . .
>
> Richard A. Posner[1]

Should groves of quaking aspen in the National Forests of southwestern Colorado be maintained for those who delight in them, "so vibrant with light and motion, forever restless, always whispering, in tune like ballerinas to the music of the air,"[2] and for ranchers, whose cows perhaps delight in the grass and shade they provide? Or should the trees be sold to Louisiana Pacific, which has figured out how to turn them into a cheaper substitute for plywood, thereby providing jobs in a not-too-prosperous area?[3] Should portions of BLM land in the Mohave Desert be open to motorcycle races that draw thousands of participants, who "really love this sort of thing"[4] and spend a lot of money in local communities? Or should they be withdrawn from off-road use as "critical habitat" for the endangered desert tortoise?

Answers to questions like these may add up to one sort of answer to the question, "How should public lands be managed?" Insofar as the uses proposed for different parcels are consistent (so that, for example, silt from a logging operation doesn't destroy a downstream fishery), these answers will constitute a coherent plan of use for public lands. But this is not the kind of answer privatization advocates give. They do not argue directly for some pattern of use, local or global. Instead, they maintain that a system in which resources are private and individuals decide how theirs are to be used is better than one in which the private use of public resources is regulated by collective decisions. That is, they take the question "How should public lands be managed?" to ask not for a giant management plan that specifies the best use of each acre, but for a description of the institutions which best constrain decisions about use.

Privatization advocates do propose to judge land-management institutions by results, but not by how closely these results fit some pattern they are prepared to specify in advance. Like politicians who tailor their pitch to their audience, they may suggest to each of various groups—environmentalists, loggers, ranchers, and others—that their interests in public lands will be better served by private management. But their basic appeal is not to some vision of how these lands should be used. Instead, they want us to agree that institutions should be judged by how productive they make resources, including those sunk into the institutions, where resources are more productive as their use better satisfies the desires of consumers. And they argue that by this criterion, private management is superior to collective management, however reformed or enlightened.

I take this appeal to productivity to be the central line of argument for privatization. In this chapter, I aim to develop it sufficiently to reveal both its depth and some openings for criticism. I begin in the first section with objections to the historical case for retention. Contemporary proponents of disposal argue that the nation picked the wrong solution to the problem of the commons, which I review in the second section. In the view of these critics, dividing public land among individual members of the public, to use as they wished, would have been preferable to regulating their individual uses of it. Under the current regulatory system, individuals have rights to use federal lands, but these rights are generally incomplete, non-transferable, and insecure. In consequence, privatization advocates claim, resources are wasted; arguments to this effect are given in the third section of this chapter. Moreover, as detailed in the fourth section, they see collective management as encouraging irresponsibility, allowing individuals to secure benefits at a discount by shifting some of the cost to others. These critics maintain that a system of complete, transferable, and secure private property rights to federal lands would make them more productive, as well as freeing for other uses the resources now sunk into managing them; some general considerations supporting this position are presented in the fifth section. Finally, in the last section, I give the argument from productivity an explicit premise-conclusion structure and note some lines of weakness.

## THE ILLOGIC OF RETENTION

Federal lands were retained in part to avoid evils associated with disposal. To the extent that such associations are correct, they may make a case for retention. Accordingly, modern advocates of privatization question them, arguing that these evils were only apparent or should not be held against disposal.

According to these apologists, at least some of what conventional wisdom vilifies as waste, speculation, and inequity was not really evil at all. Thus, they suggest, the lumbering practices of the last century that seem so wasteful to us (cutting everything to get at the clear white pine, for instance) may have made good sense when timber was abundant,[5] just as it may earlier have made sense to cut everything and *burn it* to clear land for crops.[6] We don't generally operate this way now, but that is because wood products have become more valuable so that it pays to utilize more of each tree and to reforest cutover land. Furthermore, they maintain, the transition from "waste" to "thrift" would have occurred without reserving the National Forests. As timber became scarcer, entrepreneurs would have realized that they could profit from acquiring and holding standing timber to cut when prices were higher. Eventually it would have paid to invest in reforestation and to leave less of what was cut to rot in the woods. That, after all, is what private timber companies do now on their own lands. In fact, intensive forestry makes Weyerhauser's forestland considerably more productive (of "forest products") than comparable National Forest land managed less intensively by the USFS.[7]

Holding resources in hopes of higher future prices is speculation, and advocates of privatization argue that its bad reputation is undeserved.[8] Where others look to federal managers, directed by statute to insure "a continuous supply of timber" or a "sustained yield of the several products and services," to conserve resources, they instead place their trust in speculators, who gamble that higher future demand will repay acquiring and withholding resources from present consumption. In their view, speculators are middlemen between the present and the future, giving the latter a voice it would not otherwise have in present consumption decisions. If the future turns out to be a rather short time off, as it probably was in many cases where federal land was acquired for speculative purposes, speculators look more like ordinary middlemen, who prosper by identifying valuable resources and making them available to society. The companies that assembled, divided, and sold tracts of land to settlers did what suburban developers do now. Of course, their services weren't free, but they may have gotten "land to the people" more cheaply than the average settler could have managed without them. He may actually have been better off dealing with land companies in a competitive real-estate market than locating, on his own and at considerable cost, land he could buy directly from the government, albeit at a lower price.

Skeptics may wonder how settlers who couldn't meet speculators' prices were better off. They may also be revolted by the spectacle of the well-positioned enriching themselves at the expense of the ill-favored. In response, privatization advocates can draw upon the ideas of people like Friedrich Hayek, who actually has good things to say about disparities in wealth. Hayek points out that the rich finance the development of innovations, thereby making them affordable for the rest of us.[9] For this reason and others, he maintains that intervening in the operation of the free market in order to help the poor is generally counterproductive: they usually end up worse off as a result.[10] Essentially, his position is that individuals can expect to be better off, on average, where resources are private and government intervention in the free market is minimal, though some of course will not be.[11] Although some land speculators got rich, they did so by making others, including the poor, better off than they would otherwise have been. Similar claims might be made on behalf of railroad magnates, timber barons, silver kings and other creatures of the disposal era.

To the extent that its perceived evils can't, by such arguments, be transformed into goods, privatization advocates can argue that they should not be held against disposal. Thus, economists often insist that equity is a *political*, not an *economic*, problem. If we could agree on what they were, people's basic needs might be met by gifts of cash or goods without otherwise intervening in the market. The Homestead Act provided anyone interested in farming with a gift of 160 acres. If that wasn't enough to provide a living in most of the West, it's no argument against disposal: Congress should have known better and adjusted the amount of land for conditions. Although it is not their chief concern, privatization advocates argue that equity would be better served by disposal. The average American would be better off, they suggest, if federal lands and resources were sold and the proceeds and administrative cost-savings distributed in the form of debt retirement or contributions to the Social Security system.[12]

The wholesale fraud that attended disposal does suggest that the *processes* of privatization need more attention than modern advocates of disposal have given them.[13] However, it is not much of an argument for retention, concerning as it does means and not ends. Modern advocates of disposal can claim that historical cases of fraud should have provoked more effective oversight and, in some cases, reconsideration of the conditions imposed on cash sales and homesteading, rather than inclining Congress toward retention.

Privatization advocates attribute selected environmental disasters of the disposal era—the slaughter of the buffalo and annihilation of the passenger pigeon, some deforestation and consequent erosion, the desertification of the range—not to the presence of private property but to its *absence*, to the fact that resources were held in common. Where a resource is common property, appropriatable only by consumption, nobody has an incentive to conserve it.[14] The buffalo I don't shoot for its tongue today will be shot by someone else tomorrow. Both the forest reservations and the grazing districts were a response to depredations resulting from treating federal forest and range as a commons. But wouldn't privatization also solve this problem, and at less cost? Surely individuals have an interest in maximizing the value of the resources they own. Simple self-interest would lead timber companies and ranchers to manage these lands wisely if they owned them, obviating the need for expensive federal land-management agencies.

Finally, any remaining evils can be bundled up as the unavoidable costs of achieving a socio-economic system that few would exchange for anything cheaper.[15] Of course, these costs are typically borne quite unequally: one generation's use of resources may make life for those that follow poorer in some respect, whites prospered at the expense of black slaves and indigenous peoples, etc. But perhaps an appeal like Hayek's to the welfare of the average individual ("Would you prefer living in this society or in that one, given that you didn't know when or who you'd be?") can be used to suggest that equity is less important than expected welfare.

## THE COMMONS

To the extent that such arguments dissociate privatization from the evils of the disposal era, they dispose of historical objections to it. In itself, this isn't enough to justify the resumption of disposal. What's needed is a more positive case for privatizing public lands, one that gives us reason to believe that objections *will* fail, not just that some have. I begin developing it by taking a closer look at the problem of the commons.

Privatization is recommended to environmentalists as a way of avoiding the environmental abuse that results from treating resources as common property, free to anyone for the taking. This rationale may seem obsolete. After all, federal land isn't common property in this sense any more, since its use is now regulated to avoid these very problems. However, those who advocate privatizing public lands view regulation as an inferior solution, in part because it is incomplete, creating a commons at the level of regulatory decision-making, where interested parties are free to take what they can get in the political process.

A resource is common property when anyone may use it but, accordingly, may not exclude others. Federal rangeland was a grazing commons prior to the forest reserves and grazing districts; anyone could legally run stock on it, and the federal government resisted private attempts to exclude others by fencing portions of it.[16] As long as aggregate demand for forage remains below what the range supplies, there's no problem with such a system. But when forage becomes *scarce* in the sense that aggregate demand exceeds biological productivity, there's little incentive here for anyone to conserve the range by limiting the number of stock he runs on it. In fact, individual stockmen find themselves in a notorious *prisoner's dilemma*[17] that encourages overgrazing, leaving them all worse off.

To construct it, we need only assume that grazing in excess of productivity eventually reduces productivity. There are two ways in which this might occur: forage plants might simply be grazed down to a less-productive point in their growth curve, or the productive capacity of the range might be diminished through erosion, soil compaction, succession to unpalatable species, etc.

Biological resources, such as the forage produced by a piece of rangeland $R$, typically have an S-shaped growth curve. Imagine regrowth on $R$ following a fire. Over time, forage accumulates slowly, then more rapidly, finally levelling off with plant maturity and competition for light, water, and nutrients. The forage productivity of $R$ is the rate at which $R$ produces forage. Here it rises to a maximum—the maximum sustainable yield (MSY)—and then declines. The MSY of $R$ is the greatest rate at which forage can be harvested from $R$ indefinitely, assuming that the conditions on which productivity depends (soil, rainfall, etc.) do not change.

Range forage is typically measured in animal unit months (AUMs), 1 AUM being sufficient to feed one 1-ton cow for one month. Let us ignore seasonal variation and suppose the MSY of $R$ is 10 AUM/month. Then 10 cows can be pastured there indefinitely, assuming that nothing else is eating. Adding an extra cow will increase the harvest to 11 AUM/month; the extra 1 AMU/month must be taken from forage stock. If the cattle keep eating at this rate, forage stock will eventually be completely depleted and they will be forced to get by on the new growth, if any, put out by root and stem. Or perhaps at some point short of stock depletion, the cattle economize on food-gathering effort, preferring hunger to looking for more to eat. In either case, they are eating lower on the growth curve and productivity is therefore lower than the MSY. This assumes that grazing has a negligible effect on the forage growth curve itself, but overgrazing can alter some of the factors that determine it. Local overgrazing won't diminish rainfall, but it can compact soil, increasing runoff and erosion and decreasing water retention. Livestock usually won't eat everything, and plants they avoid thus enjoy a selective advantage over more palatable species: western rangeland often goes to woody species like big sagebrush and juniper. Such changes flatten the growth curve of (usable) forage, reducing both stock and flow.

Suppose that grazing on $R$ is unregulated and that overgrazing would reduce its productivity as follows:

| | Number of cows grazing $R$ | | |
| --- | --- | --- | --- |
| | 10 | 11 | 12 |
| Total forage yield (AUM/mo) | 10.0 | 9.9 | 9.6 |
| Forage per cow (AUM/mo) | 1.0 | 0.9 | 0.8 |

Assume that, economically speaking, cows are what they eat: a cow that eats 10% less is worth 10% less. If $R$ is used by ranchers $A$ and $B$ to pasture five cows apiece, then the birth of a calf in each herd confronts $A$ and $B$ with a prisoner's dilemma. Keeping the calves on $R$ will worsen the position of both $A$ and $B$, but that is what will happen if each acts independently from self-interest. $A$ will rank possible outcomes according to the matrix below, where 5 = maintain a herd of five, and 6 = add the calf:

$B$'s choice

| 6 | 6 | |
| --- | --- | --- |
| 4.5 | 5.0 | 5 |
| 4.8 | 5.4 | 6 |

$A$'s choice

$A$ will reason that keeping the calf on $R$ is preferable to removing it no matter what $B$ does. Since $B$'s ranking is given by the same matrix with "$A$" and "$B$" interchanged, $B$ will come to the same conclusion. So they'll each end up moving from five well-fed cows to six scrawnier ones, worth less in aggregate, and to a less-productive range. Furthermore, additional opportunities to increase herd size may present additional dilemmas: if per capita yield falls by 0.1 AUM/mo for each cow added, then $A$ and $B$ will increase their herds to seven (though not to eight) if they have a chance.

The way out of the dilemma is agreement. $A$ and $B$ might agree between themselves to limit their herds to five. But if $R$ were open to other users, such an agreement could be defeated by the arrival of *C*'s cows. So this sort of agreement must be broader: society at large must agree to limit grazing on *R* to ten cows and to apportion grazing rights to *A* and *B*. Alternatively, *A* and *B* could agree to fence *R* down the middle. *A*'s stocking decisions could then be made independently of *B*'s without affecting *B*'s choices, and vice versa; and neither would be led to overstock his portion lest the other's cows eat the forage. But you can't do that if the government owns the land and tears down your fence. Again, agreement must include society; it must either transfer *R* to *A* and *B*, or give them grazing rights to *R* that provide for fencing.

The Taylor Grazing Act of 1934 embodied such agreements for federal rangeland now administered by the BLM. The federal government agreed to close the open range, fencing it into grazing allotments assigned to ranchers essentially in accord with agreements made among themselves. In most cases, an individual has exclusive grazing rights to an allotment; however, some allotments are grazed in common, the users agreeing among themselves how to apportion the permitted number of animals.[18] Stocking decisions are not supposed to be left to permittees; instead, federal range managers are to determine, generally as part of an Allotment Management Plan (AMP), "the numbers of animals to be grazed and the seasons of use"[19] so as to conserve the allotment's range.

Allotments are only part way to being private property. Ranchers can't buy them as such and don't pay property taxes on them either, at least directly. They do, however, pay for them in other ways. Federal allotments substantially increase the value of those ranches to which they are by custom attached. Ranch purchasers therefore pay for them; and operators, who could sell out for more than the ranch itself is worth, accordingly "pay" an opportunity cost that reflects their value.[20] A rancher's cows don't eat for free on her allotment, though federal forage is generally priced below market rates. Furthermore, exclusive grazing rights don't allow ranchers to close their allotments to other uses; they may have to accommodate wildlife, including hungry deer and wild horses, and they cannot exclude recreational use, oil drilling, firewood harvesting, etc. The BLM is to regulate these and other "multiple uses" pursuant to land-use plans—Resource Management Plans (RMPs)—developed with public input.[21]

## DEFICIENCIES OF REGULATION

Privatization advocates regret that this solution to the problems of the grazing commons stopped short of simply handing ranchers title to grazing allotments. Neither the rancher nor anyone else has the complete, transferable, and secure rights to federal rangeland that, in their view, would lead to its best use. One's right to *X* is *complete* to the extent that it permits one to control the use of *X*, *transferable* to the extent that one may transfer it to someone else without the approval of third parties, and *secure* to the extent that one's uncoerced consent is required to extinguish it. Rights to use federal lands are typically somewhat (1) incomplete, (2) non-transferable, and (3) insecure. As privatization advocates see it, each of these features contributes to the waste of resources.

1. Ranchers' rights to their allotments are incomplete, since they cannot run as many stock as they please or control non-grazing use. Surely, privatization advocates suggest, individual ranchers know local economic and range conditions better than district BLM range managers and could make better stocking decisions than they. Unlike trees, grass doesn't keep. If better than average rainfall causes an allotment to grow more grass than the BLM expects, the rancher won't benefit since he'll be limited by the AMP to running stock in numbers that expected rainfall will support.[22] From his point of view, the grass will go to waste. Fancy computer modelling might make federal stocking stipulations more sensitive to local conditions, but central planning is unlikely to do as well as ranchers with intimate knowledge of local conditions, or so people like Hayek argue.[23] Incomplete rights prevent the rancher making full use of his knowledge to get the most out of the land. And every other user is in the same position. For example, someone who holds a mineral lease will have to tailor operations to accommodate the BLM's idea of other appropriate uses of the area.

"But," it might be objected, "isn't the BLM in a better position to make a disinterested determination of the best mix of uses for its land than are would-be users, who are likely to be short-sighted and self-serving? And doesn't the agency itself hold what amounts to a complete bundle of rights, which it can dole out to effect this best mix?" Privatization advocates scorn such suggestions as naive. They point out that the BLM's decisions are made by individuals, who, in their view, are no less short-sighted or self-serving than the federal land users they regulate. Moreover, they argue, neither the BLM nor any other federal land-management agency harnesses the self-interest of its employees for social gain, as do the private property rights that underlie the free market. Whereas a private owner can expect to gain personally by allocating resources to their most valuable uses, often by saving them for future use, a federal land manager gains by making work for her agency, not by defending the amorphous public good or protecting posterity against insistent and powerful interests.

Preparing AMPs and RMPs keeps a lot of civil servants busy but, in the view of these critics, not very productively. Such land-use plans do not embody rational decisions about how BLM lands would best be used. At best, they validate the balance of power between those that take an interest in them. On paper, the BLM does indeed hold, or could call in, a more or less complete set of rights to the use of the lands it administers. FLPMA gives the BLM a good deal of management discretion. It has the statutory power to close areas to hunting, to cancel grazing permits, to withdraw areas from mineral leasing, to sell or exchange parcels, etc.[24] Practically, however, its authority is severely constrained by the expectations and political power of those interested in BLM lands, whether or not they have a legal right to some particular use.

2. When rights to land are dispersed, it can be costly to assemble them so as to effect a change for the better in its use. For example, it's generally a lot easier to deal with a single landowner than with her numerous heirs, whether you want the land for a subdivision or for a public park. Rights to use federal land, however, are not just dispersed; there are often barriers to transferring them from one user to another. An heir can surrender his interest in private property by accepting a sum of money from a developer, but it is not so easy to "buy out" the other interests in federal lands. If I think I could run cattle on your USFS grazing allotment more cheaply than you, I can't just buy your grazing permit from you. Instead, I must acquire your ranch, since the USFS ties its permits to particular ranches supplying "commensurate" winter forage.[25]

Changes in *type of use* are generally yet more difficult to arrange than changes in *user*. If I prefer wildlife to cattle, elk to "slow elk," I may not be able to keep your cows out of the forest *even by buying your ranch*: maybe the USFS will issue me a "non-use" grazing permit, and maybe not. Perhaps it will insist on multiple use and simply assign the grazing rights to another ranch. Robert Nelson has suggested that some grazing allotments would be better carved up into "recreational ranchettes" to be sold or leased for recreational homesites than used for grazing.[26] But there is nothing in this suggestion for the rancher, or the hunter, or the environmentalist; and without a *quid pro quo* they will oppose it. Perhaps they can be bought off in various ways—lower grazing fees, more money for game management, or more land set aside elsewhere as wilderness. But the price is likely to be high—higher, anyway, than a second-home developer would have to pay a rancher for private land.

3. Privatization advocates argue that since the rancher's rights to grazing allotments are not secure (leases are for 10 years and are subject to non-renewal, cancellation, or modification for various reasons), ranchers lack incentive to invest in range improvements, such as fencing, waterholes, and brush control, that would increase productivity. At first glance, this complaint appears to overlook provisions of federal grazing law requiring that permittees be given preference in renewals as long as their operations comply with regulations, and that they be compensated for permanent improvements if a permit is assigned to another rancher or cancelled so as to put the allotment to some other use.[27] However, the cost of securing compensation for improvements may tend to discourage investment in them, and ranchers might not be entitled to full compensation. Brush control, for example, might not be considered a "permanent" improvement. And ranchers who love their work might be willing to spend more on improvements than market considerations justify or BLM accountants would judge they're worth.[28]

Furthermore, environmentalists who want ranchers to graze their cattle elsewhere or in reduced numbers, or to pay significantly higher grazing fees, threaten their livelihood. Or so ranchers fear. Even if exaggerated, such fears divert energy and resources which would otherwise be put to better use into fending off such "takeovers." To the extent that a particular interest perceives its claim on federal lands to be threatened by the efforts of others to enlarge their share of the pie, it will invest in countermeasures. Since such threats can materialize at various levels in all three branches of the federal government—legislative, executive, judicial—there is a lot to keep an eye on. More, anyway, than interested individuals can manage on their own. Instead, they must buy into various groups—the Western Cattlemen's Association, the American Mining Congress, the American Petroleum Institute, the American Forest and Paper Association, the Sierra Club, Ducks Unlimited, the Professional River Outfitters Association, *et al.*—that follow issues and represent their interests in public lands. Were these lands privatized, the millions of dollars these groups spend fighting over the use of public resources—and keeping themselves in business—could be put to more productive uses. As it is, those who take an interest in public lands are caught in a prisoner's dilemma: they'd all be better off if they didn't have to invest in defending their interests, but, without the cooperation of all the others, none can afford to do so.

Finally, to the extent that ranchers regard their rights as tenuous, they may be tempted to "mine" their allotments by illegally overgrazing them, so as to secure now what might be denied them later. Why save for the future, if it's not going to do you any good? They may decide that the perceived risk of getting caught at it is less than the perceived risk that tighter grazing regulations, land reclassification, or other changes imposed by federal authorities in the future will put them out of business. In this way, insecure rights—or rights felt to be insecure—may contribute to degrading the range.

To the extent that individuals hold complete, transferable, and secure property rights to land, they control its use and can make full use of their knowledge for their own advantage. A rancher with a complete property right to what's now a BLM grazing allotment wouldn't have to defer to others' ideas of its proper use. He wouldn't have to tailor herd size to range-productivity estimates made by distant bureaucrats or to accommodate recreationists who forget to close gates. A transferable right to the allotment would permit anyone who thought she could make better use of it simply to make the owner an offer; a secure right would force her to do so. If our rancher preferred what a "recreational ranchette" developer offered to the satisfactions of ranching and its relatively meager income, he wouldn't need an Act of Congress to effect the exchange. Nor would he have to invest in protecting his rights from those who preferred some other use of his land: they'd have to put up or shut up.

## COLLECTIVE MANAGEMENT AND IRRESPONSIBILITY

All this suggests that privatizing federal lands would benefit ranchers, at least if they could secure title to their allotments at low cost. But what's in it for the rest of us? *All* of us would surrender rights we now have to use public lands, so that *some* of us could acquire stronger rights. Why is this a smart exchange? Even the rancher who gets title to his allotment may wonder about this when he has to pay private landowners to hunt or fish on what was formerly public land, or is simply barred from doing so. To be sure, some of the current system's costs are widely distributed, so everyone could expect to gain *something* from privatization. We could all find some other use for the tax dollars extracted from us to run the federal land-management agencies, and regulation doubtless increases the cost of some of the products of federal lands—livestock, minerals, timber—that in one form or another reach the consumer. But this doesn't really advance the argument, since I can gain something from privatization without benefitting from it—if what I lose exceeds what I gain. Personally, I'm happy to pay these modest sums for my recreational access to public lands, though others may not be. What can be said to suggest that we may expect a *net* gain, *at least on average*, from privatizing federal lands?

Theses of this sort are inherently difficult to establish in any direct way. Instead, privatization advocates proceed indirectly, ascribing virtues to private resource management and vices to collective resource management. Having touched on these alleged virtues and vices in last section, I shall now fill out the account of them. In the following section, I present private property as a solution to the problem of scarcity, a solution advertised as superior in certain respects to that of regulating the private use of public property. In the remainder of this section, I depict the current federal land-management regime as it appears to those who urge not reform but abolition.

When privatization advocates look at the federal land-management system, they see a lot of people—(1) citizens who elect the Congress, (2) federal land users who lobby it, (3) legislators who write federal land statutes, (4) bureaucrats who implement them, (5) judges who rule in disputes over implementation—all acting as they always do, viz., in their own interest, but in a system where there's little accountability to discipline self-interest.

1. Theoretically, government decision-makers are accountable to the electorate. However, according to Richard Stroup and John Baden, "[v]oters are rationally ignorant, not out of apathy, but because acquiring the necessary information to analyze bureaucratic decisions is costly relative to the impact such knowledge provides the individual."[29] Senators and representatives claim to want to hear from constituents, but it's not easy to learn enough about pending legislation to make timely and intelligent comments; besides, your call or letter will be just one of many, and your legislator has only one vote in Congress anyway. Citizens are invited to comment on management plans proposed for various federal lands, but who has time for that and what good does it do anyway? The "invitations" appear in the *Federal Register*, and your request for, say, the BLM's draft resource management plan for the San Juan Resource Area in southeastern Utah will

bring you a document several hundred pages long;[30] regardless of your input, the final plan will probably differ little from the draft, and your views and those of others will be reduced to numerical tabulations in a "Summary and review of public comment."[31]

2. Furthermore, citizen input, often amplified by organized pressure groups, tends to be irresponsible. Stroup and Baden point out that "[u]nlike the buyer who personally makes the choice between one good or service and another, the citizen who demands public services does not give up what society must sacrifice in order to provide them."[32] Neither the rancher who lobbies, perhaps through the National Cattlemen's Association or the local Grazing Advisory Board,[33] for the right to continue pasturing his cattle on federal lands, nor the wilderness lover who lobbies, perhaps through his membership in the Sierra Club, to get them out is prepared to outbid other potential users. Indeed, both are likely to object to paying anything at all to use lands they consider *theirs* in virtue of citizenship.

3. Legislators are interested in re-election and thus must, at least in appearance, deliver to their constituents (and to those who are paying their campaign expenses). So we shouldn't be surprised if Congress enacts buy-now, pay-later legislation that promises something for everyone and accommodates the special interests that control blocks of votes or pay for the television ads that deliver them. Maybe old-growth forest on federal lands in the Northwest is being cut too fast, but a lot of people are now busy doing it. Legislators who take a longer view are unlikely to be popular among constituents who prefer present to future benefits. Maybe it would be better for Congress to zone federal lands for particular uses instead of filling the statutes with multiple-use language. But that would offend someone; better to pass the buck to the agencies and the courts. Favors to special interests can often be concealed, either by cloaking them in the language of "the public interest" or by burying them in complex legislation. In any case, legislators face the voters as "package deals" in which positions on individual issues, if they are clear at all, may not loom large. Even defeat at the polls can be considerably softened by the lucrative employment opportunities that await those who know their way around the corridors of power and maintain friendships with those who still wield it.

4. Government bureaus are hardly passive instruments of legislative will. Bureaucrats are motivated by self-interest to push for a bigger budget and more authority for their bureau, since "[s]alary, position in the bureaucracy, amount of discretionary budget control, workplace amenities, and office perquisites all contribute to the bureaucrat's well-being"[34] and are likely to improve with expansion. Short of a tax revolt, there's little to check this impulse. Congress finds it hard to prune the federal bureaucracy; after all, it administers the programs that deliver goodies to constituents. Agency budgets are not financed out of agency revenues, and it's difficult to price their services anyway. Individual bureaucrats who figure out how to make do with less will be rewarded with a smaller budget next year. Far from encouraging efficiency, the system allows "bureaucratic entrepreneurs

. . . to tap the common pool of federal resource wealth and the federal treasury to exercise their individual visions and plans for bureaucratic expansion."[35] Bureaus that implement legislation frequently have a good deal to say about it, and this is certainly true of the federal land-management agencies. The congressional committees that draft federal land statutes listen to them. These statutes generally set forth general, sometimes conflicting, guidelines and give the agencies considerable discretion in implementing them. They frequently call for planning, which bureaucrats love: the endless round of study, draft, proposal, comments, revision, final proposal, implementation, and review makes work for the bureau. Public participation is a bit of a nuisance, but it helps at budget time; having largely delegated the task of legislating the use of federal lands to unelected bureaucrats, Congress is reluctant to deny funds for processes that involve the public.

5. Perhaps through oversight, privatization advocates omit the judiciary from their review of the openings government provides for the irresponsible exercise of self-interest. Federal judges, after all, are appointed for life; what sort of accountability do they have? To be sure, few of them abuse their position to enrich themselves; but they do have unusual opportunities to arrange things to their liking in other ways. One doesn't have to look very far in federal public resource law to find examples of decisions that seem dictated by personal visions of the public good. Justice William Douglas, for example, talked the Supreme Court into ruling that the act granting the Union Pacific Railroad a right of way across public lands reserved to the United States the mineral rights to the lands conveyed (the right of way plus alternate sections).[36] The 1862 act does exclude "mineral lands,"[37] but there is no reason to think this phrase signified anything other than lands identified as containing valuable mineral deposits prior to granting the patent. The Justice's assertion that "[t]he reservation of the mineral resources of these public lands for the United States was in keeping with the policy of the times"[38] is simply false. In another case, the U.S. Court of Appeals for the Tenth Circuit affirmed a District Court's injunction of a USFS timber sale in Colorado's White River National Forest, pending a decision by the President and Congress as to whether the area belongs in the Wilderness Preservation System.[39] It based its ruling on a provision of the 1964 Wilderness Act stipulating that "nothing herein contained shall limit the President in proposing, as part of his recommendations to Congress, the alteration of existing boundaries of primitive areas or recommending the addition of any contiguous area of national forest lands predominantly of wilderness value."[40] Going through with a timber sale in a roadless area adjacent to the Gore Range-Eagles Nest Primitive Area would, in the court's view, "limit" the President (and Congress).[41] In so ruling, the court took a broad view of congressional intent, seeing in the Wilderness Act "congressional acknowledgement of the necessity of preserving one factor of our natural environment from the progressive, destructive and hasty inroads of man, usually commercial in nature."[42]

Justices with different values might have taken more seriously the qualifier "herein," holding that the statute merely allowed the President to make his own recommendations.

Essentially, privatization advocates argue that the federal land-management system divorces freedom from responsibility, giving individuals opportunities to benefit in various ways while having others pay the costs. This is what Garrett Hardin would call "a commons in disguise."[43] Federal lands are no longer treated as a commons at the level of use. But a sort of commons exists at the level of regulation, where individuals are free to work at getting the rules changed. As in the commons, those with interests in the federal lands are placed in something of a prisoner's dilemma: they must expend resources on protecting their share lest they end up with less. Thus, instead of enjoying federal lands, environmentalists must spend their time fighting off threats to their interests in them. "Well," one might think, "that's their problem." But it's also a problem for those who take no interest in federal lands. Since the federal land-management system is not self-supporting, the resources of this commons include a portion of federal tax revenues. Furthermore, a decision to designate some federal land as Wilderness Area or a grazing allotment amounts to a draft on the federal treasury for the opportunity costs, and those who can engineer such designations are, in the view of privatization advocates, simply appropriating other people's resources for their own use.

## SCARCITY

From the perspective of economics, "How should federal lands be managed?" is just an instance of the more general questions: "How should we respond to *scarcity*: how should resources be used when there are not enough to go around? How should they be allocated to different uses when not all desired uses can be accommodated?"

Individuals face the problem of scarcity with respect to the resources they own or control. How shall I use my talents? To what shall I apply my labor? How shall I spend the afternoon? Shall I allocate some of my purchasing power to getting the car fixed again or toward buying a new one? Shall I use my woodlot to feed my stove or nourish my soul? To the extent that economics has advice for the individual, it is that she should think of her resources as a bundle that can be exchanged for other bundles, and that she should seek to obtain the best bundle she can through production and exchange.

Economists usually don't think of this as very demanding advice. In their view, people are self-interested, and the *best* bundle I can obtain is simply the one I *most prefer* among those available to me. The trick, as they see it, is not to get people to act self-interestedly; they will do so of their own accord in whatever sphere of freedom society allows them (and probably a bit more). Rather it is to arrange things so that the exercise of self-interest is socially productive. In particular, they suggest, we want institutions that will so constrain individual decisions that the resources available to society are used in the best way, relative to what other systems of constraints could achieve.

Now if we assume social good is no more than the good of the individuals that comprise society and that, in turn, reduces to getting what they prefer, then private property rights appear to be just the ticket. If I say all there is to say about how good a society is when I say how individuals in it fare, then what's socially productive reduces to what advances the good of individuals. If my preferences over consumption bundles define my good, perhaps because I'm presumed to know better than others both what my good is and how to rank various bundles as means to it, then I'll fare better as I acquire bundles I prefer. But isn't this more likely as more resources are private? After all, private resources may be freely exchanged.

Exchange transfers property rights: each party agrees to give up something in order to get from the other something preferred to it. Free exchange moves resources to those who value them more and in that sense makes them more productive. If the Wilderness Society has $10 million and would rather have some old-growth forest that Georgia Pacific is willing to sell for $10 million, each party will benefit from the exchange by acquiring something it values more highly than what it initially possessed. In the imagined case, preservation is evidently more highly valued than logging by the parties concerned, and is therefore the more productive use of the forest.

The prospect of getting something I like better than what I have also spurs production, i.e., the transformation of resources into more highly valued resources. People can often figure out how to make what's theirs more attractive to others: if I can't interest you in range grass, how about steak? Private gains from production can be increased until competitors catch up by increasing productivity, either by making resources go further in the same use (e.g., using automated narrow-kerf saws to cut more finished lumber out of the same logs in fewer worker-hours) or by shifting them to more highly valued uses (e.g., replanting cut-over redwood forestland with faster-growing Douglas fir—or perhaps with recreational subdivisions). The knowledge I acquire in thus advancing my own welfare becomes available to society at large. New processes and products promise monopoly profits, but they also instruct competitors, so that productivity gains are eventually passed along to consumers.

Where resources are private, I may secure what I prefer from you simply by giving up what you prefer from me. By contrast, if I want to turn public resources to a different use or to continue to enjoy a use threatened by others who do, I'll have to invest in influencing those who allocate them, a costly and uncertain business. If you and I disagree about public resource use, there's little incentive to come to terms. Each of us will wonder why the other deserves any compensation for relinquishing a claim to something he's got no real right to in the first place. Psychological barriers aside, such a deal would not be recognized by public resource managers, or by others with claims to make on these resources. Furthermore, public resource management isn't free; maintaining the system eats up a lot of resources.

If the best use of federal lands, as of all other resources, is implicit in the preferences of consumers, can we really do better than to privatize them and let the free market roll? Let's overlook the fact that federal land managers are people with interests of their own, and imagine that they are selfless servants of the public good, conceived as the good of the individuals that comprise the public. How are they to get reliable information about individual preferences and to figure out which uses might best satisfy them? The public participation required by statute gives the public an opportunity to speak for various uses of federal lands, but only a tiny segment of it does so, at least directly. Furthermore, talk is cheap, so it is not clear what public hearings reveal about individual preferences. And what is the conscientious land manager to do with all that conflicting testimony? It's certainly not obvious how to define, from divergent individual preferences (I prefer the forest primeval, you prefer clear lumber), a plan of use that can be defended as best satisfying them.[44]

Privatization, its advocates suggest, would neatly solve both these problems. I reveal my preference for *a* over *b* when I give up *b* to get *a*, and free exchange moves resources to those who value them most. Accordingly, the best way to make resource management accord with consumer preferences is to privatize the resource. Rather than wrestling with the problem of how resources are to be allocated to competing uses, government should simply institute private property rights to resources, and step aside to let consumers, on whose behalf it should be acting anyway, make these decisions. Essentially, the free-market solution to the problem of how a society might best use a batch of resources is to reduce it to individual problems by divvying up the batch. Individuals get title to them, perhaps partly via government-effected income transfers; what they do with them is then their business, assuming their titles are "clear" and non-overlapping.

Now privatization cannot be expected to *eliminate* conflict over the use of resources. Some of the difficulties public resource managers face will indeed be solved by privatization, at least in the sense of them being no longer matters of *social* concern. I may have plenty of trouble devising a consistent plan of use for my land, but, it will be said, that's my problem. Unfortunately, it may also be yours. For if I can limit *my* options in one area by what I do in another, I can often do the same for *yours*. My use of what's mine may, in effect, constrain your use of what's yours. The natural world is not so constructed that spillovers from my activity are always contained within my own space and limit only what can occur in some other part of my space. Accordingly, some problems of conflicting use in public resource management (e.g., whether the vista that greets visitors at Bryce Canyon National Park should include large strip mines on adjacent BLM land) will persist as problems of delimiting property rights.[45] Where my use of what's mine limits your use of what's yours, we shall have to decide which use takes precedence.

The view that owning something confers "the unrestricted right of use, enjoyment and disposal"[46] is widespread but naive. If property rights are to define disjoint spheres of freedom, then they cannot be rights to use one's resources just as one pleases. Instead, they must be rights to certain uses of those resources. Except in self-defense, emergency surgery, and like cases, you've no right to stick your knife in me without my consent; and I may have no right to accept hazardous waste for storage on my land. To *own X* is to be entitled to use *X* in certain ways, typically all but those prohibited by law. Fully complete property rights, conceived as allowing one to control *all* the uses of one's property, are impossible in this world, unless we are prepared to make everything the property of just one individual.

Disputes about where my rights end and yours begin, if not resolved by agreement or exhaustion, will have to be resolved by courts or legislatures or their executive agents. However, it is clear to privatization advocates what the authorities should do when private claims conflict: they should arrange for rights to go to those who value them most, preferably in a way that discourages people from misrepresenting the value they attach to them. If it doesn't cost *A* and *B* much to negotiate the transfer of a right, why agonize about who should get it? Simply assign it to one of them (the poorer, if we're into equity), and *A* and *B* themselves will negotiate its transfer to the one who values it most. Substantial transaction costs (as when *A* is not an individual but a large and dispersed group of individuals) may discourage negotiation and block such movement of rights. In such cases, the government should hire economists to figure out who values it more and make the assignment accordingly.[47]

## THE ARGUMENT FROM PRODUCTIVITY

Advocates of privatizing public lands suggest that where property rights are secure, complete, and transferable, self-interest will direct resources to their most productive uses. Complete and transferable property rights permit resources to be used—consumed, transformed in production, exchanged, reserved for future use—as their owners see fit. But they'll gain most from seeing fit to put them to their most productive uses, at least if rights are secure. So where the exercise of anyone's self-interest is constrained only by the property rights of others, we may expect resources to be utilized most productively.

The idea that self-interest may be socially useful is intriguing, partly because the means seem at odds with the ends and partly because self-interest seems to be something we're stuck with. Few would go so far as Thomas Hobbes in maintaining that "of the voluntary acts of every man, the object is some *good to himself*."[48] Often we do act on behalf of others. Even so, concern for them generally falls short of concern for self. Instead of counting "everybody . . . for one, nobody for more than one," as Jeremy Bentham advises,[49] I generally count myself for rather more than one. Even

Jesus, who seems to have thought that right action requires a selfless motive,[50] gets our attention by promising rewards for selflessness.[51]

To those troubled by the recognition that we don't love our neighbors as ourselves it may be soothing to hear that it doesn't matter; that far from diminishing social welfare, self-interest, properly constrained, is its engine; that, in fact, the yoke of constraint is absurdly easy, consisting only in respect for the property of others. Essentially, privatization advocates claim that property rights can close a gap between *is* and *ought*: the uses to which resources *are* put by self-interested individuals who are free to do as they wish with what's theirs, constrained only by the like freedom of others, are their *best* uses, the uses to which they *ought* to be put.

We may give this "argument from productivity" an explicit premise-conclusion structure as follows:

1.  Individuals are self-interested.
2.  Resources are more productive as their use better satisfies the desires of consumers.
3.  Where individuals are self-interested, resources will find their most productive uses if they are privately owned, where ownership is characterized by secure, complete, and transferable property rights.
4.  Privatizating public lands and resources would create such rights.
5.  Situations are better as the desires of consumers are better satisfied.

Public lands and resources should be privatized.

This, I think, is the central argument for privatization, and analysis of it should help us evaluate the proposal. I conclude this chapter by noting some openings for criticism. Of course, if this argument fails, its conclusion may still be true. But we shall have to be convinced in some other way that privatization is a good idea, and difficulties revealed by a close look at this argument may limit what can be expected from others.

Note first that the logic of the argument could be tighter: its conclusion does not quite follow from its premises. We must also assume that (a) the course of action with the best outcome is the one we ought to undertake and (b) the outcome of a course of action is where we end up by undertaking it. Both (a) and (b) may be questioned.

The argument from productivity is a *consequentialist* argument: actions (practices, dispositions, institutions, etc.) are justified if their consequences are better than those of alternatives. Some people—Jesus and Immanuel Kant come to mind—reject such appeals to results; instead, they insist, we are to judge actions directly by some standard of the right that does not defer to consequences. For example, in deciding whether to take someone's life, I should ask not whether what others would gain by his demise would outweigh his loss, but whether he is *entitled* to live. Non-consequentialists reject (a); so they can agree with the premises while disagreeing with the conclusion. They'll judge institutions not by how well they cause resources to be used, but by how completely they embody principles of right action. If such people go for privatization, it will be on this account, not because private property rights promote better use of resources, as the argument from productivity alleges. In particular, it might be held that in respecting their property rights we respect the integrity of persons.

By rejecting (b), consequentialists can accept the premises without agreeing to the conclusion. Surely (b)'s reading of "outcome" is too narrow. I would not decide between vacationing in Vermont and vacationing in Alaska solely by imagining how much I'd enjoy *being* in each place; I would also reckon the cost of getting there. The end result of privatizing public lands might be wonderful, but the privatization process will incur costs that consequentialists will insist on charging against benefits delivered. If such costs are great enough—or the benefits do not come soon enough— privatization will not improve on the *status quo*.

With the possible exception of premise 2, which we may regard as giving some content to a technical notion, the premises of the argument are also open to question. *Is–ought* gaps are hard to close, and it's tempting to cheat, either by idealizing *what is* or by compromising *what ought to be*. In my view, the argument from productivity does a little of both. As noted in the previous section, we cannot really make property rights complete, so premise 4 promises too much. If premise 1 means that people care only about themselves, it is false. But if it allows for wider interests, we may wonder how well they are represented in the desires of consumers, which have the form of preferences over personal consumption bundles.

If we make certain assumptions about people and property, something like premise 3 can be *proved*, provided we understand "most productive" in a certain way. However, these assumptions are idealizations: people know more than we do, their interests are tidily (if severely) pruned, and one's use of one's property never limits others' use of theirs. This suggests that self-interest operating in people as they are, constrained only by the sort of rights we can fashion, will actually direct resources to sub-optimal uses. Perhaps premise 3 can be saved by interpreting it as asserting that a realizable system of private ownership is productively superior to other realizable systems. However, I doubt that there is any way of understanding "productively superior" supports this claim and at the same time honors premise 2.

If premise 5 is true, social good reduces to how well consumers are doing in satisfying their desires. We may resolve this reduction into two components: (i) a reduction of social to individual good and (ii) a reduction of individual good to the satisfaction of one's consumer desires.

The content of (i) depends upon the account we give of "is more productive than." However, none of the standard accounts seems to embody much concern for equality: *II* can improve on *I* without doing anything for those at the bottom of the heap. Indeed, if we want to give the weakened version of premise 3 a fighting chance, we must reckon a shift from *I* to *II* as an improvement if the sum of individual gains exceeds the sum of individual losses. So *II* can improve on *I* while actually worsening the position of those at the bottom.

Reduction (ii) also seems to leave something out. Although it's not easy to characterize individual welfare, surely doing *what I'm interested in* needn't be *in my interest*, let alone that of anyone else. Even if it's generally true that I'm in the best position to know and advance my interests, it doesn't follow that people will generally do best if they are allowed to do as they wish with what's theirs, constrained only by respect for the rights of others. Can't we save the foolish and improvident a lot of grief—much more, in fact, than others thereby suffer—if we require everyone to wear seat belts, attend school, contribute to retirement programs, etc.? If we want people's interests to be in their interest, shouldn't we give some attention to the conditions under which their desires are formed?

These problems with premise 5 suggest that arrangements designed to increase productivity need not promote equality or individual welfare and that we'll need to do that in some other way. I shall, in fact, suggest that public land management can be justified and guided by such concerns.

This concludes the introductory portion of this study. I have sketched the history of federal lands and indicated how they are now managed. I have noted the most recent call for privatizing these lands and presented the arguments for doing so. A good deal of the rationale for privatization can be represented in the argument from productivity. I now turn to the issues raised by it. In Chapters 4 and 5, I explore the meaning of "more productive" and the factual issue of whether privatizing public lands would lead resources to be more productively employed. In Chapters 6 and 7, I consider normative aspects of the argument from productivity, asking what general ethical outlooks seem most receptive to such appeals and how privatization looks from them. Finally, in Chapters 8 and 9, I turn from the case for private property to the case against collective management, arguing that it is overstated and that weaknesses in arguments for privatization suggest both a defense of the current management system and some guidance for it.

## NOTES

1. Richard A. Posner, *Economic analysis of law* (Boston: Little, Brown and Company, 1972), at 11.

2. Edward Abbey, "The crooked wood," in *The journey home: some words in defense of the American West* (New York: E. P. Dutton, 1977), 206–8 at 208.

3. "Aspen clear-cutting plan raises hopes, stirs fears," *The Denver Post*, 1 October 1984, A1.

4. Jim Hayes, a motorcycle dealer and enthusiast, quoted in "Motorcyclists lose in battle with the tortoise," *The New York Times*, 17 December 1989, A45.

5. Barney Dowdle, "Why have we retained the federal lands? An alternative hypothesis," in *Rethinking the federal lands*, ed. Sterling Brubaker (Washington:

Resources for the Future, 1984), 61–73 at 70. When Dowdle looks back on the bad old days of cut-and-run logging, he sees the nation holding "a clearance sale on naturally endowed timber inventories." Id.

6. This was apparently standard practice. See Paul W. Gates, *History of public land law development* (Washington: Government Printing Office, 1968), at 531. Gates estimates that the 150 million acres of land cleared for agriculture by 1900 held 600 billion BF of timber, most of which went up in smoke.

7. John G. Mitchell, "'Best of the SOBs'," *Audubon* 76(5) (1974), 48–63 at 53.

8. See, e.g., B. Delworth Gardner, "The case for divestiture," in Brubaker, note 5 *supra*, 156–80 at 171; and Richard L. Stroup, "Weaknesses in the case for retention," in Brubaker, note 5 *supra*, 149–55 at 152.

9. "All the conveniences of a comfortable home, of our means of transportation and communication, of entertainment and enjoyment, we could produce at first only in limited quantities; but it was in doing this that we gradually learned to make them or similar things at a much smaller outlay of resources and thus became able to supply them to the great majority. A large part of the expenditure of the rich, though not intended for that end, thus serves to defray the cost of the experimentation with the new things that, as a result, can later be made available to the poor. . . . Even the poorest today owe their relative material well-being to the results of past inequality." F. A. Hayek, *The constitution of liberty* (Chicago: University of Chicago Press, 1960), at 43–44.

10. "[I]n many of the countries in which absolute poverty is still an acute problem, the concern with 'social justice' has become one of the greatest obstacles to the elimination of poverty. In the West the rise of the great masses to tolerable comfort has been the effect of the general growth of wealth and has been merely slowed down by measures interfering with the market mechanism." F. A. Hayek, *Law, legislation, and liberty* (Chicago: University of Chicago Press, 1976), Vol. II at 139.

Hayek does not, however, object to "the assurance of a certain minimum income for everyone, or a sort of floor below which nobody need fall even when he is unable to provide for himself." *Law, legislation, and liberty*, Vol. III at 55. It would be rational for everyone to agree to contribute via income transfers to maintaining such a floor, because a minimal safety net is "protection against a risk common to all" and so encourages people to take risks that benefit society.

11. Of the rules of property and conduct that underlie the free market, Hayek says "we consent to retain, and agree to enforce, uniform rules for a procedure which has greatly improved the chances of all to have their wants satisfied, but at the price of all individuals and groups incurring the risk of unmerited failure." *Law, legislation, and liberty*, note 10 *supra*, Vol II at 70. In Hayek's view, free decentralized market societies are to be preferred over alternatives because they "maximize the fulfillment of expectations as a whole." *Law, legislation, and liberty*, Vol. I at 103.

12. "[W]e propose that commercial timberlands [those acres capable of growing 240 BF of timber per year] in the national forests be sold [to] eliminate both the current mismanagement of timberlands and the rising deficit in the Social Security program." Richard L. Stroup and John A. Baden, *Natural resources: bureaucratic myths and environmental management* (San Francisco: Pacific Institute for Public Policy Research, 1983), at 122.

13. Gardner, note 8 *supra*, at 172, observes that perceptions of fraud in past disposals "will undermine any efforts to convince the public that it will be different this time," but offers nothing substantive by way of reassurance.

14. For a discussion of the dangers of treating renewable resources as common property, see Garrett Hardin's classic "The tragedy of the commons," *Science* 162 (1968), 1243–48. It is reprinted in his *Exploring new ethics for survival* (New York: Viking, 1972), which contains a more detailed analysis of the commons and alternate systems of resource utilization. For criticism of Hardin and a review of recent literature on the commons, see Michael Taylor, "The economics and politics of property rights and common pool resources," *Natural Resources Journal* 32 (1992), 634–48.

The English grazing commons cited by Hardin is an impure example of the commons, since, as tourists are reminded today, access was and is limited to members of the community. "Like any other piece of countryside, Commons, open moors, and felltops have private landowners. . . . There is a lot of confusion about Commons or Common Land. This is not land to which the public automatically has access. It is land over which certain members of the local community—the commoners—have 'rights in common'. That is, although the land is owned, locals who have registered their rights can take or use some of the produce of the soil." "Who needs to trespass anyway?," *The visitor* (Grassington, North Yorkshire: Yorkshire Dales National Park Committee, 1986), 12.

15. "Should an economic system be condemned merely because it has been costly to build? . . . The historic record is replete with examples of socialist economic systems which have been more costly to build than the U.S. free enterprise system. . . . More important, in spite of their high 'construction costs,' these economic systems do not work very well." Dowdle, note 5 *supra*, at 68.

16. Cf. the Unlawful Enclosures Act of 1885, 43 U.S.C.A. §§1061–66, and *Camfield* v. *United States*, 167 U.S. 518 (1897).

17. You and I face a prisoner's dilemma whenever our individual choices *a* and *b* are independent, the possible outcomes of these choices are *aa*, *ab*, *ba*, and *bb* as given in the matrix below, my best-to-worst ranking of them is *ba* > *aa* > *bb* > *ab*, and yours is *ab* > *aa* > *bb* > *ba*.

|  | your choice | |  |
|---|---|---|---|
|  | b | a |  |
| ab | aa | a | my choice |
| bb | ba | b |  |

The rational choice for both of us is *b*, although we both thereby end up worse off than if we'd agreed on *a*.

18. Clyde Eastman and James R. Gray, *Community grazing: practice and potential in New Mexico* (Albuquerque: University of New Mexico Press, 1987).

19. FLPMA, 43 U.S.C.A. §§1701–84, at §1752(e).

20. However, since the Taylor Grazing Act, 43 U.S.C.A. §§315–15r, at §315b, specifies that "the creation of a grazing district or the issuance of a permit . . . shall not create any right, title, interest, or estate in or to the lands," the value that federal grazing permits add to his ranch is ignored when the government compensates a rancher for taking his land. See *U.S.* v. *Fuller*, 409 U.S. 488 (1973).

21. FLPMA, note 19 *supra*, at §1712.

22. Or fewer, since a margin of safety against worse-than-expected conditions ought to be built-in. Perry R. Hagenstein, "The federal lands today—uses and limits," in Brubaker, note 5 *supra*, 74–107 at 87.

23. In Hayek's view, the free market—and free institutions generally—has evolved to solve the problem of ignorance: each of us is ignorant "of much that helps him to achieve his aims." *The constitution of liberty*, note 9 *supra*, at 22. By providing "the maximum of opportunity for unknown individuals to learn of facts that we ourselves are yet unaware of and to make use of this knowledge in their actions," free societies can utilize "more knowledge . . . than any one individual possesses or than it is possible to synthesize intellectually." Id., at 30.

Computers don't get around the problem of dispersed knowledge, since they process but don't assemble facts. *Law, legislation, and liberty*, note 10 *supra*, Vol. I at 148 (n.14). In particular, computer models of the range need to have their parameters fixed by empirical data, and Hayek would argue that such data as could be assembled would almost certainly be inferior to the dispersed, local, and sometimes inarticulate knowledge of individual ranchers.

24. See FLMPA, note 19 *supra*, at §1713 (sales), §1714 (withdrawals), §1716 (exchanges), §1732 (regulation of use, including hunting), and §1752 (grazing permits).

25. For estimates of the economic cost of restrictions on sub-leasing grazing rights, see B. Delworth Gardner, "Transfer restrictions and misallocation in grazing public range," *Journal of Farm Economics* 44 (1962), 50–63.

26. Robert H. Nelson, "Ideology and public land policy — the current crisis," in Brubaker, note 5 *supra*, 275–98 at 292.

27. See FLMPA, note 19 *supra*, at §1752(c) (renewal preference) and §1752(g) (compensation for improvements upon cancellation); and the Taylor Grazing Act, note 20 *supra*, at §315c (payment to prior permittee for use of his improvements).

28. Ranching is not a particularly good investment, judged by conventional standards of return on capital: ranches sell for much more than the value of their operations justifies, given other investment opportunities. Presumably, ranchers get much of their return on investment in the form of psychic satisfaction: they prefer ranching with low income to other activities with higher income.

29. Stroup and Baden, note 12 *supra*, at 44.

30. *Draft resource management plan and environmental impact statement for the San Juan Resource Area, Moab District, Utah* (Washington: BLM, May 1986).

31. E.g., "Sixteen percent of the comments mentioned livestock grazing or livestock-related range improvements. Altogether, 1 individual supported the proposed plan, 26 favored more restrictions, and 180 wanted fewer. About half of those favoring fewer restrictions submitted their comment by form letter." *Proposed resource management plan for the San Juan Resource Area, Moab District, Utah* (Washington: BLM, April 1989), at 89.

32. Stroup and Baden, note 12 *supra*, at 114–5.

33. FLPMA, note 19 *supra*, at §1753.

34. Stroup and Baden, note 12 *supra*, at 43.

35. Id., at 99.

36. *United States* v. *Union Pacific R.R. Co.*, 353 U.S. 112 (1957).

37. 12 Stat. 489, at §3.

38. *Union Pacific*, note 36 *supra*, at 115.

39. *Parker* v. *United States*, 448 F.2d 793 (10th Cir., 1979).

40. Wilderness Act of 1964, 16 U.S.C.A. §§1131–36, at §1132(b).

41. *Parker*, note 39 *supra*, at 797(4).

42. Id., at 795(1).

43. He so describes a proposed world food bank, on which famine-stricken

nations could draw, in Garrett Hardin, "Lifeboat ethics: the case against helping the poor," *Psychology Today* 8(4) (1974), 38 at 123.

44. Stroup and Baden, note 12 *supra*, at 64, suggest that it's *impossible* to do so: "we cannot, even in theory, establish [which are] the socially appropriate goals." They may be thinking of Arrow's theorem, which establishes roughly that there can exist no mechanism for obtaining, from rational individual preferences, a rational social preference, where in both cases rationality is characterized only by formal constraints (e.g., if everyone prefers *II* to *I*, then society prefers *II* to *I*). A clear account of the theorem and a proof by example can be found in Chapter 10 of Allan M. Feldman, *Welfare economics and social choice theory* (Boston: Kluwer-Nijhoff, 1980).

There is a vast literature on this result and what, if anything, it reveals about the rationality of social choice. One reason for skepticism is that although one might expect a rational decision on whether *II* was preferable to *I* (e.g., whether a piece of federal rangeland should be allocated to grazing or to strip mining) to turn on the merits of *I* and *II*, Arrow's approach to social choice assumes that all relevant judgments on the merits are already reflected in individual preferences, in the strong sense that my preference for *I* over *II* must have exactly the same weight in social accounting as your preference for *II* over *I*.

45. It may be possible to eliminate some of these "neighborhood effects" by merging properties. Stroup and Baden, note 12 *supra*, at 124, suggest this: "When large investors, clubs, partnerships, and corporations can purchase tracts large enough to incorporate what otherwise would be external effects, then the externalities are internalized." But there are obvious limits to eliminating conflicts between two neighbors by eliminating one of them, especially since the movement of air, water, and wildlife will make non-adjacent landowners neighbors in the relevant sense.

46. From a Texas judicial ruling, *Spann* v. *City of Dallas*, 111 Tex. 350 (1921), at 355. The text continues: "Anything which destroys any of these elements of property, to that extent destroys the property itself. The substantial value of property lies in its use. If the right of use be denied, the value of the property is annihilated and ownership is rendered a barren right."

47. In cases where $R$ is the right $R(\ell)$ to a certain level $\ell$ of use, as when $A$ wishes to vent a certain amount $\ell$ of pollution into the air, we may be able to make $A$ reveal the level $\ell'$ beyond which $B$'s loss outweighs $A$'s gain by requiring $A$ to purchase $R$ at a price designed to make $A$ quit when $\ell'$ is reached. First, we ask economists to estimate how much $B$ would have to be paid to put up with a 1-unit increase in use over $\ell$. If this is $d(\ell)$, we then charge $A\,\ell \times d(\ell)$ for $R(\ell)$.

48. Thomas Hobbes, *Leviathan*, ed. Michael Oakeshott (New York: Collier, 1962), at 105 (Chapter 14).

49. Or so J. S. Mill quotes him, *Utilitarianism, Liberty, and Representative government* (London: Dutton, 1910), at 58 (*Utilitarianism*, Chapter V). The closest approximation in Bentham to which I've found a reference (Ross Harrison, *Bentham* (London: Routledge and Kegan Paul, 1983), at 247) is "one man's interest weighing neither more nor less than another's," *The rationale of reward*, ed. R. Smith (London: John and H. L. Hunt, 1825), at 49.

50. "If you lend to those from whom you expect repayment, what merit is there in it for you? Even sinners lend to sinners, expecting to be repaid in full." Luke 6:34, *The New American Bible* (New York: Benziger, 1970).

51. "For the measure you measure with will be measured back to you." Luke 6:38. Of course, if right action requires a selfless motive, the promise of a reward can motivate but a semblance of righteousness, not the real thing.

# 4

# Productivity Standards

> When an economist is comparing alternative social arrangements, the
> proper procedure is to compare the total social product yielded by these
> different arrangements.
>
> Ronald Coase[1]

The USFS often sells National Forest timber at a loss. Although loggers may pay market price for it, the agency absorbs various costs—stand thinning, roads, sale preparation, reforestation, etc. Environmentalists view below-cost sales as evidence that "the Forest Service continues to treat timber as the number-one priority on every acre of land not otherwise designated by Congress."[2] Appealing to the multiple-use language of NFMA and other legislation, they point out that the forests are not to be managed solely for timber production and that "optimal policy requires a harmonious blend of land uses."[3]

The USFS, however, defends below-cost sales partly in the same terms, claiming that "[t]imber harvest is often an efficient tool that can be used to achieve non-timber objectives and the desired ecological conditions outlined in forest plans."[4] Its friends in The American Forest and Paper Association suggest, for example, that cutting aspen in Minnesota's Superior National Forest improves habitat for the small mammals that support the local wolf population and maintain that sales of this low-value timber "provide the most cost-effective means to provide prey for the wolf."[5] Some natural resource economists also endorse this general position, albeit more cautiously. John KKrutilla and Michael Bowes, for example, claim that "on public land, occasional timber sales below cost and timber management can be justified economically on the basis of the long-term improvement in multiple-use value that may result from harvesting."[6]

Evidently, multiple use is an accommodating ideal. Appeals to "multiple-use values" remind us that the National Forests can produce a variety of things in various "harmonious" combinations; they do not settle what "blend" of outputs is "optimal." We might be able to do this if we could agree on some standard of productivity that gives sense to claims of the general form "this use of those resources is better than that one." Since the case for privatizing the National Forests and other public lands rests largely on the claim that their resources would thereby be put to better use, such a standard would also help in assessing the proposal by clarifying what is being claimed for it.

We may roughly characterize a more *efficient* or *productive* use of resources—I shall use these terms interchangeably—as one that *gets more out* (or *wastes less*) *of* them. For example, insofar as a production process can be tuned so that the same input produces more output or the same output is achieved with less input, its inputs will be used more efficiently. However, resources can be put to different uses, for example, input to processes with different outputs. What then determines which allocation gets more out of them? Ordinarily, both "efficient" and "productive" apply to *means*: a computational algorithm is efficient as it delivers solutions relatively quickly, a legislative session is productive insofar as it delivers legislation—or perhaps good legislation, etc. What, then, is the *end* that resources serve, in terms of which their uses may be ranked as more or less efficient means?

The answer standardly given in economics is: *satisfying the desires of consumers*. Resources are whatever may be utilized to satisfy desire, and, as indicated by premise 2 of the argument from productivity, they are more efficiently employed as the product of their use is more desired. We may regard any use of resources as ultimately delivering to each consumer some amount (zero, maybe) of various products, in accord with prevailing rules of property. For example, allocating a piece of BLM land to wilderness recreation would, in conjunction with allocations of other resources, presumably deliver wilderness recreation experiences to some consumers and contemplation-of-wilderness experiences to others; allocating it to grazing would deliver a way of life to some and ultimately steaks and hamburger to others. To assess their relative productivity, allocations must be individuated in part by who gets what. In specifying a use or allocation of resources, we must say who consumes what in what quantities, for it is the preferences of consumers for certain consumption bundles over others that will determine which uses are more productive, i.e., better satisfy the desires of consumers.

Use *II* improves on use *I*, or a shift *I→II* of resources from *I* to *II* is an *improvement*, when *II* satisfies the desires of consumers better than *I*. But when is that? Suppose *I* better satisfies *my* desires and *II* better satisfies *yours*; which then better satisfies *ours*? In this chapter, I consider various attempts to answer this question and thereby to give precise content to claims of the form "*II* is a more productive use of resources than *I*." I am interested in whether any of them advance the argument from productivity: if we understand "more productive" in such-and-such a way, do we have reason to believe that privatization will make resources more productive?

## PARETO-IMPROVEMENTS

If some consumer desires what she obtains in *II* more than what she obtains in *I* and no consumer prefers what he obtains in *I* to what he obtains in *II*, then it seems pretty clear that *II* is more efficient than *I* in satisfying desires. Other things equal, such will be the case if *II* results from *I* by fine-tuning a production process that employs scarce inputs. What is known as "the Pareto criterion of efficiency" takes this to be the whole story. Use *II* is a *Pareto-improvement* over (is *more Pareto-efficient* or *Pareto-productive* than) *I* if *and only if* some consumer prefers what she obtains in *II* to what she obtains in *I* and no consumer prefers what he obtains in *I* to what he obtains in *II*. A use of resources is *Pareto-optimal* (*Pareto-efficient*) if no other use is a Pareto-improvement over it. This is the notion of efficiency that some privatization advocates have in mind when they claim that privatization would promote it. John Baden and Dean Lueck, for example, write that

> Most people do not appreciate the social value of attaining economic efficiency, perhaps because the concept is often misunderstood. In simple terms, an economic system is efficient if resources are allocated so that no one can be made better off without making at least one person worse off. It is difficult to think of a more worthy goal.[7]

The Pareto criterion is a strong improvement standard; relatively few shifts will count as Pareto-improvements. No shift *I→II* can be a Pareto-improvement if someone prefers *I* to *II*. We do require that, in comparing *I* and *II*, each consumer look only at what *I* and *II* brings to her and not at how others fare. Otherwise, envy might prevent reckoning *any* shift *I→II* as an improvement, for the envious person will prefer *I* to *II* if *I→II* is a gain for the envied individual. But even so, a great many shifts will worsen the position of someone, by her lights, and cannot be regarded as improvements by this standard. They include nearly all reallocations of public resources, such as tightening rules on mining in Wilderness Areas, shifting federal forestland in the Pacific Northwest from timber production to wildlife habitat, or expanding an air force bombing range.

If a Robinson Crusoe were to shift resources from *I* to *II*, we'd expect *II* to be more efficient than *I* in terms of satisfying desires. Here there are no desires but his to consider; and when they act at all, people attempt to satisfy their desires. Crusoe "owns" the product of the use of "his" resources, and he obviously has an incentive to use them in ways that deliver more-desired products. Secure, complete, and transferable private property rights would essentially preserve this incentive in society, where more-desired products can be had via exchange. Where rights are complete, any use of resources factors into uses to which individuals *willingly* put the resources they own; other uses are vetoed. A shift *I→II* in resource use is then the aggregate of individual shifts that would not occur unless individuals preferred them. So, as in Crusoe's case, we'd expect that *II* was the more efficient use.

What about the converse? If *II* is more efficient than *I*, can we expect to see a shift from *I* to *II*? Yes, *provided* the individual components of *II* are apparent to individuals. But why should we expect this? If I see that I can use my resources in a way that would better satisfy my desires, then I'll presumably shift them to that use. But of course I frequently don't see what's there to be seen, even if I have an incentive to do so. What's supposed to help people out here are prices: by allocating my resources in a way that maximizes return, I'll maximize my opportunities to buy what I prefer to have.

## PARETO-OPTIMALITY IN IDEAL MARKETS

Under certain assumptions, it is possible to *prove* that prices guide self-interested economic agents to allocate privately owned resources to their most productive uses, as judged by the Pareto standard. This result is known as "the first fundamental theorem of welfare economics."[8] Unfortunately, the required assumptions are too idealized for us to regard this proof as establishing premise 3 of the argument from productivity. Particularly significant departures from reality are embodied in assumptions about the independence and knowledge of economic agents.

In the world of the first fundamental theorem, self-interested consumers, producers, and resource holders act according to consumption, production, and resource-release plans chosen from those that are feasible for them. Prices guide these choices: a consumer buys the consumption bundle she most prefers, given what she chooses to spend; producers maximize profit; resource holders maximize return on the release of resources. So far, so good. But choices are also assumed to be independent in the sense that no agent's choice alters feasibility for other agents or reorders anyone's consumer preferences. So in this world, unlike ours, there are no spillovers. As a consumer, I can play my "boom box" on a commercial float trip through the Grand Canyon without making any of the other vacationers wish they'd stayed home. As a producer, I can extract gold from old mine tailings on my claims by cyanide leaching without worrying about poisoning anyone but myself. As a resource holder, I can sell timber from steep slopes knowing that the effects of erosion will be confined to my own land.

Agents are assumed to know what plans are feasible for them and the price of everything in them. In addition, consumers must have well-behaved preferences over feasible consumption plans. The epistemic burdens here can be minimized by identifying plans that are feasible for an agent with those *he knows to be available to him*. However, this is not enough to make them manageable. I certainly don't know the price of everything I know is available to me as a consumer. And I would have a lot of trouble deciding which of the possible bundles of this stuff I preferred to which, at least if my judgments had, as required, to be formally consistent. Indeed, I recall that the last time I shopped for loudspeakers, I listened to three different models and liked each of them better than the one I'd just heard previously.

Furthermore, if feasibility is limited by what agents know, though additional plans are actually available to them, the theorem is less interesting. It tells us that the allocation of resources resulting from all these individual choices is Pareto-optimal *provided prices clear the market*, i.e., provided prices coordinate individual decisions so that, for any commodity, supply equals demand. This is more likely as feasible plans are more numerous. Moreover, what is Pareto-optimal relative to some set of options may not be Pareto-optimal relative to a broader set. This raises at least the theoretical possibility of bettering the performance of the market. If God were interested in helping us out here, presumably He could do so, for His view of feasibility is presumably more inclusive than that of any economic agent.

## PARETO-OPTIMALITY IN REAL MARKETS

Theoretical possibilities, however, are not of much interest here unless we can see some way to actualize them. Calling on God, for example, is obviously not a serious policy option. This suggests a way of arguing for something a bit *stronger* than premise 3, viz., that real markets in fact allocate resources optimally.[9] Let $X$ be a possible use of resources, which we may identify with a set of plans coordinated in the weak sense that inputs to chosen production and consumption plans are available. If $X$ is Pareto-optimal, then there is no way to shift resources to some other use so that some consumer is better off while no consumer is worse off: for each possible use $Y$ distinct from $X$, some consumer prefers her $X$-plan to her $Y$-plan. Or, as it's sometimes put, no gains from trade are possible.

Now if $X$ is *not* Pareto-optimal, such gains are possible: there is some way to shift stuff around so that some consumer is better off while none are worse off. But if this is really the case, can't we expect self-interested agents to engineer these shifts, assuming that resources are freely transferable? Consider, for example, a spillover case. Suppose I operate a fishing resort on a mountain stream, and you own forestland upstream. Guided by stumpage prices, you decide to log your land. In so doing, you may make my resort a less desirable place to stay, for logging is likely to increase water temperature and turbidity, causing fish to expire or move elsewhere. If so, your action alters feasibility for me: from the same inputs (labor, electricity, etc.) I now produce a less desirable output for consumers to buy. This is the kind of situation that distances our world from that of the first fundamental theorem and suggests that its optimal allocations are beyond reach. But is this really so? If clear, cold water is worth $200/day to me, whereas you expect to net only $150/day on your logging operation, we'll both be better off if I pay you something between $150 and $200 per day to desist. Furthermore, we can expect bargaining to reveal this.[10]

The suggestion is that any non-optimality here will be corrected, more or less automatically, by self-interest and free exchange. To buy this suggestion, we must agree that where free exchange does not alter $X$, $X$ is, perhaps despite appearances, optimal. This is not as incredible as it sounds: since *is a Pareto-improvement over* is a fairly strong notion, *is Pareto-optimal* is a fairly weak one. More allocations than one might think are Pareto-optimal because it is difficult to reallocate resources without offending someone. So let us consider what might block gains in trade from $X$.

One possibility is social restrictions on transferability, for example, prohibitions against selling one's organs. However, if there is a problem here, it's not a problem for those who argue for carving the world into mine and thine. If society refuses to make body parts commodities, then they will not show up in plans, or in weakly coordinated sets of plans such as $X$. In this case, there is no set $Y$ that differs from $X$ by an exchange of an organ for whatever its cost will buy, so $X$ cannot be inferior to such an allocation.

If such restrictions on transferability are excluded, then the only thing that might block gains in trade from $X$ is their cost—the so-called *transaction costs* of exchange. These are the expenses incurred in identifying and exploiting opportunities to gain from trade. For example, if I were to purchase a camera, the transaction costs would include what I spend, in one way or another, discovering who offers the best price. To do so, I might buy next month's edition of *Popular Photography*, check the quotations in the equipment ads, and then make some long-distance calls to find out what the real price is. Sometimes transaction costs are large enough to discourage the transaction: at least one party expects to be worse off, after deducting them from what she'd gain. Such transaction-cost barriers are particularly likely in cases where transactions promise a small benefit to each of a large number of consumers. Imagine, for example, that a lot of people are each willing to pay a small amount for clear air at the Grand Canyon and other National Parks in the Southwest and that, if these small amounts were pooled, there would be more than enough to install pollution-control equipment at the offending utilities.[11] Still, this may not happen, because the cost of discovering and collecting what people are willing to pay may be too great make it worth anyone's while.

However, if it is transaction costs that block gains from trade, then it is simply a mistake to think that *gains* from trade are really possible. Appearances to the contrary, where we are must be optimal. Only by ignoring the costs of getting elsewhere can we imagine that we can do better.

Does this argument show what it seems to show, viz., that we can't improve on the performance of the free market? I think not. If free exchange won't take us from $X$ to $Y$, it doesn't follow that we can't get there in some other way, and this other way may be cheap enough to make it worthwhile. In particular, we might look to government for help with some of the large number cases. Suppose I have a piece of undeveloped land, which I'm willing to exchange for fewer dollars than my neighbors are collectively willing to pay for having it preserved as open space, but not by fewer enough dollars to induce any entrepreneur to set up the exchange. If my town were to buy it for a park with tax revenues, the cost of the exchange might be minimal. After all, government mechanisms for raising and spending money are already in place and may be quite efficient. In my town, all but a very few property owners pay their taxes on time with a minimum of prompting.

Still, it might be objected, how can we verify that such changes *are* Pareto-improvements? Taxes come from everyone, not just those who'll benefit from parks or whatever government spends them on. Moreover, in describing the land case, I *stipulated* that my price is exceeded by what my neighbors are collectively willing to pay. How is such an hypothesis confirmed in real life? Governments are quite capable of spending more for something than their citizens are willing to pay for it; how are they to get the information required to avoid doing so? About all we can suggest is public input and review in its various forms, including opportunities to vote officials out of office.

While such considerations make clear that government action *may not* improve on what bargaining among self-interested agents for the transfer of property rights would achieve, they hardly establish that it *cannot*. Accordingly, this argument does not show that free markets deliver optimality. However, advocates of privatization need not claim so much. The argument from productivity will be none the worse for being recast in terms of the relative superiority of allocation systems, especially since the complete rights called for by premise 3 are out of reach. That is, this premise can be weakened to, "Where individuals are self-interested, resources will be used more productively if they are privately owned—ownership being characterized by property rights that are secure, transferable, and as complete as feasible—than they will under any other system we can devise." So privatization advocates need argue only for the *relative* productive superiority of the market system. The fact that real markets needn't direct resources to their *most* productive use is irrelevant, if it can be shown that markets generally make resources *more* productive than do other systems. Baden and Lueck, in fact, make this point in remarking that "since there is no perfect, costless economic system, sound policy must promote the *least imperfect* system."[12] The choice is between "imperfect governments and imperfect markets," and it is not helpful to dismiss the latter "because they do not duplicate the competitive equilibrium of the neoclassical model" (i.e., do not satisfy the assumptions of the first fundamental theorem).[13]

## NET-GAIN IMPROVEMENT STANDARDS

How might the productive superiority of markets over other systems be established, if we can't do it by showing that the market *always* puts resources to their *most* productive use? Here we immediately confront a serious difficulty: the Pareto standard simply won't support such a claim. To say that resources are more productive in system $S'$ than in $S$ is presumably to say that $S'$ would—or generally would—allocate a given batch of resources to more productive uses than would *S*. But this is almost certainly false for *any* systems *S* and *S'*, if the standard of improved productivity is the Pareto criterion. Who gets what will differ between *S* and *S'*, and it's a safe bet that at least one individual will prefer what she gets under *S*. Thus, to take seriously the suggestion that the free market is more efficient than other systems, we appear to require a less demanding standard of improved productivity—one that allows improvements to occur even when some people lose. This, I believe, is what we want anyway, for Pareto-improvements are too rare to make the Pareto criterion very useful.

Unless we're prepared to break with economic theory, we must continue to view resources as means to satisfying human desire: resources are to be judged more productive as their use better satisfies the desires of consumers. So we need a defensible standard of productivity that classifies as improvements some shifts *I→II* that produce losses for some consumers, where a consumer loses by *I→II* if he prefers his *I*-plan to his *II*-plan. It would be nice to develop one that quantifies improvements so that a determination that *II* and *III* both improve on *I* also settles which of them is better.

In part, defensibility is a matter of formal constraints: *is an improvement over* should be a partial ordering of possible states of affairs, here identified with possible uses of resources. That is, it should be *transitive* (if *II* improves on *I* and *III* improves on *II*, then *III* improves on *I*) and *anti-reflexive* (*I* isn't an improvement over itself); together these features imply *anti-symmetry* (if *II* improves on *I*, then *I* does not improve on *II*). But we can also place a minimal substantive constraint on defensibility: if *I→II* is to be an improvement, losses to some must be offset by gains to others. That is, *I→II* must produce a *net* gain. The problem is making sense of this.

I can't spend the same hour working both on the Mendelssohn violin concerto and this book, so we might say that allocating the hour to music is a loss for me *qua* writer and a gain for me *qua* violinist. Here, though, the question of whether it's an improvement is presumably settled by appeal to *my* preferences, preferences that are mine not just relative to this or that role but resolve the conflicting demands of these roles. My preference for spending the hour on the Mendelssohn *rules* that the gain *to me* outweighs the loss *to me*. Similarly, allocating a piece of federal rangeland to grazing may be a gain for ranchers and a loss for recreationists. But in this case there don't seem to *be* any preferences beyond those of individuals to which we might similarly appeal to decide whether allocation to grazing is a net gain.

In the remaining sections of this chapter, I consider a number of attempts to meet this challenge, i.e., to give precise meaning to "*I→II* is a net gain," where individual preference determines individual gain and loss. In my view, none of the proposals is defensible. Moreover, these improvement standards are difficult to apply, particularly in assessing large-scale shifts. So privatization advocates will not find them particularly helpful in grounding the productivity claims they make for privatization.

## THE KALDOR CRITERION

One way we might understand "net gain" is this: $I{\rightarrow}II$ is an improvement if the winners could ideally compensate the losers and still be winners, i.e., some modification $II'$ of $II$ achieved by magically redistributing its product is a Pareto-improvement over $I$. This is the Kaldor criterion.[14] It would judge allocating rangeland to livestock grazing ($II$) rather than wildlife habitat ($I$) to be a net gain if the (human) losers under $I{\rightarrow}II$ could be fully compensated while leaving the (human) winners better off. Actual compensation is not required. In fact, since redistribution generally consumes resources, there might not be any $II'$ we could *actually* reach from $II$ that is a Pareto-improvement over $I$.

It is, of course, possible that neither $I{\rightarrow}II$ nor $II{\rightarrow}I$ is an improvement by this standard. Perhaps there is nothing a wildlife enthusiast could give that would compensate a rancher for the loss of his way of life and, conversely, nothing the latter could give that would compensate the former for replacing wild desert bighorns with domesticated cattle. What is adequate compensation in each case is up to the recipient, and people can have all sorts of idiosyncratic attachments. Used to judge proposed departures from the *status quo*, the Kaldor criterion will, in such a case, endorse the *status quo*, whatever it is. There is no inconsistency, since "endorse" here does not mean *declare better*. However, if these cases are real, if people have attachments for which there is no adequate or affordable substitute, it may not be possible to justify any significant change in federal land management, privatization included, as a Kaldor-improvement. More generally, it may not be possible to justify significant departures from any system by this criterion.

Unfortunately, we can also dream up cases that do call into question the consistency of this standard, cases in which *both $I{\rightarrow}II$ and $II{\rightarrow}I$* count as Kaldor-improvements. Imagine, for example, that resources $R$ are used to produce two goods, $X$ and $Y$, for distribution to two individuals. A given amount of $X$ and $Y$ produced might be distributed in different ways: two such ways, $I$ and $II$, are uses of $R$ that differ only in who gets what. If neither $I$ nor $II$ is Pareto-optimal, then each is a Kaldor-improvement over the other. The difficulty may be extended to Pareto-optimal cases as well.[15]

There is a quick fix available for this problem in what is known as the Scitovsky criterion: count a Kaldor-improvement $I{\rightarrow}II$ as an improvement if $II{\rightarrow}I$ isn't a Kaldor-improvement.[16] In short, use the Kaldor standard as long as it doesn't get you into trouble. The problem is that if the Kaldor criterion does lead to trouble in *some* cases, it's not clear what it has going for it in the *other* ones. Why should we regard a Scitovsky-improvement $I{\rightarrow}II$ as an improvement? The answer can't be that under $I{\rightarrow}II$ gains exceed losses in the sense that the winners could ideally compensate the losers and still be winners, for, by that criterion, $II{\rightarrow}I$ may also be an improvement. So what is the answer? If we can't understand "net gain" in Kaldor terms in all cases, why should we understand it that way in some cases?

## CONSUMER SURPLUS

Rather than trying to salvage this approach, let's explore another. Suppose we could reckon individual gains and losses on a single scale, in terms of money, say. Then their sum would be the net gain, and a positive net gain would indicate that gains offset losses and by how much. But how could we possibly assign a dollar value to individual gains and losses? The reply, at least in theory, is that *we* won't presume to evaluate these changes; instead, we'll let the affected individuals do it.

Suppose I see a listing of "Unique Western Colorado Properties" which includes: "300 acre ranch on 2 miles Dolores River, red cliffs, swinging bridge, 60 acres irrigated, orchard, petroglyphs, $300,000."[17] I'm intrigued, one thing leads to another, and I buy it from you for $275K. Assume, for simplicity, that I don't take out a mortgage. Then before the transaction, I have $275K and you have the ranch; let this be situation *I*. The transaction converts *I* into *II*: I have the ranch and you have $275K. Evidently neither of us prefers *I* to *II*, else we'd not have made the exchange (I *buy* the ranch, I don't force you to sell it). If we imagine that there is some *largest amount I'm willing to pay* (MWTP) for the ranch ($300K, say) and some *least amount you're willing to accept* (mWTA) for it ($260K, say), then evidently mWTA ≤ $275K ≤ MWTP. The difference MWTP−$275K (here $25K) is my *consumer surplus* from the transaction; it is a monetary measure of my gain from *I→II* (I'd pay up to this amount to move from *I* to *II*; I prefer *II*, less any sum up to this amount, to *I*). Similarly, the difference $275K−mWTA (here $15K) is your surplus from the transaction. The sum MWTP−mWTA of these differences (here $40K) is a monetary measure of the overall gain, assuming none but you and I are affected by the transaction.

In thought at least, the notion of consumer surplus may be generalized beyond such monetary transactions to an improvement measure for changes that benefit some at cost to others. We need simply imagine that every individual *has her price*. Individual gains and losses from *I→II* can be reckoned by MWTP or by mWTA. If *I→II* is a gain for you, we might measure it in terms of (a) the most you are willing to pay for this change or (b) the least you are willing to accept to forgo it. If *I→II* is a loss for you, we might reckon it in terms of (a) the least you are willing to accept to put up with this change or (b) the most you are willing to pay to avoid it. In each case, (a) gives the CV ("compensating variation") measure of consumer surplus; in a sense, CV assesses change from the perspective of situation *I*. In each case, (b) gives the EV ("equivalent variation") measure; in a sense, EV assesses change from the perspective of *II*.[18]

The CV measure of your gain or loss from *I→II* is the amount *cv* of money (positive, negative, or zero) for which you are indifferent between *I* and *II−cv*, where *II−cv* is the situation that results from *II* by extracting *cv* from you. If *cv* is positive, then *I→II* is a gain for you. If you have or can raise *cv* in situation *I*, you must be willing to pay it to move to *II*. The definition does not require ability to pay in advance for *I→II*. However, we must imagine that money to the extent of $cv$ can be obtained from you in $II$; perhaps $I{\rightarrow}II$ involves receiving a paying job, or a gift you can sell for $cv$. With the understanding that you needn't be able to pay in advance, we can identify positive $cv$ with your MWTP for a gain. If $cv$ is negative, then $I{\rightarrow}II$ is a loss for you, and $-cv$ is your mWTA to put up with it.

The EV measure of your gain or loss from $I{\rightarrow}II$ is the amount $ev$ of money (positive, negative, or zero) for which you are indifferent between $II$ and $I+ev$, where $I+ev$ is the situation that results from $I$ by giving you $ev$. If $ev$ is positive, then $I{\rightarrow}II$ is a gain for you, and $ev$ is your mWTA to forgo it. If $ev$ is negative, then $I{\rightarrow}II$ is a loss for you; $-ev$ is your MWTP to avoid it, and money to the extent of $-ev$ must be extractable from you in $I$.

To illustrate these notions, consider a public-resource issue, such as whether to ban motorized travel on the Colorado River within the Grand Canyon. Let $I$ be the *status quo* (motors permitted) and $II$ be the proposed change (motors prohibited). Suppose I find motors intrusive: they are noisy and smelly and remind me of what I'd take a river trip to escape from. Imagine that I'm willing to pay $100 for a ban and to accept $300 to forego it. Suppose you enjoy speed or are willing to put up with some noise in order to fit running the Grand Canyon into your busy schedule. Imagine that you are willing to pay $500 to avoid a ban and to accept $1000 to put up with it. $I{\rightarrow}II$ is a gain for me; it is worth either $100 or $300 to me, depending on whether we use the CV or the EV measure of consumer surplus. $I{\rightarrow}II$ is a loss for you; it is worth either $-$1000 or $-$500 to you, depending on whether we use the CV or the EV measure.

The *aggregate consumer surplus CV* or *EV* for a change is simply the sum of individual gains and losses, reckoned by CV or EV, for those affected by it. In the imagined case, our contribution to the aggregate would be $-$900 or $-$200, depending upon whether we are reckoning by CV or EV. Shall we therefore say that, for the microsociety constituted by the two of us, the proposed ban is not an improvement? More generally, can we hold that $I{\rightarrow}II$ is an improvement just in case $CV$ or $EV$ is positive?

Unfortunately, this proposal has serious drawbacks. (1) In general, $cv \neq ev$, and we can dream up cases where $I{\rightarrow}II$ is an improvement in terms of $CV$ while $II{\rightarrow}I$ is an improvement in terms of $EV$ (or vice versa); this forces a choice between the CV and EV measures, and the better choice isn't obvious. Even worse, for either way of reckoning consumer surplus, we can also imagine cases where *both* $I{\rightarrow}II$ *and* $II{\rightarrow}I$ count as improvements; that is, both measures seem to turn out inconsistent results, at least for abstract cases. (2) The MWTP and mWTA of individuals, if indeed there are such numbers, are not easily accessible; accordingly, it will be difficult to determine whether some proposed change is an improvement according to this standard, particularly if it is as sweeping as privatizing public lands. Finally, (3) the relation between consumer surplus and net gain is obscure; so it's unclear that we'd learn anything worth knowing about some change even if we could discover its $CV$ or $EV$. I elaborate on these difficulties in the next three sections. Some readers may prefer taking the claims of point 1 on faith to working through the somewhat technical material in the first of them.

## 1. Divergence and Inconsistency

As the example above suggests, an individual's *cv* need not equal his *ev*. As explained below, they may diverge due to (1) income effects or (2) the asymmetry between paying and being paid. This means that if we could devise CV and EV meters indicating how individuals would fare under proposed changes *I→II*, they might give different readings on how *I→II* affects them. What is worse, summing such readings across individuals might indicate that *I→II* was a net gain by one measure and a net loss by the other; an abstract illustration will be given shortly.

   1.  As your income varies, the rate at which you are willing to exchange dollars for more of some given commodity *C* may also vary. Now that I'm a rich professor, maybe I don't buy so much non-vintage jug wine. We may relate such *income effects* to the shape of one's *indifference curves* (see Figure 4–1). Let $<c,y>$ represent the best consumption bundle containing *C* in amount *c*, along with other commodities in amounts that $y will buy. Your consumption preferences can then be represented schematically by indifference curves; the points on such a curve are pairs $<c,y>$ representing bundles that are just as good from your perspective. If your income is $I_0$ and the price of *C* is $p, you will exchange dollars for *C* at rate *p* until you reach the best affordable plan $<c_0,y>$. Geometrically, this is a matter of moving from $<0,I_0>$ down a line of slope $-p$ to its point of intersection with the highest indifference curve.

   As your income varies, you may buy more, less, or the same amount of *C* depending on the shape of your indifference curves. Assume, as usual, that they are concave from below, and consider the slope of indifference curves through $<c,y>$ as *y* increases. If there is no change, there is no

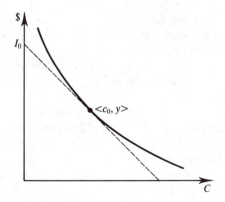

**Figure 4–1**

income effect: you will buy the same amount of *C* (aspirin, maybe) as your income increases. If they steepen, you will buy more of *C* (air travel, maybe) as your income increases (*C* is a *superior* good for you). If they flatten, you will buy less of *C* (canned pork and beans, maybe) as your income increases (*C* is an *inferior* good for you). In such cases, there is an income effect and probably also a difference in *cv* and *ev*.

In Figure 4–2, *I* = <*c,y*>, *II* = <*c',y'*>, and *I→II* is an improvement. Figure 4–2(a) represents *C* as a superior good; in this case, *cv* < *ev*. Figure 4–2(b) represents *C* as an inferior good; in this case, *cv* > *ev*.

2. More important, I think, is that MWTP is limited while mWTA is not. Suppose *I→II is a loss for you*. Then *cv* is the least you are willing to accept to put up with it; *ev* is the most you are willing to pay to avoid it, where willingness-to-pay is limited by ability to pay. If "*I+ev*" is to make sense, −*ev* must somehow be extractable from you in *I*: you must command −*ev*, either in ready cash or in the form of things that others are willing to give cash for. It's clear that for losses *cv* might be larger, indeed much larger, than *ev*. For a change that took your life, *cv* might be infinite. And even if you have your (finite) price, it might be a lot more than you could raise if you had to buy your way out of a threatened loss. Suppose, for example, a reclassification of federal land would eliminate the grazing allotment that makes some rancher's operation viable. He may value the particulars of his way of life more than anyone else does; what others are collectively willing to pay him for his allotment (= *ev*) may be a lot less than what he'd willingly surrender it for (= *cv*).

If *cv* need not equal *ev* for individuals, perhaps our social assessment of *I→II* can differ, depending upon whether we equate net gain with *CV* or with *EV*: perhaps by one measure *I→II* is net gain for society and by the other a net loss. In fact, it is not hard to dream up cases suggesting that neither *CV* nor *EV* is a *consistent* index of improvement. That is, for each of them, we can imagine cases in which *both I→II and II→I* are reckoned as improvements.

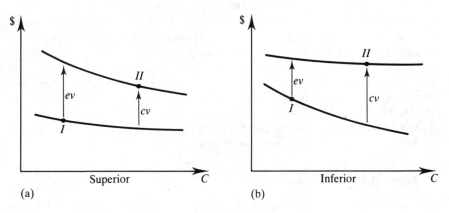

(a)                                                              (b)

**Figure 4–2**

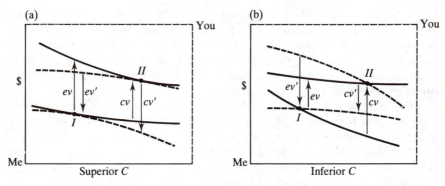

**Figure 4–3**

Imagine that you and I have the same preferences over bundles $<c,y>$, where $c$ is the amount of some commodity $C$, and $y$ is cash in hand. Suppose that $I$ and $II$ are distributions of some fixed amounts of $C$ and cash to us that are symmetric in the sense that my bundle in $I$ is yours in $II$ and my bundle in $II$ is yours in $I$. Let $I{\to}II$ be a gain for me and a loss for you. We may represent this sort of situation in a standard Edgeworth box diagram as displayed in Figure 4–3, where my indifference curves are solid and yours are dashed. Figure 4–3(a) represents $C$ as a superior good, Figure 4–3(b) represents $C$ as an inferior good. In this example, $cv$ and $ev$ are mine for $I{\to}II$, $cv'$ and $ev'$ are yours. Upward (downward) arrows indicate positive (negative) values. For $I{\to}II$, $CV < 0$ and $EV > 0$ in the superior case. From the definitions of $cv$ and $ev$, we see that $cv$ for $I{\to}II$ equals $-ev$ for $II{\to}I$. So for $II{\to}I$, $EV > 0$ and $CV < 0$ in the superior case. This suggests that these measures may assess change quite differently, since positive $EV$ says $I{\to}II$ is an improvement, while negative $CV$ says it isn't. It also suggests that $EV$ is not a consistent index of improvement, for it counts both $I{\to}II$ and $II{\to}I$ as improvements. In the inferior case, all the inequalities are reversed, suggesting that $CV$ isn't a consistent index either.[19]

A standard that assesses both $I{\to}II$ and $II{\to}I$ as improvements is not defensible. It could, I suppose, be objected that counterexamples in Edgeworth box diagrams don't necessarily represent counterexamples in the real world. If neither the CV nor the EV standard would do in *all* possible worlds, perhaps either would work well enough in *this* one. However, what appears to be the source of the difficulty—the divergence of MWTP and mWTA—also appears to be a fact.[20] Accordingly, I doubt that the burden of proof can be shifted to those who question the consistency of these consumer surplus improvement standards.

## 2. Applicability and Benefit–Cost Analysis

How are we to determine whether $I{\to}II$ generates positive $CV$ or $EV$ and is therefore an improvement according to this index? The definition suggests finding the consumer surplus of $I{\rightarrow}II$ for each individual and adding up the results. Unfortunately, the first step is problematic, since it's hard to get at people's MWTP and mWTA.

We can get some *very* limited information about other people's MWTP and mWTA from observing their exchange behavior. If I freely buy a book for \$20, then evidently the most I'm willing to pay for it is at least \$20. If I refuse your offer of \$500 for my car, then \$500 is less than I'm willing to accept for it—unless I figure I might squeeze more money out of you by pretending it is. But MWTP and mWTA are dispositional properties that we cannot directly observe. To say that \$Z is your MWTP for $X$ is to say that you would buy $X$ for any amount up to \$Z but no more, if the occasion arose and other things were equal; and similarly for your mWTA for $Y$. It's doubtful that an experiment revealing MWTP or mWTA could be devised, since the experiment itself would probably render other things unequal.

If things were clear to you, we might just administer truth serum and ask. But are they clear? I couldn't, without some thought, say what I'd be willing to pay or accept for most things. Even if it were just a box of spaghetti, I'd have to consider context: am I buying it just to restock the larder or do we need it for a dinner for which guests are expected in an hour? And for many things I doubt that the figures I'd name would bear much relation to what I'd actually do if the occasion arose. After all, people frequently drive home in new cars that cost more than they thought they were willing to spend, having perhaps accepted less than they imagined they would for the old one.

Aggregate consumer surplus is the sum of individual gains and losses, reckoned by one measure or the other. But it's not feasible to compute it by computing these individual gains and losses, just as it's not feasible to reckon the mean molecular kinetic energy of the water in a beaker by determining the speed of individual water molecules. If we want to know about the water, we use a thermometer, which responds to behavior in the aggregate. Something similar occurs in *benefit–cost analysis*, where information about MWTP and mWTA in the aggregate is derived from market prices.

To illustrate this, suppose that $I$ is the *status quo* and $II$ is a proposed western water project: say, the Parunuweap Canyon dam proposed by the Washington County [Utah] Water Conservancy District to supply water to the St. George area.[21] What people are collectively willing to pay for the various services the project will deliver, in this case water and recreation, is an index of its *benefits*. What people must collectively be paid—for labor, materials, land, etc.—to bring off the project is an index of its *costs*. The project's *net benefits* (benefits minus costs) are then taken as an index of its desirability.[22] A project with negative net benefits is a waste of resources; one with positive net benefits may also be a waste if there are other projects that would deliver greater net benefits.

A project's benefits are its $C$-benefits, summed over the various services $C$—water, flood control, recreation, hydro-electric power, etc.—

it delivers.[23] The *C*-benefits may be estimated from the market demand curve for *C*, which specifies, for each amount *c* of *C*, the price *p(c)* that would just clear the market of *c*. In the case of project recreation, *C* might be measured in user-days, and *p(c)* would be the price at which *c* user-days of recreation would be purchased by consumers, if a market in recreation services could be arranged. Although the market demand curve is theoretically the ("horizontal") sum of individual demand curves, which, in turn, can be derived from individual preference rankings of plans <*c*,$*y*>, no economist would try to construct it in this way. Instead, it is estimated from market prices: if *p* clears some real market of *c*, then *p* = *p(c)*. For example, the market demand curve for project recreation might be estimated from what people *do* pay in the form of travel costs for similar recreation. Once we have the market demand curve for some service *C* of the project, we can estimate its *C*-benefit as the area under it, up to the amount *c* of *C* the project delivers (Figure 4–4). The reasoning is as follows: it can be shown that the area below an *individual's* demand curve up to *c* is the most she is willing to pay for *c*, *provided* there is no income effect (her indifference curves over <*c*,$*y*> are vertically parallel). So, if there is no income effect for anyone who gains from *I→II*, the area under the market demand curve up to *c* will equal aggregate willingness-to-pay for the *C*-service of the project (= its *C*-benefits).

The net benefits of *I→II* would equal its *CV* provided individual gains added up to benefits and individual losses to costs. But they probably don't. The calculation of benefits assumes that there are no income effects. So if I resided in St. George and had to pay for Parunuweap water, I'd buy the same amount per month to irrigate my lawn no matter how rich or poor I became. But who can take such an assumption seriously? Costs bear even less relation to aggregate individual losses than benefits do to aggregate individual gains. What people collectively need be paid to bring off the project depends largely on what the authorities can get away with: the usual

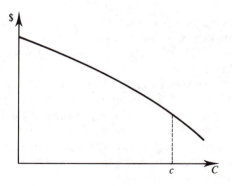

**Figure 4–4**

calculations of costs simply don't take mWTA seriously. If my land is condemned for a project, I may not be entitled to more than its market value (the most *others* would pay for it) in compensation, though I would never have freely parted with it for so little. Moreover, those who lack a recorded property right will be judged to have lost nothing for which compensation need be paid. Thus, although Parunuweap Canyon is federal land, the Washington County Water Conservancy District hasn't asked any American citizen what she'd accept to give up the opportunity she now has to enjoy it in its natural state.

As generally practiced, benefit–cost analysis does not faithfully apply the CV standard. Given the difficulties with consumer surplus, perhaps that's just as well. But standard benefit–cost analysis has its own problems. Estimates of net benefits have no clear basis in individual gains and losses and therefore no strong claim to represent net gain. We can't regard benefits as the sum of individual gains, or costs as the sum of individual losses. Why, then, imagine that net benefits represent social gain or loss at all?

## 3. Substantive Deficiencies

Let's set aside the problem of inconsistency: somehow we discover that it can't happen here, that those embarrassing cases in which *II* improves on *I* and *I* improves on *II* are confined to Edgeworth box diagrams. Let's also set aside the problem of calculating aggregate consumer surplus, if indeed there is such a number: assume that any individual's *cv* and *ev* for any contemplated change *I→II* are accessible to the analyst (imagine that for a small consideration the devil is willing to reveal them). Do we know anything worth knowing when we know the aggregate consumer surplus generated by *I→II*? Does *CV* or *EV* really measure net gain under *I→II*? There are both (1) *intra*personal and (2) *inter*personal difficulties here.

1. The CV standard reckons individual gains, and the EV standard individual losses, in terms of MWTP. But MWTP is not a plausible index of individual gain or loss. Willingness-to-pay is limited by ability to pay, and my ability to pay depends heavily on *other* people's desires. If they don't want what I have, then I can't afford to pay much to secure a gain or avoid a loss. In my view, it is crazy to judge my gain or loss simply in terms of my desires, without inquiring into their content or the conditions under which they were formed. But surely it is even crazier to judge *my* gain or loss in terms of *your* unexamined desires. Yet that is what is happening when we measure my gain by what I am willing to pay to secure it (the CV measure) or my loss by what I am willing to pay to avoid it (the EV measure). My MWTP depends upon what I can pay, and that depends on the desires of others. Thinking of loss in terms of MWTP leads, in the extreme, to the grotesque suggestion that the value of life *to its owner* should be measured by the wage it commands (e.g., that in deciding whether use of some hazardous pesticide would be an improvement, we reckon the expected loss

to farm workers in terms of wages that their untimely death or disability prevents them from earning).

If MWTP is a bad index of *individual* gain or loss, then how much confidence can one have in *aggregate* consumer surplus? If $CV$ for $I{\rightarrow}II$ is positive, then maybe $I{\rightarrow}II$ is a net gain: the price of the $I{\rightarrow}II$ is named by the losers, it can be met out of what the winners, in aggregate, are willing to pay, and each of them gains, by her lights, *at least* her MWTP. But it's not clear that a negative $CV$ indicates a net loss; imagine an investment that improves the quality of life for destitute invalids. Similarly, $EV$ seems a better indicator of net loss than of net gain.

2. Why should we think that adding my gain or loss (as reckoned by *me*) to yours (as reckoned by *you*) really measures the net (social) gain among us? To be sure, we both reckon in terms of dollars, but do dollars have the same value for each of us? If not, adding up the amounts is a bit like adding 8 degrees C to 40 degrees F and coming up with 48 degrees. The pensioner in Vittorio De Sica's film *Umberto D.* finally sells his beloved books—he needs money for food and rent. If the buyer had plenty of money, why should we think that the aggregate consumer surplus of the transaction really measures total gain? Let's agree that in this case both parties gained. The issue is: *by how much in all?* If a lire is worth more to the old man than it is to the rich buyer, then what possible significance can attach to the sum of their consumer surpluses?

There is yet another opening for questioning whether what these standards *say* is an improvement really *is* an improvement, and it is that those who lose by $I{\rightarrow}II$ need not be compensated. If $I{\rightarrow}II$ is an improvement according to $CV$, $EV$, or standard benefit–cost analysis, what are reckoned the winners' gains will cover what are reckoned the losers' losses. But even if the gains can be turned into cash, the losers needn't get any of it. In part, this complaint just reminds us why we developed these standards. Under the Pareto standard, anyone who loses by a proposed change, i.e., anyone who isn't adequately compensated for it, can block it. Even where those who'd benefit from it are willing to buy off those who lose, change won't be justified if compensation is too expensive to arrange, as it will be in many cases.

If we reject the Pareto standard because it doesn't sanction trade-offs, then we can't reject other improvement standards because they do. But it doesn't follow that all trade-offs with the same consumer surplus or net benefits are equal. Your theft of $100 from me may be neutral in terms of net benefit, but is there really nothing to choose between which of us has the $100? Of course, we generally don't include theft among the shifts $I{\rightarrow}II$ we're prepared to consider seriously, but that just suggests that net benefits aren't the whole story. Accordingly, we may wish to appeal to some notion of *fairness*, suggesting that those who lose by some change ought to receive something by way of compensation, even if the costs of paying it reduce net gain. Since the cost of adjudicating these claims will often exceed their value, we can hardly realize this ideal in each case. Often we'll just have to hope that the losers gain in the long run, that they will be among the winners in other changes. But where undeserved losses are concentrated, as when someone's house is demolished to make room for a highway, it may be possible and appropriate to make them good, perhaps out of the winners' gains.

Privatization transfers public property to private parties, and it may be argued that the public is entitled to compensation, just as private parties are when their property is taken for public purposes.[24] It may be difficult to calculate just compensation in the case of public land, especially if value is reckoned in terms of aggregate mWTA. Moreover, it will generally not be possible to make good the losses of individual members of the public; instead, the government will have to act as a trustee in receiving and managing these funds, just as it does in managing public land. However, these problems do not license giving such land to private parties at little or no cost, as some privatization advocates have urged,[25] even if it could be shown that the aggregate consumer surplus of such a transaction were positive.

## WEALTH

The last improvement standard I shall consider is associated with Richard Posner. Posner's agenda is wealth-maximization: he believes that changes $I{\to}II$ he describes as "increasing wealth" are desirable and that social institutions, such as property rights, should be fashioned to encourage them. We may associate with $I{\to}II$ various dollar-amounts, which we call "wealth changes for $I{\to}II$." My *wealth change* $\Delta w$ for $I{\to}II$ is the value (in dollars, say) I attach to what I thereby acquire, less the value I attach to what I thereby surrender. My wealth is to be preserved by the exchange of something for its value. If I own something, its value is my mWTA to surrender it; if I don't own it, its value is my MWTP to acquire it.[26] Here, $\Delta w$ is really just *cv*, with the understanding that one gains by acquiring something of positive value, and loses by giving up something of positive value that one owns. The *social wealth change* $\Delta W$ for $I{\to}II$ is the sum, taken over individuals affected by $I{\to}II$, of individual wealth changes $\Delta w$ for $I{\to}II$; $\Delta W$ is essentially *CV*. Of alternatives $II$ to the *status quo I*, we should, in Posner's view, prefer the one for which the social wealth change $\Delta W$ for $I{\to}II$ is greatest.[27]

Talk of "wealth changes" and "maximizing wealth" leads us to expect that there is something, viz., wealth, that changes and can be maximized. If so, what is it? The characterization of $\Delta w$ suggests that my wealth is the sum of the values I attach to my possessions. However, this will not do. The sum of what I'd accept for $X$, other things equal, and what I'd accept for $Y$, other things equal, is not, in general, what I'd accept for both $X$ and $Y$, other things equal, because disposing of both $X$ and $Y$ does not, in general, leave other things equal. Imagine, for example, that I'm attached to my house and its furnishings. I might be willing to sell my house for \$125K assuming I retain the furnishings and my furnishings for \$75K assuming I retain the house, but be unwilling to part with both for \$200K.

More generally, we can argue that if my wealth changes with $I{\rightarrow}II$ according to $\Delta w$, then there is *no* function $w$, defined on states individuated by what I have, that we can regard as *my wealth*, i.e., no function $w$ such that $w(I) + \Delta w = w(II)$.[28] If there were, then $\Delta w$ for $I{\rightarrow}II$ would equal $-\Delta w$ for $II{\rightarrow}I$. But since $\Delta w$ is essentially $cv$, this need not be so. Since social wealth change is just the aggregate of individual wealth changes, it follows that there is also no function defined on social states individuated by who has what that we can regard as *social wealth*. This is awkward for Posner, who wants to argue from the desirability of wealth to the desirability of wealth-maximizing institutions. It's easy to grasp an argument for some system $S$ of institutions that proceeds by claiming $S$ will generate *more W* than alternatives to $S$, where $W$ is *something desirable*. The difficulty for Posner is that wealth does not seem to fit this pattern of argument. What, then, is the form of *his* argument for wealth-maximizing institutions? This is a problem for anyone arguing that a system of private property rights is preferable to federal management because it maximizes, or increases, wealth. Evidently, the same might be said of consumer surplus.

As an improvement standard, wealth appears to have all the drawbacks of $CV$, since $\Delta W$ differs only slightly from $CV$ and not in a way that banishes counterexamples to consistency,[29] misgivings about willingness-to-pay as a measure of gain or loss, or questions about the significance of aggregating gains, so measured, across individuals. Accordingly, somehow discovering that the social $\Delta W$ for privatizing federal lands was positive would not, I think, tell us that privatization was a social gain.

## WEALTH-MAXIMIZATION AND PRIVATIZATION

Let us set aside such problems and ask if the private property rights promoted by advocates of privatization are wealth-maximizing. (Let's also speak loosely of wealth as if it were something that could be maximized.) Since $I{\rightarrow}II$ is a gain for me if my $\Delta w$ is positive, individuals have an interest in increasing their wealth and in discovering and creating opportunities to do so. Free exchange increases the wealth of the parties to it; in fact, it maximizes their wealth, relative to other opportunities known to them. However, local gains may be global losses on account of spillovers (as when I buy a stink bomb from you). More generally, there may be global gains that are not realized by the free exchange of rights, because in one way or another they are costly. In general, exchange that's free in the sense that parties willingly consent to it isn't free in the sense that it costs nothing: resources must be used to discover opportunities to gain from exchange, to reach an agreement, to transfer property rights. Better opportunities to gain from exchange may exist, but not in the imagination of those able to exploit them (maybe I could have got a better price on the stink bomb from someone else). A large-scale exchange of rights (as when a large number of people make small monetary contributions to some end) might produce a substantial wealth gain, but not enough to justify the cost of arranging it.

I have noted that the complete bundles of use-rights desired by privatization advocates are fantasies, given spillovers in consumption and production. If your use of your property is inconsistent with my use of mine, as in the fishing–logging case discussed in an earlier section, both of us can't have a complete bundle of rights. If you may cut your timber as you wish, you thereby have a right to alter the characteristics of my stream; if I may control such use of my stream, I thereby have a right to constrain your logging operation. Since our rights can't both be complete, the issue is: whose shall be incomplete?

If the costs of bargaining were low and the most we'd each pay for a right we didn't have was also the least we'd accept for it if we did, it wouldn't matter to a wealth-maximizer whether (a) I got the right to cold, clear water or (b) you got the right to log as you wish—although it would matter to you and me. If I valued fishing more than you valued logging, we'd have fishing. I'd buy the right to cold, clear water in case (b) and refuse to sell it to you in case (a). Similarly, if you valued logging more than I valued fishing, we'd have logging. As the expected cost of transferring rights increases, the wealth-maximizer will suggest secure rights (i.e., rights not alienable without consent) *assigned initially to those who value them most* and, as the cost rises further, rights that may be moved around *without* the consent of the holder in accord with some mechanisms for determining which movements will increase wealth.[30]

All this suggests that, insofar as property rights are rationalized in terms of wealth-maximization, they will be neither as simple nor as secure as privatization advocates suggest. Indeed, we might wonder whether a concern for wealth, as Posner understands it, wouldn't (1) generate a system of private rights to use public lands that's a lot like what we now have or (2) simply block privatization as wealth-decreasing.

1. A wealth-maximizer would want to place public lands, or use-rights thereto, in the hands of those who valued them most to begin with, lest transaction costs block their movement there. Perhaps this is the rationale for the suggestion of some privatization advocates that National Forest Wilderness be given to environmental groups.[31] Although its value as wilderness (judged by aggregate willingness-to-pay for its preservation) might exceed its value in other uses (judged by what its owners would accept, and other interests bid, for it), it might be too costly to assemble this dispersed willingness-to-pay into a winning bid.

This, however, is a dangerous line of thought for those who want public lands privatized. For if environmental groups can so represent the interest of numerous individuals in wilderness, why can't the same be said of the USFS? And aren't there other interests out there that should be represented as well—lovers of wild horses and burros, for instance, and others with some individually small but collectively substantial interest in aspects of federal lands? Are we sure that privatization will serve the various interests in federal lands better than does multiple use, which is supposed to allow all of us to "get what we need from the land yet leave it for other users as well?"[32] Alternatively, are we sure that a privatization program designed to represent these interests wouldn't simply replicate the current regime: the land in private hands, to be sure, but its use restricted by covenants enforced by various authorities? Since the *use* of federal lands is private, this is, essentially, a description of the current order. This line of argument suggests that a privatization program designed by a wealth-maximizer might produce a system of property rights, in what are now public lands, that is quite different from the one envisioned by privatization advocates. Indeed, it might be sufficiently clossse to the present system of use-rights to be not worth the trouble of implementing.

2. Another worry is whether getting from here to there wouldn't impose wealth losses large enough to make privatization a bad deal. Suppose we agree that $I \rightarrow II$ is an improvement if, and only if, $\Delta W$ is positive. Is $\Delta W$ for some program of privatization positive?

If we take current rights to use public land seriously, then transfer or extinction of those rights would incur wealth losses valued at what their holders were willing to accept to give them up. There are fanatics like myself out there who'll insist they'll not surrender their rights to the federal lands for any money—and not for the reason Posner thinks justifies the power of eminent domain, viz., to extort much more than what they're actually willing to accept to surrender their rights.[33]

If we don't take such rights seriously, then privatization would increase wealth: nobody would lose anything they'd a right to, and some would acquire rights they'd be willing to pay quite a lot for. But this result is of little interest without a good argument for wiping the slate clean. Wealth-maximizers like Posner don't object to extinguishing rights, but not in this way. Extinguishing an existing right always incurs a wealth loss equal to the value its holder places on it, where value is mWTA; only if these losses are offset by wealth gains elsewhere may rights be extinguished. Those who would allow rights to be transferred without their holders' consent, on a showing that doing so would increase wealth, obviously don't take them as seriously as those who'd require consent. But they take them a lot more seriously than those who are prepared simply to overlook wealth losses.

Now if I have no right to something (the Mercedes I bought with drug profits, say), then assigning it to someone else incurs no wealth loss on me, spillovers excluded. Can objection (ii) be met by arguing that rights to use public lands are, in fact, far less numerous than they appear to be? Some privatization advocates do seem to have a selective view of who has what rights to use these lands. For Baden and Lueck, for example, it appears to be long-term *income-generating* use that creates a legitimate right to use public lands, a right that should be recognized and respected by any program of privatization. They write that "individuals [who] have been using certain wilderness areas for long periods of time and have essentially established property rights to certain uses and areas [should] retain their rights. . . . Uses that would fall under this preemption clause include outfitting, guiding, and grazing."[34] Other individuals may have *interests*, but no *rights*, in public lands. Were these lands privatized, such people could, of course, purchase rights in lands of interest by outbidding other interested parties.

However, it's not easy to find a principled basis for this distinction between rights to, and interests in, uses of public land. Baden and Lueck do not explain how anyone can "essentially" establish a property right to public lands. What comes immediately to mind is John Locke's idea that one makes an unowned resource one's own by mixing one's labor with it.[35] However, federal land is hardly unowned: what you or I may rightfully do with it depends upon federal laws and regulations. To think that I can, over the years, establish some sort of property right to a bit of National Forest by laboring on it—say, by pasturing my sheep with USFS permission or growing marijuana without it—is like thinking I can acquire a property right to *your* land in the same way. Furthermore, it's not clear how, by appeal to Locke, one can distinguish between uses that generate income and those that don't, especially when Locke didn't think his argument established anyone's right to derive income from property.[36] Why should the labor he mixes with the Colorado River give an outfitter a right to run raft trips through the Grand Canyon, while someone else who does exactly the same things for her own recreation merely has an interest in such trips? There may be a good reason for the NPS to assign most of the Canyon's river-running permits to commercial outfitters,[37] but we're not going to find it in Locke's *Second treatise of government*.

The problems discussed in this chapter suggest that it won't be easy to establish the productivity of privatization, as long as resources are understood to be more productive as their use better satisfies the desires of consumers. If this is the criterion of getting more out of resources, then some alternative *II* to the present system *I* makes resources more productive if consumers on balance prefer what *II would* deliver to them to what *I does* deliver to them. By "consumers" we mean the consumers of the present system *I*, who must be projected into system *II*. "On balance" has both an individual and a social aspect. We imagine that each consumer could, if his *II*-position were made clear, decide whether on balance he preferred the resulting consumption plan to what he now has. But we also specify when, in a shift *I→II*, losses for some consumers are balanced by gains for others.

In the Pareto account, they never are. Since most shifts impose losses, this standard is not very useful. Net-gain standards require that the winners be able to meet the losers' price or that the losers be unable to meet the winners' price for forgoing gains. Some of these standards, modelled as they are on free exchange, also invest individuals with sufficient power to block departures from the *status quo*. Where the losers may name their price (as in the Kaldor, *CV*, and wealth standards), who can be sure that change won't be vetoed? After all, these accounts of the *meaning* of "resources would be more productively employed in system *II* than in system *I*" make it very hard to discover whether it's *true*. Who could imagine with any precision and confidence her consumption prospects in a system other than the actual one? If she could do this, how could she put a price on her gain or loss, and how could the policy analyst get this information? The mental construction by which we *understand* claims of the form "resources would be more productive in *II* than in *I*" does not help us much in finding reasons to believe or disbelieve them. This allows both proponents and opponents of change to take refuge in ignorance and to assert what they like with little chance of being shown to be wrong.

Privatization clearly won't increase the productivity of federal lands if the standard of improvement is the Pareto standard. Perhaps privatization would increase productivity in the sense of being a Kaldor-improvement, or generating positive consumer surplus or net benefits, or increasing wealth. These standards are so difficult to apply that such a belief may be safe from refutation. But that is not enough to commend it to anyone. Furthermore, the notions of increased productivity captured by such standards aren't particularly inspiring: there are both logical and substantive reasons to doubt that we should go for changes that they label as improvements.

If it's unclear that (a) privatizing public lands would increase productivity or (b) increasing productivity is desirable, then the argument from productivity does not succeed. Of course, what's not clear now may eventually become so. Perhaps there are reasons not yet considered for believing (a). Perhaps replies can be made to the objections to (b) that have been accumulating. In Chapter 5, I consider how privatization advocates might argue for (a), given that we can hardly verify it directly. Some of these arguments assume that systems are more productive as they more closely resemble the ideal markets of the first fundamental theorem; others suggest that empirical data confirm (a). While these arguments are by nature inconclusive, they do make it difficult to dismiss (a), particularly in the absence of conclusive reasons to think federal lands are now more productive than they'd be in private hands. The prospects for establishing (b) without qualifying it in ways that permit arguing *against* privatization are, I think, not good. I shall begin assessing them in Chapter 6.

## NOTES

1. Ronald Coase, "The problem of social cost," *Journal of Law and Economics* 3 (1960), 1–44 at VIII.

2. John Sisk of the Southeast Alaska Conservation Council, commenting on USFS administration of Tongass National Forest, in "The $64 million question," *Sierra* 78(4) (1993), 55–57 at 57.

3. *Public lands: an introduction to the agencies and issues* (San Francisco: Sierra Club, 1982), at 4.

4. *Timber sale program annual report, fiscal year 1992* (Washington: USFS, 1993), at 4. It also notes that "forest management is an investment business where monetary gains are often not realized until well into the future, but may be sufficient to cover investments at an acceptable rate of return." Id., at 13. Nonetheless, the USFS has proposed ending logging in 62 National Forests by 1998. "U.S. would end cutting of trees in many forests," *The New York Times*, 30 April 1993, A1. For a critical review of the benefits typically claimed for below-cost timber sales, see Richard E. Rice, "Old-growth logging myths: the ecological impact of the US Forest Service's management policies," *The Ecologist* 20(4) (1990), 141–46.

5. *Below-cost timber sales: the economic realities of managing our National Forests* (The American Forest and Paper Association, 1993), at IV.

6. John V. Krutilla and Michael D. Bowes, "Economics and public forestland management," *Natural Resources Journal* 29 (1989), 737–49 at 744.

7. John Baden and Dean Lueck, "A property rights approach to wilderness management" in *Public lands and the U.S. economy: balancing conservation and development*, ed. George M. Johnson and Peter M. Emerson (Boulder, CO: Westview, 1984), 29–67 at 43.

8. Its usual formulation is: *a competitive equilibrium is Pareto-optimal*, where "competitive" indicates that agents face prices and "equilibrium" indicates that supply equals demand across all commodities. However, proving the theorem requires that additional assumptions be built into the notion of a competitive equilibrium. Reasonably accessible treatments of this result can be found in Allan M. Feldman, *Welfare economics and social choice theory* (Boston: Kluwer-Nijhoff, 1980), Chapters 1–4; and Tjalling C. Koopmans, "Allocation of resources and the price system," in *Three essays on the state of economic science* (New York: McGraw Hill, 1957).

9. This line of argument is derived from Carl J. Dahlman, "The problem of externality," *Journal of Law and Economics* 22 (1979), 141–62.

10. The insight that bargaining can lead to (local) optimality in spillover cases is due to Coase, note 1 *supra*.

11. Unfortunately, the situation is far more complicated, since most of the haze and smog cannot be traced to such concentrated sources. See Steve Hinchman, "The blurring of the west," *High Country News*, 28 June 1993, 10–13.

12. John Baden and Dean Lueck, "Bringing private management to public lands: environmental and economic advantages," in *Controversies in environmental policy*, ed. Sheldon Kamieniecki, Robert O'Brien, and Michael Clarke (Albany: State University of New York Press, 1986), 39–64 at 45.

13. Id., at 55.

14. Feldman, note 8 *supra*, at 142.

15. Suppose $A$ likes $X$ twice as much as $Y$, in the sense that $A$'s marginal rate of substitution of $Y$ for $X$ is 2 (i.e., $A$ is indifferent between $<x,y>$ and $<x+z, y-2z>$, for amounts $x$ of $X$ and $y$ of $Y$), while $B$ has the opposite preference. Let $I$ use resources to produce 2 units of $Y$ and 1 of $X$, where $A$ gets $<1,1>$ and $B$ gets $<0,1>$; let $II$ use resources to produce 2 units of $X$ and 1 of $Y$, where $B$ gets $<1,1>$ and $A$ gets $<1,0>$. $I$ and $II$ are Pareto-optimal if, in each case, production is efficient in the sense that no more of either good can be produced from the given resources without producing less of the other. $I{\rightarrow}II$ produces a gain for $B$ at $A$'s expense. It is a Kaldor-improvement because transferring 0.5 of $X$ from $B$ to $A$ compensates $A$ for the loss ($A$ is indifferent between $<1,1>$ and $<1.5,0>$) while leaving $B$ still better-off than in $I$. $II{\rightarrow}I$ produces a gain for $A$ at $B$'s expense. It also is a Kaldor-

improvement because transferring 0.5 of $Y$ from $A$ to $B$ similarly compensates $B$ for the loss while leaving $A$ still better-off than in $II$.

16. Feldman, note 8 *supra*, at 144.

17. Ad in *High Country News*, 19 April 1993, 6.

18. For this account of CV and EV, see E. J. Mishan, *Introduction to normative economics* (New York: Oxford Univeristy Press, 1981), at 163.

19. This discouraging result is anticipated in the fact that $I{\rightarrow}II$ is a Kaldor-improvement if $CV > 0$. Still, the converse isn't true (in a simple exchange case where $I$ isn't Pareto-optimal, $I{\rightarrow}II$ is a Kaldor-improvement but needn't be a CV-improvement), and one might have hoped that the CV approach to hypothetical compensation avoided the troublesome cases. $I{\rightarrow}II$ needn't be a Kaldor-improvement if $EV > 0$, since the winners needn't be able to convert their winnings into cash; but this doesn't keep the EV standard from turning out inconsistent judgments.

20. Sometimes the divergence of mWTA from MWTP cannot be explained by income effects, limits on MWTP, or lack of substitutes for what one gives up. See, e.g., Jack L. Knetsch, "The endowment effect and evidence of non-reversible indifference curves," *American Economic Review* 79 (1989), 1277–84; and Wiktor L. Adamowicz, Vinay Bhardwaj, and Bruce Macnab, "Experiments on the difference between willingness to pay and willingness to accept," *Land Economics* 69 (1993), 416–27.

21. Mark Van Steeter, "Drowning Parunuweap—is there a better solution?," *Southern Utah Wilderness Alliance Newsletter* 6(2) (1989), 10. This dam, proposed for the east fork of the Virgin River, is one of many under consideration. See Marc Allred, "Damming the wild Virgin," *Southern Utah Wilderness Alliance Newsletter* 8(3) (1991), 3–6; and Mark MacAllister, "Running on empty: what's ahead for Washington County, Utah?," *Southern Utah Wilderness Alliance Newsletter* 10(2) (1993), insert 1–4.

22. The *benefit-cost ratio*—the ratio B:C of benefits to costs—does not give the same information. A project that delivered $1000 in benefits for $100 in costs (net benefits = $900; B:C = 10:1) would not be as good as one that delivered $2000 in benefits for $1000 in costs (net benefits = $1000; B:C = 2:1).

23. I ignore here the issue whether $c$ delivered at some future time should be worth less than $c$ delivered now, and, if so, what discount rate should be applied. Discount rates materially affect the calculation of benefits for projects such as dams (which are, one hopes, built to last).

24. See Richard A. Epstein, "The public trust doctrine," *Cato Journal* 7 (1987), 411–30. While Epstein thinks it would be preferable if most resources were privately owned, he takes public ownership seriously, arguing that the public must be compensated for what it gives up when public resources are privatized.

25. For Baden and Lueck, the "goal [of privatization] is not to maximize revenue, but to place management in the hands of responsible individuals," and "giveaways may be the least costly" way to accomplish this. Note 7 *supra*, at 59.

26. "Suppose I own a home . . . that I would not sell . . . for less than, say, $125,000. . . . [I]f I did not own the house—it is my principal asset—I would not be willing to pay more than $75,000 for it, because that is all I can 'afford' to pay. Is the house then worth $75,000 or $125,000? The answer depends upon whether or not I own the house." Richard A. Posner, *The economics of justice* (Cambridge, MA: Harvard University Press, 1981), at 64.

27. While I have assimilated $\Delta w$ to $cv$, it may be that Posner understands

MWTP as MWTP *in advance*. When property rights are freely exchanged, social wealth typically increases. But the wealth-maximizer would also like to arrange for the converse: ideally, if $I{\rightarrow}II$ increases social wealth, property rights should transfer accordingly. However, this program confronts an immediate difficulty. Ordinarily, we don't think property rights should transfer in cases of theft: if I *steal* something, it's not mine by right. Yet theft may not change social wealth (what you lose, I gain). What's worse, we can imagine cases in which theft is *wealth-increasing*: suppose I steal a painting I love from you—a painting you'd sell for $100K, but I'd not sell for less than $200K if I had it.

What I have reported in the text as Posner's concept of wealth-change blocks the migration of property rights in the second sort of case: my wealth increases only by my MWTP for the painting. But it isn't enough to keep an instance of theft from preserving wealth. Consider Posner's case of the diamond necklace (Posner, note 26 *supra*, at 63) worth just its market price of $10K to its owner, which a poor man steals for his wife. The thief's *cv* on the "transaction" is $10K, since he can sell the necklace for $10K; this is his MWTP to acquire it. In discussing this case, Posner observes that someone who steals generally isn't willing to pay what its owner is willing to accept. But anyone should be willing to pay $X$'s market value provided one doesn't have to do it in advance; after all, once I have $X$, I may exchange it for its market value and be no worse off than I was without it (ignore the nuisance costs here, or imagine that they are outweighed by the thrill of theft). Accordingly, it may be that Posner is thinking of MWTP as MWTP in advance. If one's wealth-increase is limited to what one is willing to pay in advance, then perhaps thefts won't preserve wealth.

However, this is an unsatisfactory solution, for it creates problems with gifts. Normally, we'd think a gift of $10K increased my wealth by $10K, but I may, of course, not be able to pay $10K to secure this gift. It won't do to suggest that I *can* pay $Y$ in advance if I'm able to borrow $Y$ on the promise of immediate repayment. For then thieves could pay in advance as well. They may be "unwilling" to—what profit is there in that, after all? But, of course, the same could be said of gifts.

A better approach, in my view, is to argue (in the manner of Hobbes) that in a society where property rights weren't reasonably secure from transfer by theft, very little wealth would be created. A theft may preserve wealth, but that does not mean society should shrug. A policy of ignoring such thefts (assuming they could be cheaply identified) might be wealth-decreasing, either by encouraging wealth-decreasing thefts or by discouraging productive activities. Posner does argue that there are cases in which theft increases social wealth. He has us imagine someone lost in the woods who breaks into an unoccupied cabin and steals food to keep himself alive. Being a person "of monetary means" (Id.), he's willing to pay more than the owner would ask, but the cost of arranging the transaction is prohibitive. Posner seems to think that in such cases rights *should* transfer, *provided* some sufficiently cheap way of identifying these cases could be devised and there is good reason to believe that countenancing such transfers would have no negative impact on wealth elsewhere. But this condition is quite demanding.

28. Note also that wealth is not a well-defined function of property rights if one's life is one's property. Since you can't take it with you, most people would be unable to name a sum that would compensate them for loss of life; its value, therefore, is undefined or infinite.

29. Posner would probably respond by suggesting that the "paradoxes" of consumer surplus are not of this world. In another connection, he remarks that "it

is theoretically possible that the initial assignment of a good might determine its ultimate assignment . . . but no one has come up with a realistic example." Posner, note 26 *supra*, at 109. However, having invoked the spectre of "utility monsters" to argue against utilitarianism, Id., at 65, Posner isn't in a good position to dismiss theoretical possibilities.

30. Where "transaction costs preclude the use of voluntary transactions to . . . move resources [to their most valuable uses], . . . alternative allocative mechanisms must be found—such as liability rules, eminent domain, and zoning." Posner, note 26 *supra*, at 70.

31. I haven't seen this argument made, although John Baden, after suggesting that wilderness areas go to environmental groups, cautions, "Any successful transfer mechanism would have to take into account . . . the benefits from reducing transaction costs." "Privatizing wilderness lands: the political economy of harmony and good will," in *Private rights and public lands*, ed. Phillip N. Truluck (Washington: Heritage Foundation, 1983), 53–70 at 69.

32. Letter from the Southern Oregon Resources Alliance in Alan M. Gottlieb, *The wise-use agenda* (Bellevue, WA: Free Enterprise Press, 1989), 141–2 at 142.

33. Richard A. Posner, *Economic analysis of law* (Boston: Little, Brown and Company, 1972), at 22.

34. Baden and Lueck, note 7 *supra*, at 55.

35. John Locke, *Two treatises of government*, ed. Peter Laslett (New York: Mentor, 1965) at 328–30 (Book II, Chapter V, §§27–8).

36. For discussion, see Chapter 7, page 164 *infra*.

37. Since 1972 annual use (reckoned in user-days) of the Colorado River in the Grand Canyon has been limited, the total being apportioned between commercial and private users in the 92:8 ratio seen that year. While these numbers are clearly arbitrary, a larger allocation of recreational space to commercial outfitters can probably be justified on grounds of equity: the average citizen probably has a greater opportunity to run the river if he needn't acquire the skills himself or acquire friends who have them.

# 5

# The Productivity of Privatization

> Land, like all other resources, is most productive when in private hands.
> The empirical evidence for this proposition is overwhelming.
>
> Steven Hanke[1]

If we agree that resources should be employed as efficiently as possible, then the case for privatizing public lands can be reduced to two issues: (1) Would privatization make resources more productive? (2) If so, is it worth the trouble?

None of the improvement standards that give definite content to (1) appear to advance the argument for it. Judged by the Pareto standard, it's clearly false: *someone* is going to prefer what federal land management delivers. Understood in terms of one of the net-gain standards, (1) may be true, but these standards are so hard to apply that we're going to have trouble justifying a belief that it is. They are too closely tied to facts about individuals (or what we hope are facts) that are inaccessible to the analyst. So we must either find a way to apply them indirectly or develop some other standard.

The indirect approach involves seeking to correlate productivity with some measurable feature of allocation systems. Were such a feature $P$ to be identified, we could determine whether $II$ was more productive than $I$ simply by comparing their $P$-values. Unfortunately, if there's something about an improvement standard that makes it hard to decide whether $II$ is productively superior to $I$, then it's also going to be hard to establish that systems with higher $P$-values are more productive, at least for any measure $P$ we can easily ascribe to them. Now we could propose *replacing* the problematic standard with whatever index is developed: "$II$ uses resources more productively than $I$" just *means* that $II$ has a higher $P$-value than $I$. The problem here is arguing that systems with higher $P$-values direct resources to uses that *better satisfy the desires of consumers*. The net-gain standards derive from *analyses* of this notion. If we abandon them because they are difficult to apply, we may at the same time break the connection between greater productivity and better satisfying desires.

Some of the arguments of privatization advocates can, I think, be construed as appealing indirectly to net-gain standards or directly to other notions of productivity. In the first four sections of this chapter, I discuss proposals that we may judge the productivity of a system by (a) how closely it resembles an ideal market or by (b) its net output or the value thereof. For the reasons outlined in the previous paragraph, I doubt that either (a) or (b) can underwrite an affirmative answer to (1).

Issue (2) is a concern because the substantial costs of altering the *status quo* argue against it unless it can be shown that they are exceeded by the benefits of change. The fact (if it is a fact) that public lands would be more productive under private management, in the sense that the uses *I* they *now* have are inferior to the uses *II* they *would* have, isn't enough to justify privatizing them. A shift from *I* to *II* will consume resources, which must be deducted from any productivity gains. Just as the nations of eastern Europe can't simply trade in their centralized economies for functioning free markets, we can't magically replace the current federal land-management system with a system of private owners. Moreover, privatization won't benefit everyone. The skills of some federal land managers will no longer be needed, and some who use public lands will judge every affordable consumption plan available to them under privatization to be inferior.

The obvious way to handle (2) is to reduce it to (1): grant that the various costs of privatization will be substantial, but argue that, once in place, a system of private management would be more productive than the current one, so that the costs of changeover would eventually be made up. Imagine that it takes 10 years to change from the current regime *I* to private management *II*, starting in 1995. Then the idea is that, although *I→II* might be a net social loss as of 2005, *II* will outperform *I* over every subsequent year, eventually making up any loss. It's a bit like constructing a dam. Until it's built, we see only costs; but these, we hope, are eventually recovered in the form of various benefits delivered by the project. The analogy is not exact because there may be no net social cost in building the dam—what some pay, others receive—whereas this is doubtful in the case of privatization.

If this *argument from future benefits* is OK, we need worry only about whether, under hypothetical private management, public lands would be more productive than they are now, i.e., we need only worry about (1). But this reduction of (2) to (1) is problematic. In the last two sections of this chapter, I discuss two difficulties, each suggesting that the promised benefits had better come pretty quickly: (i) At what rate should the future benefits of *I→II* be *discounted*? (ii) What does it *mean* to say that *II* outperforms *I* over some future time interval?


## THE ARGUMENT FROM LIKENESS TO THE IDEAL

At bottom, I think, many advocates believe that privatizing federal lands would make resources more productive by creating a system that more closely resembles the ideal markets of the first fundamental theorem. That is, where $P$ = likeness to an ideal market, $P$ indexes productivity and privatization would increase $P$. Ideal markets make resources optimally productive in the Pareto sense: no shift in use can make someone better off (from his point of view) without making someone worse off (from hers). So we might expect that as systems are more "like" an ideal market, they are more productive. The problem is to find a useful index of resemblance for which this is so. Privatizing public lands would create a system that, in certain obvious respects, resembles an ideal market more closely than the current regime. But why are these respects relevant to productivity?

B. Delworth Gardner argues that federal land management is relatively unproductive because productivity can be judged by the extent to which *market prices guide resource allocation*, while, in allocating resources, federal land managers are not guided by prices to the same extent as private landowners. An efficient use of resources, he claims, is one that maximizes the value of net output.[2] Under ideal conditions, this occurs when individual producers and resource-holders select feasible plans that maximize their profit and return. But federal land policy is not informed by prices in this way; in general, federal land managers do not seek to maximize return or profit. Indeed, "the allocation processes utilized by the agencies do not permit the informal bargaining needed to establish market prices"[3]—the prices needed to establish value and to reckon return and profit. The BLM, for example, does not decide whether a piece of federal range is best used for grazing by determining whether some rancher is willing to pay more for the right to run his livestock there than others are willing to pay for the right to use it in other ways; nor is forage sold to the highest bidder once the area is designated a grazing allotment. Grazing rights are essentially a matter of historical precedent; they are attached to particular ranches, and the fee per AUM is a national fee, determined annually by a complex formula.[4] Without market prices and appropriate incentives to use them in deciding how federal resources shall be used, Gardner argues that "the efficiency norm could be expected to be reached only fortuitously."[5]

Unfortunately, the correlation between productivity and prices claimed by Gardner is assured only in the ideal markets of the first fundamental theorem, where market-clearing prices guide self-interested individuals to a collectively optimal use of resources. His characterization of efficiency is simply read off from the proof of the theorem: if independent producers and resource-holders maximize profit and return, *the value of net output is maximal*, from which it follows that the allocation of resources is optimal, provided consumers choose the best consumption plans they can afford and prices clear the market. But where the conditions of the theorem are not satisfied, these relations are not assured. Individuals who try to maximize profit or return may not succeed; where they do, their collective efforts may not maximize the value of net output; and should this occur, it may yet be possible to make some consumer better off at no cost to anyone else.

Since the conditions of the theorem are not satisfied in this world, it's natural to wonder if in *some* cases we couldn't do better by *ignoring* market prices. Where willingness-to-pay for some use of resources (e.g., preserving the habitat of some obscure but threatened species) is diffuse and essentially uncollectible, it won't be registered in the bargaining that establishes market prices. If such willingness-to-pay is collectively significant, resources allocated by price may not be put to their most valued uses. Perhaps some of the federal land policies that look so bizarre to critics can be justified in this way.

Gardner is aware of this possibility,[6] though he's inclined to dismiss such suggestions as "largely a ruse to justify political allocations of the kind now extant."[7] However, his arguments do not show that private management would be better. They suggest only that current uses of federal lands are *sub-optimal*. This is doubtless true, but it is insufficient to establish that these lands would be *more* productive under some other system. The problem is assessing the relative importance of features that may contribute to sub-optimality. Gardner, for example, notes on the one hand that "[c]ontrary to what occurs in a private firm, a political decision maker is seldom in a position to gain personally from reducing agency cost or by selling a product to those who value it most highly, both essential to economic efficiency,"[8] and on the other hand that "[e]xternalities and public goods may distort prices in private markets."[9] But he does not explain why, as he believes, the first source of sub-optimality is *more significant than* the second.

Sometimes Gardner is more cautious, writing that "[o]nly empirical analyses can reveal whether public or private management would be more efficient in yielding public goods, and these studies have not been made."[10] Unfortunately, the empirical studies we can do are unlikely to settle anything, since it's not easy to discover what people are willing to pay for something that they have no real opportunity to buy. Consider, for example, make-believe "visibility auctions." To estimate the benefits of various pollution-control options for coal-burning power plants in the Southwest, economists have attempted to find out how much citizens are collectively willing to pay for visibility in nearby National Parks.[11] Individuals are shown photographs depicting park vistas at various air pollution levels and asked how much they'd be willing to have added to their utility bills to achieve or maintain the corresponding levels of visibility. One problem with this procedure is that nobody *has* to pay anything in these exercises, so the resulting estimates of collective willingness-to-pay for visibility in the Southwest are probably too high. On the other hand, if people were forced to pay what they said they'd pay, there'd be an incentive to take a free ride by naming a figure lower than their actual willingness-to-pay.[12] Furthermore, what one is willing to pay for something depends on what else is available: if, in addition to visibility in the Southwest, I could buy (say) grizzly habitat preservation in the Northwest, I might be willing to pay less for visibility.[13]

## WHAT IS SECOND BEST?

The difficuly with arguments from likeness to the ideal is that we don't have a good grasp of likeness. Ideal markets are defined by a number of coordinated features. If we could realize all of them, we could realize the ideal and make resources optimally productive. But we cannot do that: these features are idealized, and the best we can manage are partial realizations. How are the systems resulting from such partial realizations to be ranked in terms of productivity? In general, a Pareto-style ranking will not do. It is not generally true that *II* is more productive than *I* if some feature of an ideal market is realized in *II* to a greater degree than in *I*, and no such feature is realized in *I* to a greater degree than in *II*. If some of the conditions for an optimum are not met, it may be counterproductive to satisfy the others. For example, where there are negative spillovers like pollution, firms that individually increase profits by getting more output from the same inputs may just make matters collectively worse.

Accordingly, we may not best approximate an ideal market by doing our best to realize each of its features. Indeed, the best way to adjust for failure to realize some features (an environment that doesn't respect property lines, people who aren't omniscient, etc.) may be to *limit* the extent to which the others are realized. How we might arrange for the best when we cannot attain the ideal is known in economics as "the problem of second best." Privatization advocates assume that its solution—the closest attainable approximation to an ideal market—is private property hedged with a few covenants or easements to control spillovers and to represent diffuse but collectively significant interests in it. Barney Dowdle, for example, argues:

> Private timberlands produce multiple-use benefits too, and they do so much more efficiently than do those of government. If society wants a different mix of multiple-use outputs than would be produced if government timberlands were privatized, this should be made known and the appropriate steps taken to ensure optimal outputs. Easements can be used for this purpose.[14]

More generally, Richard Stroup and John Baden are sure that "[a] bit of tinkering on the margins will often suffice" to correct the "well-known flaws in the market picture."[15]

Unfortunately, there is little by way of argument to back up these convictions. Dowdle says nothing to support his assertion that multiple-use benefits are *more* efficiently produced by private management. Stroup and Baden propose just a bit of tinkering because they believe that more than that will introduce inefficiencies that dwarf those it's supposed to address. They observe, correctly, that "we must accept an imperfect solution" and that "[t]hough markets are imperfect, their failures do not automatically imply that collective action is better."[16] In their view, remedies for the inefficiencies of real markets that involve "[r]elinquishing private rights and the rule of willing consent in favor of collective action"[17] are generally worse than the disease. Like Gardner, they point to features of collective management in general, and federal land management in particular, that absorb resources. But they do not show what needs to be shown, viz., that these resources are wasted, that in one way or another we are "spending" more to correct problems than the corrections are worth.

So one may wonder if more than just a bit of tinkering isn't in order. Perhaps, indeed, the regulated use of public lands approximates what would be achieved by a system of covenants and easements designed to contain spillovers and evade transaction costs. If so, it's hard to see why we should bother to privatize them, especially since it's hard to imagine how legal instruments like easements or covenants could replace agency decisions informed by the knowledge of land-management professionals and the changing preferences of public-land users.[18]

Privatization advocates will ridicule the suggestion that federal management might actually be efficient, relative to what other systems could achieve. But it is harder to refute than they imagine. It won't do simply to point to clear cases of unproductive federal management, even if we can be pretty sure the resources in question would have been more productive in private hands. For some bad results can be expected from any system. But what about persistent patterns in federal management, such as relatively low return—often negative, in fact—on the release of resources? Can't we agree that these practices are inefficient and would not persist under privatization?

Unlike the resource holders and producers of idealized markets, federal land managers don't seem to maximize return on the release of resources (or profit on resource-release operations). Many USFS timber sales cost more to administer than they realize in revenue: the timber isn't worth much to begin with, and the roads the USFS builds to get at it are expensive. A private timber company that operated this way would go out of business. Wouldn't it make more sense to forget about logging such stands and instead invest in the intensive forestry of more accessible and productive ones? Similarly, grazing fees do not cover the cost of the BLM grazing program. Even if some BLM districts make money on grazing, the return on grazing may be lower than if the land were put to some other use—leased, say, to private hunting clubs for stocking with game more challenging than "slow elk," as cattle are sometimes described.

But it is not clear that such practices really are inefficient, relative to private management. The USFS and BLM can argue that timber and grazing programs produce more than sawlogs and forage. Supposedly, logging and grazing are integrated with other uses of federal lands, and at least some of the cost of timber and grazing programs can be charged against providing for those other uses. The USFS views forest roads as providing access to *all* of the resources of the National Forests. Cheaper roads could be built to get timber out, but such roads might be more prone to erosion and wouldn't be as useful for other purposes (such as enabling backpackers to drive their low-clearance automobiles to Wilderness trailheads). Supporters of government timber and grazing programs can also claim that, in helping to preserve valued ways of life, they produce non-standard but valuable goods.

Marginal logging and grazing on federal lands may be quite important to those whose way of life depends upon it, and perhaps to others who value their national heritage. Driving in to the Needles section of Canyonlands National Park in Utah, we were once enveloped by sheep, herded down the road by horsemen straight out of the 19th century. They were not, it seems to me, the only beneficiaries of federal grazing policies on the road that day. If we can spend public funds to preserve historic buildings and battlefields that "remind us of who we are as a people,"[19] then we can also subsidize threatened ways of life.

I do not imagine that such considerations add up to a productivity case *for* federal management. I am suggesting only that privatization advocates are still some distance from establishing what they take to be obvious, viz., that federal land management is relatively inefficient.


## PRODUCTIVITY JUDGED BY NET OUTPUT

We might have an easier time comparing the productivity of systems if productivity didn't depend on who gets what. "Productivity" suggests production, which is usually treated separately from consumption in textbook expositions of microeconomics. Couldn't we understand an alternative to the present system to be more productive insofar as it simply produces more from a given batch of resources, regardless of who consumes the final output? Perhaps this is what Stroup and Baden had in mind when they wrote that "[m]aking the pie bigger is what efficiency is all about."[20]

The trick is to understand "produces more" in a way that preserves the connection between greater productivity and better satisfied consumers. In the idealized models of the free market where the first fundamental theorem holds, equilibrium prices make this connection. If each producer produces so as to maximize her profit, then producers can't collectively produce more from the inputs collectively available to them: an increase in the output of some commodity requires that the output of some other commodity be decreased. Since prices clear the market, what's produced is consumed. Furthermore, while different mixes of production outputs are feasible, none will better satisfy consumers, if "better" is understood in Pareto terms: a shift to any different mix will leave at least one consumer with a plan he considers inferior. If these models represented actual markets, federal lands would be most productive if they were private—though not yet in a sense justifying privatization, since no significant change from the present system would be a Pareto-improvement. But since the models aren't of this world, we can't depend on actual market prices coordinating production and consumption in this way.

Is there some sense of "produces more" for which we can argue both that (i) systems better satisfy the desires of consumers as they produce more and that (ii) under private management, public lands will produce more? Suppose we simply designate certain desired commodities $C, \ldots$ individuate uses of a given batch *B* of resources according to the amounts of these commodities forthcoming as (net) outputs, and propose that *B* is more productive in use *II* than in use *I* if *II produces more than I of at least one of the commodities C, . . . and less of none of them* (or, as I shall say, *II produces "more" of everything than I*). By identifying *I* and *II* with the uses to which different systems put *B*, we'd then have a criterion for judging the relative productivity of systems.

However, this Pareto-style approach is not too promising because (1) if every desired commodity is on the list, (ii) is false; and (2) if some desired commodity isn't on the list, (i) is false. Indeed, (i) is false regardless.

1. It's going to be hard to show that we'll get "more" of *everything* from federal lands under privatization. Indeed, if the products of federal lands are finely differentiated, we'll certainly get less of some things: make any number of changes in the land or access to it, and people won't be able to enjoy it as it was. The only way to make (ii) at all plausible is to amalgamate the various products of these lands into broad types: board feet of lumber, pounds of beef, days of recreation, etc. For some such grouping of products, it may be possible to show that privatization would make federal lands produce "more" of everything. But so what? If we're prepared to lump things together in this way, we may observe that cabernet vineyards would be more productive if they were replanted to gamay, since the latter yields more tons of *grapes* or gallons of *wine* per acre. This approach makes the productivity of systems turn on the way in which their outputs are grouped, not on how well they satisfy the desires of consumers. Would Sequoia National Park's Mineral King valley be better utilized if leased to Disney Enterprises for a ski development?[21] Yes, if the output is *recreation*, measured in visitor-days; no, if it is *skiing* and *wilderness recreation*, similarly reckoned, for the former will displace the latter. If what we mean by "thing" is *recreation*, then Disney's management will produce "more" of everything; if what we mean is *skiing* and *wilderness recreation*, it won't. So what *should* we mean if we want to know what use of Mineral King best satisfies the desires of consumers?

2. If every commodity desired by some consumer or other is included in the list, then half of (i) is true: systems that produce "more" of everything will better satisfy the desires of consumers, assuming distribution is such that consumers end up with "more" of everything. If some desired commodity is omitted, we cannot be sure of this. I may not prefer a consumption plan that gives me more of certain commodities, even ones I want, if I have to accept less of others. However, even if we reckon output in terms of *every* desired commodity, the other half of (i) is false: often we can better satisfy the desires of consumers by shifting resources from the production of one commodity to another. If consumers prefer *C'* to *C*, then redirecting inputs from the production of *C* to the production of *C'* may better satisfy the desires of consumers. Yet this sort of improvement is ruled out when we propose to understand "is more productive than" as *produces "more" of everything*.

We could get around problems (a) and (b) if we had a desirability index $v$ for commodities $C$. Then the sum of net outputs $c$ of commodities $C$, weighted by their desirability $v(C)$

$$V = \Sigma_C \, v(C) \times c$$

would indicate how highly net output is *valued*, and we could count *II* more productive than *I* if the net output of *II* were more valued than that of *I*. But where are we to find this index $v$? If $v(C)$ is the market price of $C$, then $V$ is Gardner's measure of productivity. But the market price may not index relative desirability to consumers; this is assured only in ideal markets. Here in the real world, spillovers and transaction costs may distort prices. A shift in production that increases the value of net output, as reckoned by market prices, need not better satisfy the desires of consumers in any defensible sense.


## THE PRODUCTIVITY OF RANGELAND

In spite of such conceptual shortcomings, net-output accounts of productivity are attractive because they permit productivity claims to be tested. By comparing the outputs of comparable land and other resource inputs under private and federal management, we may hope to get empirical evidence for or against the thesis that privately held resources are more productive. In this section, I consider Gary Libecap's use of this method to argue that rangeland is more productive under private management.

Libecap believes that privatizing public rangeland would increase its output of standard commodities like livestock while at the same time improving its condition, and he claims that empirical data support his view. There are two problems with his argument. First, what Libecap argues *for* is short of what he should establish, namely, that privatization would increase productivity. Second, the data he cites do not support his weaker claim. I shall say a bit about the first problem and then devote most of the section to the second problem.

If Libecap could show that private range produces "more" of everything than comparable public range, his argument would establish the productivity of privatizing federal rangeland. But his data are weakly relevant only to the weaker hypothesis that privatizing rangeland would increase *output* of *selected* commodities (e.g., beef on the hoof, reckoned in pounds per acre). The output standard of productivity, by contrast, runs in terms of *net* output of *all* commodities. If more beef could be had from the range at no cost, all would be well. But typically producing more livestock involves squeezing wildlife out and/or expensive "range treatments" to alter vegetation. We should not be impressed with a showing that private range produces more beef on the hoof per acre than comparable public range unless variable inputs (labor, etc.) are also comparable and the other services of rangeland are undiminished. Since this is unlikely, it would be nice to be shown that the *value* of net output is greater for comparable private range (e.g., that the cows that compete with desert bighorn sheep for water and forage are more *valuable*). The closest Libecap gets to establishing this is to argue that rangeland will be in better shape under private management. However, range condition is not a very good index of the level at which various services are actually provided. A healthy range is capable of supporting more cattle or more wildlife, but what it's actually used for will depend upon who's in charge. Accordingly, showing that privatization would improve range condition will not, by itself, show that privatization would produce "more" of everything.

In fact, Libecap does not do too well in arguing that privatizing federal range would (i) improve its condition or even (ii) increase its output of cattle. His case for (ii) is based on a 1925 USDA study, comparing cattle on private range in west Texas with those on largely (92%) public range in New Mexico and Arizona in terms of weight-gain, calf mortality, etc. From the data presented there, Libecap estimates that private ownership of the range "would have increased the value of the cattle stock in Arizona and New Mexico . . . by at least 8%."[22] That is, the same land would have produced cattle whose market value was greater by at least 8%. But this estimate, if correct, does not support the hypothesis that rangeland will be more productive of cattle under private ownership than it is under federal management. The data confirm an expectation that a given piece of rangeland will, in the long run, support more cattle under private ownership than as an *unregulated commons*, for that is the how BLM range was "administered" prior to the Taylor Grazing Act of 1934.[23] But they do not show that privatizing public range would improve upon the present system of *regulated* grazing, which after all evolved in response to the problems of the commons.

The same oversight damages Libecap's empirical case for (i). Observing that "their political power gave stock owners formal, near proprietary rights to federal lands for nearly thirty years" after the Taylor Act instituted a system of grazing rights to BLM lands, Libecap writes that "[i]n 1936, 42% of the land was classified as fair, good, or excellent; in 1966, 67% was so classified."[24] While this suggests that the range is healthier under quasi-private ownership than as a commons, it does not show that privatization would conserve the range better than the present system of multiple-use management. Furthermore, Thadis Box, the source of Libecap's data on range condition, is not so reassuring about the rancher as conservationist. Let's do Libecap a favor and use Box's Table 7 (BLM land, to which the Taylor Act applied) instead of Table 4 (all federal rangeland):[25]

*% of rangeland in condition class*

|      | Excellent–good | Fair | Poor–bad |
|------|----------------|------|----------|
| 1936 | 1.5            | 14.3 | 84.2     |
| 1966 | 18.9           | 51.6 | 29.5     |

This makes Libecap's rosy picture look even rosier: only 16% of BLM land in excellent, good, or fair shape in 1936 vs. 70% in 1966 after 30 years of quasi-private management. However, these gains are largely an artifact of aggregation. Most of the improvement came from lifting rangeland out of the poor–bad category into the fair category; relatively little made it into the excellent–good category. Furthermore, an understanding of what such terms as "fair" mean further weakens Libecap's case.

Box explains the range-condition categories in his table as involving (in descending order) *moderate, material,* and *severe or extreme* depletion.[26] He does not explain these labels in turn, but "depletion" probably means depletion relative to climax plant community. According to the Soil and Conservation Service (SCS), "range condition is determined by comparing existing plant communities with the presumed climax plant community for a specific range site, regardless of the value of individual plants or the plant community for specific uses."[27] To determine the condition of a site, one first asks what climax plant community would exist at the site. For each climax species $s$, one then estimates *climax production C(s)* and *actual production A(s)*, both in kilograms of dry weight per hectare (kg/ha) per year. If $B(s)$ is the *smaller* of $A(s)$ and $C(s)$, the fraction

$$\Sigma_s B(s)/\Sigma_s C(s)$$

converted to a percentage, indexes "how closely the plant community resembles the climax plant community for the range site."[28] Condition categories may then be defined in terms of this index. The SCS uses a quartile system: excellent is 76–100%, good 51–75%, fair 26–50%, and poor 0–25%.[29] Box's categories suggest a quintile system: excellent, 80%+; etc. But in any case, enlightened self-interest operating for thirty years with "near proprietary rights" doesn't seem to have done much to enhance the condition of BLM rangeland. At best, four-fifths of it was producing forage at less than 60% of ecological potential, and nearly a third at less than 40%.

Privatization advocates can respond by (1) accepting the data and making excuses, or by (2) questioning their significance. Libecap does both.

1. He conjectures that although the Taylor grazing licenses were "secure," they didn't grant the actual "property rights to the land" that would have encouraged more investment in range improvement.[30] This is conceivable, but a number of considerations argue against it. The Taylor Act requires that ranchers be compensated for range improvements in the (unlikely) event their grazing licenses are transferred to others.[31] Furthermore, since ranchers grazing federal lands pay no property taxes on it and their grazing fees are assessed far below those charged for private rangeland,[32] they should have relatively more to invest on range improvements than their propertied counterparts. Finally, private rangeland isn't in very good shape. Some 98% of the range in six Great Plains states is non-federal,[33] almost all of that private; yet the USFS estimated that in 1976 only 15% of this land was in good or excellent condition, with 31% in fair condition, 39% in poor condition, and 15% in very poor (bad) condition.[34]

A more likely explanation for the limited gains under the Taylor regime is that on most BLM land, range improvement probably isn't a very good economic investment. The forage available from these arid and semi-arid rangelands was never very great. In its pristine condition, the Great Basin–Colorado Plateau semi-desert is estimated to have produced 0.33 AUM of usable forage per acre per year,[35] so that roughly three acres would be required to feed one cow for a month. Unregulated grazing dropped this to 0.11 AUM per acre-year by the 1930s; under the quasi-privatization of the Taylor era, forage production rose only slightly to 0.13 AUM per acre-year by 1971.[36] Other BLM rangelands are more productive, but some are even poorer: in general, they are the unselected, unreserved leftovers from the long process of disbursing federal lands. To restore this range to its former meager productivity, substantial investments must be made (including income lost by curtailing grazing during a long recovery period). Most ranchers couldn't afford them, nor could they talk banks into lending the money: the expected return is just too small.

A recent study of USFS, BLM, state, and private range in Rich County, Utah,[37] suggests that the condition of the range depends more on how much its owners are willing to invest in management than it does on whether they are private individuals or public agencies. It also suggests that if investments are made to maximize expected return, then investments will not be made in range improvements, except perhaps by ranchers who love their work and are basically indulging in consumption. The USFS spent the most managing its Rich County rangeland (considerably more, no doubt, than it recovered in grazing fees) and had the best range to show for it. For their rather smaller but roughly equal investment, the BLM and private ranchers got roughly the same poor quality range. State rangeland was in the worst shape; Utah law requires that state lands be managed to maximize revenue, and forage is a pretty low-value commodity.

2. Having himself cited range-condition estimates to argue that the condition of BLM range improved during the Taylor era *because* ranchers were granted "near proprietary rights" to it, Libecap is also prepared to question such data when it suits his purpose. He suggests that, to justify its own existence and management practices, the BLM has essentially manufactured an overgrazing case against ranchers by comparing existing conditions to a hypothetical pristine state that never in fact existed.[38] In his view, "[t]he land deterioration conditions cited by the BLM . . . likely reflect long-standing trends of *natural* erosion which could be altered only at high social cost."[39] The only evidence Libecap offers for this original thesis is a review by Thomas Vale of pioneer journals, indicating that to those raised in the humid East much of the intermountain West looked dry and brushy.[40] Of course, pristine conditions are hypothetical, but that does not make them purely conjectural. Data collected from plots of range fenced against livestock for decades, isolated "relict" areas protected by topography from stock, and experiments correlating growth of native grasses and shrubs with such variables as soil-type and moisture give range

scientists a pretty good idea of the natural potential of various types of rangeland.[41]

It's true that range-condition data from 1936 and before are a lot softer than more recent data, so it's hard to be sure how much improvement has really occurred under various types of management. One may also question the standard of improvement implicit in the range-condition index. The index measures production relative to potential, but "potential" here means climax vegetation community, and that will interest some people more than others. For environmentalists, who value natural communities, range with a higher index is better. Those who have other plans for the range may think otherwise; they may pay attention to range-condition studies only insofar as they "provide a basis for predicting the extent and direction of changes that can result in the plant community because of specific treatment or management."[42]

To be sure, a low range-condition index generally indicates that past overgrazing has left short rations for the present. Suppose, for some site, big sagebrush would contribute only 10 kg/ha to annual production at climax, but contributes 1000 kg/ha at present; what goes into the numerator of the range condition index for this site will be 10 kg/ha. The 1000 kg/ha does not appear anywhere, except by the absence from the numerator of all that climax production it has replaced, generally growth more palatable to livestock. However, in some cases, original species have been (or could be) replaced by others that stock can eat. Cheatgrass is an exotic annual,[43] so a site's production of it won't appear in either numerator or denominator of the condition index; but it may contribute substantially to forage usable by stock in the spring. Cheat isn't a particularly welcome addition to the range community: the mature plant is inedible. But other exotics may provide better forage for livestock than species of the climax community. Just as Midwest farmers prefer corn and soybean monocultures to the original prairie community, western ranchers may prefer to manipulate the range toward more of these species. The fact that such changes will, other things equal, lower the range-condition index won't bother them a bit.[44]

Productivity relative to climax community is not what Libecap has in mind when he alleges that private range is more productive than federal range. As in the world of the first fundamental theorem, prices tell ranchers how best to utilize the range; use "consistent with wealth maximization"[45] will be its most productive use. If this looks to the range scientists like overgrazing, well, so much the worse for science. Warning of the threat of "potentially disruptive scientific management of livestock operations"[46] posed by the BLM's multiple-use charter, Libecap writes that:

> the emphasis of bureaucratic managers on achieving targeted biological sustained-yield goals conflict[s] with more flexible harvest practices desired by ranchers. . . . To the extent that the market signals followed by ranchers reflect social preferences and costs, bureaucratic interference reduces production and wealth.[47]

Libecap has no doubts about market signals reflecting social preferences and costs, at least when property rights are secure, transferable, and complete. Essentially, we are to trust the market to direct resources to their most productive uses.

Unfortunately, ranchers tempted by market signals to ignore ecological conditions are awkward reminders that real people don't behave like the agents of the first fundamental theorem. Real people are often ignorant of production feasibilities. No rancher knows, for example, just how much rain is going to fall, and where and when, and hence how many sheep or cattle his range can support this year. Moreover, our estimates of what's feasible are often colored by hopes. If feedlots are paying high prices for cattle, the prospect of making some money and getting out of debt may lead a rancher to believe that his range can indeed support more stock, that extension agents who counsel otherwise don't know what they're talking about, that the recent drought is over, etc.

To conserve the range, ranchers must make stocking decisions based not on hope but on ecology. The number of animals and seasons of use must be adjusted to match forage production, which varies principally with moisture. The pioneers believed, disastrously, that "rain follows the plow;" Libecap appears to believe that it follows the commodity and capital markets. He writes that "[a] rise in expected livestock prices or interest rates leads ranchers to increase the number of animals placed on the range, . . . depleting the forage stock. A fall in expected prices brings herd liquidation, light harvesting, and a recovery of vegetation."[48] But for most BLM rangeland, this reassuring scenario has no basis whatever in ecological reality; arid land responds to market-driven forces not like a pendulum but like a ratchet. According to Box:

> The plants of arid regions have evolved under a system of shifting and nomadic browsing geared to spotty rainfall patterns. Attempts to change the pattern of use and to obtain greater yields of animal products many times lead to a deterioration of the plant community and a loss in the composition of the more stable plants. Heavy continuous grazing by one class of domestic animals may lead to the disappearance of the more desirable plants from the ecosystem. Arid ecosystems are delicately balanced, and for the most part, succession is extremely slow. Once an ecosystem has been disturbed or altered it seldom heals itself within the lifetime of a man. Artificial revegetation of damaged ecosystems is also difficult because of the rigorous climatic and biological constraints of the system.[49]

Under such unforgiving ecological conditions, we can expect market incentives to produce overgrazing and deteriorated range, unless individual freedom is limited by regulations that limit the number of stock to what our best information suggests the range can support. In theory, this is how federal rangeland is administered. If it is not in better shape, it is because ranchers have too much, not too little, to say about how their grazing allotments are used.

## DISCOUNTING FUTURE BENEFITS

I turn now to problem (2): if we grant that private resources are more productive than public resources and that productivity should be maximized, we are still some distance from endorsing privatization, for we need to argue that the costs of privatizing federal lands are not so large as to outweigh the benefits. The obvious route to this conclusion is the argument from future benefits. However, there are difficulties for this argument which I shall discuss in this section and the next.

Suppose that, once in place, system $II$ would, in fact, outperform system $I$ over each future year, and that we know this. Standard economic analysis discounts the future benefits of $I{\rightarrow}II$ at the real rate of interest. The issue is: should we spend \$$X$ now to secure some certain benefit $y$ years from now that will then be worth \$$Y$, corrected for inflation? If instead we invested \$$X$ at rate $r$, we'd have \$$(1+r)^y X$ after $y$ years; hence, $Y$ had better exceed $(1+r)^y X$. Alternatively, the *present value* \$$Y/(1+r)^y$ of \$$Y$ delivered at the end of year $y$ (i.e., what we'd have to invest now to get \$$Y$ then, assuming $r$ is constant over the interval) had better be greater than $X$. For fixed $r$, present value declines as delivery time $y$ increases. Even at modest interest rates, benefits delivered in the not-too-distant future aren't worth a lot in the present. For example, at 5%, the time required to halve the present value of a future benefit is only about 14 years.

Here \$$X$ is the imagined changeover cost of privatization, the difference between what the losers are collectively willing to accept and what the winners are collectively willing to pay. Should this sum be "invested" in privatization? If the benefits of privatization start coming in year $y_0$ and are valued at \$$Y$ (paid at year-end) annually thereafter, then the present value of these benefits is

$$\Sigma_{y_0 \leqslant y} \$Y/(1+r)^y = \$Y_0 \, (1+r)/r$$

where $Y_0 = Y/(1+r)^{y_0} = $ *the present value of \$Y* paid at end of year $y_0$. If $r$ is 5% and $y_0$ is 14 years, then the present value of privatization is only about $\$10 \times Y$. Accordingly, modest returns from privatization starting some years hence may not be enough to offset large start-up costs. Let us consider two ways in which this worry might be addressed.

1. One might object to identifying the discount rate with the real rate of interest, arguing that it should be *zero*. When future benefits are discounted at rate 0, they are not discounted at all, so the assumed benefits of privatization would eventually exceed its cost. The argument might go as follows: "The real rate of interest is based on a real preference that individuals have for present over future benefits. But the basis for such time-preference is uncertainty, whereas the benefits of privatization are not uncertain. It is not appropriate to discount a *certain* benefit at the real rate of interest, if that rate is based on uncertainty. If we can show that privatization would *in fact* yield a stream of benefits valued at \$$Y$ annually commencing after $y_0$ years, this benefit stream should not be discounted."

On this view of time-preference, individuals prefer present to future benefits (or future to present costs) because the present is more certain than the future. Suppose I have one free admission to the local cinema. I may prefer using it today to using it tomorrow, either because it's somewhat less probable that I'll be able to use it tomorrow (maybe I'll get sick or be hit by a truck), or because I'm not sure I'll be as interested in seeing the film tomorrow (maybe something better will come along or I'll just not feel like going). That is, I may judge on the basis of expected utility that it's better to see the film now: it is less probable (I judge) that I'll get as much out of deciding to go tomorrow as I'll get out of deciding to go now. Of course, I might change my mind if you were to pay me for deferring my visit to the cinema; and what you had to pay, relative to my valuation of going now, would determine my personal rate of interest in this case.

Unfortunately, there are at least two things wrong with this argument. (i) It confuses what the real rate of interest *should* be with what it *is*. I am inclined to agree that the only *rational* basis for discounting the future is uncertainty. It is very hard to make any sense at all of the idea that *merely occurring in the future* can reduce the value of some experience. Someone who thinks to himself, "I'll enjoy the film just as much tomorrow, but that won't be as good as seeing it now," just isn't paying attention. However, the real rate of interest may partially reflect an *irrational* preference for the present;[50] the fact that a belief makes no sense is, unfortunately, not enough to prevent people from holding and acting on it. If people are willing, on some rational basis or none, to pay interest, then it would be foolish not to consider whether $X was better "invested" in privatization or in some interest-bearing account. (ii) It's not possible to avoid uncertainty: we can't *now* show that privatization would, in fact, produce these benefits. Like my enjoyment of the film tomorrow, they are to some degree conjectural: the process of privatization might, in various ways, be derailed, and private management itself might turn out to be less desirable than we thought.

2. One might question the appropriatenesss of judging an "invest-ment" of $X (say, in privatization) by what $X *would* return in an interest-bearing account, when we can't really get hold of $X and so invest it. $X is the cost of privatization, but it is not as if we have $X and can choose to "invest" it in privatization instead of treasury bonds. $X is just the difference between what the losers demand and the winners are willing to pay. Perhaps we can think of the losers as having $X "invested" in the *status quo*, but it is not in liquid form.

Now to this it might be objected that we *could* raise $X by taxation. Once we had it in hand, we could compare "investing" it in privatization (by paying off the losers) with investing it in an interest-bearing account, and find privatization the better investment only if $Y_0(1+r)/r$ exceeded $X$, just as originally maintained. But this does not follow, since the "investment" in privatization is different. Here we are imagining that "investing" in privatization involves taxation to compensate the losers, whereas this was not originally contemplated. Accordingly, the objection has no bearing on privatization without compensation.

## MAKING SENSE OF FUTURE BENEFITS

Hypothesis 2 may undercut the rationale for discounting the benefits of privatization and thereby meet *one* objection to the argument from future benefits. But there are others. Since we are thinking of performance in terms of productivity, *II* outperforms *I* over some future year $y$ if *II* is more productive than *I* over $y$. Presumably, this means that a magical shift $I \rightarrow II$ is a net gain over $y$. We are to imagine that each consumer $i$ of *I* can decide whether on balance she'd prefer spending year $y$ in *II* rather than in *I* and by how much: she can put a dollar-value $V(i)$, positive or negative, on the shift $I \rightarrow II$. Then $I \rightarrow II$ is a net gain over $y$ if the sum of these values $V(i)$, taken over all individuals $i$, is positive. But there are a number of serious problems with this picture.

1. It's not clear that any consumer could do what it requires of him. I occasionally wonder how my life would have differed had I taken a job I turned down in 1970 for the one I now have. I imagine that had I taken it, there is some definite way my life would have gone. Assuming that I could somehow see myself as I am (*I*) and as I would have been (*II*) over the course of some year $y$, could I then say that *II* is better (or worse) for me than *I* over $y$ and, if so, by how much? I'm quite sure I couldn't—I usually can't even answer the standard political campaign question, "Are you better off than you were four years ago?" I may be able to say that in certain respects things are better and in others they are not, but it's hard to know whether the gains collectively outweigh the losses; and even if I could figure *that* out, I certainly couldn't *quantify* a net loss in terms (say) of how much I'd have to be paid to put up with it.

Sometimes I can say, with what I suppose is authority, that some year was better for me than another. Thus, I'd probably rank any "normal" year over one I had to spend in bed with some debilitating illness. The limiting case of this is existence vs. non-existence. A year in which I'm alive will generally be better for me than a year in which I'm not. This is irrelevant when I'm trying to compare the years of my actual life, but not when I compare a year of my actual life with the corresponding year of some life I might have had, since it may be a year I *wouldn't* have had in that life. Suppose that, had I taken that other job, I would have died in an auto accident ten years later; then I won't be too keen to move from the *status quo* to where I'd now be had I taken that job. In fact, I might think no amount of money sufficient to compensate me for *that* change of state. Now if, to assess some proposed change $I \rightarrow II$, I'm supposed to compare how I fare in the actual situation *I* over year $y$ with how I would have fared over $y$ in the hypothetical situation *II*, and I would not have existed in *II* over year $y$, then we're going to have trouble understanding $I \rightarrow II$ as a net social gain. I'm not going to be crazy about *II*, and if those who'd indeed fare better in *II* than in *I* over *y* have to meet my price in order for *II* to outperform *I* in *y*, *II* may not outperform *I*. This suggests (b).

2. If net benefits are assessed in this way, they eventually become *negative*, contrary to what is required by the argument from future benefits. It won't be too many years before quite a few of the people who exist to enjoy the *status quo I* (whatever it is) would not have existed, were we now to undertake an alteration *I→II* in it. The reason may be either deaths in *II* that would not have occurred so soon in *I* (as illustrated by my hypothetical auto accident) or births in *I* that would not have occurred at all in *II* (I would not have been born, had my parents conceived their first child on another occasion). We may expect any significant change in the *status quo* to have such effects. Therefore, it won't be too long before we'll have a problem seeing *II* as outperforming *I*: the losers will demand too much. Indeed, beyond some future year *y*, there will be *only* losers, since *nobody* who exists in *I* at *y* would have existed in *II* at *y*.[51]

The difficulty might be avoided if *II* had, in year *y*, a *definite slot* for each *I*-individual who exists in year *y*. Then to compare *II* and *I* over *y*, each individual merely projects herself into her *II*-slot. But what is my *II*-slot for year *y*? If it is to help solve the problem, it cannot be year *y* of the life I would have enjoyed, had *I→II* occurred, for the problem is precisely that, had *I→II* occurred, I might not be around to enjoy *y*. Perhaps we could think of it as how things *would in fact* go for me in *II* in the course of year *y*, if I were magically set up in *II* at the beginning of *y*, as if I'd spent the previous part of my life there. However, we can imagine being set up in *II* in quite different ways, just as we can imagine being born into different circumstances. The choice of initial conditions will significantly affect how things *would in fact* go for me in *II* in the course of year *y* (imagine that I'm homeless and alcoholic as of 1 January) and therefore my assessment of this hypothetical shift *I→II*. So what assumption are we to make about these initial conditions? If I couldn't have spent the previous part of my life in *II* (as will be the case where I owe my existence to *I*), there doesn't seem to be *anything* that anchors our choice of initial conditions.

Unless there is some way around this problem, the prospect of private management outperforming the present system indefinitely (and so eventually recouping any set-up costs) is a mirage. Those who argue for the productivity of privatization had better show that transition losses are made up quickly. And even such a showing may not be convincing. Why, after all, should we go for a change *I→II* if at *some* future time the cumulative net gain is positive, when it eventually becomes negative, as the above considerations suggest it will? Sooner or later, *I→II* is going to be a net loss, judged by individuals in *I*, since as time goes on more and more of them would not have existed in *II*.

3. Since *I→II* may alter preferences, "Which do I prefer (and by how much)?" is an ill-defined question. Consider again the case in which I compare my present life with the life I would have had, had I taken that

job. Here I am to judge my actual and hypothetical consumption in terms of my preferences over consumption plans, asking whether I'm better off here or there. Now by "my preferences" do we mean my actual preferences or my hypothetical preferences? It would be incredible if they were the same, but *different preferences may turn out different rankings of I and II*. Had I taken that job—it was in Las Vegas—I might have developed an interest in gambling strategies and now be working for a casino, a life that has as little attraction to me now as (we may suppose) my present life would have to me as I might now be. Would 1990 (say) have been better for me had I taken that job? Well, it depends upon where I stand in making the judgment.

Or suppose *I→II* is privatization. From the perspective of the *status quo*, it looks to me like a loss, for I now enjoy recreational use of public lands without having to pay much for it. But when options close, people often develop other interests. Were I unable to hike where I please in the West without going through a lot of nonsense getting permission from its new owners, I might take up gardening and pretty soon not care much about hiking anyway—there's always something I miss harvesting by being away, weeds take over, woodchucks break in, etc. Or perhaps, given the opportunity, I'd buy a recreational ranchette and become what Edward Abbey terms "an instant redneck."[52] Maybe privatization would look OK to one of these hypothetical future extensions of myself.

Any significant change is likely to alter preferences. But unless preferences are stable under *I→II* in the sense that an individual's *I*-preferences at any time are no different than her *II*-preferences, we may well have individuals assessing *I→II* as a loss from the perspective of *I* and as a gain from the perspective of *II*. Accordingly, *I→II* may look like a net social loss from the perspective of *I* and a net social gain from the perspective of *II*. Is there some reason to pick one of these perspectives over the other? We can't really dismiss *II* as hypothetical—as if that made a difference—for if we are considering which future to actualize, both *II* and the continuation *I* of the *status quo* are hypothetical. If we cannot solve this problem, appeals to productivity will decide nothing—unless we are prepared to cut productivity loose from preference. More generally, appeals to preferences will not help—unless we are prepared to say that some are better than others.

In this chapter and the previous one I have been preoccupied with two questions: (1) What does it *mean* to say that one use of a given batch of resources is more productive than another, assuming that the account must honor the idea that resources are better used as they better satisfy the desires of consumers? (2) Is there reason to believe, as proponents allege, that privatizing public lands would, in such a sense, improve the use of resources? I do not believe that we yet have a satisfactory answer to (1), and the less-than-satisfactory answers we can devise do not seem to help us answer "Yes" to (2).

I am not claiming that the resources held by the current public land-management system cannot be better employed, or even that they wouldn't be better employed if public lands were privatized. It may be that in some defensible sense of "better used" privatization *would* cause resources to be better used; perhaps this could even be shown. I have argued only that it is harder than one might think to give sense to "use *I* better satisfies the desires of consumers than use *II*" and that, in terms of the available standards, it has yet to be shown that resources would better satisfy the desires of consumers were public lands to be privatized.

Beyond this issue of fact, however, lie issues of value: are better uses of resources *worth* arranging for, if uses are held to be better as they better satisfy the desires of consumers, however that is made out? In other words, is premise 5 of the argument from productivity true—or true with qualifications that privatization would respect? Could the property rights that privatization advocates call for be justified, not as promoting productivity, but for some other reason, such as protecting autonomy? In Chapter 6, I discuss some general conceptions of value to which privatization advocates might appeal in rationalizing their commitments. In Chapter 7, I assess such appeals.

## NOTES

1. Forum, "Privatizing public lands: the ecological and economic case for private ownership of federal lands," *Manhattan report on economic policy* 2(3) (Manhattan Institute for Policy Research, 1982), at 4.

2. "Economic efficiency in production simply means that given scarce resources shall be employed in such a way that the value of net output (in more technical terms, the willingness to pay for output less the opportunity costs of the inputs) will be at a maximum." B. Delworth Gardner, "The case for divestiture," in *Rethinking the federal lands*, ed. Sterling Brubaker (Washington: Resources for the Future, 1984), 156–80 at 158.

3. Id., at 160.

4. In language reminiscent of joke headlines like "Legislature sets value of $\pi$ at 3.0," the Public Rangelands Improvement Act of 1978, 43 U.S.C.A. §§1901–8, states at §1905 that "Congress finds fair market value for public grazing equals the $1.23 base established by the 1966 Western Livestock Grazing Survey multiplied by the result of the Forage Value Index (computed annually from data supplied by the Economic Research Service) added to the Combined Index (Beef Cattle Price Index minus the Price Paid Index) and divided by 100."

5. Gardner, note 2 *supra*, at 161.

6. "Informal market transactions do not permit the interests of nonnegotiating parties to be included. If it were costless to bring third parties into the negotiations, they would be included, and no problem would exist. Unfortunately, the transaction costs are often prohibitive. . . . [I]n principle, it must be granted that private decisions will not take these spillover effects into account and political decisions just might." Id., at 164.

7. Id., at 175.

8. Id., at 161.

9. Id., at 176. A public good is one that cannot be supplied to just one consumer; when "consumed" by one, it is "consumed" by all, willy nilly. National security and clean air are standard examples. Public goods violate the independence condition of the first fundamental theorem: one consumer's choice of a consumption plan with a particular level of some public good imposes that level on other consumers.

10. Id., at 174.

11. William Schulze, et al., "The economic benefits of preserving visibility in the national parklands of the southwest," *Natural Resources Journal* 23 (1983), 149–73. Visibility auctions are an instance of what is known as "contingent valuation" (sometimes abbreviated "CV"), i.e., valuation contingent on a hypothetical market. For a description and defense of this method, see Robert Cameron Mitchell and Richard T. Carson, *Using surveys to value public goods: the contingent valuation method* (Washington: Resources for the Future, 1989). For another illustration of its use, see Jonathan Rubin, Gloria Helfand, and John Loomis, "A benefit–cost analysis of the northern spotted owl," *Journal of Forestry* 89(12) (1991), 25–30.

12. Various schemes for determining how much of some public good to buy and how to get people to pay what they're willing to pay for it are outlined in Chapter 6 of Allan M. Feldman, *Welfare economics and social choice theory* (Boston: Kluwer-Nijhoff, 1980). All have theoretical or practical drawbacks.

13. My 1985 Colorado individual income-tax return form invites those entitled to a refund on withholding to dedicate a portion of it to any of three programs (nongame wildlife, domestic abuse, and the U.S. Olympic Committee). The revenue thereby generated for any one program was doubtless lower than it would have been had the other two options not been available.

14. Barney Dowdle, "The case for privatizing government owned timberlands," in *Private rights and public lands*, ed. Phillip N. Truluck (Washington: Heritage Foundation, 1983), 71–83 at 82.

15. Richard L. Stroup and John A. Baden, *Natural resources: bureaucratic myths and environmental management* (San Francisco: Pacific Institute for Public Policy Research, 1983), at 118.

16. Id., at 51.

17. Id. See also Chapter 4 generally.

18. Robert Nelson observes that "the public and private land systems seem to be gradually converging, as governments increase their control over the use of private land through zoning and other regulations, and as private rights proliferate on public lands," though it is not clear how much of this process can be rationalized as increasing productivity. Robert H. Nelson, "The subsidized sagebrush: why the privatization movement failed," *Regulation* 8(4) (1984), 20 at 43.

For misgivings about our ability to write and enforce "restrictive covenants that would cover all future contingencies," see Dolores T. Martin, "Divestiture and the creation of property rights in public lands: a comment," *Cato Journal* 2 (1982), 687–90 at 689.

More generally, John Francis notes that "[a] shift to the market requires careful development of rules governing property. Every indication is that the range, diversity, and sophistication of public lands interests at both the national and subnational level are such that the development of an elegant market solution might prove legislatively elusive." John G. Francis, "Public lands institutions and their discontents," in *Federal lands policy*, ed. Phillip O. Foss (New York: Greenwood Press, 1987), 61–76 at 72.

19. Representative David Bonier (D-MI), arguing for federal protection of the few remaining old major-league baseball stadiums, in Claire Smith, "Writing happy ending for four storied parks," *The New York Times*, 18 July 1993, H7.

20. Stroup and Baden, note 15 *supra*, at 126. Some critics of economic approaches to environmental policy see the enemy in the same terms. Mark Sagoff, e.g., writes: "The allocation of resources has to do with how they are used; the distribution has to do with who uses them or benefits from their use. . . . Some economic theorists who write about the environment assume that natural resources should be used in . . . the way that maximizes efficiency. . . . Once the pie is as big as we can make it, we may distribute it in the way we then decide is just or fair." *The economy of the earth* (Cambridge: Cambridge University Press, 1988), at 57–8.

21. In 1969, the USFS, which then had jurisdiction over Mineral King as part of Sequoia National Forest, approved a plan submitted by Walt Disney Productions to develop a ski resort in the valley with overnight accommodations for 1500 visitors. The Sierra Club sued to block the lease in a celebrated case that broadened criteria for legal standing. *Sierra Club* v. *Hickel*, 433 F.2d. 24 (9th Cir. 1970); *Sierra Club* v. *Morton*, 405 U.S. 727 (1972). Disney eventually withdrew its proposal, and in 1978 Congress enlarged Sequoia National Park to include Mineral King.

22. Gary D. Libecap, *Locking up the range: federal land controls and grazing* (San Francisco: Pacific Institute for Public Policy Research, 1981), at 27.

23. A productivity difference of only 8% suggests that ranchers were overgrazing their own lands as well. According to estimates cited by Thadis Box, 85% of private rangeland declined in quality from 1905 to 1935. Thadis W. Box, "The arid lands revisited—one hundred years since John Wesley Powell" (Logan, UT: Utah State University 57th Annual Honor Lecture, 1978) at 19 (Table 3).

24. Libecap, note 22 *supra*, at 46.

25. Box, note 23 *supra*, at 19 (Table 4) and 20 (Table 7).

26. Id., at 19 (Table 4, Note (b)).

27. *National range handbook* (Washington: Soil Conservation Service, U.S.D.A., 1976), at 305.1(c).

28. Id., at 305.5.

29. Id., at 305.5(a).

30. Libecap, note 22 *supra*, at 72.

31. "No permit shall be issued which shall entitle the permittee to the use of such improvements constructed and owned by a prior occupant until the applicant has paid to such prior occupant the reasonable value of such improvements to be determined under rules and regulations of the Secretary of the Interior." 43 U.S.C.A. §315c.

32. Libecap, note 22 *supra*, at 55–60.

33. *An assessment of the forest and range land situation in the United States* (Washington: USFS Forest Resource Report No. 22, 1981), at 163.

34. Id., at 159 (Table 5.1).

35. N. E. West, "Great Basin–Colorado Plateau sagebrush semi-desert," in *Temperate deserts and semi-deserts*, Vol. 5 of *Ecosystems of the world*, ed. Neil E. West (Amsterdam: Elsevier, 1983), 331–49 at 338.

36. Id.

37. Michael Loring and John P. Workman, "The relationship between land ownership and range condition in Rich County, Utah," *Journal of Range Management* 40 (1987), 290–93.

38. Libecap, note 22 *supra*, at 71.

39. Id., my emphasis.

40. Thomas R. Vale, "Presettlement vegetation in the sagebrush–grass area of the intermountain west," *Journal of Range Management* 28 (1975), 32–36.

41. E.g., Jack D. Brotherson, et al., found that plots fenced against grazing for 40 years had significantly more grass and less bare soil than adjacent plots that had experienced moderate to heavy grazing over that period. "Effects of longterm grazing on cryptogam crust cover in Navajo National Monument, Arizona," *Journal of Range Management* 36 (1983), 579–81.

Michael H. Madany and Neil E. West found that grazed mesa tops in Utah had more trees and shrubs and less grass than similar mesa tops inaccessible to livestock; they suggest that grazing enables woody seedlings to sprout in dense perennial sod. "Livestock grazing–fire regime interactions within montane forests of Zion National Park, Utah," *Ecology* 64 (1983), 661–67.

42. *National range handbook*, note 27 *supra*, at 305.3.

43. See Aldo Leopold, "Cheat takes over," in *A sand county almanac* (New York: Ballantine, 1970), 164–68.

44. Box, in fact, observes that "[r]ange in low seral stages may be more valuable to society than climax or excellent stages." Thadis W. Box, "Rangelands," in *Natural resources for the 21st century*, ed. R. N. Sampson and D. Hair (Washington: Island Press, 1990), 101–20 at 113.

45. Libecap, note 22 *supra*, at 67.

46. Id., at 53.

47. Id., at 83.

48. Id., at 68.

49. Box, note 23 *supra*, at 6.

50. Marion Clawson and Jack L. Knetsch claim that "even pefectly certain future income is less highly valued than present income." *The economics of outdoor recreation* (Washington: Resources for the Future, 1966), at 258. Of course, income that's "perfectly certain" may not seem so to its recipient.

51. This line of argument assumes either that (a) no person could have developed from a different pair of gametes or (b) no person could have had a different genetic endowment. It has been used to suggest that we have neither a duty to compensate anyone for wrongs done to not-so-distant ancestors (because their descendants owe their very existence to the actual course of history) nor a duty to future generations (because whatever we do to discharge such a duty will alter the identity of future persons).

F. A. Hayek argues in "History and politics," his editor's introduction to *Capitalism and the historians* (Chicago: University of Chicago Press, 1954), 3–29 at 16, that capitalism did not worsen the position of the poorest because "the proletariat which capitalism can be said to have 'created' would not have existed without it . . . ; it was an additional population which was enabled to grow up by the new opportunities for employment which capitalism provided." Hayek does not rest his case on this observation, preferring to argue that capitalism raised the average level of welfare.

For problems in the notion of obligations to future generations, see Thomas Schwarz, "Obligations to posterity," in *Obligations to future generations*, ed. R. I. Sikora and Brian Barry (Philadelphia: Temple University Press, 1978), 3–29; and Part IV, "Future generations" of Derek Parfit, *Reasons and persons* (Oxford: Clarendon, 1984).

52. Edward Abbey, "Free speech: the cowboy and his cow," in *One life at a time, please* (New York: Holt, 1987), 9–19 at 19.

# 6

# Rationalizing Economic Values

> Economic values are created only as people desire things, and are but a
> reflection of these desires.
>
> Marion Clawson and Jack L. Knetsch[1]

The argument from productivity alleges that privatizing public lands would
make them—and the resources now committed to their management—
more productive. I have spent the last two chapters interpreting and
evaluating this factual claim. In my view, there is no sense of "more
productive" for which it is both interesting and clearly true. But if there
were, it would not immediately follow that public lands should be privatized.
In order to reach normative conclusions, we need normative premises. In
the argument from productivity, these are essentially that situations are
better as resources are more productively employed and that we should
arrange for the best possible situation. In this chapter I consider how such
assumptions might be rationalized.

## VALUE JUDGMENTS

One of the attractions of productivity, I suspect, is that it seems to offer a
way of evading this task, a way of taking values into account without taking
sides. People disagree about ends, for example, about whether old-growth
forest is best reserved for spotted owl habitat, or cut on a sustained-yield
basis, or liquidated to improve quarterly reports to stockholders, or carved
into woodland estates. It would be nice to resolve such disagreements by
demonstrating the superiority of some particular end. But a demonstration
would be an argument from normative principles, and such principles
themselves are disputable. How, then, can policies or institutions designed
to promote some particular end, such as preserving spotted owl habitat, be
defended? Though they might be rational *relative* to that end, how is the
end itself to be rationalized? Better to sidestep the problem by letting
individual consumers rank ends (I prefer other consumption plans to those
I characterize as "poor"), seeking only arrangements (such as private
property rights) that serve whatever preferences they might have.

    While there are certainly difficulties here, it is a delusion to think we
can avoid them by deferring to the desires of consumers. When privatization

advocates claim that public lands and resources would be more productive under private management, they aren't merely *describing* what they take to be facts. In their view, the proper response to this information is not "How interesting!" but "Let's privatize these lands!" If you argue that we *should* privatize public lands *because* doing so will make them *more productive*, then you must believe that greater productivity is desirable. If you think that social institutions should be designed to secure the most efficient use of resources, where one use is more efficient than another insofar as it better satisfies the desires of consumers, then you must *value* satisfying desires and hold some view about how the desires of different individuals are *best* satisfied when they are incompatible.

If we are asked to join you in these normative commitments, then you owe us an account of why they are *better* than others we might make. Given that people can desire anything at all, what precisely *is* good about satisfying desires? Alternatively, what do desires have to be like, in content or history, to make satisfying them worthwhile? Should someone's desire for a vacation home count just as much as a homeless person's desire for a safe place to sleep? Should we judge how much someone's desire counts by how much she is willing to pay to have it satisfied? Wouldn't such a formula fail to honor Bentham's ideal by making those who are lucky "count for more than one?" Such questions must be faced and the misgivings that lie behind them quieted if a commitment to efficiency is to be rationalized.

These issues receive little notice and less attention from privatization advocates. Part of the reason is that they are not moral philosophers but economists, and economists typically regard this sort of normative inquiry as unscientific and unprofessional. B. Delworth Gardner, for example, remarks that "[o]ften analysts make assumptions that egalitarian distributions are better than highly concentrated ones, but these assumptions are simply value judgments about which science has little to contribute."[2] Economics is supposed to be science, and science is supposed to be "value-free." Just as we may study how religious convictions influence people's lives without endorsing any of them, economists may grant that individual values regulate individual behavior, but refuse to pass judgment on them. The various productivity standards are non-judgmental about individual preferences, and one could regard judgments of relative productivity ("*II* makes resources more productive, or utilizes them more efficiently, than *I*") as purely descriptive and therefore "scientific."[3]

In such uses, "productive" and "efficient" function as technical terms with no normative force. However, economists pay attention to productivity or efficiency because they regard more productive or efficient arrangements as *better*. When they advertise efficiency improvements as *improvements*, as they cannot resist doing, or *recommend* some course of action because it will enhance productivity, they unavoidably make value judgments. If science must be value-free, then those who recommend increased efficiency cannot pretend they are speaking as scientists.

One may try to worm out of this by viewing recommendations as hypothetical: "You should do $Y$" is elliptical for "*If* you want $X$, you should do $Y$." Richard Stroup and John Baden, for example, offer the assurance that "[w]e do not, of course, advocate a particular standard of equity; rather, we attempt to explain the efficiency and the equity implications of alternative institutional arrangements."[4] But this is disingenuous. Stroup and Baden are not merely arguing for the conditional imperative "if you want efficiency, go for privatization!" They are not just advising those with a taste for efficiency how best to gratify it. Increased productivity is not, in their view, something we can just take or leave. They value increased productivity and think *the rest of us should too*.

Value judgments are often dismissed as merely subjective. In this view, when I describe $X$ as good (or bad) or $Y$ as right (or wrong), I am not telling you anything about $X$ or $Y$ but merely something about myself, namely, that I have favorable (or unfavorable) attitudes toward $X$ or $Y$. While I believe that subjectivism is untenable,[5] I shall not argue for that here. It is enough for my purposes if we are prepared to act *as if* there were a fact of the matter, accessible to rational inquiry, about $X$ being good or bad, and $Y$ being right or wrong. Even those who regard values as subjective (i.e., as features of subjects) can behave as if they were objective (i.e., were features of objects or relations between objects and subjects), provided they value rationalizing their commitments and care enough about the opinion of others to take criticism of those commitments seriously.

Without such inclinations, people who seek to enlist others in some cause, such as privatizing public lands, are unlikely to get very far, at least if enlistment by conscription is prohibited. If I want to bring you around to my view that $X$ should be done, I have to give you reason to value doing X. To some extent I must rationalize doing $X$, and in a way that appeals to your values. That is, I must appeal to some general conception of value that invests $X$ with rightness and which, I suggest, is *your* conception. I must also be prepared for you, or some third party who prefers $Y$ over $X$, to question my rationalization by pointing to ambiguities in, or unwelcome implications of, this general conception, or by asking what rationalizes it in turn. If I wish to persuade you, such objections must be answered. To dismiss them with remarks like "That's just your opinion" or "That's just a va⸳ ⸳e judgment" is clearly inappropriate in this situation, since you will naturally wonder why they do not apply with equal force to my own views.

A good illustration of the sort of rationalization I have in mind is given by Richard Posner. Recall that Posner proposes to judge change by its impact on wealth: we should think $II$ better than $I$ if $\Delta W$ for $I \rightarrow II$ is positive, and we should aim for institutions that encourage such shifts. Now wealth will strike many people as a strange thing to want to maximize, so Posner attempts to rationalize wealth-maximization by appeal to more general conceptions of value. He essentially argues that wealth is a *surrogate* for two things of more obvious value, viz., happiness and autonomy, and that if we wish to promote *both* of them, we cannot do better than to arrange for wealth-maximizing institutions. The argument appeals to the strengths and weaknesses of ethical theories built around promoting happiness (classical utilitarianism) or upholding autonomy (Kantianism):

> What makes so many moral philosophers queasy about utilitarianism is that it seems to invite gross invasions of individual liberty. . . . But uncompromising insistence on individual liberty or autonomy regardless of the consequences for the happiness or utility of the people of the society seems equally misplaced and unacceptable. Hence there is increasing interest in trying to combine utilitarianism and the Kantian tradition in some fashion. . . . The ethics of wealth maximization can be viewed as a blend of these rival philosophical traditions. Wealth is positively correlated, although imperfectly so, with utility, but the pursuit of wealth, based as it is on the model of the voluntary market transaction, involves greater respect for individual choice than in classical utilitarianism.[6]

This argument cannot be assessed without knowing more about the traditions Posner invokes. I shall review them in this chapter and propose a somewhat different "blending." The point I wish to make here is that the value of things like wealth requires explanation in terms of more basic values.

I now turn to considering what explanations of this kind might be given for the things privatization advocates value, beginning with productivity. Insofar as we can bring the argument from productivity under the wing of some respectable ethical theory, its normative claims will be secured; insofar as we can't, we may develop a normative basis for criticizing it. The theory that seems most hospitable to it is a version of utilitarianism: we are to arrange for maximizing the good of individuals, where one's preferences define one's good. However, the appeal to productivity is not the only appeal that privatization advocates could make, and utilitarianism is not the only ethical theory with some claim to respectability. Indeed, in contrasting the "legalized coercion of the government apparatus" with the "rules of willing consent" that govern exchange of private property,[7] privatization advocates may be appealing to liberty and autonomy. The ethical theorist most closely associated with respect for autonomy is Immanuel Kant. I discuss his views later on in the chapter, in the course of developing certain objections to utilitarianism.


## UTILITARIANISM

By "utilitarianism" I mean a family of theories that share the following features.

(u1) *Right reduces to good: what's right is what produces the greatest (net) good.* In assessing the rightness of actions, policies, or institutions, we typically consider their effects: consequences matter. Utilitarian theories hold that consequences are *all* that matter: what's right or appropriate is what *maximizes utility*, i.e., where the utility of $X$ is the good consequent to $X$ minus the bad. In *act* utilitarianism, $X$ is an individual action. Usually, just those acts that maximize utility are held to be right, while the rest are wrong, although we might instead rank actions as more or less appropriate by the utility they produce. In *rule* utilitarianism, $X$ is a practice or institution (or, better, a set of practices or institutions); the appropriate $X$ is that which would generate the best consequences overall, and actions are right as they issue from the appropriate X, though they may not individually maximize utility.

(u2) *Social good reduces to individual good: utility is aggregate net benefit to individuals.* An action (practice, institution) $X$ will typically produce some good and some bad for a given individual, and the impact will be different for different individuals. To estimate X's utility, we estimate X's net benefit for each affected individual and sum them to get aggregate net benefit. An individual is whatever has a good of its own and thus can be harmed or benefitted in a way that does not resolve without residue into harm and benefit to others, so it's trivial that what's good is ultimately a matter of what's good for individuals. The substantive claim here is that collections of individuals are not themselves individuals in the relevant sense: there is no good that resides irreducibly in groups or collectives of individuals. We may speak of policies benefitting some groups and harming others, but this means no more than that on balance the individuals that comprise these groups are benefitted or harmed.

(u3) *Individual good reduces to individual valuation: one's values define one's good.* My good is not a matter of my being a good person or conforming to some notion of what people ought to be or to strive for. To reckon my good in terms of how saintly or virtuous I am is to confuse my good with that of others and to give no account of either. To reckon it in terms of how fully I've developed my "potential," individual or "human," leaves mysterious why I should be interested in what is after all supposed to be *my* good. Instead, utilitarians judge my good in terms of something I can be presumed to value, such as my happiness or the satisfaction of my desires.

These features, u1–u3, give a unified account of the right and the good, though hardly an unproblematic one. Some of its difficulties are of the kind we expect when philosophers subject ordinary notions—such as that of the consequences of an action—to critical scrutiny. Others arise because utilitarianism seems at odds with other glimpses of moral truth. I shall consider u1, u2, and u3 in turn. The main problems with u1 revolve around (a) the nature of consequences and our ignorance of the future and (b) the claim that only consequences matter. I discuss (a) in the next section and (b) in the following one. Kant's notion of respect for persons, which appears to involve rejecting (b), is explored in the next section. After briefly discussing u2 in the following section, I finish the chapter with three sections on u3. In the first two of these, I consider preference and classical utilitarianism, which differ in the account they give of individual good; in the third, I suggest that these accounts require correction in the direction of Kant.

## JUDGING CONSEQUENCES

If actions, procedures, or institutions are to be judged by the good they achieve, then we need to be able to determine what they do or would achieve. There are two difficulties here.

1. *Estimating the future course of events.* If we were to do or conform to $X$, then we imagine that events would unfold in some way, call it "the $X$-future." But just what is this way? Let's put aside any problems there might be in determining the goodness of the $X$-future: imagine that we possess a goodness meter capable of giving us reliable readings on possible futures, provided we can get hold of them. The problem is how we are to obtain these inputs for our meter.

2. *Deciding how much of the X-future to ascribe to X.* It does not seem correct to *identify* $X$'s consequences with the $X$-future, since the $X$-future owes its shape to many contingencies other than $X$. Had I not left my keys in the car at the mall, you wouldn't have gone joyriding in it, and that kid on the bicycle you hit would still be alive. My carelessness (or even my going shopping) certainly contributed to the tragedy, but it's odd to hold that against it when your contribution seems so crucial. It would be nice to apportion causal responsibility for the $X$-future to $X$ and the other actions or practices that shape it, but it is not clear how.

In view of these problems, we can hardly arrange for the best possible future by maximizing the utility of each and every action. Point 2 suggests that "maximizes utility" can't be meaningfully predicated of individual actions. Even if it can, point 1 suggests we're unlikely to discover which they are. If we attempt to choose between individual actions on this basis, we'll almost certainly fail to maximize utility. We're likely to invest more time and effort in acquiring information than the information is worth, to disappoint others' expectations by acting on the basis of idiosyncratic estimates of the likely course of events and its net value, and to exploit ignorance to "justify" all sorts of self-serving actions.

Accordingly, act utilitarianism does not seem to construe maximizing utility in a very helpful way. The future is the result of individual actions, but we obviously cannot arrange for the best possible future by asking, at each opportunity, which of the actions open to us maximizes utility. Even if "the consequences of $X$" designates something, we're going to have a lot of trouble figuring out what it is. Rule utilitarianism looks a bit more promising, since we expect it to be much easier to determine whether some action conforms to some rule, practice, or institution than to determine whether it maximizes utility. To reduce difficulty 2—the problem of isolating $X$'s consequences—we should think in terms of *systems* of rules, practices, or institutions. Where $X$ is a system, perhaps $X$'s consequences can be identified with the $X$-future. Point 1 is still problematic: if we have trouble answering the question "For each alternative $X$, what is the $X$-future?" where "$X$" ranges over actions we might take in some situation, we're also going to have trouble with it where "$X$" ranges over practices or systems of practices we might follow.[8] Accordingly, rule-utilitarian arguments for a particular system of rules, practices, or institutions are bound to be somewhat conjectural. However, we frequently have some basis for predicting some effects of a marginal change in the present system (e.g., whether human suffering would be reduced if the rule "Don't kill other people, except under conditions C" were modified by expanding the list C of excusing conditions to include certain types of euthanasia).

If we want a system of rules that maximizes utility, we must take into account their *use*. Rules by themselves produce no utility; people must live by them. Rules that are very complex or that seem to demand great sacrifices are not good candidates for including in a system that will maximize utility in practice. On the other hand, simple rules do not seem equal to the complexity of human affairs. In many cases, we'll have to work pretty hard to bring situations under some rule or other, and where this can be done in different ways (so that we are directed both to do and not to do $X$) we'll have to judge which is the best way. Accordingly, some moral philosophers argue that the correct utilitarianism is neither act nor rule utilitarianism, but a mixture of the two. Richard Hare, for example, thinks that maximizing the good calls for a two-level moral system.[9] The "intuitive level" is defined by a body of fairly simple rules (like "Don't kill people," "Tell the truth," "Keep your promises," etc.) that we internalize if we are well brought up and which govern most of our moral business. The "critical level" is constituted by the idea that such rules are to serve the good: the rules we choose to do our moral business with should be selected on the basis of their utility in practice, and the inevitable conflicts between them should be decided by estimating what action would maximize utility.

## DOES THE RIGHT SERVE THE GOOD?

If what's right is what does the most good, then we ought to do what we can to maximize utility. That this standard may be difficult to apply is no reason to reject utilitarianism. Instead, one must argue that right can't be reduced to good in this way. It's not hard to make people uneasy about the utilitarian reduction. In assessing actions, we often look *backward* rather than *forward*. Suppose that $X$ maximizes utility; can $X$ be the right thing for me to do if I *promised* to do otherwise? Can $X$ be the right thing for you to do if, in view of my past conduct, I *deserve* otherwise? Furthermore, isn't the *reason* for which $X$ is done relevant to our assessment? Surely many will concur with David Hume here: "'Tis evident, that when we praise any actions, we regard only the motives that produced them, and consider the actions as signs or indications of certain principles in the mind and temper. The external performance has no merit."[10]

For a utilitarian, neither the motive nor the history of an action is *directly* relevant to its evaluation. John Stuart Mill claims that "[h]e who saves a fellow creature from drowning does what is morally right, whether his motive be duty, or the hope of being paid for his trouble."[11] The fact that by doing $X$ I keep a promise I made to you is not a reason to do $X$, at least from an act-utilitarian perspective, except insofar as not doing $X$ will disappoint you or erode trust more generally. That the punishment fit the crime—or that the innocent not be "punished"—is not dictated by some notion of a fitting response (e.g., taking the lives of those who take life, or making those who litter clean up a mile of roadside) but by the idea that punishment should deter would-be offenders or rehabilitate the criminal.

But it does not follow that utilitarians must be indifferent to the motive or history of actions. It's standard procedure for those who advance some ethical theory to claim that our considered ethical judgments are compatible with it. Thus, utilitarians may argue that by following certain rules (like "Keep your promises"), or developing certain dispositions or traits of character (like honesty or kindness), one can most effectively promote the good of individuals. They may even suggest that our actions will be most efficient in this sense when we forget that such rules and dispositions are merely means and instead act from a sense of right shaped by them. Since there is normally a close connection between my motive and what my action achieves, utilitarians will care about motives. They will dismiss as fantasy the idea that we might be able to arrange things so that people acting from purely selfish motives are led "by an invisible hand" to produce the best possible result.[12] A world in which the only motive for saving people from drowning is the expectation of monetary reward, in the form of either direct payment or not losing one's job as a lifeguard, is a world in which more people drown. Furthermore, an overriding concern for self is unlikely to make people happy. As Mill remarks, "When people who are tolerably fortunate in their outward lot do not find in life sufficient enjoyment to make it valuable to them, the cause generally is, caring for nobody but themselves."[13]

None of these utilitarian maneuvers would impress Kant, who explicitly denies that the right can be understood in terms of the good: "the moral worth of an action does not lie in the effect expected from it nor in any principle of action that needs to borrow its motive from this expected effect."[14] Instead, a moral action requires a moral motive: one must act, not from inclination, but from duty, from a sense that one's action is called for by the "moral law". And what does the "moral law" call for? Kant's answer is contained in his Categorical Imperative, of which he gives four supposedly equivalent formulations. The one that appeals most directly to autonomy is the respect-for-persons version, RP: "Act in such a way that you treat humanity, whether in your own person or in the person of another, always at the same time as an end and never simply as a means."[15]

RP derives from Kant's view that rational agency is the source of value in the world. Without rational agents—individuals capable of choosing their own ends after rational deliberation and initiating a sequence of events designed to secure them—there would be nothing of value. To treat a rational agent as a mere means to one's own ends, as if it had none of its own, is to violate its nature. Indeed, Kant would characterize such actions as "contradictory," inasmuch as one is denying agency at the very same time one is engaged in it. However, one needn't buy such "justifications" in order to find RP appealing, for it seems to account for our moral intuitions about certain cases in a direct and satisfying way. By contrast, utilitarian accounts are apt to seem roundabout and contrived.

A lot of resistance to utilitarianism derives from the worry that policies designed to maximize aggregate net benefits could leave some individuals very badly off: simply imagine that others gain more than they lose. Once we start thinking in terms of aggregating benefits, we'll wonder why a trivial gain for each of a large number of people can't outweigh a terrible loss for one: why not throw a few Christians to the lions if the crowds are big and enthusiastic enough? A particularly arresting suggestion is that utility would be increased by a policy calling for sacrificing an individual whenever transplanting her organs would save (say) two others. Whatever your view of individual good, wouldn't such a policy give us *more* of it? Now a lot of people would nevertheless consider such a policy to be odious, and RP seems to rationalize this feeling. For surely the individual who is sacrificed is not thereby being treated as an end but as a mere means; we are not regarding her as the author of a life, but simply as an organ bank. So we seem to have a case in which utilitarianism conflicts with our intuitions, while Kant's view not only accords with, but seems to explain, them.

A utilitarian may respond by arguing that utilitarianism is not in conflict with intuition in this case: the proposed policy is not an implication of the theory, because it would make people nervous and that tips the utility balance against it. Now against this line of defense it might be pointed out that if my nervousness has a rational basis, it must be that I'll be more likely to be an involuntary organ donor than an organ recipient, and that's obviously impossible if this policy is followed. Still, the utilitarian can observe that policies are implemented by people, and who would be willing to trust others to make such a decision?[16] History, after all, gives us good reason to worry about the readiness of some—among them can be found both social engineers and free-marketeers—who march under the banner of maximizing utility to accept costs to others as "necessary." Accordingly, it might be best (i.e., maximize utility) to build some safeguards into the program of maximizing aggregate net benefits. In particular, we might try to secure for each individual some minimum level of welfare and freedom defined by a system of rights and entitlements.

Some of these rights (e.g., the right to life) will protect individuals against being *made use of* in certain respects, even in cases where it may be argued that doing so would increase utility. However, the utilitarian will not justify rights in such Kantian terms, but in terms of their utility. For example, she may point out that when I violate $A$'s rights, I generally not only harm $A$ but contribute to eroding respect for rights, either in others by example or in myself through habituation and self-deception. Perhaps the cost to $A$ here is indeed outweighed by some benefit to $B$, but when we add these other expected costs, we'll have a good utilitarian reason to refrain from violating *A*'s right in all but very exceptional cases (where it will be hard to argue *against* violating it).

Many utilitarians have, in fact, claimed that rights and entitlements securing some of "the essentials of human well-being"[17] are part of the system of institutions that maximize utility. Early in *On liberty*, his celebrated defense of individual rights, Mill declares, "I forgo any advantage which could be derived to my argument from the idea of abstract right, as a thing independent of utility. I regard utility as the ultimate appeal on all ethical questions."[18] Of course, one may wonder if Mill wasn't mistaken about the consistency of *On liberty* with *Utilitarianism*. In particular, if "equal amounts of happiness are equally desirable,"[19] won't equal rights maximize utility only on the assumption that people are capable of the same amount of happiness? However, it is open to Mill to argue that no better system could be devised, in part because any system that allowed for discriminating between people on the basis of their capacity for happiness would invite abuse.

Nonetheless, this whole line of argument will strike some people as both flimsy and off the mark. Are judgments of right and wrong really hostage to such contingencies? Suppose God informed us that utility would indeed be maximized by sacrificing *A* and distributing her organs to *B* and *C*; would we agree that that was the thing to do? Or suppose the Word is that, just as utilitarians claim, utility would not be maximized by sacrificing *A*; is *that* the reason not to sacrifice *A*? Doesn't Kant's Imperative give us a *better* reason?

## RESPECT FOR PERSONS

What exactly is the content of RP? What is it to treat someone "always . . . as an end and never simply as a means?" Libertarians who invoke the authority of Kant to argue for a system of "negative" rights against interference, tend to pass over the first part and concentrate on the second, as if treating *A* as an end was to be achieved merely by *not* treating *A* simply as a means. We treat people simply as a means when we coerce, deceive, or otherwise manipulate them. Individual rights protect us against some of this: there are certain things you may not do without my willing consent. If I have a veto over your use of my person and other property, then you must take *me and my goals* into account; by respecting my rights, you avoid treating me simply as a means in certain respects.

To the extent that negative rights against interference honor the first part of the formula, it is by giving each individual a sphere of freedom to fill as she wishes with her own life. But this falls rather short of Kant's intention; he clearly intends the first part of the formula to do some work:

> Now humanity might indeed subsist if nobody contributed anything to the happiness of others, provided he did not intentionally impair their happiness. But this, after all, would harmonize only negatively and not

positively with humanity as an end in itself, if everyone does not also strive,
as much as he can, to further the ends of others.[20]

Appealing to such passages, Onora O'Neill argues that RP requires acting
"on principles that do not undermine but rather sustain and extend one
another's capacities for autonomous action" and that we "share and support
one another's ends and activities at least to some extent."[21] Since humanity
is unlikely to flourish amid ignorance or grinding poverty, shouldn't we add
some "positive" rights, for example, to education and basic necessities, to
the negative ones in the libertarian bundle? Negative rights, of course, must
be qualified accordingly; I will have a duty to contribute some of what's mine
in aid of those less fortunate.

There is another reason for thinking that negative rights cannot embody
the whole of Kant's conception of respect for persons, and that is his
inclusion of "my own person" in RP. Among those I am to respect is myself;
it is not just others that I am to treat as an end, but also myself. Now, of
course, this is a little odd: how can actions I take as a rational agent *fail* to
meet this standard? If what makes manipulating another person wrong is
that I ignore his ends, then how can my pursuit of ends be wrong insofar as
it affects only myself? Answering this question requires appealing to the
notion of rational agency; there are various ways in which I can act and yet
fail to live up to this standard, depending upon what is packed into it.

The weakest reading of "rational" is the pursuit of consistent ends by
efficient means. Given that I have chosen consistent ends, ends not at odds
with one another, I am rational insofar as I select appropriate means. This
is the way in which economists typically understand rationality. Ludwig von
Mises, for example, writes that "the economic problem [is] to employ the
available means in such a way that no want more urgently felt should remain
unsatisfied because the means suitable for its attainment were employed—
wasted—for the attainment of a want less urgently felt."[22] However, this
weak reading may be strengthened in two ways, both of which Kant would,
I think, insist upon.

The first takes seriously the *agency* part of rational agency: if I am to
act as a rational agent, it must be that *I* am the one who selects my ends.
To be worth *my* pursuit, my ends must be authentically *mine*, not things I
want because you have manipulated my desires or because they spring willy
nilly from my subconscious. Von Mises doesn't seem to care where my ends
come from. He remarks that "[t]he murderer whom a subconscious urge
(the *Id*) drives toward his crime and the neurotic whose aberrant behavior
seems to be simply meaningless to an untrained observer both act; they like
anybody else are aiming at certain ends."[23] This is certainly not Kant's view,
and it's hard to see why ends of this sort deserve respect, even where they
do not involve *using* others, as in the case of the murderer.

The second way of enriching the notion of rationality is to hold that
there are some additional constraints on what it is rational to choose as one's
ends. Von Mises insists that "[t]o apply the concept *rational* or *irrational* to

the ultimate ends chosen is nonsensical."[24] But Kant would disagree. He believes that for someone "to indulge in pleasure rather than to bother himself about broadening and improving his fortunate natural aptitudes" would be to deny his rationality: "as a rational being he necessarily wills that all his faculties should be developed."[25] The basic idea is that one can waste not only one's *means* but one's *life* (such as, Thomas Nagel suggests, in "the cheerful pursuit of a method of communicating with asparagus plants"[26]). Surely we *ought* to choose ends that are *worthy of our nature and gifts*.

Now, of course, this is a very difficult conception. What exactly *is* worthy of us? Is there some way of answering this question that leaves room for agency? Perhaps we could think of $A$'s gifts as defining a class of lives *fitting for A*, one of which $A$ then *makes her own* through her choice or construction of it. Presumably, there should be some "fit" between the individual's gifts and her life. It would be certainly irrational for someone of my modest scientific and musical talents to pursue a career as a physicist or concert violinist. Perhaps it would also be irrational in this sense to neglect certain gifts by allowing the labor market and one's consumer interests to dictate one's career choice. Suppose, for example, that Antonin Dvorak had decided that the butcher's trade his father wanted him to pursue was, in fact, his best option. I am inclined to think that not only *we*, but *he*, would have been the worse for such a choice.

It would be nice to say more about what makes a possible life *fitting*, but I don't think we need a very exact understanding to suggest that respect for humanity in one's own person is not going to be promoted by the libertarian's system of negative rights. These rights *merely* protect certain aspects of rational agency; they do not *promote* other aspects. A sphere of freedom does not assure that my ends are mine or that they are worthy of me. To serve these aspects of rational agency, we must look elsewhere.

I conclude this section by observing that, in appealing to rational agency to work out the implications of RP, we appear to have regained a utilitarian perspective, albeit one with a non-standard notion of the good, viz., rational agency. For have we not been considering how to *promote* rational agency, asking, for example, whether restricting some aspects to enhance others wouldn't produce an *overall gain*? If so, we have not succeeded in developing an alternative to u1 after all. From this perspective, RP may not be the last word: perhaps we needn't *always* treat others as ends and not mere means. There may be cases in which *using* people can be justified as promoting rational agency; perhaps Sherlock Holmes's deception in "The adventure of Charles Augustus Milverton" is one of them.[27]

## SOCIAL GOOD

I now turn to the second feature of utilitarian theories: social good reduces to individual good. I have already considered an objection to the standard reduction, taken as a guide to action: in some cases, maximizing aggregate net benefits seems to involve *using* people. Another objection is implicit in my discussion of the shortcomings of negative rights: maximizing aggregate net benefits won't respect agency, if it can be done while leaving some people very badly off.

This is the problem of utility vs. equality. Unless we can appeal to something like diminishing marginal utility, there is no reason to think that utility is maximized by equalizing circumstances. Set aside misgivings and suppose that utility is an increasing function of income (perhaps because utility is happiness and money buys happiness). If everyone's utility function is *identical* (from the same income, A and B get exactly the same utility) and the *rate* at which A's utility increases *declines* as A's income rises (the assumption of diminishing marginal utility), then it's easy to show that utility will be maximized when income is divided equally among the population. But the assumptions required for this happy result are not compelling. Indeed, it's not even clear that guaranteeing people a *minimum* income is consistent with maximizing utility.

If there are problems with the *standard* utilitarian reduction of social to individual good, what about the general idea that social good is nothing over and above the good of individuals? Is there some difficulty with that as well? Here I think the utilitarian is correct. It's not part of his theory that collectives are of no importance, or that we cannot speak of one society being better than another. But the good of society is, in his view, instrumental to the good of individuals: we can't argue that X contributes to the good of society Y without arguing that X makes Y's members better off in some way.

It does not follow, however, that to maximize utility, actions or policies must be *directed* toward making individuals better off. On the contrary, acting on behalf of collectives—one's family, church, community, firm, profession, nation, etc.—conceived as things over and above their members, may be more effective. A somewhat risky example is going to war: those who think about the appalling costs to individuals may prefer to opt out, to negotiate concessions, to have "peace in our time," perhaps at greater cost to individuals in the long run. The basic point is that we may do better in securing certain ends if we do not aim at them directly. Reflect again on the "paradox of happiness:" those who seek happiness are almost certain to end up with less of it than those who do not.

Such "false target" arguments—the best way to get X is to aim for Y instead—may enable the utilitarian to absorb all sorts of apparently non-utilitarian elements into his theory. The difficulty with them, of course, is that it's hard to *establish* that aiming for something other than utility (by holding rights inviolate, or thinking of collectives as having a good of their own) really is the best way to maximize it. Such arguments tend toward argument by assertion. However, it may not be possible to rationalize such aims in a more direct way. Can we really take seriously the notion that collectives have a good of their own?

If something has a good of its own, what must it be like? People can abuse their cars and their children, but it is only the latter that have anything at stake. The harm I do my car by red-lining the engine or never replacing the coolant is no more than harm I do to myself or other people, whereas I cannot imagine that this is so when I harm my daughter. She has her own point of view, in terms of which things matter. Unlike my car, she is not indifferent about what happens to her; things are pleasant or unpleasant for her, in accord with, or contrary to, her wishes. The relation between her enjoying or desiring something and its being good for her need not be simple; children sometimes enjoy what we'd describe as sexual abuse, though in later life they rarely recollect the experience with pleasure. To assess the impact of something on your welfare, we may need to appeal to what you would feel or desire if suitably informed and rational. But without involving you in the assessment by some such appeal to your point of view, it's hard to be sure that we aren't confusing *our* good with yours.

If, as this suggests, feelings or desires are required for a good of one's own, then collections of individuals won't qualify. However important they may be for the individuals comprising them, collectives do not seem to have a point of view. Members of a family may make sacrifices for it, but it—as a collective, distinct from its members—cannot benefit from them: it lacks the desires or feelings in terms of which harm or benefit may be understood.

This, however, is not true of some non-human animals, and the utilitarian approach forces consideration of how our actions or practices affect their welfare. When deciding between actions or practices, we can't restrict consideration of their consequences to the impact on humans, but must estimate how anything with a good of its own might be affected. If utility is reckoned in terms of happiness, practices that make animals suffer for our benefit—factory farming, toxicity testing, medical research—may not maximize utility relative to other practices and will therefore be unjustified by utilitarian reasoning.[28] This strikes some people as sufficiently ridiculous to constitute an objection to utilitarianism. Posner, for example, remarks that "there is something amiss in a philosophical system that cannot distinguish between people and sheep."[29] Unfortunately, he does not tell us just what is amiss, nor why non-human animals should count for as little as they do in the system he prefers (since they command no wealth, they count for absolutely nothing in their own right).

It's one thing to suggest that one must have feelings or desires if one is to have a good of one's own; it's another to give a precise account of the notion. The simplest way of accounting for the importance of feeling or desire is to make it *constitutive* of individual welfare: simply judge one's welfare either by the level of one's pleasure or happiness, conceived as a quantifiable psychological state, or by the extent to which one's desires are satisfied. Classical utilitarianism incorporates the first suggestion (we're to maximize happiness), preference utilitarianism the second (we're to maximize the satisfaction of desires). While both conceptions of individual good honor u3, both are problematic. Some of the problems are internal, relating to just what account is being given of individual welfare and what it would mean to maximize the good of individuals, so conceived. Others are external, relating to whether this account can be correct.

## PREFERENCE UTILITARIANISM

While preference utilitarianism seems to be the preferred variety nowadays, it has serious shortcomings. The most obvious is explaining how getting what one wants can enhance one's welfare, given that people can want all sorts of things—alcohol and other drugs, power, hollandaise sauce, retirement, riches, the latest in consumer electronics, adulation, etc.—that aren't good for them. How can anyone seriously maintain, without qualification, that my preference for $X$ over $Y$ (or the fact that I want $X$ more intensely than I want $Y$) makes my desire for $X$ more worth satisfying? Evidently some constraints must be placed on the content of desires, or their formation. The usual suggestion is information: my desires should be informed by knowledge of what it would be like to satisfy them. This leads, at the limit, to Henry Sidgwick's proposal that "a man's future good on the whole is what he would now desire and seek on the whole if all the consequences of all the different lines of conduct open to him were accurately foreseen and adequately realized in imagination at the present point of time."[30] But it also suggests that what rationalizes satisfying desires may be *satisfaction*: how it *feels* to pursue and achieve one's ends. If so, preference utilitarianism collapses into classical utilitarianism.

It is also hard to give any clear sense to the notion of maximizing the satisfaction of desires, either for an individual or for a collection of individuals, and thus to be sure that preference utilitarianism is an intelligible theory. Imagine two alternative courses of action, $I$ and $II$; what can it mean to say that $II$ better satisfies desires than $I$?

Consider first the individual case: when does $II$ better satisfy my desires than $I$? Let us simplify the problem by supposing that I have considered the matter and prefer (i.e., more intensely desire) $II$. Does it follow that $II$ better satisfies my desires than $I$? As Richard Brandt points out,[31] this is not obvious. Suppose that, as often happens, my desires change with time: I now prefer $II$, but some years hence I prefer $I$ (imagine that $I$ and $II$ diverge only later; Brandt's example is someone deciding at age six that "he would like to celebrate his fiftieth birthday by taking a roller-coaster ride"[32]). Which preference is decisive, given that I have different ones at different times? If my good is a matter of having my desires satisfied, isn't my good ill-defined? Isn't Sidgwick's characterization of my future good either empty or incoherent, inasmuch as what I'd desire *now* if suitably informed need not be what I'd desire *later* if suitably informed? *My future good*, as determined at some later time $t$, need not coincide thereafter with *my future good*, as determined now, even if I manage to live from now to $t$ in accord with the latter plan.

We have run into this problem before, in trying to make sense of the

argument from future benefits in Chapter 5. Even if it could be resolved in
a non-arbitrary way, we'd still have to give sense to maximizing the
satisfaction of the desires of a collection of individuals. We can do so in
terms of one or another of the various productivity improvement standards
discussed in Chapter 4, but none of them is satisfactory. The Pareto standard
is too strong, since we can better satisfy desires in this sense only if we can
avoid offending anyone. We can avoid complete immobility only by
disregarding certain ways in which one might take offense—such as seeing
the poor remain poor, observing you enjoying what I'd like, or being
assaulted by spillovers. The net-gain standards in effect measure intensity
of desire by willingness-to-pay. But this is completely loony. Willingness-
to-pay presupposes ability to pay and that, rather than more intense desire,
is what puts old violins in the display cases of collectors rather than in the
hands of musicians.[33]

## CLASSICAL UTILITARIANISM

The classical utilitarian view of individual welfare seems to be that there is
a real-valued function $H$ of individuals $A$ and times $t$ for which the following
are true: (1) $H(A,t)$ is the level of $A$'s happiness at $t$; (2) $A$'s welfare
$W(A,\Delta t)$ over the time span $\Delta t$ is given by the area under the $H(A,t)$-curve
over $\Delta t$; and (3) how $A$ and $B$ together fare over $\Delta t$ is given by $W(A,\Delta t)$
$+ W(B,\Delta t)$. Each of these features invites protest. Is there any identifiable
psychological state—my happiness—quantifiable as required by (1)? Our
experience—joys, miseries, and the more usual episodes that are neither—
seems too varied to be squeezed into such an index. Are we to agree that
my anguish on learning of a friend's suicide differs only in intensity and
duration from the pain of dislocating my thumb? Can how I fare over some
interval—the rest of my life, perhaps—really be judged by how I feel, as
(2) indicates? If so, how can it be "better to be a human being dissatisfied
than a pig satisfied; better to be Socrates dissatisfied than a fool satisfied,"
as Mill claims?[34] Finally, what sense can be made of there being some
common unit of happiness, in terms of which happiness may, at least in
principle, be summed across individuals, as in (3)?

The last difficulty is the one that most impresses economists: if we can't
make *sense* of measuring aggregate happiness, let alone do it, then we had
better find some other index of welfare.[35] However, this problem may not
be intractable. Brandt proposes to give sense to interpersonal comparisons
of happiness by first reducing the problem of making *inter*personal
comparisons to the problem of making *intra*personal comparisons and then
explaining how that is to be done.[36] He thinks of $A$'s level of happiness at $t$
as, roughly, how badly $A$ wants whatever she's experiencing at $t$ to continue.
Brandt argues that $A$ can, if $A$ attends to it, analyze her experience at a time
$t$ into elements that are pleasant, unpleasant, or neither, and that $A$ can
quantify these contributions. Quantification here involves assigning (a) to

neutral elements, the value 0; (b) to elements that would add (or detract) equally from one's experience, the same positive (or negative) value; and (c) to elements that would add (or subtract) an amount of pleasure equal to the joint contribution of other elements, the sum of the values assigned them. $A$'s choice of a unit is immaterial, provided we can compare $A$'s unit with $B$'s. This Brandt proposes to do by carefully matching $A$ and $B$ for, say, thirst, getting each to say how bad it is according to their individual measures, and then equating these values, i.e., normalizing the intrapersonal scales so that (say) this experience of thirst is $-1$ on each.

Brandt's proposal does not provide a basis for comparing the happiness of humans with that of non-human animals, since the latter can't construct intrapersonal scales. It does, of course, involve assuming that equal deprivation produces equally unpleasant mental states in $A$ and $B$, and that we can arrange for equal deprivation by carefully matching $A$ and $B$. So the proposal will be rejected by those who doubt the existence of other minds, think that people can be deliriously happy when they give every sign of being miserable, etc. What's more worrisome, I think, is whether intrapersonal scales can be constructed as Brandt proposes.

The difficulty is that elements may not jointly contribute the sum of their values, as required by (c). Brandt's example involves dining at a restaurant where a string quartet is playing. He suggests that where the "increment from eating parfait is just equal in pleasantness to a combination of hearing the quartet and gazing at an attractive lady, the latter two having already been judged equal and given the number 1,"[37] the increment may be assigned the value 2. This assumes that hearing the quartet doesn't *enhance* the pleasure of gazing at the lady, that in combination these elements do not contribute more to my total enjoyment than the sum of their separate contributions. Yet this seems unrealistic.

It's also not clear that one can make the required estimates. Suppose the positive elements of my experience at the moment include eating the parfait, hearing the quartet, and gazing at the lady. Brandt seems to call for my imagining doing none of them, adding on various combinations to the remaining elements of my experience, and then comparing the results; otherwise it is not clear what is meant by the parfait increasing my enjoyment by as much as the quartet and the lady together. But this exercise seems too difficult. Perhaps I could make estimates at the margin, judging, say, that stopping the music, given the presence of the lady and the parfait, would diminish my enjoyment by about as much as the lady's departure, given the music and parfait. But these are not the required estimates.

Still, surmounting such difficulties—thereby giving *sense* to the classical utilitarian picture, at least for humans—does not seem out of the question. The problem of the contented pig, however, raises doubts about whether it can be *correct*. If my good is my happiness and I get more pleasure from a swinish existence than from any alternative open to me, isn't the life of a pig the life for me? Mill, who didn't see much in the life of a contented pig, tries to save utilitarianism by suggesting that, in estimating happiness, pleasures should be weighted by their quality,[38] those of the pig or the fool being of a rather low order. His suggested criterion of quality is the preference of competent judges: "Of two pleasures, if there be one to which all or almost all who have experience of both give a decided preference, irrespective of any feeling of moral obligation to prefer it, that is the more desirable pleasure."[39] He adds that it is a "sense of dignity"[40] that keeps us from preferring the "lower pleasures."

Unfortunately, this seems to save classical utilitarianism by replacing it with something else. If the value of happiness is to be decided by preference, why not forget happiness and reckon welfare in terms of desire (if we can make sense of doing so)? But Mill's proposal goes beyond preference utilitiarianism too, for the fact that A prefers X to Y (desires X more intensely than Y) will indicate that X is better than Y for A only if A is a competent judge (i.e., knows both X and Y), in fact, only if the *majority* of competent judges would prefer X to Y. Mill's appeal to dignity suggests that certain pleasures are unworthy of us, whether we prefer them or not. My good is no longer what I *do* value; it is what I *ought* to value.

But why ought I? Unless it can be shown that my life will be more satisfactory to me or others if I pursue the higher pleasures, the explanation isn't going to be utilitarian. Mill does remark that "there can be no doubt that [a noble character] makes other people happier, and that the world in general is immensely a gainer by it,"[41] but he clearly does not want to rest his case for higher pleasures on their instrumental value. Sometimes he seems to suggest, contrary to his statement of the problem, that those who pursue the higher pleasures just get *more* pleasure: as we pursue higher pleasures, we enlarge our *capacity* for pleasure. If we feel more dissatisfied, that is because our happiness has increased less than our capacity; but it *has* increased.[42] On the other hand, he says, "A being of higher faculties requires more to make him happy,"[43] which suggests that more is required to achieve the same level of happiness. Note that it won't help here to abandon classical for preference utilitarianism. After all, people are quite capable of desiring what Mill would call "lower pleasures," even of preferring them to the higher.

## INDIVIDUAL GOOD

A natural response to challenges like Mill's contented pig is to look for conditions under which we *would* be willing to identify my good with my happiness—or with the satisfaction of my desires. To introduce such conditions is to depart from utilitarianism, unless it can be argued that I'll be happier if they are satisfied. Mill's appeal to dignity suggests a departure in the direction of Kant. However, those who start from utilitarianism will probably want to stop short of Kant; they will think his conditions go too far toward imposing an external standard. I simply don't have enough to say about what *my* good consists in, if my choices are limited by Kant's idea of what's worthy of me.

Some of Mill's remarks in *On liberty* suggest the following proposal: how I feel or how far I can satisfy my desires is a reliable index of how well I'm doing *provided* I'm following a plan of life of my own devising, where my construction is informed by an understanding of my gifts and circumstances and the possibilities they define. Sketchy as it is, this formula has some attractive features. It doesn't identify my good with someone else's idea of what's worthy of me. At the same time, few who make choices informed by other options will, one imagines, opt for the life of a pig. And a plan of life, which of course could allow for spontaneity, should help discipline wayward and destructive desires.

Moreover, the formula seems to have some practical import, at least in the weak sense of guiding inquiry into how to pull off what it calls for. It strongly suggests that social policy will best advance individual welfare if it is directed to enabling everyone to make an informed choice of the direction of her life and to pursue her plan, constrained only by a like freedom for others. So, among other things, we should consider what sorts of institutions can help inform choice. Surely the lives of others, real and fictional, are the primary source of ideas for our own. So we should think about how to make these other lives accessible to individuals and how to encourage their diversity. Here we might consider aspects of diversity, asking what sort of social arrangements would nurture them. For example, one model for accessible *cultural* diversity might be a city with diverse and flourishing ethnic communities, whose citizens view their own communities with pride and those of others with interest. We could then consider what stands in the way of approaching this ideal and how we might get around such obstacles. In this way, we might be able to develop what may seem to be a rather vague proposal into some useful policies.

Utilitarians could claim such a formula as their own, derived as it is from Mill. He argues that freedom to construct one's own life is essential if each is to attain his "fair share of happiness."[44] The lives of others (other "experiments of living,"[45] as Mill thinks of them) are a valuable source of information about options and their likely results, but only I can discover what best fits my "circumstances and character,"[46] presumably by discovering what is most satisfying to me. Although choice informed by models and experience won't *guarantee* a happier life, it may be argued that no better system for promoting happiness could be devised.

However, the proposal should also appeal to those who are persuaded (by Mill's contented pig, Robert Nozick's experience machine,[47] and the like) that no purely "subjectivist" account of individual good is viable, and who are attracted to more Kantian views. For it might be argued that where choice is informed in this way people will be more likely to choose a *fitting* life, a life that fits their individual natures and potentials. Mill himself claims that freedom is essential if people are generally to "grow up to the mental, moral, and aesthetic stature of which their nature is capable."[48] On such a view, happiness is at best an *index* of welfare, a sign that we have "come down where we ought to be,"[49] as the Shaker hymn has it.

Or it might be urged that it is not the expected consequences of the choice which validate it, but its conditions: the fact that it is the choice of a rational agent made under conditions that respect such agency. Respecting your agency is partly a matter of not allowing my idea of what's appropriate restrict your options. But such "benign neglect" is not enough. We do not respect agency in the full sense unless we are prepared to work toward lifting other limitations on options, such as poverty and ignorance, and toward improving people's ability to understand and assess the options they have.

People who are interested in foundations will not want to leave it at that. They will not be satisfied until they have decided which, if any, of these rationales is correct and how a full account of it might qualify the proposal. However, if we agree that something like it is reasonable, we may not need to choose between different rationales. Indeed, if we can get Kantians and utilitarians to agree that it's desirable for people to shape their own lives under conditions that will help them choose wisely, so much the better. We can proceed to considering how we might best arrange for that with the backing of these ethical traditions. Presumably, this goal dictates both extensive individual liberties and various measures designed to improve the prospects that they will be well used. The latter, revealed through the sort of inquiry sketched above, might include entitlements to education and basic necessities, the encouragement of diverse ways of life, the protection of our cultural, artistic, and natural heritage, and continuing public debate concerning how such commitments are best realized.

There is clearly some tension here between not getting in people's way and enlarging their options and ability to make informed choices. All of the measures just mentioned cost something in terms of individual freedom; directly or indirectly, they limit what people might otherwise do. Some people—like the developer whose taxes support designation of historical districts that place valuable building sites beyond his reach—pay twice. There is certainly room for debate about how far we should restrict individual freedom generally in the interest of seeing that it is not wasted. However, it's important to see that there's something worth debating here. Neither Kantianism nor utilitarianism justifies indifference to what individuals make of their freedom, even where others are not at risk.

I think we can now glimpse the outline of an ethical case against privatizing public lands, which I shall fill out in the final chapters.

First, argue that privatization does not follow from plausible versions of Kantianism or utilitarianism. At best, private property rights only incompletely institutionalize concern for rational agency or individual welfare. What they miss is important and must be provided for in some other way. Respect for rational agency, one's own and that of others, requires more than respecting property rights (or, more generally, negative rights against interference). Privatization might help consumers get what they want, but arranging for better satisfying desires can be expected to enhance individual welfare only if those desires are well formed. In the next chapter,

I shall elaborate on why concern for agency or welfare can't be reduced to respect for property rights, which, accordingly, must be supplemented with other institutions.

Second, argue that the current federal land-management system helps meet this need, so that privatizing public lands would, from either ethical perspective, be a poor exchange. If, as I have suggested, both Kantianism and utilitarianism call for giving people freedom to shape their lives, under conditions that encourage wise choices, then both Kantians and utilitarians should view privatization as a mistake. The current system serves aspects of agency and welfare that are, at best, not promoted by freedom in the market and, at worst, threatened by it. In the last chapter, I shall defend collective management of public lands in such terms.


## NOTES

1. Marion Clawson and Jack L. Knetsch, *The economics of outdoor recreation* (Washington: Resources for the Future, 1966), at 214.

2. B. Delworth Gardner, "The case for divestiture," in *Rethinking the public lands*, ed. Sterling Brubaker (Washington: Resources for the Future, 1984), 156–80 at 159.

3. Perhaps this is what Gardner means in describing economic efficiency as a "scientific paradigm." Id., at 158. However, this does not distinguish efficiency from equity, for it is possible to develop standards that give precise meaning to claims of the form "*II* is fairer than *I*." See Allan M. Feldman, *Welfare economics and social choice theory* (Boston: Kluwer-Nijhoff, 1980), Chapter 8.

4. Richard L. Stroup and John A. Baden, *Natural resources: bureaucratic myths and environmental management* (San Francisco: Pacific Institute for Public Policy Research, 1983), at 2.

5. If "*X* is good" *means* I approve of *X*, then it is hard to make any sense at all of (a) wondering whether *X* is good or (b) commending *X* to others. Unfortunately, objectivism also has its problems: if values are "out there," (a) how do we apprehend them and (b) why should apprehension lead to valuing? The classical statement of these difficulties is David Hume, *A treatise of human nature*, ed. L. A. Selby-Bigge (Oxford: Clarendon, 1888), at Book III, Part I, Section I. For recent attempts to get around them, see Geoffrey Sayre-McCord, ed., *Essays on moral realism* (Ithaca: Cornell University Press, 1988).

6. Richard A. Posner, *The economics of justice* (Cambridge, MA: Harvard University Press, 1981), at 65–66.

7. Stroup and Baden, note 4 *supra*, at 3. In "The privatization debate: an insider's view," *Cato Journal* 2 (1982), 653–62 at 662, Steve H. Hanke describes "[t]he real issue in the privatization debate" as "the choice . . . between private property and individual freedom versus public ownership and serfdom."

8. Arguing generally against attempts to rationalize the social order, F. A. Hayek writes: "Nor can the choice of the appropriate set of rules be guided by balancing for each of the alternative set[s] of rules considered the particular predictable favourable effects against the particular predictable unfavourable effects, and then selecting the set of rules for which the positive net result is greatest; for most of the effects on particular persons of adopting one set of rules rather than

another are not predictable." *Law, legislation and liberty* (Chicago: University of Chicago Press, 1976), Vol. II at 3.

Although he explicitly rejects utilitarianism (Id., at 17–23), Hayek's argument for liberty and free institutions fits the rule-utilitarian model. He holds that: (a) the average individual will be better off, i.e., will be more likely to attain her ends, as individuals are free to use their local knowledge in pursuing their ends; (b) social institutions should serve individuals: where we can see how to modify the social order to do better by them in this sense, we should do so; and (c) critical reflection on historical "experiments" in social organization indicates that certain institutions, viz., constitutional democracy and the free market, will best serve individuals.

9. R. M. Hare, *Moral thinking* (Oxford: Clarendon, 1981).

10. Hume, note 5 *supra*, at 477.

11. John Stuart Mill, *Utilitarianism, Liberty, and Representative government* (London: Dutton, 1910), at 17 (*Utilitarianism*, Chapter II).

12. Adam Smith's claim is not so extravagant. "By preferring the support of domestic to that of foreign industry, he intends only his own security; and by directing that industry in such a manner as its produce may be of the greatest value, he intends only his own gain, and he is in this, as in many other cases, led by an invisible hand to promote an end which was no part of his invention. . . . By pursuing his own interest he frequently promotes that of society more effectually than when he really intends to promote it." *An inquiry into the nature and causes of the wealth of nations*, ed. Edwin Cannan (New York: Modern Library, 1937), at 423 (Book IV, Chapter ii, Paragraph 9).

13. Mill, note 11 *supra*, at 13 (*Utilitarianism*, Chapter II). For a tale of liberation from self-absorption, see Tolstoy's *Resurrection*. "It was so different in the old times, when the only center of interest of Dmitri Ivanovitch Nekhludof was himself and everything bored him to extinction. Now all his occupations were centered in the affairs of other people and not his own, and everything interested and charmed him, and there was always enough to do." Lyof N. Tolstoy, *Resurrection* (New York: Crowell, 1911), Book II at 113 (Chapter 30).

14. Immanuel Kant, *Grounding for the metaphysics of morals*, James W. Ellington, trans. (Indianapolis: Hackett, 1981), at 13 (A401).

15. Id., at 36 (A429).

16. T. M. Scanlon suggests that *some* rights have a utilitarian basis in mistrust. "Rights, goals, and fairness," in *Theories of rights*, ed. Jeremy Waldron (Oxford: Oxford University Press, 1984), 137–52 at 151.

17. Mill, note 11 *supra*, at 55 (*Utilitarianism*, Chapter V).

18. Mill, note 11 *supra*, at 74 (*On liberty*, Chapter I). "To have a right . . . is, I conceive, to have something which society ought to defend me in the possession of. If the objector goes on to ask, why it ought? I can give him no other reason than general utility." Id., at 50 (*Utilitarianism*, Chapter V).

19. Mill, note 11 *supra*, at 58 (*Utilitarianism*, Chapter V, second note).

20. Kant, note 14 *supra*, at 37 (A430).

21. Onora O'Neill, "The moral perplexities of famine and world hunger," in *Matters of life and death*, 2nd edn., ed. Tom Regan (New York: Random House, 1986), 294–337 at 323–24.

22. Ludwig von Mises, *Human action: a treatise on economics* (New Haven, CT: Yale University Press, 1962), at 207.

23. Id., at 12.

24. Id., at 884.

25. Kant, note 14 *supra*, at 31 (A423).

26. Thomas Nagel, "Death," in *Mortal questions* (Cambridge: Cambridge University Press, 1979), 1–10 at 5.

27. Arthur Conan Doyle, "The adventure of Charles Augustus Milverton" *The complete Sherlock Holmes* (Garden City, NY: Garden City Books), 667–80. To gain knowledge that will allow him to save his client from ruin, Holmes woos her blackmailer's maid with false promises of marriage.

28. For a utilitarian view of our relations to non-human animals, see the writings of Peter Singer, e.g., *Animal liberation* (New York: New York Review, 1975) and *Practical ethics* (Cambridge: Cambridge University Press, 1979).

29. Posner, note 6 *supra*, at 53.

30. Henry Sidgwick, *The methods of ethics* (Chicago: University of Chicago Press, 1962), at 111–12 (Book I, Chapter 9).

31. Richard Brandt, "Welfare: the concept, measurement, and interpersonal comparisons," *A theory of the right and the good* (Oxford: Oxford University Press, 1979), 246–65 (Chapter 13), at 247ff.

32. Id., at 249.

33. "The orthodontists are driving up the cost of instruments to the point where young musicians simply can't afford them." Joseph C. F. Lufkin, consultant to Sotheby Parke Bernet, a New York auction house, quoted in "Early violins, the latest in collectibles," *The New York Times*, 14 January 1979, C2.

34. Mill, note 11 *supra*, at 9 (*Utilitarianism*, Chapter II). For a thought-experiment that challenges *any* identification of my good with how things feel or seem to me, see Robert Nozick's discussion of the experience machine in *Anarchy, state, and utopia* (New York: Basic Books, 1974) at 42–5.

35. Kenneth Arrow, e.g., writes: "The viewpoint will be taken here that interpersonal comparison of utilities has no meaning and, in fact, that there is no meaning relevant to welfare comparisons in the measurability of individual utility. . . . Indeed, the only meaning the concepts of utility can be said to have is their indications of actual behavior." *Social choice and individual values*, 2nd edn. (New Haven, CT: Yale University Press, 1963), at 9. Arrow is here laboring under the self-imposed burden of *verificationism*, the doctrine that identifies the meaning of a statement with its empirical content, identified in turn with the set of observations that would verify it. This doctrine is too strong: many statements we understand quite well, including the doctrine of verificationism itself and most scientific claims, have no empirical content in this sense.

36. Brandt, note 31 *supra*, at 253ff.

37. Id., at 255.

38. ". . . some *kinds* of pleasure are more desirable and more valuable than others. It would be absurd that while, in estimating all other things, quality is considered as well as quantity, the estimation of pleasures should be supposed to depend on quantity alone." Mill, note 11 *supra*, at 7 (*Utilitarianism*, Chapter II).

39. Id., at 8.

40. Id., at 9.

41. Id., at 10–11.

42. "Whoever supposes . . . that the superior being, in anything like equal circumstances is not happier than the inferior . . . confounds two very different ideas, of happiness, and content. It is indisputable that the being whose capacities of enjoyment are low, has the greatest chance of having them fully satisfied; and a

highly endowed being will always feel that any happiness which he can look for, as the world is constituted, is imperfect." Id., at 9.

43. Id., at 8.

44. Mill, note 11 *supra*, at 125 (*On liberty*, Chapter III). "A man cannot get a coat or a pair of boots to fit him unless they are either made to his measure, or he has a whole warehouseful to choose from: and is it easier to fit him with a life than with a coat, or are human beings more like one another in their whole physical and spiritual conformation than in the shape of their feet?" Id.

45. Id., at 115. Mill argues that we benefit from the freedom of others, since we can learn from their example. "There is always need of persons not only to discover new truths, and point out when what were once truths are true no longer, but also to commence new practices, and set the example of more enlightened conduct, and better taste and sense in human life." Id., at 122.

46. Id., at 116.

47. See note 34 *supra*.

48. Mill, note 11 *supra*, at 125 (*On liberty*, Chapter III).

49. The context is:

'Tis the gift to be simple, 'tis the gift to be free
'Tis the gift to come down where we ought to be
And when we find ourselves in the place just right
'Twill be in the valley of love and delight.

Aaron Copland, *Old American songs*, First set (London: Boosey and Hawkes, 1950).

# 7

# The Ethics of Privatization

> In essence, the argument in principle for disposal of the public lands is this: Each person knows best what is best for him or her, and, therefore, the best system is one that permits the real preferences of individuals to be revealed and implemented. With rare exceptions, the ideal mechanism for implementing these preferences is a private marketplace where each individual expresses his or her desires through bidding. Private ownership advances this goal, and public ownership impedes it.
>
> Joseph L. Sax[1]

Insofar as arguments for privatization can be read as appealing to general ethical conceptions, they acquire greater depth and, perhaps, respectability. The argument from productivity suggests a rule-form of preference utilitarianism: by changing institutions (in this case, by substituting private property rights for collective management of public lands), we'll promote people's welfare by enabling them better to satisfy their desires. But we can also glimpse in the recommended institution of private property rights a more Kantian commitment: where I can acquire what's yours only with your willing consent (and generally in exchange for something of mine you value more), I can't treat you simply as a means, at least in certain respects.

However, in my view, such appeals do little to advance the argument for privatization; on the contrary, they reveal weaknesses in it. The property rights recommended by privatization advocates provide for individual freedom but not for its wise use. They do not help people to treat humanity *in their own persons* as an end or to form desires *worth* satisfying. There is an opening here for arguing that privatization is a bad idea, not because the current system, despite appearances, is relatively efficient or the cost of dismantling it is too great, but because what we'd get is inferior in a more basic sense to what we now have. Public land management promises greater protection of our natural and cultural heritage than the market—at least if we can resist the seductive suggestion that it be *marketized*, i.e., that we aim to allocate the resources of public lands as would an ideal market. Furthermore, the opportunity to define and defend values in public debate rather than simply buying what we happen to prefer (and can afford) is one we should, in our own interests, preserve.

It is primarily on such grounds that I oppose privatizing public lands. To get this argument off the ground, we must allow that *what I'm interested in* can differ from *what's in my interest*. I shall spend much of this chapter meeting objections to such a distinction and arguing that the free market can't be expected to help people take an interest in what's in their interest. In the first two sections, I consider utilitarian and non-utilitiarian justifications of property rights and indicate why they are of little help to privatization advocates. In the middle two sections, I review grounds for criticizing desires and consider objections to limiting people's freedom for their benefit. In the final two sections, I indicate why markets can't be expected to alter preference for the better and how non-market institutions might help to do so.

## THE EFFICIENCY CASE FOR PROPERTY RIGHTS

Those who advocate privatization generally do so in the belief that private property rights are the best solution to the problem of scarcity. Where wants outrun the resources available to satisfy them, the best social response, they claim, is to divvy up the resources by establishing property rights in them held by individuals. The resources of public lands are certainly scarce in this sense; there is no way to manage them so as to please everyone. So suppose we disregard various claims—some a matter of legal right, others based on expectations deriving from historical use—that might constrain what we may do with these lands and simply view them as comprising a big pot of resources at the disposal of society. What should we do with them? Privatization advocates suggest that instead of having land-management agencies administer this pot for our benefit, we should simply divide it up. Don't we know better than they what we want?

More generally, they argue that a free market based on private holdings will generate the best allocation of whatever resources are available to society. We will, of course, have to invest resources in maintaining such a system: property rights must be secure, contracts enforceable, competition insured, etc. Additional social investments, for example, in public roads, education, pollution control, R&D, etc., may be justified on grounds of efficiency or equity. But such investments should advance the satisfaction of desires—or perhaps, in addition, their more equal satisfaction. Of any proposed departure from the free market, we should ask: is this going to enable people to do better in terms of satisfying their desires? Investments designed to *improve* people's desires, rather than improving their chances of satisfying the ones they have, will be rejected. In the view of privatization advocates, when I seek to "improve" your desires, I am simply confusing my good with yours.

This line of argument is utilitarian: a system of private property rights to federal lands is recommended for its effects, reckoned in terms of the good of individuals. The best society is that in which individuals fare best, and, it's claimed, they'll fare best if they are free to pursue their individual ends in a free market. Individual good is conceived in terms of desire-satisfaction: individuals fare better as they consume according to plans they prefer. The part of this argument that most interests me is its identification of my good with the satisfaction of my desires. But I shall first consider other grounds on which it might be criticized.

Utilitarianism reduces the right to the good, which it identifies with the good of individuals. The efficiency argument for property rights takes these individuals to be human beings: it is only their welfare that counts for anything. This assumption invites challenge from two directions. First, one might argue that certain *groups* of human individuals—families, communities, societies, nations, etc.—are not just instrumental to the welfare of their members, enabling them to secure benefits not otherwise available. Instead, they have a good of their own: they may prosper or decline, and their fortunes do not reduce without residue to the fortunes of their members. Second, one might similarly propose that some *non-humans* (or systems with non-human components) may be harmed or benefitted in a way that does not resolve into human harm and benefit; accordingly, they should not be regarded simply as resources. Abusing non-human animals may be bad for the humans who do it, but it's worse for the victims; and similar claims have been made on behalf of trees, rivers, ecosystems, etc.[2]

I shall not raise such objections, partly because it's difficult for me to make sense of them and partly because I believe that much of their force can be preserved with a sufficiently broad notion of the good of human individuals. I have heard it claimed that midwestern farmers practice "plant slavery," but it is hard to see why manipulating the natural tendencies of plants and ecosystems counts as injuring *them*. They don't mind, and it's not because they have been engineered into the life of a contented pig: they simply don't have the equipment to experience any sort of life. If *A* is not a conscious subject, there seems to be no *point of view* we can ascribe to *A*, and thus no way of quieting the doubt that what we claim to be in *A*'s interest merely reflects our own interest in *A*. Since there is no reason to believe that trees, rivers, ecosystems, or groups of humans are conscious, there is no reason to think that any of them has a good of its own. If so, utilitarians need worry only about the good of humans and certain other animals.

However, "*X* has no good of its own" does not entail "We should regard *X* merely as a resource or a tool." It may, in fact, be that we'll do ourselves the most good by treating *X as if* it had a good of its own that constrains our use of it. Ernest Partridge, for example, argues that "fundamental to the human condition is a need to care for things outside oneself"[3] and that the natural world can help satisfy this need:

> paradoxically, wild species are valuable "to us" precisely to the degree that they are valued and admired not for *our* sake and gratification but for *themselves*—for *what* they are. . . . To the degree that we "lose" our self-awareness in the contemplation of the wild—and thus cast aside the impudent question, "But what good is all this to *us*?"—to that degree we gain the fullest advantages of visiting wild places, or even merely knowing that they exist, free, undisturbed, and wild.[4]

This sort of argument suggests that concern for human welfare, broadly conceived, may have roughly the same implications as concern for the imagined good of trees, families, ecosystems, nations, *et al*.

Accordingly, I shall not challenge the efficiency argument for property rights on the ground that such rights serve only *human* good. However, since its reduction of social to individual good is a bit vague, one may worry that property rights won't do much good for *some* of us. We can assure that individuals are free to pursue their ends in a market economy in many *different* ways, simply by altering who has what property to begin with, and some distributions of property rights will leave some people pretty badly off. What I can get in a free market is obviously limited by what I have to offer in exchange and how costly it is to effect transactions. Even being able to sell her *teeth* didn't do poor Fantine much good,[5] and the difficulty of converting dispersed willingness-to-pay into ready cash will frustrate purchase of such public amenities as the "rural character" that people who live in my town say they want preserved.

I'm inclined to think that there's some basis here for objecting to privatization, though I shall not put much weight on it. Privatization advocates will insist that grossly unequal holdings or transaction-cost barriers to the movement of resources do not argue against property rights but only against certain distributions of them. This may be true, but the fact that we can *talk* about arranging for equity in holdings, or about getting around barriers to the movement of resources by putting stuff into the hands of those who value it most to begin with, does not mean that we can or will *do* these things. Nor is it out of the question that, in replacing one system of rights to use federal lands with another, we'll actually make holdings *more* unequal and *raise* transaction costs. Let us consider the problems of (1) equity and (2) transaction costs more closely.

1. Privatization advocates, who aren't very explicit about how federal lands would pass into private hands, do not emphasize distributional issues. Perhaps this is because, like many economists, they think of equity as a political issue, not an economic one. The general idea is that society can adjust for unequal holdings and still enjoy the productivity of a market economy by redistributing income through the tax system.[6] If we agree that someone should have an annual income of $X to meet her basic needs or to support her addiction to live performances of grand opera, then we can tax ourselves to provide it. Redistribution, no doubt, has limits. As taxes become "confiscatory," people are said to lose their incentive to work, or at any rate to report their income. However, unless redistribution is suspected of having some significant effect on productivity, economists generally take little professional interest in it; it is someone else's problem.

To correct what is perceived as inequity, economists prefer grants of cash, rather than goods and services, because cash is more efficient. Why have the government act as a purchasing agent for individuals, buying stuff it thinks they need, when they can do that themselves? This service is expensive, and there will inevitably be some mismatch between what the government supplies and what individuals want or need. Partly for this reason, few economists would be impressed with the suggestion that various public land policies, such as nominal charges for recreation and various commodities, promote equity by providing services for those who can't afford to pay fair-market value. Other things equal, they'd prefer to see the resources managed for maximum return, which could then be distributed in the form of decreased taxes or direct subsidies. And if federal land managers are to maximize return, why have federal managers at all? After all, we can expect private resource holders to maximize return without special instruction. Their property and operations could be taxed to subsidize those thought to be in need, whether they be inner-city residents who now benefit little from federal land policies or ranchers whose way of life may owe a good deal to them.

But isn't this just so much talk? It may be true that we *could* do as well or better by the needy if public lands were privatized, but that does not mean that we *shall*. If doing $X$ and $Y$ would promote some good $Z$, it doesn't follow that doing $X$ alone will promote $Z$. As it is, privatization will close public lands to many who now enjoy their use. Some will not be able to buy the same services in the private market, either because they lack the means or because those particular services are simply no longer available or are not for sale. It is only too easy to imagine the "blissful seclusion" and "unspoiled privacy" now within the reach of anyone willing to walk into a National Forest restricted to "a select few" who are willing and able to pay for an exclusive estate or resort.[7] Privatization will worsen the position of some, whether or not there is a "privatization dividend" in the form of greater net government revenues, which are then distributed to the needy. Furthermore, the fact that we can *imagine* some way of making privatization promote greater equity gives us absolutely no reason to think it will happen. The poor seem to be always with us, ever handy to advocates of various policies.

2. Because transactions can be costly, privatization will also make it more difficult for some consumers to satisfy certain desires. In many cases where people are willing, in aggregate, to meet the owner's price to preserve a wild beach, say, the cost of closing the deal—identifying these people, getting them to pay what they're actually willing to pay rather than taking a free ride with less, creating some legal entity that will hold the property in trust, etc.—will block it; the beach will end up being sold to a developer. In effect, such transaction costs remove certain goods from the market: you will not be able to acquire that beach, even in partnership with others, whether you want it for walking on a winter's day or merely for the satisfaction of knowing that that piece of the natural world is beyond the reach of "progress." This is the conventional economic argument for public parks, zoning for historic districts, government support of the arts, etc.: it is too costly to bring willing buyers and sellers together.[8]

Or suppose your use of your property spills over onto mine, as in the logging and fishing case discussed in Chapter 4, and you'd be willing to stop in exchange for what I'd be willing to pay to have you stop. Then we'd both be ahead if I paid and you stopped; this exchange would put resources—my stream, your woods, and whatever resources my payment commands—to uses that better satisfy our desires. However, it may be costly to negotiate such deals, particularly where more than two parties are involved, and these costs may be high enough to block beneficial exchange of resources. If these cases could be anticipated in advance of privatizing public lands, we might adjust the initial pattern of holdings accordingly: maybe I should get, along with my trout stream, a property right in your woods that allows me to veto certain uses of it. But, of course, we can anticipate only a few of the cases in which spillovers direct resources to sub-optimal uses. So again one might argue for a government presence: instead of having parties negotiate directly for the exchange or qualification of private property rights, have them make their case for use-rights to public land to some agency like the USFS, whose economists could then estimate what use of resources best satisfied the desires of consumers.

I don't know whether privatization would, in practice, promote equity and efficiency, though I doubt that misgivings on this score can be shown to be groundless. What interests me more at this point is why anyone should care one way or the other. After all, the sort of preference utilitarianism that seems to rationalize efficiency isn't very inspiring, and it doesn't help much to introduce corrections for equity. If resources are more efficiently used as they better satisfy desires *but no constraints are placed on the content or origin of desires*, why is efficiency worth promoting?[9] Wouldn't it be better to *waste* the resources I command than to use them to support a *wasted life*, such as one of dissipation? If equity is conceived in terms of equally satisfying the desires of different people, however that is made out, then isn't the value of equity also conditional? If some desires *I* may have are more worth satisfying than others, more worth committing resources to satisfy, then the same will be true of *us*. Before we arrange for better or more equitably satisfying desires, shouldn't we first inquire into the conditions under which people are likely to form desires worth satisfying and then attempt to arrange for those conditions?

## NON-UTILITARIAN ARGUMENTS FOR PROPERTY

This problem cannot, I think, be evaded by moving to a non-utilitarian perspective. Respect for persons, I have argued, requires more than respecting negative rights against interference, just as concern for welfare does. In this section, I contrast utilitarian and non-utilitarian approaches to property rights and indicate why privatization advocates can expect as little support from the latter as from the former.

A standard criticism of utilitarianism, noted in the previous chapter, is that it does not seem to respect persons. Utilitarians have attempted to meet this objection by arguing that rights have a utilitarian justification. But where this justification runs in terms of efficiency, as in Harold Demsetz's account, rights needn't embody much respect for persons. Demsetz develops the solution to spillovers associated with Ronald Coase into a general rationale for property rights: "the primary function of property rights is that of guiding incentives to achieve a greater internalization of externalities."[10] Suppose you and I use a lake to which nobody has a property right: you use it for bird watching, I use it for target practice. My use may harm you (as when my skeet shooting frightens away your waterfowl) or benefit you (as when I practice on the snapping turtles that take your birds). But these harms and benefits are external to my decisions: I don't lose by harming you or gain by benefitting you. Property rights internalize these external harms and benefits: I pay for harms I impose and am paid for benefits I confer. If I have shooting rights at the lake, then I may blast away as I wish, but I thereby lose whatever you're willing to pay me to forgo that pleasure; if instead you have birding rights, then I must pay you for the harm I impose. In either case, we can expect there to be less shooting at skeet and more shooting at snappers.

To the extent that harms and benefits are internalized, I have an incentive to act so as to maximize aggregate net benefits. I'll take harm and benefit to you into account because our property rights convert them into harm and benefit to me. So it may look as though property rights designed to internalize externalities institutionalize respect for persons: insofar as property rights internalize externalities, they lead me to take you into account. Furthermore, Demsetz's notion of property rights is broad enough to include all the rights anyone would want to ascribe to individuals, for "property rights specify how persons may be benefitted and harmed, and, therefore, who must pay whom to modify the actions taken by persons."[11]

But if the rationale for property rights is internalizing externalities (or, more generally, maximizing aggregate net benefits), rights needn't go to those who'd have them if their function were to uphold respect for persons. It seems to be a matter of indifference to Demsetz whether I'm a free man or a slave (whether I own my labor or you do), as long as "ownership includes the right of sale"[12] and enterprising slaves can negotiate to buy their freedom on the basis of "the expected return to them of being free men."[13] If I'm your slave and you refuse my best bid for freedom (perhaps because I can't find anyone willing to invest much in my freedom, perhaps because you enjoy lording it over me), then you value the right to command my labor more than I do, and it will stay with you. If there's reason here to prefer that I hold this right to begin with, it's not that my holding it will prevent you from treating me simply as a means. It's either that my labor is worth more to you when I hold it (because I'll work harder) or that transferring rights may be costly. For Demsetz, the difference between freedom and slavery is simply a difference in the distribution of wealth.

Property rights constructed on such a utilitarian basis can't embody respect for persons, even if respect for persons is stripped of Immanuel Kant's idea that I owe myself respect. If you hold rights to my labor or other aspects of my person (as in the infamous *droit du seigneur* of folklore and opera), then I must pay you to secure respect for my person. And whether I can acquire these rights does not depend on me but upon others: upon whether what others are willing to pay for the resources I command (or would command, if I had those rights) exceeds what you are willing to accept to give them up. We may say that if you retain rights to my person, it is because you value them more; but that may be only because the value I attach to something can be no more than what I can pay for it. Anyone who thinks of certain rights as embodying respect *owed* to individuals will find this totally bizarre.

Demsetz could respond to this sort of criticism by removing such "personal" rights from the scope of his theory: let them be justified by appeal to respect for persons, but appeal to efficiency to justify the others— the ordinary ownership of *things* that come to mind when we speak of property rights. However, what emerges from this sort of justification may not be very much like our ordinary idea of ownership. Ordinarily, to own something is to *control* a more or less complete bundle of rights to use it. What's required by the efficiency approach to property rights is that each use-right be held by someone. But there is no reason to assign the whole bundle of use-rights to one person (for example, to give one of us title to the lake rather than, say, giving me the right to shoot on Saturdays and you the right to watch birds on Sundays), unless divided ownership wastes resources. To be sure, divided ownership might raise the cost of assembling certain rights; or it might raise the cost of resolving conflicts between uses. On the other hand, undivided ownership is also costly. Owners of bundles of use-rights are likely to regard them as indivisible, so I'll typically have to buy rights I don't want in order to get the ones I do. Even where owners are willing to divide ownership, it may be costly to do so. If we're going to re-shuffle bundles via exchange, why not save the exchange costs and, wherever possible, simply assign use-rights to those who value them most at the outset?

On this view of property, federal land management already gives us property rights in public lands, save that they are generally non-transferable. Maybe privatization would shift the distribution of use-rights in a productive way, but showing as much is a very messy business. Is there no way to justify a stronger and more ordinary notion of ownership, which might at the same time advance the privatization argument? If we think of owning $X$ as *controlling* its uses, then ownership looks like the exercise of agency. Can we perhaps argue that respect for persons, for rational agents, demands carving up public lands into private domains for individuals to control?

This approach does not look promising to me. In the previous chapter I argued that respect for persons includes respect for agency in one's own person, which obviously cannot be institutionalized in any system of negative rights against interference. Later in this chapter I shall suggest that certain features of the federal land-management system promote respect for agency in one's own person. Moreover, this system appears to provide plenty of room for the exercise of agency. I am free to use public lands in many ways; I may also participate in the political and legal processes that fix what uses are permitted.

One may try to argue from persons to property in other ways, but I doubt that any argument of this kind can underwrite privatization. The most celebrated of these arguments is John Locke's: by mixing my labor with some "unowned" resource, I make it *mine* in certain respects.[14] But Locke is really no help to privatization advocates. John Christman has pointed out that Locke himself did not think his argument justified what Christman calls "full ownership."[15] If I mix my labor with $X$, I acquire a use-right to $X$ and may rightfully exclude your use of $X$; but I do not thereby acquire a right to *transfer X* to you or to *derive income* from $X$ in other ways, rights entailed by full ownership of $X$. In Locke's view, any right to transfer and derive income from property arises from a *social* contract, and such contracts may differ. Federal land management would be OK with Locke, at least insofar as it recognizes historical use-rights. Indeed, he explicitly indicates that his argument does not apply to land that is "common by Compact, i.e., by the Law of the Land."[16] He intends it to cover only such appropriations from what God gave to mankind in common as occur before the establishment of civil society.

Furthermore, privatization according to Locke is subject to a couple of provisos, which in effect require that my removal of $X$ from the common not worsen the position of anyone else. As I argued in dismissing the Pareto criterion, there is certainly no reason to think that public lands could *now* be privatized without worsening the condition of *somebody*. The only way to make it remotely plausible that nobody will suffer is to reckon condition in terms of something like income. But this is misguided, since my condition can be worsened by rendering some consumption plans infeasible, even if my income increases, as when you close my favorite fishing stream. And it won't work anyway, since *somebody's* income is sure to be lower than it would otherwise have been.

Arguments like Locke's aren't strong enough to justify privatizing federal lands because they basically aim to show that private property is *permissible*, not that it's *required*. To argue from persons to privatizing public lands, one would have to show that retention was (i) a violation of persons (ii) best redressed by allowing individuals to appropriate public lands. But the prospects for establishing either (i) or (ii) appear to be nil.

## GROUNDS FOR CRITICIZING DESIRES

I have suggested that appeals to efficiency beg the question of why we should care about better satisfying desires, given that people can desire anything, and that certain aspects of federal land management can be justified as investments in bettering desires. Similarly, appeals to individual liberty beg the question of how we, who are not so fortunate as Minerva, are to acquire the wisdom to use our freedom well; it makes sense to sacrifice some freedom in order to learn how to use what remains, and some of the limitations on liberty that collective management entails may be justified in this way.

Now this line of argument presupposes a distinction between what I *do* desire (value, take an interest in, etc.) and what I *should* desire (value, take an interest in, etc.). Let us recall the possible grounds for such a distinction.

Suppose I desire something; on what basis could this desire be criticized? The easy answer is: getting what I want involves some sort of harm to others, as when I want you dead. When privatization advocates claim that establishing a free market in the resources of public lands will better satisfy the desires of consumers, they don't mean these. They agree that such desires don't count and will want the rights that underlie the market to protect people from them.

Now is the easy answer the *whole* answer? Or may we sometimes say that, regardless of its implications for others, my desire for something is one I shouldn't have? On what basis could such a judgment be made? Again, there is an easy answer, viz., *consistency*: if my desire for $X$ conflicts with my desire for $Y$ (I love rich food, but I also want to lower my LDL cholesterol level), then something has to give. However, consistency is not a very strong constraint; I can clean up inconsistencies and still end up with strange desires. Is there any basis for judging consistent desires, however strange, to be *inappropriate*?

One kind of affirmative answer appeals to *autonomy*: desires I have but which I have not *authored* are desires I should discount. If I want something, not because I have fitted it into a considered plan of life, but because you have it or I'm addicted to it or clever advertising creates in me a desire for it, then *I* have no reason to get it. Such desires are not *mine* at all. A second sort of affirmative answer appeals to *welfare*: desires whose satisfaction would diminish my welfare are not good for me and on that account are desires I should not have. This line of argument presupposes some account of individual welfare. Happiness is the usual suggestion, for we frequently revise our preferences on the basis of how it felt to satisfy some desire. Yet a third type of affirmative answer appeals to *excellence*: desires that are not worthy of my gifts or the kind of thing I am are desires I shouldn't have. This approach needs some account of worthiness; if it's a matter of "being all I can be," then we need some account of that.

Autonomy, welfare, and excellence are all very difficult notions, and there may be tensions between them. Nonetheless, they have a real pull, and it's worth trying to incorporate them into a condition of appropriateness for desires. At the end of the previous chapter, I suggested that desires might be rationalized by a plan of life of one's own devising, informed by an understanding of one's gifts and circumstances and the lives they make possible. This proposal respects autonomy, inasmuch as the individual has the last word: there is no ground for objecting that a desire for something which passes the harm and consistency tests is nonetheless a desire I should not have, *provided* I have arrived at it in this way. However, the proviso reflects concern for welfare and excellence, since someone whose plan of life was suitably informed would be more likely to live a rewarding and worthy one.

This is a sketchy standard, but I don't think it's vacuous or implausible—though perhaps its plausibility owes something to its sketchiness. It does appear to have some general policy implications. If I'm to devise a plan of life informed by an understanding of its possibilities, I'll need some help: living examples, a chance to try various things on for size, retreats to gain perspective, some sort of safety net, etc. A wide variety of government programs—education for all, whether they want it or not; grants for the arts; nature preserves; compulsory seat belt laws; historic preservation; federal land policies that subsidize certain activities or ways of life; etc.—can, I think, be justified in part as helping us to make better choices for ourselves.


## PATERNALISM

The idea that my desires may be inappropriate, that my interests may not be in my interest, will strike many people as dangerous. For it seems to open the door to paternalistic intervention, or to manipulation excused as such. Friedrich Hayek observes that it is "possible to declare almost any interest a general interest and to make large numbers serve purposes in which they are not in the least interested."[17] Richard Stroup and John Baden complain about "[t]he intellectual violence directed at individual freedom by [the] elitist view [that] preferences expressed in and by the market are often wrong."[18] Even social institutions designed to enable the individual to make good use of his freedom will involve restricting it, either directly or indirectly. I have to wear a seat belt, or be prepared to pay the fine; I can't buy a condominium on the rim of the Grand Canyon, no matter how much I'm willing to pay; I must contribute, via taxes, to the support of the arts and the lifestyle of western ranchers what I would otherwise spend on other things; I have to devote time to debating the costs and benefits of various proposed restrictions on freedom.

Although critics are correct in pointing out that restricting people's freedom for their benefit is a risky business, it is not easy to show that a concern for individuals is best served by letting them fend for themselves in a free market defined by freely transferable property rights to whatever we can imagine transferring. In this section, I consider and respond to a couple of objections to benefitting people by restricting the scope or operation of the market. The first denies that it makes sense to restrict people's freedom for their benefit, the second that we can pull it off.

1. The boldest defense of freedom against limitations designed to improve people's use of it is simply to refuse to distinguish between what's in my interest and what I'm interested in. Who, it may be asked, makes this

distinction? Isn't it always somebody *else*, who is merely imagining herself in my position and rejecting my choices because they are not the ones she'd make? Doesn't the distinction rest on a confusion of her good with mine?

I do not believe so. Anyone who steps back from his own life will recognize the distinction. With sufficient detachment, we'll see ourselves pursuing things that, on reflection, seem unworthy, or at least unworthy of the amount of attention we give them. I wish I had a Leica R6 and spend time monitoring its astronomical price in photo equipment ads, although on reflection I doubt that I'd be any happier if I had one or take discernibly better photographs than I now do with my ancient Pentax. And there are doubtless lots of other weaknesses that critical self-examination would expose in my case. People often recognize that they are in the grip of various compulsions, addicted to alcohol, drugs, unhealthy foods, success, consumer goodies, etc., that they would be well rid of. The fact that it does not occur to others to question the direction of their lives is not, alas, good reason to think that all is well with them.

As I have suggested, it's hard to divorce my good completely from my desires, to make sense of something's being in my interest which I wouldn't freely endorse, given enough information, critical skills, etc. But the qualification is crucial. What's in my interest is what I would, *under certain conditions of "rational choice,"* take an interest in. It's not easy to describe these conditions exactly, much less bring them about. Still, by analyzing our own failures, considering what might be learned from history, and sifting the accumulated wisdom of those who have observed the human condition from antiquity, I think we can make some progress—enough anyway to be skeptical of claims that people don't need any help making rational choices because their choices are already rational. Richard McKenzie, arguing against mandatory seat belt laws, insists that "[t]he vast majority of these people [who don't wear seat belts] have decided that they prefer to take the risk of more serious injury in the event of an accident in order to remain unencumbered and more comfortable without their seat belts buckled."[19] But it is quite beyond belief that these "decisions" are rational. People are generally ignorant of basic physics and accident statistics. Moreover, even if I have this information, it needn't *inform* my decisions, since many of us operate under the illusion that "it can't happen to me." Our subjective estimates of probabilities frequently bear little relation to relative frequencies. There may be reason to oppose mandatory seat belt laws, but only those who are desperate will look for it in the rationality of motorists' choices.

McKenzie, like most economists, understands "rationality" in a rather weak sense. Consumers choose rationally if they buy the best bundle they can afford, where "best" means most preferred and preference is formally well-behaved (transitive and anti-reflexive). Thus, Fred Glahe and Dwight Lee claim that you can choose to drink crank-case oil and not be irrational unless you pay a higher price for it than you had to.[20] More generally, people are rational if they maximize utility in the weak sense that there is no course of action they could have chosen that, on balance, they prefer to what they do choose. Only the formal constraint on preference keeps this notion of rationality from collapsing into triviality, since when people act at all, they do what they most prefer: that is what distinguishes agency from mere behavior. The problem with it is that preferences are taken as given, no questions asked. It's hard to find in McKenzie and other critics of attempts to protect people from their irrational tendencies much concern for the substance of preferences or the conditions under which they are formed. Glahe and Lee, in fact, dismiss the idea that preferences can be irrational as *self-serving*, noting that "it is common to derive satisfaction from comparing your preferences to other people's preferences and smugly concluding that you are more rational than most."[21]

2. A more promising defense of the market against restrictions in scope or operation would concede the obvious—that what I want and what's good for me may be different and that for this reason my choices may be irrational—but argue that we cannot do better by people than to secure the sort of liberties that define the free market. It is not possible to arrange things so that my choices are always rational, my interests always in my interest, but, it might be urged, the market system comes closer than the competition. This is basically a rule-utilitarian argument to the effect that people will, on average, though not of course in every case, be better off if their freedom is constrained only by duties to respect the liberties of others and to contribute to maintaining the system of liberties from which they benefit. It is supported by positive and negative considerations.

On the positive side, freedom to make mistakes is also freedom to correct them; people can learn from their errors and those of others and then change course, at least if they don't need society's approval. Glahe and Lee observe: "We can all recall exchanges we have made that we regretted after the fact. But people learn from their experiences, and only the most accomplished incompetents would consistently engage in voluntary exchanges that detracted from their well-being."[22] Like many economists, they seem to understand preference in terms of (expected) satisfaction: I prefer $X$ to $Y$ *because* I expect more satisfaction from $X$.[23] My preferences are, as it were, working hypotheses about what will bring me happiness, to be adjusted as necessary: if $X$ proves disappointing, I'll probably alter my preference for it. If my good is happiness, as this suggests, am I not *generally* in the best position to know what contributes to it and what doesn't? Can we really hope to improve on this feedback system? I may misjudge my interests, but can *you* do better for me? And even if you can, how do I know that? As every parent knows, it's not easy to get people to acquiesce to choices they think aren't *theirs*, even when they're for the best.

On the negative side, attempts to improve people's use of their freedoms by directly or indirectly restricting them are apt to be counterproductive, at least in the long run, or simply to benefit some at the expense of others. Restrictions on freedom tend to lead to further restrictions; start with seat belt laws, the thinking goes, and pretty soon people will be talking, without apology, about requiring cowboys to wear riding helmets. Government programs of all sorts tend to enlarge themselves, and at some point they will start to consume more than they deliver; I doubt that the USFS would have much difficulty finding work for twice as many employees as it now has or that it would be long before it wished for more. Finally, allowing government to "take sides" by promoting certain preferences or deciding that certain resources are best used to help people make better choices seems to put some, maybe all, of us at risk. The Wise Use people and others charge that land-management agencies are subject to "capture" by those with "elitist" agenda. The Professional River Outfitters Association urges customers to complain to their senators and representatives about a proposed River Management Plan regulating float trips through the Grand Canyon:

> Our taxes pay salaries to the same Park Service bureaucrats who are trying to shut us off the river. All they can say is they want everyone to have "a wilderness river running experience". Obviously, *they* presume to decide what that will be, and you're going to get *that* or *nothing at all*.[24]

In the same vein, Nathan Edelson warns of allowing the National Parks to become "virtual fiefdoms" for preservationists, whose "approved list" of park activities do not, in his view, include "going car camping with your family, having a drink in a park dining room with a great view, or staying overnight in a bed with sheets at a park lodge."[25]

Such arguments justify caution, but they hardly show that we should give up on the idea of modifying people's freedom for their benefit. That people can learn from their mistakes is clearly no argument against laws mandating the use of seat belts or prohibiting the use of crack cocaine. Those who are dead or addicted are in no position to learn from their mistakes. But aren't these rather special cases? Surely the argument that mistakes are largely self-correcting looks better when we put them aside, particularly when we ask what it is that we might do instead. Still, their own choices can lead people into a position somewhat analogous to that of the addict: a life that is not very rewarding but from which it is difficult to extricate oneself. Perhaps you've never experienced anything better; or perhaps, like a friend who douses much of what he eats with hot sauce, you've become so habituated that you no longer recognize alternatives as better; or perhaps you do see that life could be better but there are now too many obstacles. Mistakes of this sort won't be self-correcting.

Whether we can collectively do anything to head them off or to fix them later is another matter, but I do not think the problem is hopeless, at least if we don't demand too much of solutions. If rational choices are those people make under the "right" conditions, then we need only seek to identify these conditions and to secure them for everyone. Assuming that we may expect better choices as actual conditions approach the "right" conditions, we should aim to improve the conditions under which people choose and act. It is not hard to come up with plausible hypotheses about what contributes to rational choice. Some of them appear to have little bearing on the issue of privatizing public lands. For example, while we surely want people to feel that they *have* a future and that their choices *matter* to it, the many things we could do to restore hope to the millions of people trapped in places like the South Bronx seem to be largely independent of what happens to, or on, federal lands. But other hypotheses seem relevant.

Surely people are more apt to choose wisely if they can step back and critically reflect on the direction of their lives. Some progress can be made toward such critical detachment, I suggest, by involving people in determining the use of some resource held in common—public lands, the family vacation, town property-tax revenue, the community orchestra's rehearsal time, and so forth. If you are to bring others to your point of view, you must first figure out what your view is and then how to make it attractive to them. Clarifying things for yourself, imagining how others will react, devising arguments that will persuade them, anticipating objections, and so forth are all exercises in critical thinking and detachment. And there is likely to be some transfer of these skills to situations in which it is oneself whom one must persuade.

Furthermore, certain things have the power to take us out of ourselves, to release us from unrewarding preoccupations while at the same time engaging our interest and curiosity. Institutions that preserve these things for such restorative "use" can be regarded as investments in bettering desires or improving the use of our freedom. Consider what Edward Abbey says about one of the sandstone arches in Arches National Park, Utah:

> A weird, lovely, fantastic object out of nature like Delicate Arch has the curious ability to remind us—like rock and sunlight and wind and wilderness—that *out there* is a different world, older and greater and deeper by far than ours, a world which surrounds and sustains the little world of men as sea and sky surround and sustain a ship. The shock of the real. For a little while we are again able to see, as the child sees, a world of marvels. For a few moments we discover that nothing can be taken for granted, for if this ring of stone is marvelous then all which shaped it is marvelous, and our journey here on earth, able to see and touch and hear in the midst of tangible and mysterious things-in-themselves, is the most strange and daring of all adventures.[26]

It would, I think, be hard to construct a better argument for the National Parks that protect such features.

What Abbey means by "a different world" is the non-human, natural world. But a similar case can be made for preserving various human artifacts—a stone wall in the New England woods, ghost figures staring from pictographs in the canyons of the Southwest, Shaker furniture, a portrait by John Singer Sargent, the voices of Appalachian mountain folk in song, Chicago's Monadnock Building, the desolate site of the massacre at Wounded Knee. Such things may also open our eyes, this time to a different world of human experience, certainly wider and perhaps deeper than one's own.

## LEAVING IT TO THE MARKET

If those who see themselves in a "world of marvels" are less likely to waste their time here, then concern for individuals dictates concern for the marvels of the world, human and natural. Unfortunately, the protection of our natural and cultural heritage can't be entrusted to the free market. Even if the most valued use, reckoned in terms of aggregate willingness-to-pay, of some resource is its contribution to this heritage, transaction costs will often block that use. Without zoning restrictions, the city block now graced by a Louis Sullivan or Henry Richardson building would be put to more profitable use, a parking garage, perhaps. Without museums subsidized by taxes—or the corporate grants that so displease free-marketeers who believe the business of firms is profit-maximization—their paintings, sculpture, and other artifacts would be dispersed to private collections and generally inaccessible. It is government intervention, not private initiative, that honors Theodore Roosevelt's advice on the Grand Canyon: "Leave it as it is. You cannot improve on it. The ages have been at work on it, and man can only mar it."[27]

Furthermore, it's not at all clear that actual consumer preferences dictate the preservation of these things. Imagine an idealized market without the friction of transaction costs, where things really are put to their most highly valued uses; can we be sure even that the Grand Canyon would be left as it is? A sense of wonder is one of the "things of the child" that people tend to lay aside as they grow up. Unfortunately for us, we often come to adulthood with little appreciation for things that enrich life and, what is worse, little interest in discovering what they might be. I'm not thinking only of the disadvantaged; there are plenty of others who are badly brought up. Money talks, and if these are the people with money, we shouldn't expect too much from a system advertised as "encouraging the movement of resources to more highly valued uses."[28] Those aspects of our heritage threatened by our foolish preferences will evidently be protected only by taking them, in one way or another, off the market.

Its champions ascribe many virtues to the free market, but the ability to improve people's preferences isn't among them. They will insist that the market is *neutral* with respect to preferences, that it is driven by, but does not alter, them. As in the world of the first fundamental theorem, the uses to which the market directs resources are simply the resultant of the uses to which individual participants direct theirs, where one allocates the resources one controls so as to realize consumption plans one prefers. If preference formation really is exogenous to the market, we obviously can't look to *it* to better people's preferences. An environment conducive to forming better preferences will have to be provided for in ways other than by simply instituting private property rights—and the scope and meaning of such rights restricted, if necessary, to make room for them.

Wilderness, for instance, is sometimes seen as a sort of spiritual resource. A sojourn "back of the beyond" may, as Abbey suggests, restore one's sense of wonder and proportion. One can follow Christ and others into the wilderness—if there is some—to gain detachment from and perspective on one's life; those who have made such a retreat often recall the experience as helping them find a "place to stand." The preservation of things that are wholly other and not subject to us—whether we enjoy them or not—is an exercise in humility and self-restraint. Suppose we were impressed by such suggestions (rather than, say, by Joseph Conrad's *Heart of darkness*) and wanted to save the remaining islands of wilderness. Should we listen to privatization advocates and defer to the market? That would be to defer to the very preferences we suspect may need improvement. Suppose one of these islands of wilderness contains oil worth a lot of money: more than what people in aggregate are willing to pay to keep it wild, enough even to induce a private owner like the National Audubon Society to sell out.[29] Then the market, i.e., people's preferences, will dictate its development. If we suspect that preferences may in this way operate against their own improvement, we'll have to look for a way around them, and the market, insofar as it's preference-driven, is not a promising place to look.

## IS THE MARKET NEUTRAL?

Ideology is one thing, reality another. Surely it's a bit naive to view real markets as neutral instruments of individual preference. Surely my preferences owe something to my environment, which of course includes the economic environment. There are at least three potentially bad influences here: (1) advertising, (2) consumer sovereignty, and (3) free-market ideology.

1. The party line on advertising is that it *informs* but does not *manipulate* preference. According to Ludwig von Mises, for example, advertising lets me know of the existence of a new product, but it's completely up to me whether I buy it and keep buying.[30] The notion that advertising just gives consumers information will certainly seem quaint to marketing departments, advertising agencies, and psychologists. The goal of advertising $X$ is to sell $X$; and causing people to want $X$, if it can be pulled off, will sell more $X$ than simply providing them with information about $X$. There seems little doubt that, within limits, sophisticated advertising can make people want things. Surely nobody imagines that Marlboro's dominance of the American cigarette market is due solely to the product rather than the associations created by its advertising campaign.

One might try to save the claim that advertising doesn't alter preferences by viewing marketing as part of production: what consumers buy is not $X$ as it comes off the assembly line but $X$ as it is then presented by the marketing department. For example, people who buy Marlboros don't just buy cigarettes but participation in the mythic rituals of the old West, and their preference for enjoying a bit of fantasy while they smoke explains why the same cigarettes in other packages at the same price wouldn't sell as well.

Now there is something in the idea that advertising alters products to satisfy preferences, but not enough to insulate preference from the operation of the market. What people bring to the market is not a well-defined preference ranking; one could hardly develop that without knowing what's available. Nor can we imagine that my preferences are determined solely by my nature and what's available and owe nothing to their interaction. People bring to the market not only well-defined preferences but inchoate longings, which advertisers attempt to shape and focus. Curiously enough, von Mises' own psychology of action seems at war with his conviction that advertising doesn't alter tastes. In his view, "[t]he incentive that impels a man to act is always some uneasiness,"[31] to which one responds by surveying alternatives to one's present situation and choosing that which one calculates will best remove or diminish this sense of unease. The cause of this uneasiness may be external and beyond one's control. In particular, its source could be advertising, a good deal of which seems designed to foster dissatisfaction with what one has.

2.   Stroup and Baden write that in the market system, "individuals gain by doing what others desire most."[32] My incentive to put the resources I command to their most productive use is that I'll thereby realize the greatest return, to use as I wish. It's this incentive that's supposed to make private landowners good stewards, since

> [a]ny erosion of productive land, any scarring of scenic land, or any destruction of habitat valued by scientists and clubs . . . reduces the owner's wealth . . . by lowering the land's asset value. Land values—that is, the present capitalized value of *all* future services from the land—hold the owner accountable.[33]

Let's set aside various problems with this argument—the fact that spillovers may allow me to shift some costs to others, that transaction costs may prevent the most productive use from yielding the greatest return, that positive interest rates discount the value of future services and, in effect, give the future little voice, that "most productive" has no more normative force than "most desired"—and consider only the tension in the claim that "individuals gain by doing what others desire most." Don't I risk *my* individuality in attempts to gain by doing what *you* desire most? Doesn't it take a pretty strong-minded individual to resist the inducements of the market, to step back and ask where *I* am in all these transactions, making sacrifices to get a job doing what *others* want done so that I can buy what *others* want to sell me?

Doing what others desire most is supposed to be a *means* to satisfying my own desires. If I release the resources I hold (labor, land, etc.) to their most valued uses, I'll be able to buy into the best consumption plan. Unfortunately, in determining which uses are most valued, I may neglect to consider myself. The most valued use of my time isn't writing computer programs at $X$/hour, even if nobody will pay more than $X$ for an hour of my time, if that hour is more valuable to me in some other use than anything

I could buy for $X$. Money values, such as the highest wage my labor could command, reflect *other* people's preferences; they tell me nothing about mine. Yet it's easy to overlook this. It's of course conceivable that those who tell us that they can't afford to take a day off (or that, despite their convictions, they can't afford to refuse employment in the liquor or defense industry) are operating according to some considered plan of life. But it's more likely that, like those Henry David Thoreau saw "buying and selling and spending their lives like serfs,"[34] they have simply lost their grip on who they are.

Even von Mises does not paint a very pretty picture of consumer sovereignty:

> Neither the entrepreneurs nor the farmers nor the capitalists determine what has to be produced. The consumers do that. . . . Their buying and their abstention from buying decides who should own and run the plants and the farms. . . . They are merciless bosses, full of whims and fancies, changeable and unpredictable. For them nothing counts other than their own satisfaction. They do not care a whit for past merit and vested interests. If something is offered to them that they like better or that is cheaper, they desert their old purveyors. In their capacity as buyers and consumers they are hard-hearted and callous, without consideration for other people. . . . The entrepreneurs, capitalists, and farmers have their hands tied; they are bound to comply in their operations with the orders of the buying public. . . . In the conduct of their business affairs they must be unfeeling and stony-hearted because the consumers, their bosses, are themselves unfeeling and stony-hearted.[35]

With such defenders, does the market need critics? Indeed, this sort of observation is apt to lead people to wonder if something *entirely different* from the market wouldn't serve us better. At the least, we need to consider what social institutions might help to counteract these tendencies to callousness and self-absorption.

3. Free-market ideology, insofar as it informs attitudes, isn't so benign either. The free market may harness self-interest for the public good, but the *idea* that we do best for all by doing best for ourselves isn't healthy for anyone. If the system enables us to do good by doing well, then why worry about doing good at all? I can simply look out for Number One, assured that I shall thereby best look out for others. Now, to be sure, my interests may be directed toward others. I may prefer giving $X$ to Amnesty International or Oxfam to spending it in some other way, or I may choose not to work overtime so that I can spend time with my family or volunteer at the local soup kitchen. So if looking out for Number One is a matter of satisfying my desires, it may involve looking out for others.

Unfortunately, these other-directed interests get little support in an ideology that views all values as "personal, individual, and arbitrary," as von Mises puts it.[36] In his view, the businessman who gives a "distressed friend . . . a job in his office, although he does not need his help or could hire an equivalent helper at a lower salary" is just making a personal consumption decision,[37] one not objectively better or worse but just *different* from others he might have made, like spending the money at the track. There is little encouragement here for the other-regarding concerns that seem necessary for rewarding lives.

More generally, talking as if what's in my interest is simply what I'm interested in just makes it less likely that I shall want what's good for me. People—I include myself, of course—are only too willing to believe that they know what's best for themselves. For our sakes, this comfortable belief needs to be challenged, not ignored or encouraged. We all need to stop occasionally and critically consider the direction of our lives and the utility of our attitudes. We need to realize that if others can waste their lives, we can too. If we don't follow Thoreau to Walden, we need to keep in mind why he went there:

> I went to the woods because I wished to live deliberately, to front only the essential facts of life, and see if I could not learn what it had to teach, and not, when I came to die, discover that I had not lived.[38]

I can hear the free-marketeers—some of them, anyway—objecting: "Yes, but what has all this to do with the organization of economic life? Are we to have a market or not?" The answer, I think, is: "Yes and no: a market, but one operating in a matrix of social institutions designed to correct for its limitations and costs." Given a choice between the free market and socialism, conceived as poles, I'd take the market. The arguments of Hayek and others for decentralization seem perceptive, and the world's experiments in central planning have not been inspiring. But surely our options are not limited to (1) a market in everything that could be a commodity, with only such regulation as can be justified as productivity-enhancing, and (2) a planned economy, in which the production and distribution of everything is arranged by some central authority in accord with somebody's notion of who should get what.

Some restrictions on the scope and operation of the market may be justified as being in the interests of individuals regardless of their interest in them. Some things surely ought to be off limits to buying and selling. John Stuart Mill argued that people shouldn't be permitted to sell themselves into slavery;[39] he also thought everyone should get "an education fitting him to perform his part well in life towards others and towards himself," whether he could afford it or not.[40] Things that can help us improve our preferences—things like wilderness with the power to take us out of ourselves—are also candidates for non-commodity status, particularly if threatened by current preferences. Continuing debate on where the market is to end and other institutions begin can also get our attention and encourage critical reflection on the distance between what we *do* and *should* want. Although one might wish for more civility in public debate and decision-making, the "harmony and good will"[41] that private property is supposed, by contrast, to foster, strike me as stifling.

Individual freedom does not come with instructions, and it is difficult for individuals to do it justice. In the free market I may use my knowledge for my own ends, but if these ends are ill conceived it is not going to do me much good. For some, indeed, market freedoms are not at all liberating; we don't need the detachment of popes to recognize that consumerism is a form of slavery.[42] It is to institutions *outside* the market that we must look for help in learning to choose wisely and to avoid this sort of enslavement. I am suggesting that public lands contribute to meeting this need. Federal land classifications can protect some of our natural and cultural heritage, while debate over what classifications are appropriate forces us to articulate and, at least to that extent, reflect on our values. I shall have more to say about this in Chapter 9, after meeting some general criticism of collective resource management in Chapter 8.

## NOTES

1. Joseph L. Sax, "The claim for retention of the public lands," in *Rethinking the public lands*, ed. Sterling Brubaker (Washington: Resources for the Future, 1984), 125–48 at 130–31.

2. See, e.g., Christopher D. Stone, *Should trees have standing?* (Los Altos, CA: William Kaufmann, 1974); John Rodman, "The liberation of nature?," *Inquiry* 20 (1977), 83–131; Aldo Leopold, "The land ethic," in *A sand county almanac* (New York: Ballantine, 1970), 237–64; Kenneth Goodpaster, "On being morally considerable," *Journal of Philosophy* 75 (1978), 308–25; Paul Taylor, "The ethics of respect for nature." *Environmental Ethics* 3 (1981), 197–218.

3. Ernest Partridge, "Nature as a moral resource," *Environmental Ethics* 6 (1984), 101–30 at 118.

4. Id., at 121–2.

5. Victor Hugo, *Les miserables* (New York: Heritage, 1938), Vol. I (*Fantine*) at 180ff (Book V, Chapter 10). John Troyer brought this literary example to my attention.

6. What is known as "the second fundamental theorem of welfare economics" is often taken to show that there is no theoretical tension between equity and efficiency. It states roughly that, under certain restrictive conditions, *any* Pareto-optimal set of feasible plans can be sustained by price-governed production and exchange, provided we move income around appropriately. For a precise statement and proof, see the references cited in Chapter 4, note 8.

7. Quoted phrases from "Hawk isn't for everyone. For which a few of us will be eternally grateful," advertisement for Hawk Inn and Mountain Resort ("where privacy is the ultimate luxury"), *The New York Times Magazine*, 24 June 1990, 20.

8. "The philosophy behind wilderness and national park creation is based on the notion that, if left alone, under-investment in preservation will occur due to both free-rider problems and sheer transaction costs associated with raising capital from the thousands of individual beneficiaries." Peter Nickerson, "Markets for preservation: old-growth and Forest Service auctions," *Land Economics* 66 (1990), 473–77 at 476.

Milton Friedman accepts this sort of reasoning for city parks, since access to their amenities is hard to control, but not for isolated national parks like

Yellowstone, where, he argues, it is easy to make visitors ante up simply by charging admission. Being unable to imagine any other justification for public ownership (e.g., that people who never visit Yellowstone might value its existence), a curious lapse in one so adept at manufacturing justifications, Friedman concludes that such parks should be left to the private sector: "If the public wants this kind of activity enough to pay for it, private enterprise will have every incentive to provide such parks." *Capitalism and freedom* (Chicago: University of Chicago Press, 1962), at 31.

9. Mark Sagoff has similar misgivings. In *The economy of the earth* (Cambridge: Cambridge University Press, 1988), at 107, he says flatly that "the efficiency criterion has no normative basis at all." In order for a more efficient or productive arrangement to be better, Sagoff suggests, it would either have to (1) make people better off or (2) be such as to secure their consent. But "the efficiency criterion has no demonstrable connection with any substantive or normative conception of welfare" (105–6); nor can it be shown that we consent, actually or hypothetically, to be ruled by such a criterion (107ff).

10. Harold Demsetz, "Toward a theory of property rights," *American Economic Review* 57 (1967), 347–59 at 348.

11. Id., at 347.

12. Id., at 349.

13. Id., at 348.

14. John Locke, *Two treatises of government*, ed. Peter Laslett (New York: Mentor, 1965), at 329 (Book II, Chapter V, §27). It is not quite correct to see Locke as laying down conditions on the rightful appropriation of unowned resources, since his view was that the earth was originally the *common property* of mankind, a restricted gift from the Creator to be used for the benefit of all. For a discussion of the implications of this for the social regulation of private land, see Kristin Shrader-Frechette, "Locke and limits on land ownership," *Journal of the History of Ideas* 54 (1993), 201–19.

15. John Christman, "Can ownership be justified by natural rights?," *Philosophy and Public Affairs* 15 (1986), 156–77.

16. Locke, note 14 *supra*, at 333–34 (§35).

17. F. A. Hayek, *Law, legislation and liberty* (Chicago: University of Chicago Press, 1976), Vol. II at 1.

18. Richard L. Stroup and John A. Baden, *Natural resources: bureaucratic myths and environmental management* (San Francisco: Pacific Institute for Public Policy Research, 1983), at 40.

19. Richard McKenzie, "Seat belt laws strangle rights," *The Denver Post*, 9 February 1985, A14.

20. Fred R. Glahe and Dwight R. Lee, *Microeconomics: theory and applications* (New York: Harcourt Brace Jovanovich, 1981), at 114.

21. Id.

22. Id., at 158.

23. They write, e.g., that "the consumption of goods provides satisfaction" and appear to believe that the satisfaction I expect or get from a bundle of goods determines its place in my preference ranking, although they have the standard doubts about quantifying satisfaction and thus saying by how much I prefer $X$ to $Y$. Id., at 102.

24. Quoted in George Cameron Coggins and Charles F. Wilkinson, *Federal public land and resource law* (Mineola, NY: Foundation Press, 1981), at 715.

25. Nathan Edelson, "Conservationists vs. National Park visitors," *The New York Times*, 12 October 1985, at 27.

26. Edward Abbey, *Desert solitaire* (New York: Ballantine, 1971), at 41.

27. From a speech delivered at the Grand Canyon in 1903, quoted in François Leydet, *Time and the river flowing: Grand Canyon* (San Francisco: Sierra Club, 1964), at 84.

28. Stroup and Baden, note 18 *supra*, at 3.

29. Editorially supporting proposals to open the Arctic National Wildlife Refuge to oil exploration and development, *The New York Times* asks: "Is it worth $32 billion to avoid modest ecological damage to this small strip of tundra? That is 100 times the amount Washington spent in 1986 to acquire land for national parks; it is 10 times the annual budget of the national forests and parks combined. If Congress were to hand $32 billion to environmental groups to invest as they wished, they would have many higher priorities before protection for a sliver of the Arctic National Wildlife Refuge." "Is this icy strip worth $32 billion?," *The New York Times*, 17 February 1988, at A22. The sum of $32 billion is the editorial's estimate of what consumers would realize in savings over buying oil from other sources, assuming that environmentalists are right and only 3.2 billion barrels—200 days' national supply—of it are to be found in the refuge.

30. Ludwig von Mises, *Human action* (New Haven: Yale University Press, 1962), at 321.

31. Id., at 13.

32. Stroup and Baden, note 18 *supra*, at 3.

33. Id., at 103.

34. Henry D. Thoreau, *Walden* (Princeton, NJ: Princeton University Press, 1971), at 208. The context is: "Let not to get a living be thy trade, but thy sport. Enjoy the land but own it not. Through want of enterprise and faith men are where they are, buying and selling and spending their lives like serfs."

35. von Mises, note 30 *supra*, at 270–1. This is just one of many judgmental passages in *Human action*, notwithstanding von Mises's claim that all valuation is "personal" and "arbitrary," note 36 *infra*.

36. Id., at 387.

37. That is, if he "owns the whole firm." Otherwise he's mismanaging other people's resources. Id., at 241.

38. Thoreau, note 34 *supra*, at 90.

39. John Stuart Mill, *Utilitarianism, Liberty, and Representative government* (London: Dutton, 1910), at 157 (*On liberty*, Chapter V).

40. "Is it not almost a self-evident axiom, that the State should require and compel the education, up to a certain standard, of every human being who is born its citizen? . . . [I]f the parent does not fulfill this obligation [to provide for the instruction and training of the child's mind], the State ought to see it fulfilled, at the charge, as far as possible, of the parent." Id., at 160.

41. John Baden, "Privatizing wilderness lands: the political economy of harmony and good will," in *Private rights and public lands*, ed. Phillip N. Truluck (Washington: Heritage Foundation, 1983), 53–70.

42. "In the civilization of the rich countries, where there is not only a practice but also a mentality of consumerism, each person can become a slave of this system of life." Pope John Paul II, quoted in "Consumerism a form of slavery, pope says" *The Denver Post*, 17 December 1984, C14.

# 8

# Self-interest and Collective Management

> The public sector provides no incentives for politicians and bureaucrats to resist pressures from special interests or to manage natural resources efficiently.
>
> Richard Stroup and John Baden[1]

Arguments for privatizing public lands that appeal to the virtues of markets don't look very good under close inspection. The free market may, in some sense, maximize the satisfaction of desires. The property rights which define it may, to some degree, institutionalize respect for persons. But such justifications are quite incomplete, for they do not explain how we are to encourage respect for humanity in one's own person or the formation of desires worth satisfying. Before enlarging the market by privatizing public lands, we should ask whether we wouldn't thereby eliminate institutions that help do this. I have suggested that this is indeed the case.

It doesn't quite follow that privatization is a bad idea, for under scrutiny the federal land-management system may not look very good either. The extravagant claims privatization advocates make for markets create unrealistic expectations, but privatization might still improve on what we now have, if that system were as fundamentally flawed as critics like Stroup and Baden allege. In that case, the good I see in it might be outweighed, and we'd have to look for other ways to achieve that good. So in this chapter I consider attacks on the current regime, attacks which appeal to problems that are supposedly inherent in the collective management of resources and are therefore remediable only by privatization. A good deal of it concerns the claim, made by premise 1 of the argument from productivity, that individuals are self-interested. Like the philosophical thesis of determinism,[2] this one challenges us to give a reading that is both true and non-trivial.

As detailed in Chapter 3, privatization advocates argue that, while self-interest rules everyone's behavior, the current system doesn't constrain it in a socially productive way, for it allows people, particularly those with a role in shaping public land policies, to gain by shifting costs to others. After reviewing this argument in the first section, I suggest in the second section that, if self-interest were really as advocates of privatization conceive it to be, privatization would be a hopeless cause and an ineffective remedy to these problems. In the third section, I question the underlying conception of self-interest, arguing that the sense in which people act from self-interest lessens the challenge of disciplining it. While individuals do attempt to promote their own interests, these interests are generally not selfish. Even the sorts of things that people seek for themselves, like status or happiness, must be achieved, and achievement demands something of them. In the fourth section, I note that we generally achieve happiness or status in particular roles, by meeting their performance standards. Accordingly, the picture that privatization advocates draw of self-interested people manipulating the current system for personal gain is distorted. Now these critics may concede that roles bring some accountability into the system, but deny that it's enough or of the right sort. For don't we want public land management to serve the public interest, i.e., the interests of the various members of the public, and wouldn't a market in the services of public lands be more responsive to it? In the fifth section, I review replies to the effect that some of our interests are interests in collective action and therefore could not be satisfied in a market. In the last section, I respond to the criticism that such interests are illegitimate because they are coercive.

## THE EVILS OF COLLECTIVE MANAGEMENT

Politicians who indulge in negative campaigning attempt to make themselves look good by making their opponents look bad, and much of the privatization literature essentially mounts a negative campaign against the federal land-management system. Most privatization advocates don't have a high opinion of government generally; they view it as wasteful and coercive by nature, and prefer as little as possible. Every American taxpayer contributes to the support of federal programs, but some benefit a lot more from them than others. A defense contract may increase everyone's security, but some, in addition, get high-paying jobs, another term in Congress, etc. Those who create and administer government programs owe their livelihood to them, and they are often in a position to protect their interests. Other potential beneficiaries may find that it pays to invest in getting or preserving their "share" of the pie, rather than in more socially productive activity. From this perspective, public land management looks like a way of forcing taxpayers at large to contribute to the benefit of a rather smaller group: those who devise and administer management policies and those who receive the services of public lands. In addition, the system encourages unproductive jockeying for benefits. Surely, privatization advocates suggest, we can't imagine that there's no better way to use the resources committed to, and by, this process. Wouldn't the *average* citizen be better off under privatization?

As summarized here, the argument doesn't specify the standards by which we're to judge when resources are better used or people are better off, but its force is largely independent of the choice of standards. The picture it presents of government in action is disturbing whether you think resources are better used as they better satisfy the desires of consumers, or promote better desires, or better secure respect for persons, or whatever. Basically, the argument is that the institutional structure of public resource allocation doesn't constrain the exercise of self-interest to good effect. As Stroup and Baden remind us, "[t]he world is populated by self-interested individuals constantly seeking ways to make themselves better off,"[3] and they, "not large groups or societies, make decisions regarding resource use."[4] We can't expect those who make such decisions to act against their own interests: of the affordable options, they'll choose the one they most prefer.

In the view of critics like Stroup and Baden, the federal land-management system makes too many options affordable for some people. In various ways, decision-makers can shift some of the costs of their decisions to others. Consequently, public land policy tends to serve not the public interest, whatever that might be, but the self-regarding interests of those who have a hand in shaping it: lobbyists, legislators, agency administrators, and others. Furthermore, where public resources are allocated to private use, as they are here, I can gain by getting government to transfer rights to use them from you to me. Stroup and Baden comment that this is "a negative sum game in which the resources spent by some in generating and by others in opposing transfer activity lead to a *net* loss. The private gain of one is more than offset by the other's loss coupled with the unproductive waste of resources used in the process."[5]

The spectacle of people attempting to gain at the expense of others, using resources to increase or hold onto their share of the pie rather than to enlarge it, is not uplifting. Moreover, one's regard for a system that gives people opportunities to "influence the distribution of wealth"[6] in this way won't be increased by noting that such opportunities are not equal, that some people enjoy a positional advantage. However, before concluding that things could hardly be worse, we should ask if this depiction of government in general, and federal land management in particular, isn't a bit of a caricature and whether privatization would solve the problems to which it draws attention.

## IS PRIVATIZATION A REMEDY?

One difficulty with the argument is that if things are as bad as all that, privatization wouldn't do much good—and it's futile to push for it anyway. If, as Stroup and Baden maintain, it's rational for citizens to be ignorant and unconcerned, what chance does *any* proposed reform have? If it's foolish for me, as an individual, to spend time trying to get the current system to put public lands to the uses I prefer, then surely it's even more foolish to take time from more pressing concerns to lobby for privatization. My expected return from this investment of effort is zero at best and more probably negative, unless I get some satisfaction from the effort. And *that* I can also get from working within the current system for however it is I think public lands should be used.

And if I could snap my fingers and have privatization, what then? Opportunities to gain by appropriating other people's things would hardly disappear. In the world of the first fundamental theorem, firms maximize profits because those who own them are self-interested consumers who exercise effective control over their operations. But, except for tiny owner-operated firms, this is fantasy. In general, the owners of firms hire managers to run them. Unless an individual owner controls a large block of stock, she has very little control over what managers do. If she doesn't like the way "her" employees are running things, she can neither give them different instructions nor fire them; such decisions are collective, not individual. All she can do is pay her broker to sell her stock and invest the money elsewhere. As is well known, large corporations (such as U.S. auto manufacturers) offer enterprising managers many opportunities to gain at the expense of other managers and owners. Much of the criticism privatization advocates level at government also applies to them.[7]

If, under the present system, people can gain by getting the rules changed, they can also do so under privatization. Private property rights are defined, upheld, and respected by people. Are we to imagine that privatization will somehow convert self-interest into reverence for the property of others, that the smart money will no longer be invested in attempts to change, or get around, the rules? If the "forces of simple self-interest" are really as "relentless" as Stroup and Baden claim,[8] why would people let the mere fact that what they want belongs to someone else stop them?

The simplest sort of non-market transfer activity is, of course, theft. But I can also take what's yours by getting the state to "attenuate" your rights, or by threatening to do so. Stroup and Baden mention height restrictions on buildings, of which they evidently disapprove.[9] But what precisely is going to stop people from attempting to impose such restrictions on the property of others? A friend of mine was threatened with a lawsuit unless he lowered the roofline of the house he was building in Colorado Springs; his neighbor-to-be thought it would degrade his view of the mountains and was prepared to spend a lot of money to defend his claim in court. Not wanting to spend years in rental housing and who knows how much in attorney's fees contesting the suit, my friend had his house redesigned and the roof trusses he'd already bought sawed up into kindling.

A less direct approach to getting others to do as *you* wish with *their* property without paying them for it is to push for zoning regulations. An appeal to the public interest—in, say, not having wetlands filled or city streets turned into canyons—can sometimes get the authorities to rule out certain uses of property generally. Courts are averse to takings, but it doesn't follow that they are eager to defend private property by throwing out laws that restrict its use or by ruling that such restrictions require compensation. They may simply find a way to rule that restrictions and prohibitions *aren't* takings.[10]

Getting tarred with your own brush is one of the hazards of negative campaigning. Of course, it may be that less sticks to you. So while privatization wouldn't eliminate opportunities to gain from transfer activities, perhaps it would still reduce them. Unfortunately, relying on negative arguments tends to make people lazy, and they frequently have little to say when it turns out, inevitably, not to be a matter of black and white. Privatization advocates need to explain why the energy now directed to transfer activity in the public sector wouldn't simply be redirected to transfer activity in the private sector, if public lands were privatized. So far they have not done so.

## SELF-INTEREST

I have just argued that we cannot expect privatization to banish the evils of collective managment. Here I shall argue that these evils are not as great as privatization advocates would have us believe. I cannot claim much first-hand experience with government, and it may be that I am willing to think better of people than they deserve. But surely there is something a bit fantastic about these critics' vision of the federal land-management system as just another theater in Thomas Hobbes' "war of every man against every man,"[11] where self-interested individuals attempt to wrest advantage from others. Surely this is a distortion. Decision-makers do ask themselves, "What's in it for me?" But that is not the only question they ask. Nor should we agree that there is no accountability in the present system, that only the rule of willing exchange, whereby I must give up what you want in order to secure from you what I want, can effectively discipline self-interest.

In order to think that welfare economics has much to do with welfare, you've got to conflate *what's in my interest* and *what I'm interested in*. Something similar is going on here, I believe: "self-interest" is being read both as *interest in self* and *the self's interests*. When people act, we may say that they choose the alternative they most prefer, all things considered: they do what they most desire or take an interest in, given perceived constraints. If "self-interest" refers to the self's interests in this way, then it is true, though pretty uninteresting, that people are self-interested or act from self-interest. The claim that people are self-interested in the sense of acting always out of an interest in self, that they act always on their own behalf, seems more exciting. But to the extent that it is more exciting, it is also false. Most of our actions are not decided by answering the question "What's in it for me?", unless this question means simply: *which of the options do I prefer, all things considered?* To confirm this, consider your own decisions.

In the world of the first fundamental theorem, consumers are self-interested in a fairly strong sense. Because their choices of consumption plans are assumed to be independent, they can essentially care only about their own consumption. Gifts or charity could be understood as personal consumption: if *A* lets *B* fish on *A*'s land for nothing when the going rate is $50/day, then *A* is (a) releasing this resource to *B* at $50/day and (b) consuming the income of $50/day by giving it to *B*. However, to avoid influencing the consumption decisions of others and violating the independence assumption, gifts must be completely insignificant—a stick of chewing gum, maybe, not a day's fishing. The people of this hypothetical world are not much like us, as even privatization advocates will admit. Indeed, Stroup and Baden tell us that "[t]o assert that individuals are primarily motivated by self-interest merely suggests that when individuals evaluate the projected impact of an action, their first question is, 'How will that action affect the things I value?'"[12] Given this understanding of "primarily motivated by self-interest," it's difficult to argue with their claim that "[i]ndividuals, on average, are predominantly self-interested."[13] Indeed, since I can value *anything*, including satisfying *your* desires, the qualifiers "primarily," "on average," and "predominantly" do no work at all here. However, this notion of self-interest doesn't tell us much about what self-interested individuals are likely to do. After all, Mother Teresa—along with everyone else—is self-interested in this sense.

In order to make government look bad, Stroup and Baden make the apparently stronger assumption that government decision-makers are motivated primarily by interest in self: of the options that their environment allows them, they will pick the one they expect will maximize their personal gain. I say "apparently stronger" because it is hard to understand "personal gain" in a way that makes it both true and interesting that people generally attempt to maximize personal gain. If personal gain is reckoned in terms of wealth, status, or happiness, then either it is false that people generally attempt to maximize personal gain or nothing very exciting follows from it.

Nobody I know is primarily interested in amassing wealth, and I doubt that my acquaintances are unrepresentative or that something strange happens to people when they enter government service. It's as silly to think that Justice Douglas's opinion in *U.S.* v. *Union Pacific* was motivated by some expectation of tangible personal gain as it is to think that Stroup and Baden wrote *Natural resources* for the royalties. Though changes in public land policy may affect the distribution of wealth, to imagine that concern for personal wealth *accounts* for most of the interest in public lands is to falsify people's motivations. When John Muir grumbled about the time and effort he spent on the letters and essays that helped build the movement for National Parks,[14] he certainly was not complaining about the burdens of wealth. You will never understand why he and his present-day disciples act as they do if you think they are interested in amassing or securing wealth. This is also true of many whose interest in federal lands appears to be more "commercial." Ranchers, for example, do not seem to be wealth-maximizers; they would be wealthier if they sold out and did something else.[15]

I am assuming here that "my wealth" means something like the market value of my possessions. This is the popular understanding of "wealth." It may be possible to save the thesis that what generally governs my actions is an interest in increasing my wealth if we move to Richard Posner's understanding of "wealth" (my wealth is the sum, taken over things $X$ that I own, of what I'm willing to accept for $X$) and beyond (let the range of "$X$" include also the various bits of "stock" I have in the present body of federal land policies, for example, the opportunity that I *or others* have to hike in Olympic National Park). As argued in Chapter 4, "my wealth" is then probably ill-defined, but let's overlook that. Perhaps we can still make sense of my wealth *changing* by some amount $\Delta w$ and hold that people always seek to maximize $\Delta w$. However, this move drains the notion of wealth of nearly all explanatory value. To say I'm interested in increasing my wealth is to say little more than that I'm interested in having my desires satisfied, desires which could be quite impersonal, like Muir's desire to preserve wilderness. To say that I take an interest in public lands because public land policies have an impact on my wealth is then to say no more than that I take an interest in them because I take an interest in them.

People may be after status or happiness, but, again, the sense in which this is so does little to advance the argument that our public land-management system allows self-interest to run amok. The picture of self-interest operative here seems to be of people who are after $X$ manipulating institutions to secure $X$ for themselves. But neither status nor happiness is a likely candidate for $X$, for neither of them functions as a thing apart, an end independent of the means by which it is secured. This is obvious in the case of status. Nobody can acquire status *simpliciter*. It is always status in some role—parent, federal judge, conductor, Mafia boss—where roles come with standards of excellence that individuals can do little to alter. There is nothing threatening about individuals who are interested in status, as long as these standards of excellence are socially productive.

The pursuit of happiness is similarly constrained. The classical utilitarians thought that happiness was, in fact, what people sought: what accounts for my choosing $X$ over $Y$, thereby revealing a preference for $X$ over $Y$, is the expectation that choosing $X$ will make me happier. This seems to reduce the self's interests to a particular interest in self, viz., an interest in securing happiness. But even if true, it's not very exciting, for my happiness is not independent of its pursuit. For most people, getting happiness is not like getting to Chicago: there is not a multiplicity of routes to the same end. I may prefer eating to going hungry, but not if I have to steal from you to do so; in such a case, taking your loaf will not make me happier. John Stuart Mill goes so far as to say that the way we get it is "part" of happiness. While, in his view, "there is in reality nothing desired except happiness," we come to desire other things "for their own sake," finding that we cannot obtain happiness without them.[16]

For most people, doing well in the roles they take on or fall into—parent, scholar, church-member, manager, citizen, judge, volunteer fireman, forest ranger, spouse, member of Congress, technician, etc.—is part of happiness. Now people may *assume* particular roles because they think them efficient means to happiness. They may, for example, choose a particular career because they reckon that it will enable them to live comfortably. Or they may join a church, not from conviction, but because they wish to be well-regarded. But very few people can play a role for long without living it. Roles demand certain things of us, and it is difficult to sustain them if we continue to think of them merely as a means to something else. They come with their own standards of performance, and living up to these standards usually displaces whatever motivated our choice of the role in the first place.

But if that was an expectation of happiness, can't one's subsequent choices—going to see your child's school play instead of relaxing at home, assigning your students a paper that will be no fun at all to grade, taking time to compose a letter to your senator, listening to repetitive testimony at public hearings, agreeing to organize a fund-raising activity for your church because it's your turn, rendering a professional opinion that your department-head will not welcome, etc.—still be rationalized as promoting happiness? After all, had I not so chosen, I'd *feel* bad about not living up to the responsibilities of the roles I've assumed. Such explanations seem to me to reverse cause and effect. To a large extent, my roles define for me who I am, and *I* cannot be happy except by doing well in them. If I think some role requires $X$ of me, I'll be most unlikely to explain my doing $X$ in terms of expected happiness. Instead, I'll talk the language of duty or character: I did $X$ because I thought I ought to, because I couldn't live with myself if I didn't. I shall not generally yield to suggestions that I change roles because I'd be *happier* with the new one. What's more likely to move me in this direction is the realization that I'm not doing *well by* a particular role.

## ROLES AND ACCOUNTABILITY

Those who look at the federal land-management system and see only self-interested individuals manipulating institutions for their own advantage seem to have a curiously static view of interests. We are to imagine that individuals are active and institutions passive; that people bring to their social roles some set of desires and values, formed elsewhere, that rule their performance in them; that such roles, while useful in satisfying such interests, have no power to alter them; that compromise never develops into consensus but merely balances opposed forces. But this is incredible. Atoms persist unchanged through various molecular associations, but that is not true of people. Anyone who looks back at his own life will recognize that his desires have been shaped by his affiliations. Successful marriages, for example, require compromises, and those compromises are often institutionalized in altered preferences; we all know couples who have grown together.

Stroup and Baden ridicule the idea that "culture can 'rewire' people so that the public interest becomes self-interest."[17] But there's little doubt that the roles they assume can and often do, in effect, "rewire" people so that their interests include doing well in these roles, which often include promoting institutional goals. Government bureaus capture administrators, for better (Walter Hickel[18]) or worse (Casper Weinberger[19]). Collectives— whether families, academic departments, firms, communities, government agencies, orchestras, clubs, military units, etc.—can hardly prosper as long as their members regard them as merely instrumental to their own prosperity. There must be a sense of shared enterprise, which of course is not something an individual can *bring* to it. Its members must identify with the collective and revise their preferences accordingly. Smart business managers worry about how to instill a sense of loyalty to the firm and pride in one's work. And I suspect that many executives defend their companies against takeovers and government regulation not primarily because they fear they'll end up worse off under the new regime; rather, their sense of *who they are* owes so much to their association with the firm that they take threats to it, or attacks on it, personally.

I am not suggesting that their other interests never influence the way in which people do their jobs or act out their roles. Nobody who teaches at a university can imagine that staffing or curriculum decisions are made only with a view to providing the best education possible, given the available resources. The distribution requirements that are supposed to give students a good general education, whether they want it or not, reflect inter-departmental politics as well: departments that don't have a piece of the action face falling enrollments, loss of positions, and perhaps absorption by other departments. Individual departments offer large lecture-format introductory courses with machine-graded multiple-choice exams, despite misgivings about the passive and inarticulate learning they promote, because such courses free faculty for upper-level and graduate teaching, or research, or spending weekends with their families. Such decisions reflect a variety of concerns and interests. What I reject is the idea that the operative ones are *personal* in some interesting sense. There simply is no sphere of personal interests, external to all of one's roles, that directs one's performance in them. Aside perhaps from basic needs for food, shelter, and medical care, it's hard to find interests that one has that are not interests one has *qua* parent, teacher, researcher, etc.

In itself, this is not much of a reply to critics who see government staffed by individuals who do whatever they can get away with to advance their interests. They can still maintain that *other* interests, whatever their source or content, are apt to overwhelm the interest people take in the responsibilities of their position. Maybe it's better that Colonel Oliver North abused his office for patriotic reasons rather than for personal gain, but it isn't *much* better. What difference does it make if the interests of decision makers are "personal" or "ideological"? It is still *their* interests, and not the *public* interest, which are controlling. "Indeed," William Dennis and Randy Simmons suggest, "it is precisely when actions are the most 'selfless' that they are most irresponsible, for then they are least related to the real needs of real people."[20]

This objection may be partially met by arguing that people generally do take their jobs and the responsibilities of their positions seriously—that the interest people take in doing a good job is not just one of many. I've observed that it's hard to play any role without living it, and for most of us the work we do is not just another role. People, in fact, often have a lot of trouble developing interests *outside* their work; their retirement is a disaster. I wouldn't expect those who thought of their jobs as purely a source of income to enjoy them much; yet surveys indicate that something like 80% of Americans like their work. My university colleagues generally work much harder at teaching than a cynic would predict, knowing that they are tenured and can expect little financial reward for the extra effort. I realize that such considerations fall rather short of a *proof* that people generally take the responsibilities of their positions seriously and that their interest in doing a good job is strong enough to push their other interests aside. But can those who imagine that things are otherwise—that wherever government decision-makers have discretion, their other interests dictate their choice— offer even as much in support of their view?

Of course, this argument does not justify the public land-management system. Doing a good job in a bad cause may just make things worse. However, to the extent that the argument succeeds, it shifts concern from personnel to institutions. We can then debate public land management in conventional terms: What should public land policies achieve? What sort of institutions are efficient means to these ends? What should be the mission of agency $A$, and how should $A$ be structured to implement it? Is the tension between agencies with different missions creative or destructive? If professionalism of one sort or another is to keep decision-makers on the straight and narrow, how do we achieve it? Do the people coming in have the right professional training? What ideology comes with an academic degree in forestry, ecology, range management, recreational education, economics, etc., and is it appropriate? Does the agency encourage or discourage professional judgment?

Furthermore, it suggests that there's more accountability in the system than critics like Dennis and Simmons, who think of accountability in terms of the consumer's budget constraint, imagine. We can say, if we like, that federal judges are accountable to none but themselves; but that does not mean that they will act irresponsibly. I imagine it's quite difficult to be a federal judge without thinking of yourself as such and realizing that your position creates many opportunities to make a fool of yourself: your written opinions will be closely read, overturned or upheld, cited as precedent or dismissed as quixotic, discussed—for better or worse—in the law journals or ignored as routine.

Of course, federal judges are unusually exposed, and others may find it easier to evade the responsibilities of their roles. Imagine a citizen considering whether to take a vacation day to attend an NPS hearing on a proposed management plan for a nearby National Park; a member of Congress considering how far she's prepared to go in committee mark-up sessions to resist language that surrenders federal claims to water rights for

Wilderness Areas; a USFS district ranger considering whether some allotment in his district is being overgrazed and whether he's prepared to take the heat if he rules that it is and orders a reduction in some rancher's herd. Still, I imagine that in such cases self-respect often functions like a critical audience. To the extent that people see themselves as citizens, legislators, forest rangers, etc., to the extent that they identify themselves with such roles, their self-respect will demand that they do their best by these roles.

It would be nice if we could devise empirical tests for these arm-chair speculations, but that will be difficult. A researcher trying to determine the relative frequency with which people live up to the responsibilities of their roles must have access to a representative sample of choice-situations and know what choice a particular role indicates in each of them. I've spoken of roles as if it were clear just what they demand in a particular situation, but often it is not. Furthermore, one's roles may conflict, requiring an assessment of their relative importance. Any survey will reflect the researcher's judgment about what situations are significant and what duty demands in each.

Consider, for example, trying to determine the extent to which legislators meet their responsibilities as legislators. Unfortunately, the role of legislator is not as simple as, say, the role of a violist in an orchestra. Legislators are expected to play a number of roles, few of which come with well-defined performance standards, though they certainly have enough content to generate tensions: legislators are to represent their constituents but also make law in the broader public interest. Even interest groups have trouble rating legislators. Recorded floor votes often give a very incomplete picture of the positive or negative contribution a legislator has made to the cause, whatever it is. Legislation is generally shaped in committee, and committee members—or those to whom they owe favors—have more to say about its shape than others; it may come to the floor under rules that limit or prohibit amendments. Whatever your interest, not all legislation of interest is equally important; and judging how important it is—whether $A$'s good vote against $X$ is worth as much to you as $A$'s bad vote for $Y$—is difficult. But the researcher who wants to rate a legislator's performance, not as an environmentalist or defender of family values or whatever, but as a *legislator*, has more serious problems. It's not that we can say *nothing* about what distinguishes good from bad legislators; but what we can say doesn't translate easily into an account of what a good legislator would have done in a given situation.

## THE INTERESTS OF THE PUBLIC

Such difficulties leave us free to wonder about the extent to which professionalism and self-respect discipline one's non-professional interests. It's clear why privatization advocates and other critics of government want to believe that such constraints are weak and ineffective; it's less clear that such a belief is reasonable. However, "bashing" bureaucrats is only part of their assault on government. They may argue as follows: "OK, set aside venality; imagine even that government decision-makers always act professionally and that professional judgments leave little room for the intrusion of other values. Then public land management will reflect the interests embodied in the institutions of the public land-management system, including the professions of its personnel. But these interests do not add up to the public interest. 'The public interest' means no more than the interests of the several members of the public, and many of these interests won't be represented in public land management. Those on the losing side of decisions—whether legislative floor votes, agency rule-making, or judicial rulings—do not have their interests embodied in policy."

Since wants outrun resources, we can't arrange to satisfy everyone's interests. But, it will be said, the market is more "democratic" than the winner-take-all system we now have, since it allows for a sort of proportional representation of interests. As Stroup and Baden remark: "in the private sector the citizen can 'vote for' tires made by one company and toasters made by another. His choices in the market are precisely recorded."[21] Even if the federal land-management system were staffed by individuals wholly committed to serving the public interest, we should, according to Dennis and Simmons, expect allocations inferior to those of the market. The reason is that land managers lack both information about the real interests of the public and appropriate incentives to correct misinformation. In their view, only when decision-makers "capture the effects of a policy" by prospering when things go well and suffering when they go badly, can we expect policy to be well-informed. As it is "the costs to the decision-maker of misinterpreting available information approaches zero," so "policies will maximize social value by chance, if at all."[22]

One weakness of this argument is that the market is a peculiar sort of democracy, inasmuch as its governing principle is "one buck, one vote." Possibly this objection could be met by income transfers, although it's not clear just what sort of "equality" such transfers should achieve: should I have more to spend than you if my needs are greater, or my tastes more expensive? However that may be, the argument is vulnerable on other grounds. Those who say that the interests of the public would be better served by a market in privately owned resources than by the current federal land-management system must identify (a) one's interests with one's desires and (b) one's desires with one's wants *as a consumer*.

It does not seem to occur to Dennis and Simmons that (a)'s identification is dubious and consequently that meeting people's actual wants in the fullest possible way might not maximize social value. For them, being "other-interested" means no more than being interested in meeting the wants of others. Since the other-interested person is often in a poor position to know what others' wants are, she generally ends up imposing her own wants on them, substituting what she "thinks people ought to value for what is really valued."[23] I have questioned (a)'s equation of one's welfare and the satisfaction of one's desires in the previous chapter and shall return to the matter in the next. Here I want to challenge (b)'s conception of one's desires.

Not all my interests are consumer interests, satisfiable by acquiring some consumption bundle. This is true even if my consumption bundle is enlarged to include what others get as well. Some of my desires make essential reference to collectives like *my country*. I may want to participate in the political life of the nation (e.g., to have my say in how federal lands are to be managed), and I may want it to do something (e.g., to preserve our cultural and natural heritage, or to pay restitution for our treatment of Native Americans). Such desires are not desires for commodities and cannot be satisfied in the market, regardless of how much wealth I command. To propose, as privatization advocates do, that the market be enlarged at the expense of the political sphere is simply to ignore such interests. They cannot be satisfied at all if government is restricted to (efficiently) securing private property rights, insuring competition, lowering transaction costs, and (if we're generous) moving income around.

This sort of argument has been made by Joseph Sax[24] against privatizing federal lands and by Mark Sagoff[25] more generally against the idea that government should merely arrange for the most productive use of resources, i.e., that it should secure the property rights from which markets arise and limit its intervention in them to correcting discrepancies between the real and the ideal (e.g., preserving competition by anti-trust actions, and controlling spillovers by taxing emissions). Their arguments do not turn on a distinction between what people want and what's good for them. They appeal not to desires that people *should* have, but to desires they *do* have, desires that can't be satisfied in markets.

Sax argues that insofar as people's desires legitimate private property rights and the market, they *also* legitimate collective management of federal lands. People want autonomy and prefer certain consumer goods to others. Hence the individual rights that define a private sphere and underlie the market. But people also want to participate in collective action and prefer that collectives act in certain ways; indeed, "one preference people can, and do, have is to yield some of their autonomy *in order* to obtain the benefits of collective action."[26] Hence the political rights that define a public sphere and underlie more-than-minimal government. Insofar as the case for privatizing public lands rests simply on people's desires (we should arrange to maximize the satisfaction of desires), it must confront the awkward fact that privatization *could not* promote the satisfaction of anyone's desire to have a say in how *our* lands are to be managed or anyone's desire that *we* manage them in one way rather than another.

Suppose I want our nation to preserve the old-growth forest that yet stands on federal lands; suppose also that instead of merely hoping this will happen, I want to help bring it about by writing to my legislators or speaking at a public hearing. None of these desires could be satisfied under privatization. Old-growth forest might be saved by private purchase, but not by our nation or through my participation in its political processes. If federal lands were privatized, I might support such purchases by sending money to groups like Save the Redwoods League or The Nature Conservancy. But making monetary contributions to private organizations cannot satisfy my desire to participate in the processes whereby the nation assumes responsibility for preserving its natural heritage. Nor would the fact that old-growth forest is thereby preserved satisfy my desire that the nation do it: a desire *that Y do X* is not satisfied merely by *having X done*.

If such desires can't be dismissed as irrational—and privatization advocates hesitate to tell anyone that her desire for *X* is irrational—then we'll have to argue that they are relatively weak, that privatization would better satisfy people's desires even though it could not satisfy these. If you reckon better satisfying people's desires by the Pareto standard, this is hopeless. If you reckon it by one of the net-gain standards, then you have a very messy problem: it is not clear whether privatization would better satisfy people's desires, even if those desires for collective action are excluded. Furthermore, standards which assess the strength of desires in terms of willingness-to-pay seem inappropriate here. One who desires that *we* act in some way does not want it decided on this basis. That is like deciding whether it's OK for some people to keep others as slaves by determining whether what those who think people should not be bought and sold are collectively willing to pay for the freedom of slaves exceeds what their masters are collectively willing to accept to free them.

Sagoff claims that people have different preferences *qua* consumer and citizen:

> I used to buy mixers in returnable bottles—but who can bother to return them? I buy only disposables now, but to soothe my conscience, I urge my state senator to outlaw one-way containers. I love my car; I hate the bus. Yet I vote for candidates who promise to tax gasoline to pay for public transportation. . . . The political causes I support seem to have little or no basis in my interests as a consumer, because I take different points of view when I vote and when I shop.[27]

We may be able to arrange things so that individuals take a particular point of view and reveal the preference associated with it. If I have an opportunity to vote in a referendum, I may reveal a preference for limiting cash transactions to $100 so as to make life harder for drug dealers. If I can only buy or refrain from buying, I may reveal the opposite preference insofar as I patronize merchants who *don't* have such a policy, because their prices are lower.[28]

Some economists suggest that, since I must put my money where my mouth is, I reveal my *true* preference in the latter case. Hence their suggestion that we may discover whether people *really* want the Arctic National Wildlife Refuge preserved by determining whether what they are collectively *willing* to pay, say in the form of higher pump prices for gasoline, to keep the refuge off-limits to oil and gas development exceeds what they *would* collectively have to pay to forgo the use of the cheaper oil we imagine would be found there. But, in Sagoff's view, this is false: if I reveal a consumer preference, it is simply because I am encouraged (or forced) to think and act as a consumer. Since my preferences derive from my roles and there is no "single comprehensive role the individual plays,"[29] there is *no true preference to be revealed*: no preference that is simply *mine* and not mine *qua* consumer, *qua* citizen, *qua* parent, etc.

It follows that it *makes no sense* to speak of maximizing the satisfaction of preferences, unless preference is relativized to some role. Improvement standards which reckon preference in terms of willingness-to-pay can at best tell us only what course of action best satisfies the desires we have as *consumers*. The fact, if it is a fact, that privatization would, in such terms, improve on the *status quo* tells us only that such desires would be better satisfied by privatizing public lands. The desires we have as *citizens* would not be better satisfied, because their satisfaction requires institutions that privatization would eliminate.

At best, my citizen interests (which have roughly the form "I want us to do *X*") will be represented by corresponding consumer interests ("I want *X* done"). But these representations are incomplete because their satisfaction conditions are weaker. If I think that our nation ought to acknowledge the injustice of its treatment of Japanese-Americans during World War II by designating the site of the detention camp at Manzanar as a National Historic Park, I certainly would not be satisfied if the area were given to representatives of the Japanese-American community and a private memorial established by donations from the victims of our policies. Furthermore, consumer surrogates of citizen interests are unlikely to hold their place in my consumer preference-ranking without the political institutions that support citizenship. Imagine, improbably, that my interest in having some undeveloped federal land preserved as wilderness is recognized simply by giving me title to it and that I am able to pay the local property taxes. Then I may indulge my interest in wilderness by refusing offers from those who want to develop the land in various ways. But it's likely that, with the disappearance of the institutions that nurture it, my commitment will weaken. I'll begin to think about what I could do with the money—and why not, since the land is *mine*?

The arguments of Sax and Sagoff seem to me effective in refuting the suggestion that, since "the public interest" means no more than the interests of the public, government in general and federal land management in particular, serve the public interest only insofar as they arrange for maximizing the satisfaction of consumer interests. The problem is that members of the public have other-than-consumer interests, some of which *require* government institutions for their satisfaction. Those who think we'd be well-rid of such institutions must justify ignoring these interests. To do so, privatization advocates must go beyond the mere existence of desires and argue that some are either illegitimate or not in the best interest of those who have them.

## CHALLENGING CITIZEN INTERESTS

The standard challenge to the legitimacy of the interests Sagoff imagines I have as a citizen points to their coercive implications. I think that *we* should preserve the Arctic National Wildlife Refuge as part of *our* natural heritage; you think *we* should open it to oil and gas exploration to enhance *our* national security. My "we" and "our" include you, and yours include me. One of us will be forced to accept a decision he doesn't like.[30] Privatization advocates have no quarrel with voluntary associations; like other people, they belong to churches, amateur theater guilds, service clubs, the PTA, professional associations, etc. Though it may be costly in various ways to do so, one may withdraw from a voluntary association if one objects to the way it does business or to the actions it takes. It is much costlier, perhaps even impossible, to renounce one's citizenship and move elsewhere if one doesn't like the way things are done in the USA.

One might try to justify the commons in intent, if not in effect, by observing that it does not *impose* a pattern of resource-use on anyone. When the private use of public land is *regulated*, this is not the case. If I can't bend the rules or get them changed, then I may do as I wish only by becoming an outlaw and risking the sanctions imposed on those caught breaking the law. Alfred Coleman thought he could read federal mining law so as to secure himself a 720-acre homesite in California's San Bernardino National Forest, but the authorities wouldn't go along with it; he lost not only his house— the USFS had it demolished—but the money he spent taking his case to the Supreme Court.[31] Since the rules governing the use of federal lands are made in a complex system of institutions, challenging their interpretation or getting them changed is difficult and costly. If Sequoia National Park were private property, those who wished to turn giant sequoias into tomato stakes might simply strike a bargain with the landowner; as it is, they might as well forget it.

That's fine by me, but there are many other federal land policies that aren't. I'd like to see the demolition of Glen Canyon Dam and the ecological restoration of the canyons drowned by its reservoir, Lake Powell. But there is no chance at all of selling this vision of the best use of Glen Canyon to Congress. At least until Lake Powell is silted up, this notion will remain the stuff of fantasy.[32] Despite reforms legislated in 1990,[33] the USFS will continue to regard Alaska's Tongass National Forest not as the nation's largest rain forest but as a source of pulp and plywood. Although I disapprove of Tongass timber sales, I have to live with them. In fact, I must help to pay for them through my federal income tax, since, like many federal land programs, this one operates at a loss. Were the Tongass private property, I'd be able to bid, along with others, for the uses I prefer.

Doubtless a lot of the forest would thereby be allocated to pulp and plywood production. But, with the elimination of federal subsidies for logging, wouldn't it be less? Besides, I'm also bidding for *that* use every time I buy photographic film or plywood sheathing. In any case, I wouldn't be forced to pay for uses I didn't want.

Dennis and Simmons remark that it is a "serious question . . . whether it is at all appropriate for people to use the power of a democratic, constitutional government to impose their values on society through the allocation of natural resources."[34] They prefer the transactions of the free market, where exchange requires the consent of both parties. Indeed, a standard defense of the market is that it frees us from the whims of dictators or central planning agencies, enabling each to live according to his own values. Ludwig von Mises remarks:

> A dictator may deem the conduct of the consumers rather foolish. Why should not women be dressed in uniforms like soldiers? Why should they be so crazy about individually fashioned clothes? . . . The democracy of the market consists in the fact that people themselves make their choices and that no dictator has the power to force them to submit to his value judgments.[35]

To the extent that environmentalists, ranchers, timber interests and others succeed in getting the federal land-management regime to enforce their visions of the best use of particular public lands, do we not have a dictatorship of taste?

Unfortunately, this line of argument fails to do what it sets out to do, namely, to distinguish citizen interests from consumer interests. Both have coercive implications, or near enough, so it cannot be on *this* basis that interests I have *qua* citizen are ruled out as illegitimate while those I have *qua* consumer are not.

While arguing that the market permits one to live according to one's own ideals, von Mises concedes that this may be difficult, given that "in his capacity as a producer every man depends either directly—e.g., the entrepreneur—or indirectly—e.g., the hired worker—on the demands of the consumers."[36] Still, he points out:

> If a man has a weighty reason for defying the sovereignty of consumers, he can try it. . . . Nobody is forced to go into the liquor industry or into a gun factory if his conscience objects. He may have to pay a price for his conviction; there are in this world no ends the attainment of which is gratuitous. But it is left to a man's own decision to choose between a material advantage and the call of what he believes to be his duty.[37]

What von Mises means by "forced" seems to be what Friedrich Hayek understands by "coerced," namely "such control of the environment or circumstances of a person by another that, in order to avoid greater evil, he is forced to act not according to a coherent plan of his own but to serve the ends of another."[38] In this view, coercion is not simply a limitation of freedom; I am coerced only when someone narrows my options in order to serve his ends. Where options are limited by impersonal forces, as they are in a competitive market, there is no coercion.

I suppose that citizen interests count as coercive by this account. But it is not clear that we should be upset by this, since it is not clear what ethical significance there is in the distinction between coercive and non-coercive arrangements. Why should we object strenuously to slavery but shrug at slave wages? Hayek has an answer to this, but it is essentially a utilitarian appeal to the greater benefits we may expect from limiting intervention in people's affairs to prohibiting their coercive use of others. As such, it may be opposed by appeals to the utility of additional restrictions on people's options, such as those that follow from taking citizen interests seriously.

If "coercion" is understood more weakly as *restricting options*, then consumer interests are also coercive. Serving them requires an apparatus of property rights which restrict freedom and which one is required to support whether one likes it or not. Your freedom is a constraint on mine; when courts rule against me in disputes over where yours ends and mine begins, I'll have to go along with it—and help pay for enforcing any court order against me. Privatizing public lands would enlarge the private sphere at the expense of the public sphere: decisions now made collectively would be made individually. If I value the freedom I now have to participate in collective decision-making more than the freedom to bid in an enlarged market, then in terms of freedom I'd lose by privatization. If *we* choose privatization, *I'll* be forced to accept less.

The argument is no better if we understand "coercion" as the illegitimate restriction of options, for it fails to establish that citizen interests are, while consumer interests are not, coercive in this stronger sense. A proof that people have individual rights that are necessarily violated when others pursue the interests they have as citizens would show such interests to be illegitimate. But nobody has come close to giving such a proof. Assertions of rights do not count as establishing them, and whether rights are rationalized in utilitarian or in Kantian terms—as contributing to welfare or as embodying respect for persons—this line of argument seems totally unpromising.

Privatization advocates are not in a good position to argue that people's citizen interests are bad for them. Their view is that when I criticize *your* desires, I generally do no more than observe that they aren't *mine*. They permit themselves to question the interests of others only on the basis of inconsistency or inefficiency. Accordingly, they may observe that my citizen preferences are at odds with my consumer preferences, and suggest that I "get it together." If I really feel strongly about car dealers who let people buy BMWs with sacks full of twenty-dollar bills, I should take my business elsewhere, realizing that when I buy a car, I'm buying a bundle of services that can include peace of mind. Or they may suggest that some of the things I desire as means to other desired things are not very efficient means, that I could get what I ultimately want in some "cheaper" way. Thus, an economist I know wonders why I hang onto my senile jeep when I could rent one at less expense for the few days a year I use it.

Sagoff could resist appeals to consistency by arguing that even where we can conceive my consumer and citizen preferences to be opposite—*qua* consumer, I prefer *X* over *Y*; *qua* citizen, I prefer *Y* over *X*—they are not in a strict sense inconsistent. The content of the latter is *we should do Y, not X*. It may follow that I should do *Y*, not *X*, but that is consistent with a preference for *X* over *Y* (I should stop smoking; I even agree that I should; but I prefer not to). Still, there is something peculiar about this. If I agree that I should do *Y* instead of *X*, I seem to be committed to the prescription *let Y, not X, happen*! So how can I, except by inattention, maintain my preference for *X* over *Y*, which appears to entail the opposite prescription *let X, not Y, happen*!?

In any case, the most that an appeal to consistency or efficiency can accomplish is an adjustment of citizen and consumer desires; it cannot banish the former. Perhaps I'll agree that someone like myself who deplores suburbanization and lobbies the town Planning and Zoning Commission to encourage cluster-housing surrounded by open space rather than sub-divisions with 1-acre lots shouldn't want to build a new house on a nice lot; so instead I purchase an older house and fix it up. Or perhaps I'll admit that I drive my car more than a good environmentalist should; so I begin commuting to the university by bicycle and arrange to car-pool to a hearing so that I can speak against a proposed expressway. But I need not give up my desire to participate in the political life of my community or nation, or my wish that it act in certain ways.

Such rejoinders are defensive. They may blunt attacks on collective management from those who urge privatization, but they don't yet make much of a positive case for the federal land-management system. To point out that people desire collective action as well as individual consumption, or that privatization and private property are themselves coercive, is to defend the *status quo* as *no worse than* the proposed alternative. This might be defense enough, considering the costs of replacing it with something else. However, we can do a bit better by arguing that the current regime is *superior* to what privatization would bring us. Privatizing public lands—or managing them as if they were private—is not in anyone's interest, whether or not it would better satisfy some of the interests he happens to have. In the final chapter I shall add to what I have already said in support of this claim.

## NOTES

1. Richard L. Stroup and John A. Baden, *Natural resources: bureaucratic myths and environmental management* (San Francisco: Pacific Institute for Public Policy Research, 1983), at 23.

2. Determinism claims roughly that the past determines the future, or somewhat more precisely that initial conditions determine subsequent conditions. For discussion of whether there is some way of understanding "determines" so that the thesis is both true and interesting, see John Earman, *A primer on determinism* (Dordrecht: D. Reidel, 1986).

3. Stroup and Baden, note 1 *supra*, at 55.

4. Id., at 8 (I've reversed the order of the clauses).

5. Id., at 13.

6. Id., at 3. The context is: "Government is able to engineer huge wealth transfers with a minimum of violence. There is, naturally, competition for control of that exploitative potential. . . . In most systems, the best investment available to individuals is in the political process. By influencing government, one can influence the distribution of wealth."

7. Joseph Sax makes this point in "The legitimacy of collective values: the case of the public lands," *University of Colorado Law Review* 56 (1985), 537–57 at 555.

8. Stroup and Baden, note 1 *supra*, at 26.

9. Id., at 8.

10. See, e.g., *Just* v. *Marinett Co.*, 56 Wis. 2d 7, 201 N.W. 2d. 761 (1972). However, courts are less inclined to do so than they once were: Presidents Reagan and Bush were able to appoint a lot of like-minded federal judges, and "anti-taking" legislation has made headway at the state level. See "Environment laws face a stiff test from landowners," *The New York Times*, 20 January 1992, A1; and "Resolving property 'takings'," *The New York Times*, 23 August 1992, C1. Two recent Supreme Court cases on regulatory takings, *Nollan* v. *California Coastal Commission, 483 U.S. 825 (1987), and Lucas* v. *South Carolina*, 112 S.Ct. 2886 (1992), are discussed in Sandra Bailey, "Land use regulations and the takings clause: are courts applying a tougher standard to regulators after *Nollan*?" *Natural Resources Journal* 32 (1992), 959–75. For somewhat different views on the regulatory takings issue, see "Look who's taking," *Sierra* 78(5) (1993), 43; and Wallace Kaufman, "The cost of 'saving': you take it, you pay for it," *American Forests* 99(11–12) (1993), 17.

11. Thomas Hobbes, *Leviathan*, ed. Michael Oakeshott (New York: Collier, 1962), at 101 (Chapter 13).

12. Stroup and Baden, note 1 *supra*, at 4.

13. Id.

14. Edwin Way Teale, ed., *The wilderness world of John Muir* (Boston: Houghton-Mifflin, 1976), at xiv.

15. ". . . [B]eef prices . . . remain so low that ranchers receive a lower return on their investment than they could obtain in the non ranch economy." William E. Martin, "The distribution of benefits and costs associated with public rangelands," in *Public lands and the US economy: balancing conservation and development*, ed. George M. Johnston and Peter M. Emerson (Boulder, CO: Westview, 1984), 229–56 at 237.

16. John Stuart Mill, *Utilitarianism, Liberty, and Representative government* (London: Dutton, 1910), at 35 (*Utilitarianism*, Chapter IV).

17. Stroup and Baden, note 1 *supra*, at 29.

18. Secretary of the Interior (1969–71) in the Nixon Administration. There was little in Hickel's background in Alaskan politics and real-estate development to suggest that he would take his stewardship of federal lands and resources as seriously as even environmentalists concede that he did.

19. Secretary of Defense (1981–89) in the Reagan Administration. "Cap the

Knife" came to the Pentagon with a reputation for budget cutting as Secretary of Health, Education, and Welfare (1973–75), but found it hard to say "No" to anything on the wish-lists of the various armed services.

20. William C. Dennis and Randy T. Simmons, "From illusion to responsibility: rethinking regulation of federal public lands," in *Controversies in environmental policy*, ed. Sheldon Kamieniecki, Robert O'Brien, and Michael Clarke (Albany, NY: State University of New York Press, 1986), 65–84 at 72.

For a somewhat different view, see William R. Dorgan and Michael C. Munger, "The rationality of ideology," *Journal of Law and Economics* 32 (1989), 119–42. Dorgan and Munger argue that ideological voting in the legislature can serve both the personal interests of the legislator (in being re-elected) and the needs of her constituents (despite its often being at odds with their preferences). Roughly, the argument is that ideological voting solves the problem of rational ignorance; it maintains a persona that enables voters to make a semi-informed choice at the polls without having to invest resources in finding out what candidates think about specific issues.

21. Stroup and Baden, note 1 *supra*, at 24.

22. Dennis and Simmons, note 20 *supra*, at 72.

23. Id.

24. Sax, note 7 *supra*.

25. Mark Sagoff, *The economy of the earth* (Cambridge: Cambridge University Press, 1988).

26. Sax, note 7 *supra*, at 544. "However much people may value having their individual preferences implemented, they are also very interested in expressing themselves through collectivities, though doing so demands a price, and often a quite heavy one, in individualism." Id., at 548.

27. Sagoff, note 25 *supra*, at 52–53.

28. The example was suggested by a story on a New Haven shoe store owner broadcast on National Public Radio's *Morning edition* for 17 September 1990. As his part in the war on drugs, the owner posted a notice in his display window to the effect that drug money wasn't welcome. People applauded but evidently spent theirs elsewhere—the story indicated that the owner was filing for bankruptcy.

29. Sagoff, note 25 *supra*, at 55.

30. Sagoff claims that my preferences as a member of some group G are judgments or beliefs about what any G-member should, as a G-member, want: their form is "*We* should do $X$." Where members of G differ in their beliefs, "they must deliberate together to determine who is right and who is wrong. This way of finding the will of the community may require a vote; the vote settles a logical contradiction between beliefs." Id., at 55.

It is not clear to me whether Sagoff thinks that such a vote can *make it true* that we should do $X$. He appears to hold that it can, provided $X$ is "consistent with a sense of decency and compassion for which there is no analytical or methodological substitute." Id., at 121. After noting that "regulation may strive to make the conditions under which people live and work cleaner, safer, more natural, and more beautiful, because these goals reflect public values and represent a shared conception of what we stand for as a nation," Sagoff claims that such goals are "not hard to justify on ethical or aesthetic grounds." Id., at 101. Do these ethical or aesthetic justifications appeal to public values, or are they different? Could public values be aesthetically or ethically *incorrect*?

31. *United States* v. *Coleman*, 390 U.S. 599 (1968).

32. For an incomplete literary realization, see Edward Abbey, *The monkey wrench gang* (Philadelphia: Lippincott, 1975).

33. Under provisions of the Tongass Timber Reform Act of 1990, 104 Stat. 4426, the USFS is to renegotiate long-term timber contracts and sell only enough timber to meet market demand; some additional portions of the National Forest were given Wilderness protection, but most of it is slated for clear-cutting.

34. Dennis and Simmons, note 20 *supra*, at 82 (note 6).

35. Ludwig von Mises, *Human action* (New Haven: Yale University Press, 1962), at 387.

36. Id., at 286.

37. Id.

38. F. A. Hayek, *The constitution of liberty* (Chicago: University of Chicago Press, 1960), at 20–21.

# 9

# Marketization

> Bureaus specialize in the supply of those services that some collective organization wishes to augment beyond that supplied by the market and for which it is not prepared to contract with a profit-seeking organization.
>
> William Niskanen[1]

As noted toward the end of the previous chapter, the very existence of collective values or citizen interests adds to doubts that privatizing federal lands would better satisfy our desires. But it may also be argued that we are *better* for having such concerns and, accordingly, that privatization would not be in our interest, inasmuch as it would eliminate opportunities for developing them.

Joseph Sax observes that "at a moral and ethical level, collective values can be judged just as personal preferences can be,"[2] though he refrains from judging them. In discussing the desire to be a part of some larger enterprise, he speaks the language of social psychology, not ethics: "there is a great deal of evidence to suggest that one of our strongest urges is to identify ourselves with a source of moral or communal authority, and to subordinate our autonomy to it; that we draw strength from values external to our purely personal convictions; and that we draw values from collective solidarity."[3] Yet Sax clearly thinks that instead of denying this part of "human nature,"[4] we should arrange for its *constructive* fulfillment. And he evidently thinks that giving people the opportunity to join with others of like mind and debate the use of public lands in a broadly democratic system does so.

Mark Sagoff's views are similar: other things equal, it's good for people to develop and pursue common ends. As something of a Kantian, he thinks of communal action as at once constrained *and called for* by respect for persons. The constraint is partially embodied in certain basic rights that communal action must not violate; for example, death threats made by Idaho ranchers against USFS personnel in a controversy over grazing are clearly out of bounds.[5] But Sagoff would argue that respect for persons demands more than merely securing the person and other property of each individual. For it is in the roles they assume that individuals develop the interests and values that give them a sense of who they are, that define them as persons, that give direction and purpose to their lives. To deny individuals a public sphere where they may deliberate and work with others to shape their communities and thereby themselves is to stunt their growth.

We may put the case for public lands briefly and baldly in this way: the present system is preferable to privatization, not because it better satisfies desires, but because in various ways it helps us form better desires. We may benefit from joining with others to define and pursue common ends and from having to defend our vision of the best use of public lands against the arguments of those with a different vision. We may also benefit from the policies that result from these democratic processes.

After filling out this argument a bit in the first section, I shall spend the rest of this chapter considering its implications for public land management—or more precisely, its negative implications. My target here is marketization in its various forms. My general position is that if we look to public land management to help us form better desires, then we should not be impressed by appeals to economic rationality and consumer sovereignty, for these take desires as given. In the second and third sections of this chapter, I consider the impact of marketization on natural and cultural values. In the fourth section, I explore the idea that, while National Parks and Wilderness Areas might be reserved for the sort of "use" I have in mind, multiple-use lands should be zoned for productivity. In the fifth section, I suggest how concern for both natural and cultural values might guide multiple-use management of public range and forest. In the final section, I briefly consider a weaker version of privatization, viz., enlarging the role of private contractors in the management of public lands.


## BETTERING DESIRES

It is difficult for individuals as individuals to have much impact on public land management. To do so, one must join with others, either inside or outside government. What may begin as a purely personal interest—saving a favorite hiking area in a National Forest from being clear-cut, for example, or keeping a mill that depends on federal timber in business—is likely to be enlarged and refined in the process. The agenda I take to a meeting is unlikely to be adopted as the group's plan of action without modification, and, though I may not agree with all the changes, I'm unlikely at the end to see the issue in just the same way I did at the beginning. I won't get the group to work toward what *I* want unless I can argue that it's what *we* want: if I speak of what I want, I get a hearing only because others assume I am speaking as a group member. They will be quick to discount my advice if it appears that this is not so. Even the most self-serving desires are apt to be transformed by this necessity: it's the rare individual who can *use* groups without becoming part of them and adopting their interests as her own.

Of course, it does not follow from the fact that one's interests change in this way that they change for the better. It's only too easy to imagine associations by which one's interests are transformed for the worse, where the values shaped and strengthened by association with others are evil. However, those that come most readily to mind—street gangs, the Ku Klux

Klan, etc.—tend to operate outside both the law and democratic institutions. Internal dissent is not tolerated, and dealings with other groups are generally limited to commercial transactions in which nobody is required to justify anything.

By contrast, those interested in public lands are forced to articulate their interests, to make a case for them, to anticipate and respond to criticism. The federal land-management system gives interest-groups numerous opportunities to advance their visions of the public interest by appealing to legislators, administrators, or judges. Those with different visions must be ready with their own arguments. Federal land-management statutes are drafted by a democratic legislature, generally only after years of proposals, hearings, lobbying, amendments, etc. These statutes often require public hearings on the regulations that land-management agencies write pursuant to them; their actions are subject to judicial review and legislative oversight. Courts have moved some distance toward the view that public resources are to be managed as a public trust, and are readier to hear challenges to the exercise of that trust; legislators and administrators have duties to the public and must be prepared to justify their actions with more than the simple *assertion* that they are acting in the public interest.[6]

The current public land-management system encourages—perhaps even forces—us to articulate and reflect on our values. We should welcome such opportunities, whether stepping back in this way leads us to change the direction of our lives, locally or globally, or to reaffirm it. They are rather less likely to come our way in the market, where it is considered bad form to ask consumers to justify their choices, where "Why do you want $X$?" is at best a request for information that will enable a supplier better to serve a customer. I am not suggesting that grocery cashiers be instructed to challenge shoppers on the contents of their shopping carts, foolish though their selections may be. I am suggesting that we don't need more of give-the-customer-what-he-wants, no-questions-asked than we already have. Modifying the market in this direction is unworkable; maintaining a parallel system where people are forced to do business differently is not.

If fashioning public land policy can contribute to better desires, so can the policies themselves. Some critics regretfully observe that under current management policies public lands do not supply goods and services in the amounts they imagine would be forthcoming, were commodities produced, exchanged, and consumed in an ideal market. They go on to suggest either privatization or marketization. But there is nothing to regret about current management policies not directing resources to their most productive uses if the deviations can be justified as investments in bettering people's desires. Friedrich Hayek defends the market as enabling individuals to make use of the knowledge of others for their own ends.[7] However, insofar as public land policies summarize the conclusions of open inquiry into what sort of management would be most in our interest, inquiry in which citizens must articulate and defend their visions of the public good, the current system also enables individuals to benefit from the knowledge of others.

Suppose we reflect that it's a good thing for people to be taken out of themselves once in a while and observe that exposure to the otherness of the natural world is a particularly effective way of achieving this detachment; and suppose we note that the market system encourages neither detachment nor the desire for it, and indeed that satisfying consumer desires for lumber, minerals, vacation homes, etc., requires subjugating nature. Then we might well consider setting aside National Parks and Wilderness Areas, limiting recreational development of them, banning overflights by aircraft, enforcing pristine air-quality standards for them, using devices other than price of admission to ration their use, etc. Or suppose we reflect that it's good for people to compare others' sacrifices with their own, to reflect on the uses and abuses of power, to wonder about human progress and their own contribution—or lack thereof—to it. Then perhaps we'd do better to preserve historic battlefields as memorials rather than letting the real-estate market convert them into shopping malls and planned recreational communities. Or suppose we conclude that individuals and individuality flourish in communities and ways of life with links to the past or roots in the land; and suppose we notice that these are threatened by what John Wesley Powell called "the rapacity of individuals,"[8] which the market does little to discourage. Then we may turn to historical zoning and subsidized, but regulated, grazing of federal lands.


## MARKETIZING NATURAL VALUES

When it suits their purpose, some environmentalists can be heard appealing to economic rationality—condemning deficit timber sales, below-market grazing fees, water projects with weak benefit–cost ratios, and the like—and calling for the marketization of federal land policies. For example, in a letter to *The New York Times*,[9] Johanna Wald of the Natural Resources Defense Council writes: "Instead of seeking to privatize publically owned lands, we are pressing for fair-market value from the sale of forage and timber grown on them." This, she maintains, would "bring a measure of good economic and environmental sense to a critical problem in public-land management," namely, overgrazing. Unfortunately, what makes good economic sense may make none at all to environmentalists, and they are asking for trouble if they commit themselves to economic values by arguing for an end to below-market grazing fees rather than for an end to overgrazing. They should notice that their adversaries in the Wise Use movement make similar appeals to economic rationality in arguing for an end to deficit operation of the Wilderness System, economic impact statements for preserving endangered species, demand-based recreational facilities in National Parks, etc.[10]

Wald's appeal to the market is strange, because it cannot be relied upon to deliver what environmentalists want—or indeed what *any* interest group wants. What the market delivers in the Pacific Northwest are not preserves of old-growth forest but quick profits from its liquidation. The Japanese and others are willing to pay premium prices for unmilled logs. Timber concerns like the Pacific Lumber Company were attractive targets for takeovers, since the junk bonds sold to finance acquisition could be retired by "reducing inventory," i.e., clear-cutting the woods.[11] Nor do market forces seem to be keeping private timberlands within New York's Adirondack Preserve "forever wild." A developer acquired 96,000 acres of them when Diamond International Corporation was dismembered after a leveraged buy-out.[12]

Richard Stroup and John Baden claim that "it is not the profit motive that has resulted in poor resource management. Rather, poorly defined and enforced property rights have generated faulty signals regarding the value of resource inputs which, in turn, have led to inefficient resource management."[13] But what Stroup and Baden understand by "poor resource management" is not at all what environmentalists have in mind. By "poor" they clearly mean *inefficient*, where resource management is efficient insofar as it satisfies the desires of consumers—and not merely *certain* desires of those consumers who regard themselves as environmentalists. Environmental values will be promoted by efficient markets only to the extent that environmental quality can be purchased in the form of commodities that consumers prefer to others. If they prefer to enjoy "wilderness" from the comfort of home—or producers can't figure out a way to profit from a demand for the real thing that may be large in aggregate but is individually small and dispersed—then the market is going to produce second-home developments rather than Wilderness Preserves in the Adirondacks.

The standard response is to attribute environmental problems to the imperfections of real markets, which we may correct if we are clever enough. The goal of marketizing public land management is approximating an ideal market in the resources of public lands. But not even an ideal market can, I think, be married to the ideals of environmentalists.[14] Do they really want natural values regarded as commodities, to be "produced" as dictated by supply and consumer demand? Is the value of wilderness, for example, to be determined by the desires of consumers, by what they are collectively willing to pay for its services? Is the reason to designate an area "Wilderness" simply that preservation better satisfies the desires of consumers than other uses to which its resources might be put, or is it that we expect that preservation will contribute to *bettering* these desires? If the latter, shouldn't we want natural values safeguarded from the operation of the market, rather than submitted to its "judgment?"

To get a better idea of what marketization might involve, environmentalists should look at Randal O'Toole's *Reforming the Forest Service*.[15] O'Toole argues that the USFS, like all bureaus, tends to do what maximizes its budget.[16] Accordingly, we should seek to arrange things so that government agencies can maximize their budgets only by spending their income in socially productive ways. In O'Toole's view this is not true of the USFS now. Current law allows the agency to prosper by operating the National Forests as tree farms, though in most of them mature timber is worth less than it costs to grow and harvest, even if we don't include as costs the value of forest services that are not, in consequence, delivered. Under provisions of the Knutson–Vandenberg Act of 1930[17] the USFS is allowed to retain from gross timber-sale receipts what it estimates it needs for reforestation, thinning, and wildlife-habitat management at the sale site. The Forest Roads and Trails Act of 1964[18] permits retaining, as "purchaser credits," the cost of designing and building roads to get the timber out. The USFS thus has an incentive to sell timber on steep slopes (a larger reforestation budget) in remote roadless areas (a larger road budget), where costs, both monetary and environmental, are likely to be high but are not borne by the agency.

Environmentalists will nod in agreement, but O'Toole's notion of social productivity is different from theirs: it is just the economic notion of productivity or efficiency. Although he is not as explicit as he might be about his normative commitments, O'Toole's ideal is, I think, the ideal market. His discussion of perfect markets suggests that he has no reservations whatever about *their* social productivity;[19] the problem, as he sees it, is just that real markets are imperfect. However, he argues, these market failures may be mitigated by various devices.

O'Toole proposes that the USFS be replaced by public corporations, which would run individual National Forests. Their budgets would be a fixed share—he suggests two-thirds[20]—of *net* receipts from the sale of forest services, and they would be largely free to offer and price these services so as to maximize budgets by maximizing net receipts. Commodities like timber and forage would be sold only if it were "profitable" to do so. Revenue would have to cover costs, and managers would quickly learn to count as a cost the net revenue lost by not selling competing services instead. O'Toole lumps these non-commodities together under the heading of "recreation." He argues that modest recreation fees—averaging, say, $3/visitor-day—would bring in more net revenue than timber and forage in most National Forests.[21]

Recreation functions here as a surrogate for non-commodity values in the National Forests, but O'Toole recognizes that it is not a completely adequate one. In his terms, what people are willing to pay for non-commodities exceeds the collectible recreation fees, since some of these non-commodities, such as wilderness and wildlife, can be "enjoyed" without actually visiting a roadless area or seeing a grizzly. Accordingly, the amount of such non-commodities "produced" by a National Forest is likely to be "sub-optimal" if they can be sold only as recreation. To correct the operation of the market here, O'Toole would allow a "minimum of prescriptive legislation" like the Wilderness and Endangered Species Acts.[22] Existing Wilderness Areas would be administered by trusts according to provisions of the Wilderness Act. These trusts could enlarge the Wilderness Areas they adminster by outbidding other interests for the development rights to roadless areas of the National Forests, using money raised by fees assessed for the use of these areas.

O'Toole's proposals are designed to approximate a perfect market in the resources of the National Forests, a market in which resources are "put to their highest and best uses."[23] But environmentalists are unlikely to agree that the uses of the National Forests which maximize net revenue in O'Toole's system are their highest and best uses. What people are collectively willing to pay for recreation in much of the Pacific Northwest is less than they're collectively willing to pay for its timber; only by invoking the Endangered Species Act on behalf of creatures like the northern spotted owl could we hope to protect non-timber values there.[24] Wildlife that's not endangered or threatened will count in management decisions only to the extent that it can "pay its way" by attracting paying customers—hunters, fishermen, photographers, bird-watchers, etc.[25]

Although the trusts that would manage Wilderness Areas would be "obligated to obey the terms of the Wilderness Act and to maximize wilderness values,"[26] they could, given O'Toole's casual reading of the act,[27] maximize wilderness values by selling "resources in the wilderness, including grazing permits and minerals" and then using the proceeds to finance expansion of the areas, since "[t]otal wilderness values might be increased if the acres added through purchase of development rights exceeded the acres disturbed."[28] In recreation, as more generally, "[a]llocations between uses would be based on willingness to pay."[29] By this criterion, Mineral King valley, now part of Sequoia National Park, should certainly have been turned over to Walt Disney Productions for recreational development.[30] A recreational use O'Toole does not mention, but for which some people would be willing to pay a great deal, is vacation homesites. Leasing particularly scenic areas for second-home developments might well be the way to maximize net revenue from them, just as the National Inholders Association claims: "recreation residences . . . provide the highest income per acre of any recreation use of the forests."[31] O'Toole remarks that "hikers would be able to choose between using an area open to off-road vehicles or paying a premium to hike in areas with no off-road vehicles,"[32] as if it were only fair that those who seek refuge from a world of machines should pay more than those who seek to enlarge its extent.

Finally, while the federal government would retain title to the National Forests in order to make it easier to correct problems O'Toole hasn't foreseen,[33] public participation in management decisions would be limited to commercial transactions. O'Toole tells us that forest management plans

> will be oriented to identifying and making the best use of opportunities to generate income through sales or leases of timber, recreation, and other resources. Public involvement in the plans will be in the form of proposals to use, lease, or contract parts of each forest for various purposes. For example, a hiking organization might propose to maintain trails, collect fees, and monitor recreation in a particular area in exchange for paying the forest a share of the receipts.[34]

If marketization has an environmental downside, it could still be a good deal, even for environmentalists. Some of the environmental problems with O'Toole's proposal are also problems for the present system. The National Forests of the Pacific Northwest now seem to be zoned for timber, and non-game wildlife doesn't get much attention anywhere. Nonetheless, I think that environmentalists—and others—should not, in the end, go for marketization.

O'Toole believes marketization would make the USFS or its successors "more responsive to public demand and changing tastes,"[35] and I think he is probably right. Indeed, marketization has the potential of making public land policy even *more* responsive to consumer demand than privatization. Private owners, after all, have the option of refusing all bids; because they own the land, they are not just one consumer among many.

Privatization schemes that give conservation groups control of certain public lands have been criticized for this reason. Dolores Martin fears that privatization would not "necessarily lead to an improvement in efficiency." In her view, "[t]he underlying argument for divestiture is that bureaucratic managers do not bear the consequences of the resource mismanagement while the discipline of the private market would force resource owners to take these consequences into account." But "non-profit clubs," should they end up owning formerly public lands, "may be equally unresponsive to opportunity costs," operating, as they do, "within their ideological framework."[36] Martin's view appears to be that willingness-to-pay should rule and that willingness-to-accept should not be allowed to stand in the way: if I own an acre of old-growth redwood forest for which Georgia Pacific is willing to pay $20K, I should ask myself not "Do I prefer enjoying the land to what $20K will buy?" but "Would I bid more than $20K for this if I didn't own it already?"

Of course, there are ways of getting the attention of private owners, such as property taxes.[37] However, marketization allows us to avoid owners and their idiosyncratic tastes entirely. Public resources could, under such a system, be allocated to those who are willing to pay most for them, without having to equate anyone's MWTP with the much higher mWTA she might demand as an owner.[38]

Consumer sovereignty, however, has no place among the ideals of environmentalists. They should be interested not in better satisfying changing tastes but in changing tastes for the better. Nobody who thinks, as they do, that experiencing the natural world *elevates* taste, that

> From these our interviews, in which I steal
> From all I may be, or have been before,
> To mingle with the Universe, and feel
> What I can ne'er express, yet cannot all conceal,[39]

I become a *better* person, can agree that such opportunities should be available on a fee-for-service basis, in the amounts that clear a market driven by actual tastes. An artificial market purged of the veto power of landowners should not reassure them in the least.

Furthermore, buying and selling the services of public lands in a market is a poor substitute for public participation in public land management. In O'Toole's scheme, people would continue to enjoy some of the benefits of collective action, since some of the organizations that now lobby for particular uses of public lands would presumably transform themselves into purchasing agents for these services. But significant benefits would be lost. No one need hear anything that challenges one's assumptions and thereby encourages one to think more critically about them. The present system allows us to think that arguments matter, and this is beneficial even if it turns out that they matter a lot less than we hope. In O'Toole's system, it will be clear to everyone that what counts is willingness-to-pay. Finally, marketization would deny us the sense that we were acting as a nation to determine the best use of national resources.

## MARKETIZING CULTURAL VALUES

We also jeopardize cultural values when we treat the resources on which they depend merely as commodities. Regretting that ranchers do not enjoy the legal protections accorded endangered non-human species, Patrick Jobes writes:

> The way of life and the feelings of persons are the genuinely unique characteristics of humans, and these are the characteristics which have emerged as most negotiable or ignored when decisions on land use are made. . . . Certainly the variety of life styles deserves protection as much as do the lives of lesser species.[40]

Jobes is worried about the vulnerability of ranching to changes in federal grazing policy. For it is the liberality of that policy that prevents the extinction of this way of life. Most public-land ranchers are not "welfare parasites," as Edward Abbey once described them;[41] they work too hard for too little money. That is the problem. Left to the tender mercies of the market without the subsidies now accorded them, many ranching operations would go under. Robert Nelson remarks that "as a producer of myth the public lands are probably managed very efficiently; the rangeland program involves very minor sums compared with the billion-dollar agricultural subsidies to preserve the illusion of the yeoman farmer."[42] This sounds a bit dismissive; but taken seriously, it suggests a reason to resist marketizing grazing policy.

Other resource-based cultures are also threatened by market forces. The citizens of Roslyn, Washington, value a way of life centered around timber. They may not care whether logging old-growth forest threatens the northern spotted owl, but they do care about logging. Yet to protect itself from takeovers, the Plum Creek Timber Company is itself doing what corporate raiders would do if they acquired it: raising profits by logging the land it owns around Roslyn "at a rate that will leave no standing commercial timber for several generations."[43] Those who live there might preserve their way of life by buying out the company's stockholders, who demand increased profits as a means to satisfying their own consumer desires. But a satisfactory offer is quite beyond their means. It is very unlikely that these people would be any better off if the land around Roslyn were National Forest managed by O'Toole's marketized USFS. For who but the citizens of Roslyn would be willing to pay much for sustained-yield logging there?

Finally, consider water. Powell thought the best use of the arid lands of the West was to support ranching *communities*. He envisioned settlements with grouped residences, surrounded by sufficient land to support the community through grazing. The land was not to be fenced into private range, but used in common. Rights to sufficient water to grow winter forage in irrigated fields should, he maintained, "go with land titles" lest the water essential to maintaining the community be sold.[44] Rather than entrust his vision to the vagaries of the market, Powell submitted it to Congress in 1878 in the form of draft legislation. But Congress would have none of it, and in consequence western water, tied neither to communities nor to the land, now "flows uphill toward money."[45] Water rights ultimately go to the highest bidder and water that might have sustained agricultural communities is diverted to Los Angeles, Las Vegas, Phoenix, and Denver. The only thing that seems to bother O'Toole about this is that the transfer of water rights is often impeded by provisions of state water law.[46]

Exactly the sort of thing Powell anticipated and tried to head off is now occurring in northern New Mexico, where the state is in the process of "adjudicating" water rights. Spanish water law and custom ties water to land, just as Powell proposed. Individual landowners get a share of the water delivered by an *acequia* (irrigation ditch) as *parciantes* (shareholders); individual *acequias* get a share of the water delivered by nature, generally by a river. The necessary *acequia* maintenance is shared by the *pariciantes*, who supply *pions* (workers) in proportion to their share of the water. Water not used by some individual is shared among the others. When nature does not deliver enough water, everyone makes do with less: shares are adjudicated by negotiation, the elected *comisionados* (commissioners) of different *acequias* agreeing to some formula for splitting the available water between *acequias*, the water alloted to each being then divided among its *parciantes*.

The aim of the state's quite different adjudication process is to vest transferable water rights in individuals. Farmers or other legal entities like corporations and Indian reservations get legal rights to water, which they may then sell to anyone. A right to so many acre feet of water per month entitles one to draw from the source up to this amount per month, if it is available. One need not worry about whether doing so takes *all* the water left by more "senior" users, leaving none for more "junior" users. As may be imagined, the adjudication process sets community against community, and negotiation gives way to bitter litigation. Furthermore, making water a commodity owned by individuals destroys the communities built around *acequias.* As individual *parciantes* sell their water rights to urban developers and water districts, these communities lose both the members and the water that sustain them.

Stanley Crawford, writing from his own experience in the governance of an *acequia*, makes the case against treating water as a commodity this way:

> Without water rights a *parciante* ceases to be one, and a ditch loses thus a member, a taxpayer, a *pion*, a potential worker, a potential officeholder. . . . [T]he pressure to convert water from the uses of subsistence agriculture to municipal-industrial uses for the cities of Santa Fe, Albuquerque, and Las Cruces [endangers] something irreplaceable of a political and cultural nature. . . . There are few other civic institutions left in this country in which members have as much control over an important aspect of their lives. . . . [W]e should be saying that water is essential for keeping our communities together, and such is its main use now—as the substance around which a most remarkable tradition of self-governance adheres. To this, even agricultural use may be secondary.[47]

## PROTECTING LAND VALUES

Public lands give us opportunities to consider and support aspects of individual welfare and agency that are apt to be ill-served by the market. We should not squander them by uncritically following the advice of some economists that we manage these lands for productivity. Even if it could be shown that a perfect market would, say, allocate the remaining old-growth forest on federal lands in the Northwest to logging, it does not follow that it should be cut.

We might, of course, conclude that in some cases there is nothing to be gained by directing public resources away from the uses to which a free market would put them. In such cases, we might seriously consider privatization, as the BLM does in selling off odd bits of federal land. But in most cases, public land management should not be dictated by the "wisdom" of the market. This is perhaps clearest in the case of National Parks and Wilderness Areas. Such classifications preserve lands from the commercial uses to which they would otherwise be put, and even those who advocate privatizing federal lands often make an exception of these. But if the justification for designating some area a National Park or a Wilderness Area runs in terms of bettering desires, not better satisfying desires, then we should not look to consumer demand for guidance on how to manage it.

Bil Gilbert expresses a popular view when he writes: "Some may like snowmobiles in national parks and others may not, but it's a matter of personal taste, not a question of ecology or morality. Backpackers camping in the wilderness are no better, worse or natural than a family vacationing in a parking lot in their camper."[48] But those who see the National Parks and Wilderness Areas as institutions that help elevate taste cannot take this

"I'm OK, you're OK" attitude. If it's really no better to hike into Olympic National Park to spend a season in the wilderness than it is to park the camper in a parking lot and watch TV for the duration, aren't we allocating resources rather foolishly in declaring Olympic's billions of board feet of timber off-limits to logging?

I agree with Gilbert that the National Parks are threatened by "creeping silliness,"[49] but it is not of the sort he imagines. What is silly is Gilbert's reading of "parks are for people" as "parks should give people what they want," a reading unfortunately given weight and respectability by economics. The fact that more people would visit Canyonlands National Park if they could play tennis or party at a night club there—or perhaps tour a high-level nuclear waste repository on the way in[50]—is no reason at all to supply these facilities. Similarly, it is ridiculous to decide whether it's worth requiring scrubbers on coal-burning power plants in the Southwest by determining whether their cost exceeds what citizens say they're willing to pay to achieve certain visibility levels at the Grand Canyon and other parks.[51]

But aren't National Parks and Wilderness Areas a special case? Sax remarks that "however obvious it may be to many people that the United States should own and control Yellowstone National Park or the Lincoln Memorial, it is far from self-evident why the United States should also have charge of hundreds of millions of acres of rather ordinary land."[52] And one might object: "Yes, I see the argument for National Parks and Wilderness Areas. But how much denial of consumer sovereignty do we need? Let's settle on the extent of the National Park and Wilderness Preservation System and manage the rest of the federal lands on a rational economic basis. If possible, privatize them; if not, maximize their productivity by marketizing their management." This may be the attitude of some who press for "release" language in legislation creating Wilderness Areas in the National Forests. The idea is that roadless areas not thereby designated Wilderness be released to logging, mining, recreational development, etc., under the multiple-use doctrine. It may also be the view of some privatization advocates. Gary Libecap, for example, writes that "BLM lands are typically arid brush and grassland suitable for grazing, but with few of the park-like qualities commonly associated with some national forest areas."[53] Perhaps he'd be willing to exempt "park-like" areas from his call for privatization.

However, several considerations argue against zoning public lands so that whatever isn't a National Park or Wilderness Area (say) will be managed for productivity or simply disposed of.

First, we're not in a position to say that the National Park or Wilderness Preservation System is finished, that we have all the National Parks or Wilderness Areas we shall ever want to carve out of public lands. Sometimes it takes a while to develop appreciation for certain landscapes, such as those proposed for inclusion in a Great Basin National Park in eastern Nevada. Perry Hagenstein remarks that while "most of the federal lands with characteristics that *now* would qualify them as national parks or national wildlife refuges have been reserved for these purposes[,] . . . as interests in the federal lands change, there will certainly be some candidates for parks or wildlife refuges among the present national forest and public [BLM] lands"[54] Economists may try to represent such interests as "option values:" if what we're collectively willing to pay to preserve the option of establishing a park at some future time exceeds what we're collectively willing to pay for some other use, then it makes sense to preserve that option. But if National Parks and Wilderness Areas are justified as investments in bettering desires, this will not do. If consumer preferences shouldn't determine whether we establish a National Park or Wilderness Area, then they shouldn't determine whether we preserve the option to do so either.

Second, if nature is good for us, why write off what isn't enclosed in National Parks and Wilderness Areas? If we assess federal lands in terms of their aptness for promoting self-renewal, etc., we won't find that they fit neatly into two categories, which we can label "Parks and Wilderness" and "Other." At best, we'll see a continuum with (say) the Grand Canyon at one end and who knows what at the other. If the productivity of "non-Park" lands is to be maximized, it is likely that natural values will be respected only insofar as they have value as commodities. So logging will be prohibited in the watershed of a trout stream only if what people are collectively willing to pay to fish it exceeds what they are willing to pay for the timber, and it can actually be collected in the form of user fees.

Third, we ought to protect cultural as well as natural values. There may be certain ways of life that are rewarding for those who practice them and enrich the experience of others, but which are threatened by market forces. To preserve them, subsidies may be required and appropriate, and one form of subsidy we might consider is use of public lands. Some who might qualify for such subsidies now benefit from public land and resource policies. Think of ranchers who lease federal range for marginal operations at less than the going market-rate for forage; of prospectors who owe their livelihood to luck, toil, and the liberal provisions of federal mining law; loggers who depend on deficit federal timber sales; farmers who couldn't make it without subsidized irrigation. Now, of course, the subsidies that such individuals in effect receive may not be the most efficient means of preserving the cultural values they embody. Like farm subsidies, these are not targeted very carefully. The major beneficiaries may be large corporations or individuals whose way of life is neither particularly admirable nor in jeopardy.[55] But it is entirely appropriate to consider supporting valuable ways of life through public land policies.

Such arguments can also be turned against less extreme proposals. Nelson, for example, argues for zoning federal lands broadly into *recreation* or *commodity production* lands.[56] Recreation lands would be retained in public ownership—National Parks, Wilderness, and other "'critical areas' for the whole nation" by the federal government, the rest transferred to the states and thence perhaps to counties.[57] Commodity lands would be sold or leased on a long-term basis. Nelson's zoning principle is the value of outputs: "[d]ecisions to allocate land to one use should reflect at least an implicit calculation that this use has a higher value than others—including appropriate values for nonmarket outputs."[58] In his view, a good deal of USFS and BLM land should be classified as recreation land.[59] On much of it, investment in commodity production now exceeds the value of the commodities produced, as does the estimated value of recreational use. However, highly productive forestland in the Northwest, promising energy areas, valuable recreational homesites, and productive rangeland would be prime candidates for commodity designation. The allocation of resources on commodity production lands would be left to private producers and the free market, though "nonmarket objectives" could be pursued "by regulatory means and by financial incentives offered to the private sector."[60]

Everyone will agree with Nelson that "each parcel of public land should be put to the use with the highest social value."[61] The issue is how this is to be determined: do we defer to "expert analysis,"[62] presumably by economists, or work it out in the political process? Nelson does not say how certain outputs are to be valued, noting that "there is much uncertainty about the correct price at which to value [recreation and other nonmarket uses]."[63] If values are to be reckoned in terms of willingness-to-pay, then all public land will be zoned for productivity, and previous criticisms apply. If some determinations of value should be made politically, as Nelson suggests may be appropriate in the case of "the value of a wilderness area, or the importance of protecting habitat for endangered species,"[64] then it is not clear how Nelson's zones will differ from present land classifications.

Their administration, however, would differ and not clearly for the better. Surely it is easier to pursue "nonmarket objectives" in a multiple-use regime than it is in a regulatory regime. Transferring USFS and BLM lands to the states and on to counties would further decentralize their management. But Phillip Foss reminds us that:

> decentralization means delegation of authority to local elites. Such elites will ordinarily represent (or be sympathetic to) commodity user groups (mining, ranching, or timber interests). Recreationists, environmentalists, and, to a lesser degree, hunters and fishermen are likely to be transients from the outside. Consequently their influence in local decision making is likely to be minimal.[65]

As it is, federal "field personnel [tend] to 'marry the natives,'" as Foss puts it,[66] and local interests generally have more to say about how public lands are used than do other members of the public.

## MULTIPLE-USE MANAGEMENT

Zoning for productivity might tidy up the messy world of multiple use, but I remain to be convinced that it would be an improvement. "Multiple use," of course, promises more than multiple use can deliver; it suggests that competing claims to public lands can somehow be happily reconciled, that we can make room for natural and cultural values as well as consumer interests. But obviously these claims will frequently pull policy in different directions. When the West Coast Alliance for Resources and Environment speaks for the "people of the redwood heartland," whose "culture here is a fragile ecosystem all its own, made up of hardworking people and the land" that is "worth protecting," it is speaking against the designs that environmentalists have on the region's public forests.[67] Supporting the way of life of ranchers means giving their cattle the run of the land, to compete with wildlife for water, forage, and territory, to foul streams and trample vegetation, to impose upon those who seek solitude and renewal. These impacts can be reduced by reducing the number of stock permitted, but such reductions may force ranchers out of business. Despite what ranching interests say, consumers probably would not suffer as a result. Federal grazing programs supply only about 10% of the nation's beef-calf stock[68] and cost taxpayers millions of dollars to administer. If federal range were closed to grazing tomorrow, producers in the South and Midwest would quickly make up the difference; and, after an initial rise, beef prices would fall back. Furthermore, consumers would have more to spend if they could somehow recover the tax revenues the USFS and BLM now sink into the grazing programs. Finally, there are doubtless other uses of some grazing allotments that interest some consumers more than cheap hamburger; they might be better served by leasing this land to hunting clubs or vacation-home developers. Our interest in these uses, however, is likely to be opposed by our other interests.

Difficult as it is to know what shape multiple use should take on particular lands, we should not throw up our hands and in one way or another turn the problem over to the market to settle. That way of resolving conflicting claims on scarce resources simply ignores some of them. If the interests of consumers and the distribution of income are to decide the use of public lands, they'll be put to those uses that people are in aggregate willing to pay most for. It would certainly be amazing if the uses selected in this way were those most in our interest. I think we are much more likely to approach this ideal if we ignore the siren calls of economic rationality and instead work at articulating and debating the merits of competing claims.

Economists will no doubt complain that we are not given any yardstick like productivity with which to judge the merits of competing claims. As B. Delworth Gardner points out, "[i]t is not very helpful to reject this framework without having another as an acceptable substitute."[69] It is true that the goal of bettering desires, of empowering people to construct rewarding lives for themselves, does not translate into some standard by which alternatives may be easily judged. However, as I have argued, the same might be said of productivity, and in any case it can't be helped. Furthermore, this goal is not devoid of content. At the very least, it suggests what sort of considerations are relevant in judging alternatives and thus sets the terms of debate. If you think that I am wrong in suggesting that experiencing the otherness of nature and working with others to preserve what remains of it can help people fashion rewarding lives, then at least we agree on what it is I am supposed to be wrong about. You can explain just where my mistake is, I can respond, and perhaps together we can make some progress toward refining the question and resolving it.

Moreover, I believe, perhaps foolishly, that we can achieve a fairly broad consensus on preserving the cultural and natural values of the public lands and that such a commitment can guide us to satisfactory resolutions of some contentious issues. If you have a sufficiently selective and sympathetic ear, you can discern some basis for agreement among those who are now slugging it out over federal grazing and timber policy. Both environmentalists and their adversaries profess to believe in multiple use, the former insisting that "environmental and esthetic values as well as economic and sociological factors must be taken into account,"[70] the latter agreeing but reversing the order of the clauses. If we are persistent in reminding them of this shared verbal commitment, we may hope to construct something of substance from it.

In some cases, these reminders may have to be pointed. Ranchers and loggers, for example, claim to love the land, yet their typical reaction to suggestions that their operations threaten natural values is denial: overgrazing is a myth perpetrated by academic bean-counters;[71] if ranchers really abused the land, they'd be out of business;[72] spotted owls do just fine in second-growth;[73] the decline of salmon fisheries must be due to something other than logging-induced siltation of their spawning streams;[74] etc. They need to be called on this. While environmentalists give lip service to social and economic values, their effective vision of Aldo Leopold's land community[75] often seems to be strangely empty of people. They need to be asked whether they don't in fact view the rural West as a playground for yuppies, as critics allege,[76] and if not, how public land policy can help sustain both natural values and rural ways of life. Those who do think in terms of pristine natural communities where humans are spectators but not participants need to be reminded that few of these remain; that fewer still are large enough to be sustained without human intervention, buffers, and the cooperation of local residents; that achieving sustainability by buying up surrounding land and restoring it to its pre-settlement condition is generally out of the question; and that dealing with local people with a sense of place is likely to be more productive than dealing with recreational developers and absentee corporations.[77]

If we want to resolve the grazing controversy in a way that honors both cultural and natural values, we would aim to keep ranchers in business while improving the range. If the range condition is to be improved, then herd-size must in many cases be reduced and ranch incomes will fall, unless ranchers are in one way or another compensated. It should be possible for people who agree on the importance of these values—and they, I suggest, should be all of us—to devise a suitable compensation scheme and to find the money in the federal budget, especially since we are not talking about a lot of it. This solution, of course, will not appeal to people who think the free market should be the arbiter of values. But such a position is not consistent with allegiance to cultural or natural values, neither of which is likely to be promoted by a free market in the services of federal rangeland. Higher grazing fees may remove cows, but not pressures on federal rangeland, as ranches give way to recreational subdivisions full of people who want to ride ATVs over "their" public lands.

A resolution of the controversy over logging old-growth forests on public lands in the Northwest that preserves both the forests and timber communities is more difficult. The practices halted by legal actions on behalf of the spotted owl, which convert old-growth to even-age stands of Douglas fir to be harvested at 50–70 years, clearly will not do. However, it may be possible to sustain both old-growth forests and a way of life by shifting to "high-quality forestry," which aims at producing a very desirable forest product: the clear, strong, close-grained wood of trees 150–200 years old. In this regime, individual trees would be cut to maintain mixed-age stands, which would also receive periodic thinning and pruning. This is the type of forestry favored by environmentalists.[78] It is also promoted by some timber activists, who note that it "has a greater in-the-woods job creation potential than other harvest and plant regimes."[79]

However, it is an expensive and somewhat risky strategy. Since its high-quality product is delivered far in the future, high quality forestry is very unlikely to maximize net revenue. Moreover, many forest economists would argue that it is ridiculous to base present policy on assumptions about what people 200 years from now will want; instead, we should meet today's needs.[80] They point out that even now technology is providing substitutes for what the forests of the Northwest no longer supply, such as 80-foot I-beams made of wood strands and glue.[81] Furthermore, we cannot be certain that high-quality forestry will maintain the integrity of old-growth forest, and it may be argued that it is foolish to gamble that it will.

Nonetheless, I think those who take natural and cultural values seriously should be willing to pay some money and take some risks. They will reject the idea that forests are to be managed to maximize net revenue or return on capital. They will have difficulty imagining that high-quality wood for veneers, paneling, and the like, won't command a high price when it is a lot scarcer than it is today. They will point out that high-quality forestry does meet a present need of timber communities. They will demand monitoring of indicator species like the spotted owl and be prepared to change course if indicated, but they will not give cultural values so little weight that conjectures about what might happen to the owl outweigh them.

## CONTRACTING OUT

Those who advocate privatizing public lands want them transferred to private ownership. But public land management might be privatized in ways that fall short of this. At present, it is twice-removed from the market. Under current management policies, public lands are made to deliver various services in amounts other than what we'd expect were they privately owned. And in many cases public land agencies do not hire private firms to deliver these services, but do it themselves. Architects and engineers employed by the NPS design visitor centers and roads; park rangers collect entrance fees, direct traffic, and lead nature walks. USFS employees design forest roads, trails, and campgrounds; they fight fires, mark timber for sales, and replant cut-over or burned areas. It is worth considering whether it wouldn't be better to contract-out some of these services.[82] Competition might lower their cost or improve their quality. Furthermore, agencies that maintain staff for in-house work have to find work for them to do; for example, the "roading" of National Forests is no doubt driven in part by the large USFS engineering department.

Of course the agencies now do a lot of contracting-out. The USFS does not deliver pulp, plywood, and lumber; it essentially hires private loggers to cut the trees and truck them to the mills. Apart from providing campgrounds in most National Parks, the NPS is not in the business of feeding and housing visitors; it contracts with concessionaires to provide these services to the public. The BLM does not mine coal or produce calves; it leases its land to private individuals, who use it to produce these commodities. But more might be done. The USFS has recently developed a new "recreation strategy" for the National Forests, in which "private investors will be sought to develop camping areas, resorts, marinas, ski areas and other projects."[83]

Some critics of the current system have even suggested contracting-out the *management* of large pieces of federal land. O'Toole's proposal that individual National Forests be managed by public corporations, funded from National Forest revenues, fits this description. So does Marion Clawson's long-term leasing plan.[84] He suggests that forestlands capable of producing 1,000 board feet of lumber per acre per year at maturity be leased in 90,000-acre blocks for 100 years; terms would be initial payment of the market value of standing timber plus an annual rental of 5% of the value of the land and immature timber. Clawson pretty clearly thinks that such "productive" forestland is generally best used for timber production, but he proposes allowing those who think otherwise to bid for up to 30,000 acres of such a block on the same terms. Conditions on use designed to protect water quality, wildlife, etc., might also be written into the lease.

Privatizing the management of federal lands in Clawson's way doesn't differ much from transferring title to private parties, but under covenants designed to promote various public purposes. Indeed, the chief difference between Clawson's proposal and those of privatization advocates is that Clawson, like O'Toole, *has* a proposal: rather than calling vaguely for the disposal of federal lands, he has thought through how it might be done. But much of my criticism of privatization and O'Toole's in-house version of it applies as well to Clawson's, and I shall not reiterate it here.

What, though, of suggestions that the federal land-management agencies should simply oversee the private use of public lands and leave the business of providing services to the private sector? Although I do not have supporting data, I suspect that the economies to be realized from more contracting-out are quite small. Most of the people employed by the NPS and USFS to collect park or campground fees, clear trails, issue backcountry permits, fight fires, reseed clear-cuts, lead nature walks, direct visitors to the rest rooms, etc., are seasonal employees, hired, often locally, at modest wages as they are needed and budgets permit. It is unlikely that adding middlemen to this process would deliver these services more efficiently, particularly when close supervision is required.[85]

Furthermore, insofar as the firms that contract to supply services are interested in maximizing profits, they may seek to increase the demand for these services in ways that conflict with the mission of the agencies that employ them. National Park concessionaires, for example, are interested in constructing facilities which will draw customers but have nothing to do with the purpose of the parks, and in fact are inimical to it. MCA, for example, wanted very much to build a convention center in Yosemite Valley. I'm sure there's a lot of money to be made by entrepreneurs with ideas on how to jazz-up the park experience, if only the NPS would surrender its interpretive programs to the private sector. But that's just the trouble, isn't it?

While it's nice to see the USFS take time from planning timber sales to give thought to recreation, I have similar misgivings about its new "recreation strategy," the "ultimate goal" of which is "consumer satisfaction with more, high-quality recreation services."[86] If Kampgrounds of America, Inc. (KOA) builds and runs campgrounds in the National Forests, they will doubtless look like KOA campgrounds across the nation, complete with street lights, hookups for mobile homes, flush toilets, swimming pool and playground, a store where you can rent a video for the evening, and other facilities designed to "meet customer preferences."[87] I should think it preferable to offer people a different sort of experience, one that asks more of them but promises greater rewards: access too rough and narrow for mobile homes, a quiet walk, the scent of pine and willow, a simple meal, the murmur of a creek, the call of an owl, a view of the stars.

As I conclude my critique of the privatization proposal, I am a bit bemused to find myself defending our public land-management system. Can I, who have so often despaired of federal land policy and federal land managers, actually believe what I have written here? I can indeed, in part because I am defending a *system of institutions*, not all the policies that issue from it, in part because the alternative is worse.

Although it is easy to complain about public land policies, it is not easy to describe a system for making and implementing them that is clearly better than the one we have. After all, it gives all who take an interest in public lands numerous opportunities to make their case to the public, in Congress, at the agencies, and before the courts. Those with other views listen carefully and respond, lest silence be taken for concurrence. The better arguments may not prevail in every case, but over time weak policies will be exposed and modified. Anyone can easily imagine policies they think better; it's harder to imagine how one would get them adopted, while allowing others with different visions the same opportunity.

Relative to what might reasonably be expected, I also think that federal land management has been pretty good. There is certainly room for improvement: some National Parks are overdeveloped and overcrowded, BLM and USFS rangelands are not in good shape, the USFS talks multiple use but thinks timber, etc. But such shortcomings should not blind us to the achievements of the federal land-management system. There is good reason to believe that, without it, much of what we now regard as our natural and cultural heritage would not exist, or would exist only in a diminished form. If we grant its value, we must, I think, be grateful for the system which has preserved it.

I have argued for this system in rather general terms, suggesting that in various ways it contributes to bettering desires. I shall add here a personal testimonial: I think I've probably spent the best days of my life on federal lands—bushwacking up Salt Creek in Canyonlands National Park to meet, across the centuries, the gaze of the All-American Man pictograph; hunting for minerals in the abandoned mine dumps of Colorado's San Isabel National Forest as a kid; pursuing a look at whatever might be around the next bend in Dark Canyon, Utah; circling Mt. Bonneville in Wyoming's Wind River Mountains; climbing through lifting clouds to Spire Point in the North Cascades of Washington; hearing boulders thud against bedrock as runoff waterfalls poured down 3,000 feet of canyon wall to the Colorado River below Toroweap; walking the footpath of those who once lived there back in time to the magical Hensley settlement at Cumberland Gap National Historic Park. Federal land policy has made such experiences possible, and it would, I think, be tragic if dissatisfaction with the current system led to changes that denied our children such opportunities.

It's usually a mistake to believe things couldn't be worse, and a critical examination of the case for privatization suggests that things would indeed be worse if public lands were privatized. In itself, this is not a particularly exciting conclusion, since at present few take the proposal seriously. However, the same cannot be said for the economic ideas behind it. Appeals to productivity and economic rationality are quite respectable and seductive. They are likely to continue to make inroads on federal land policy.

Marketization in various forms is, I think, not a remote possibility. Its rationale is essentially that of privatization, and its effects will be similar. Institutions and policies that in various ways encourage reflection on desires will be replaced by others that, at best, serve them. Opportunities to work with others to develop and realize visions of the best use of public resources will be replaced by opportunities to purchase what we most prefer of the available and affordable commodities. In my view, this is a poor exchange and should be resisted. If markets are good, other things equal, it does not follow that enlarging their scope must be better, for that may not leave other things equal. That, I have argued, is the case here.

## NOTES

1. William Niskanen, *Bureaucracy and representative government* (Chicago: Aldine Atherton, 1971), at 18.

2. Joseph Sax, "The legitimacy of collective values: the case of the public lands," *University of Colorado Law Review* 56 (1985), 537–57 at 557.

3. Id., at 545.

4. Id.

5. "In west, a showdown over rules on grazing," *The New York Times*, 19 August 1990, A1.

6. See Joseph Sax, "The public trust doctrine in natural resource law: effective judicial intervention," *Michigan Law Review* 68 (1970), 471–566; and Charles F. Wilkinson, "The public trust doctrine in public land law," *U.C. Davis Law Review* 14 (1980), 269–316.

7. F. A. Hayek, *The constitution of liberty* (Chicago: University of Chicago Press, 1960), Chapter 2.

8. John Wesley Powell, *Report on the lands of the arid region of the United States* (Cambridge, MA: Belknap, 1962), at 50. Of course, we may also agree with Henry M. Stanley that "[i]ndividuals require to be protected from the rapacity of communities." *The autobiography of Sir Henry Morton Stanley* (Boston: Houghton Mifflin, 1909), at 530.

9. *The New York Times*, 27 January 1986, A26.

10. See Goals 22, 18, and 11 in Alan M. Gottlieb, *The wise use agenda* (Bellevue, WA: Free Enterprise Press, 1989), at 15, 12, and 8. Like environmentalists, the Wise Use people are somewhat selective in their appeals to economic rationality. Goal 10, e.g., urges that provisions of MUSYA, 16 U.S.C.A. §§528–31, be invoked to assure that "no timber harvest plan may be identified as 'below cost.'" Id., at 8.

Some environmentalists are more cautious than Wald about endorsing economic principles. To improve the legal guidelines for writing and implementing National Forest management plans, Dennis Baird of the Sierra Club's Public Lands Committee suggests "clarifying and supplementing the generally non-existent economic suitability section of the regulations." He then observes that "[s]ince this is a double edged sword (look at western Oregon, for example), these improvements should make it clear that economic suitability tests should never be the tool for final land allocation decisions. This language should also not be used to preclude sales below-cost." "Improving the Forest Service regulations," *Public Lands: Newsletter of the Sierra Club Public Lands Committee* 7(1) (1989), 6–7 at 7.

11. "They cut redwoods faster to cut the debt faster," *The New York Times*, 2 March 1988, A16. The take-over of Pacific Lumber and its impact on the company's logging practices is reviewed in Lisa H. Newton and Catherine K. Dillingham, *Watersheds: classic cases in environmental ethics* (Belmont, CA: Wadsworth, 1994) at 115–17.

12. James Howard Kunstler, "For sale," *The New York Times Magazine*, 18

June 1989, 22 at 25. The New York State Constitution's stipulation (Article XIV, Section I) that the preserve remain "forever wild" applies only to state lands within its boundaries.

13. Richard L. Stroup and John A. Baden, *Natural resources: bureaucratic myths and environmental management* (San Francisco: Pacific Institute for Public Policy Research, 1983), at 41.

14. For skepticism about the possibility of free-market environmentalism, see Thomas Michael Power and Paul Rauber, "The price of everything," *Sierra* 78(6) (1993), 87–96. If the Sierra Club's Executive Director has similar doubts, you would not guess it from his defense, in the previous issue of *Sierra*, of environmentalists against charges that they are "anti-market." See Carl Pope, "Market free-for-all," *Sierra* 78(5) (1993), 22.

15. Randal O'Toole, *Reforming the Forest Service* (Washington: Island Press, 1988).

16. The thesis that bureaus, both public and private, behave as if they were individuals that seek to maximize their budgets is developed in Niskanen, note 1 *supra*.

17. 16 U.S.C.A. §§576–76b, at §576b.

18. 16 U.S.C.A. §§532–38, at §535(2).

19. O'Toole, note 15 *supra*, at 103.

20. Id., at 213.

21. Id., at 209–10. Some recreation fees—such as those for big-game hunting and running popular whitewater rivers—would far exceed the $3 average. A "basic dispersed recreation permit," good for admission to, and certain activities in, a National Forest, could be modestly priced because "[t]he real income would be generated from hunting and fishing permits and concentrated use fees." Id., at 209. "Trips on . . . popular rivers, such as Idaho's Salmon, might sell for $25 to $50 per day." Id., at 208.

22. Id., at 194. That O'Toole's rationale for such prescriptive legislation does not go beyond conventional economic thinking is suggested by the following passages:

"[M]arkets may not provide an optimal amount of wilderness. This is partly because many people place an 'option demand value' on wilderness—that is, they may not expect to use wilderness soon, but they wish [i.e., are willing to pay] to have the option to do so. In addition, . . . there are some 'public goods' aspects of wilderness—many people would benefit from the existence of wilderness [i.e., are willing to pay something for preserving it] even if only a few people pay the costs [i.e., pay user fees]. . . . For these reasons, it may be necessary to provide some protection for wilderness and wild lands above that which would be provided by the market." Id., at 210.

"Certainly, some resources cannot be bought and sold in a marketplace. Endangered species is the major example in the national forests. Although society may want to protect all species, contributions to an endangered species would necessarily be voluntary and would probably [presumably in virtue of the free-rider problem] be insufficient to protect such species as the red-cockaded woodpecker and northern spotted owl. Prescriptive legislation may be needed in such cases." Id., at 201.

23. Id., at 103.

24. "Ruling on owl stirs new hope for trees," *The New York Times*, 18 November 1988, A16. In this case, *Northern Spotted Owl* v. *Hodel*, 716 F.Supp. 479

(D.Wash., 1988), the district court ruled that the government acted illegally in ignoring the testimony of its scientists on the issue of whether to list the northern spotted owl as an endangered species. See also "Concern about spotted owl leads to ban on timber sale," *The New York Times*, 25 May 1991, A11. In this case, *Seattle Audubon Society* v. *Evans*, 771 F.Supp. 1081 (D.Wash., 1991), the district court blocked federal timber sales in order to prod the government to issue management plans for protecting the owl.

For discussion of these cases, see Mark Bonnett and Kurt Zimmerman, "Politics and preservation: the Endangered Species Act and the northern spotted owl," *Environmental Law Quarterly* 18 (1991), 105–71; Elizabeth A. Foley, "The tarnishing of an environmental jewel: the Endangered Species Act and the northern spotted owl," *Journal of Land Use and Environmental Law* 8 (1992), 253–83; Kathleen E. Franzreb, "Perspectives on the landmark decision designating the northern spotted owl (*Strix occidentalis caurina*) as a threatened species," *Environmental Management* 17 (1993), 445–52.

For discussion of owl-protection costs, see Herbert E. McLean, "Paying the price for old growth," *American Forests* 97(9–10) (1991), 22. For analysis of economic impact studies, see V. Alaric Sample and Dennis C. LeMaster, "Economic effects of northern spotted owl protection," *Journal of Forestry* 90(8) (1992), 31–5. For graphical presentations of economic impacts, see "Owls, trees, and jobs: the Timber Summit," *The New York Times*, 2 April 1993, A22.

25. "Populations of [non-game] species may increase or decrease, but as long as they did not approach threatened or endangered status, there would be little cause for concern." O'Toole, note 15 *supra*, at 210.

26. Id., at 216.

27. "Subject to valid rights then existing, effective January 1, 1984, the minerals in lands designated by this chapter as wilderness areas are withdrawn from all forms of appropriation under the mining laws and from disposition under all laws pertaining to mineral leasing and all amendments thereto." Wilderness Act of 1964, 16 U.S.C.A. §1131–36, at §1133(d)(3).

28. O'Toole, note 15 *supra*, at 216.

29. Id., at 205.

30. See Chapter 5, note 21.

31. Letter in Gottlieb, note 10 *supra*, 69–83 at 72.

32. O'Toole, note 15 *supra*, at 205.

33. "[P]ublic lands should be retained in public ownership so that public demand can easily correct any unexpected or unintended effects of reforms." Id., at 194.

34. Id., at 217.

35. Id., at 194.

36. Dolores T. Martin, "Divestiture and the creation of property rights in public lands: a comment," *Cato Journal* 2 (1982), 687–90 at 689.

37. In a forum on "Privatizing public lands: the ecological and economic case for private ownership of federal lands," William Tucker remarks, "I love this idea of just selling [wilderness to environmentalists] or giving it to the Audubon Society and letting them pay taxes on it and see[ing] what they do with it." *Manhattan report on economic policy* 2(3) (Manhattan Institute for Policy Research, 1982), at 11.

38. For comparison of allocation by "traditional markets in which buyers and sellers must agree on prices" vs. the "willingness to pay approach . . . in which resources go to those willing to pay the most for them, even if the owners refuse

to sell their rights," see Mark Sagoff, "Some problems with environmental economics," *Environmental Ethics* 10 (1988), 55–74; quoted passages at 56.

39. George Gordon (Lord Byron), *Childe Harold's pilgrimage*, Canto IV, Stanza 178.

40. Patrick C. Jobes, "Comments on the protection of an endangered species," *Journal of Range Management* 32 (1979), 328.

41. Edward Abbey, "Free speech: the cowboy and his cow," in *One life at a time, please* (New York: Henry Holt and Company, 1988), 9–19 at 12.

42. Robert H. Nelson, "The public lands," in *Current issues in natural resource policy*, ed. Paul R. Portney (Washington: Resources for the Future, 1982), 14–73 at 73.

43. "Where have all the forests gone?," *The New York Times*, 15 February 1989, A16. Roslyn's misfortune is not unique; Champion International did the same thing on its checkerboard lands in western Montana. See "A land deal leaves Montana heavily logged and hurting," *The New York Times*, 19 October 1993, A1.

44. Powell, note 8 *supra*, at 54.

45. From an illustration for "Demystifying water: technocracy or democracy?" *Earth notes* 1(3) (University of Colorado Environmental Center, 1985), 1 at 1. Commenting on proposals to allow water delivered by federal irrigation projects in California to be freely sold, BuRec Commissioner Dennis Underwood observed: "Who holds the most money potentially controls the water. First you take away from farmers, then small cities. Where does it stop?" "Farmers in west may sell something more valuable than any crop: water," *The New York Times*, 6 April 1992, B9.

46. O'Toole, note 15 *supra*, at 190.

47. Stanley Crawford, *Mayordomo: chronicle of an acequia in northern New Mexico* (Albuquerque: University of New Mexico Press, 1988), at 175–77. For discussion of adjudication, see Chapter 8 generally. For misgivings about the extent to which water markets protect social and environmental values generally, see Arthur H. Chan, "To market or not to market: allocating water rights in New Mexico," *Natural Resources Journal* 29 (1989), 629–43; and Helen Ingram and Cy R. Oggins, "The public trust doctrine and community values in water," *Natural Resources Journal* 32 (1992), 515–37.

48. Bil Gilbert, "Alone in the wilderness," *Sports Illustrated* 59(14) (3 October 1983), 96–112 at 112.

49. Id.

50. In defending its choice of Davis Canyon as one of several possible sites for such a facility, the Department of Energy characterizes opponents as "traditionalists [who] have taken the position that any industrial development near a National Park is an unacceptable change that would keep visitors away." It responds by citing visitation data from "analogous situations" to show that "properly controlled industrial facilities are accepted by the majority of the public and . . . do not keep the vast majority of visitors from a rewarding leisure experience." *Draft environmental assessment: Davis Canyon, Utah* (Washington: DOE, December 1984), at 5–90.

51. William D. Schulze, et al., "The economic benefits of preserving visibility in the national parklands of the southwest," *Natural Resources Journal* 23 (1983), 149–73. Some economists do wonder if value is captured by willingness-to-pay. See Thomas H. Stevens, et al., "Measuring the existence value of wildlife: what do CVM estimates really show?", *Land Economics* 67 (1991), 390–400; Robert E. Kohn, "Measuring the existence value of wildlife," *Land Economics* 69 (1993), 304–8; and

Thomas H. Stevens, *et al.*, "Measuring the existence value of wildlife: reply," *Land Economics* 69 (1993), 309–12.

52. Sax, note 2 *supra*, at 537–38.

53. Gary D. Libecap, *Locking up the range: federal land controls and grazing* (San Francisco: Pacific Institute for Public Policy Research, 1981), at 78.

54. Perry R. Hagenstein, "The federal lands today—uses and limits," in *Rethinking the federal lands*, ed. Sterling Brubaker (Washington: Resources for the Future, 1984), 74–107 at 83.

55. Bil Gilbert comments that "the Sagebrush Rebellion wasn't created by and for 100-head-of-sheep men in the Bighorns, but rather by and for men who hire somebody else to run their 1,000 head of cattle on 50,000 acres of BLM land. . . . They may have started in the cattle business, but in many cases they have bought a ranch because it is a good Western, macho possession and tax shelter. They now also have a few oil wells, some coal leases, a GM dealership in Denver, a piece of a Phoenix shopping center and/or a condominium complex on Maui. You are much more likely to find them mending fences in the state legislature than wrestling with barbed wire out there in the sagebrush; listening to Wayne Newton in Vegas than to a harmonica around a mesquite campfire." Gilbert, note 48 *supra*, at 103.

56. Nelson, note 42 *supra*, at 70.

57. Id., at 62.

58. Id., at 59.

59. Id., at 71.

60. Id., at 68.

61. Id., at 33.

62. Id.

63. Id.

64. Id.

65. Phillip O. Foss, ed., *Federal lands policy* (New York: Greenwood Press, 1987), at xix.

66. Id. "If you live in a place like Sheridan [Wyoming], you want the community to do well, you want the people to say hello to you in the cafe. And if you've just cut a guy's income by 10 percent—which is what reducing the number of cattle involves—he's not going to be happy." Tom France of the Northern Rockies National Wildlife Federation, speaking of social pressures on USFS district rangers, in Elizabeth Royte, "Showdown in cattle country," *The New York Times Magazine*, 16 December 1990, 60–70 at 66.

67. Letter in Gottlieb, note 10 *supra*, 60–68 at 64–5.

68. William E. Martin, "The distribution of benefits and costs associated with public rangelands," in *Public lands and the US economy: balancing conservation and development*, ed. George M. Johnston and Peter M. Emerson (Boulder, CO: Westview, 1984), 229–56 at 233.

69. B. Delworth Gardner, "The case for divestiture," in Brubaker, note 54 *supra*, 156–80 at 159.

70. *Our public lands: an introduction to the agencies and issues* (Sierra Club, 1982), at 1.

71. "I remember federal range users in Worland, Wyoming. Their allotments were cut back. What happened was that some bleep from an Eastern college came out and stuck a wire basket over a three-foot-square piece of ground and counted the blades of grass inside the cage. He comes back the next summer and says there

are 15 fewer blades of grass and therefore your allotment will be cut." Senator Alan Simpson (R-WY), quoted in Gilbert, note 48 *supra*, at 103.

72. "If we destroy the land, we're out of business." Wyoming rancher Jim Hendry, quoted in "Higher grazing fees have ranchers running scared," *The New York Times*, 12 September 1993, C5.

73. "[O]wls have been found living in suburban back yards. . . . The largest spotted owl population in Washington state is found in the second growth forest that surrounds Wenatchee." Larry Mason, "The Forest Conference is a good beginning, but there's much more to be done" (Forks, WA: Washington Commercial Forest Action Committee, 6 May 1993) at 12 ("Science").

74. "I personally don't believe logging is a major problem for fisheries." Larry Mason, "The forest conference" (Forks, WA: Washington Commercial Forest Action Committee, 1993), at 4.

75. Leopold argued that we ought, for our own good, to step down from "conqueror of the land community to plain member and citizen of it," but he certainly thought of citizens as participants in the life of the community. Aldo Leopold, "The land ethic," in *A sand county almanac* (New York: Ballantine, 1970), 237–64 at 240.

76. "Some in the highly urbanized East see the West as a land mass to be managed, not for multiple use and the economic well-being of those who live here, but as a playground to be enjoyed by urbanites." William Perry Pendley, "No so-called 'sustainable' fixes are required," *EPA Journal* 18(4) (1992), 37–39 at 38.

77. For discussion of The Nature Conservancy's "bioreserve" initiative, which seeks to preserve natural communities by enlisting the aid of their human components, see John Lancaster, "Saving the parks isn't enough," *Journal of Forestry* 90(3) (1992), 20–1. For its application to the Texas hill country, see "Novel strategy puts people at heart of Texas preserve," *The New York Times*, 31 March 1992, C1; and Betsy Carpenter, "The best-laid plans," *U.S. News and World Report*, 4 October 1993, 89.

78. "Long rotations provide better quality wood and protect other values, such as wildlife. . . ." *Our public lands*, note 70 *supra*, at 5.

79. Mason, note 73 *supra*, at 6.

80. See, e.g., R. W. Behan, "Forestry and the end of innocence," *American Forestry* 81(5) (1975), 16.

81. See "Transforming scrawny trees into sinewy lumber," *The New York Times*, 12 September 1993, C9; and Dede Ryan, "Engineered lumber," *Journal of Forestry* 91(11) (1993), 19–20.

82. The Southeastern Utah Association of Local Governments recommends "Privatization" in the sense that "All services provided on federal lands including parks and monuments shall be provided by the private sector in-so-far as practicable." Letter in Gottlieb, note 10 *supra*, 26–30 at 29. For a remarkably cautious recommendation of contracting-out in general, see David F. Linowes, et al., *Privatization: toward more effective government* (Washington: President's Commission on Privatization, 1988), 243–44.

83. "Aid is asked on recreation in forests," *The New York Times*, 17 February 1988, B5. The strategy urges USFS employees to "[b]e creative in attracting new sources of financing for recreation investments. We want investors to seek us out as attractive opportunities to provide quality public service while realizing a reasonable return." *The National Forests: America's great outdoors: National recreation strategy* (Washington: USFS, 1988 & 1992), at 13.

84. Marion Clawson, *The federal lands revisited* (Washington: Resources for the Future, 1983), at 204ff.

85. For what may happen when contract trail maintenance isn't closely supervised, see Sally Reid, "Trail maintenance: a wolf in sheep's clothing," *Public lands: Newsletter of the Sierra Club Public Lands Committee* 8(1) (1991), 14–15.

86. *National recreation strategy*, note 83 *supra*, at 6.

87. Id., at 13.

# Index

Parenthetical numerals refer to notes; for example, "75(2)" refers to note 2 on page 75.

Abbey, Edward, 75(2), 127, 170, 171, 209
accountability
  by budget, 10, 188
  in collective management, 10, 63, 66–69,
    188–90
  and property rights, 63, 173
  and roles, 186–89
  and self-respect, 189
  *see also* cost shifting
*acequia*, 210
acreage of
  BLM lands, 22(3), 44
  federal lands; 3, 22(3)
  land grants; *see* land grants
  National Forests, 37
  National Grasslands, 38
  National Wildlife Refuges, 43
  NPS lands, 41
  Wilderness, 47
acreage limitations
  of disposal legislation, 32, 33, 49(6), 49(13)
  for federal irrigation, 34–35, 49(13), 50(28)
action
  and preference, 168
  self-interested, 183
  selfless, 187
  von Mises on, 173
  wealth-increasing, 185
addiction, 167, 169
Adirondack Preserve, 205, 222(12)
advertising, 165, 172
agent, rational, 139
aggregate net benefit, 95, 136, 140
air pollution; *see* emission; visibility
Alaska, 6, 22(3), 22(7), 23(14), 36, 37, 43, 44,
  47, 50(37), 52(59), 53(78), 54(92),
  55(114), 74, 194, 198(18)
Alaska National Interest Lands Conservation
  Act (ANILCA)
  ANWR provisions, 24(27), 53(90)
  Tongass provisions, 52(59)
  Wilderness provisions, 47, 55(114)
Alaska Native Claims Settlement Act, 22(3)
Alaska Statehood Act, 22(3), 50(37)
Albuquerque (NM), 211

All-American Man, 220
allocation
  by free market, ix, 9, 17, 56, 69–71, 85–86,
    111, 157, 171, 223(38)
  political, viii–ix, 10, 48, 71, 112, 180–81
  by willingness-to-pay, 208, 223(38)
allocations
  individuation of, 82, 115–16
  relative productivity of, 82
Allotment Management Plan (AMP), 62–63
Alm, Alvin, 29(87)
American Forest and Paper Association, 65, 81
American Mining Congress, 65
American Petroleum Institute, 65
Amnesty International, 174
AMP; *see* Allotment Management Plan
ANILCA; *see* Alaska National Interest
  Lands Conservation Act
animal unit month (AUM), 60
animals
  good of, viii, 145, 158
  and interpersonal utility comparisons, 148
  livestock; *see* livestock
  and utilitarianism, 145
  wild; *see* wildlife
Antiquities Act, 41
anti-reflexive, 88
anti-symmetric, 88
anti-trust, 191
ANWR; *see* Arctic National Wildlife Refuge
Appalachian Mountains, 31
Arches National Park, 170
Arctic National Wildlife Refuge (ANWR), 6,
  24(27), 43, 178(29), 192, 194
argument from
  anecdote, 20
  future benefits, 110
  likeness to the ideal, 110
  productivity, 73
Arizona, 22(7), 24(18), 25(34), 118
Arrow, Kenneth, 79(44), 154(35)
Arrow's theorem, 79(44)
aspen, 56
AUM; *see* animal unit month
autonomy, 134, 139, 165

autonomy (*Cont.*)
  and collective action, 191, 199(26), 201
  and property rights, 19, 135, 152(7)
  *see also* coercion; freedom; respect for
    persons

Baden, John, 26(38), 30(104), 30(105),
    66–68, 76(12), 78(34), 78(35), 79(44),
    79(45), 83, 87, 102–3, 106(25), 108(31),
    113, 115, 152(7), 166, 173, 178(28),
    178(41), 179–84, 186, 190, 198(6), 205
Baird, Dennis, 221(10)
Bankhead–Jones Act, 38
Barrick Gold Strike Mine, 50(24)
*Belville Mining Company* v. *U.S.*, 51(44)
benefit–cost
  analysis, 95–97
  ratio, vii, 106(22), 204
benefit stream, 123
Bentham, Jeremy, 72, 79(49), 133
Berle, Peter, 16
Berlin, Irving, 22(3)
Bighorn mountains, 225(55)
bioreserves, 226(76)
BLM; *see* Bureau of Land Management
BLM lands, 4, 43–45
  area of, 22(3), 44
  ecology of, 122
  land treatments, 7, 117
  management objectives for, 37
  pristine condition of, 120
  range condition, 118–20, 220
  and Sagebrush Rebellion, 7
  state claims to, 25(34)
  Wilderness acreage, 47
Blue Ribbon Coalition, Inc., 25(31)
Bonier, Representative David, 130(19)
bonus bid, 45
Boston (MA), 18
Bowes, Michael, 81
Box, Thadis, 118, 122, 130(23), 131(44)
Brandt, Richard, 146–48
Brooks, John, 51(48)
Brotherson, Jack, 131(41)
*Bryant* v. *Yellen*, 50(27)
Bryce Canyon National Park, 71
budget maximization, 205, 222(16)
buffalo, 43, 59
building-height restrictions, 182
Bureau of Land Management (BLM), 4,
    43–45
  authority, 63
  budget, 44
  as central planning agency, 63
  and County Movement, 11

  grazing program, 6, 34, 62, 111, 114, 121
  history, 44
  land treatments, 7
  land-use plans, 27(67), 62
  mining law administration, 5, 37, 44
  multiple-use management, 4, 37, 44, 62,
    114
  as referee, 45, 63
  wilderness review, 47, 55(114)
  *see also* BLM lands; federal grazing fees;
    federal grazing permits; FLPMA
Bureau of Reclamation (BuRec), 26(41),
    224(45)
bureaucratic
  entrepreneurs, 68
  expansion, 67, 169
  goals, 67, 205
  incentives, 67–68, 205–6
BuRec; *see* Bureau of Reclamation
burros, wild, 5, 24(19), 101
Bush, President George, 198(10)
Byron, Lord, 224(39)

Cabinet Mountains, ix
California, viii, 5, 22(7), 34, 41, 53(66),
    54(93), 194, 224(45)
*California Coastal Commission* v. *Granite
    Rock Company*, 23(15)
*California Oregon Power Co.* v. *Beaver
    Portland Cement Co.*, 26(54)
California Outdoor Recreation League,
    25(33)
*Camfield* v. *United States*, 23(12), 77(16)
Canada, 43
Canyonlands National Park, ix, 42, 115, 212,
    220, 224(50)
Cape Cod National Seashore, 18–19
capitalism; *see* free market
Carlin (NV), 50(24)
Carlsbad Caverns National Park, 25(32)
Carson River, 9
Carson Sink, 10
Carter Administration
  Alaska national interest lands withdrawal,
    42
  federal water projects, 5
  MX missile basing, 5
  OCS leasing policy, 23(16)
  synthetic fuels program, 5
Carter, President Jimmy, 5, 41
Catron County, 11, 12
cattle; *see* livestock
Center for the Defense of Free Enterprise,
    28(73)
chaining, 7

Champion International Corporation, 224(43)
charity
  as consumption, 183
  efficiency of, 159
cheatgrass, 121
checkerboard lands, 35, 54(93), 224(43)
Chicago (IL), 170, 185
Christman, John, 164
citizen
  interests, 193–94
  preferences, 192, 199(30)
Clarke–McNary Act, 38, 51(44)
Class I air quality area, 6
classical utilitarianism, 147–49
  and preference utilitarianism, 146
  and pursuit of happiness, 185
  and wealth, 135
Clawson, Marion, 12, 14, 131(50), 132, 218
Clean Air Act
  1977 amendments, 6
  1990 amendments, 29(91)
  and National Parks, 6, 24(21)
Cleveland, President Grover, 38
climax plant community, 119
Clinton Administration
  grazing fee proposals, 29(100)
  on privatizing highways, 13
  and user fees, 16
Clinton, President Bill, 13
coal
  federal, 5, 6, 45
  reservation of, 22(3), 45
  severance tax on, 23(14)
  stripmining of, 51(44), 71
coal lands
  sale of, 54(99)
  withdrawal, 45
Coal Lands Act, 22(3)
Coase, Ronald, 81, 105(10), 162
coercion
  and bettering desires, 151
  by citizen interests, 194
  by collective management, 152(7), 195
  by consumer interests, 174, 195
  government, 180
  nature of, 195–96
  paternalistic, 166–69
  and respect for persons, 141
  and rights, 196
  see also autonomy; freedom; respect for persons
Coleman, Alfred, 194
collective management
  and coercion, 152(7), 195

evils of, 66–69, 180–81
collective values; see citizen interests
collectives
  good of, 158, 187
  and respect for persons, 201
  utility of, 144
  voluntary, 194
Colorado, 22(7), 23(12), 56, 68, 129(13), 220
Colorado Plateau, 120
Colorado River, vii, 42, 91, 103
comisionado, 210
commensurate forage, 64
commercial timberland, 76(12)
commodities
  aggregation of, 116
  body parts as, 86
  desirability index for, 117
  natural and cultural values as, 205–6, 221
  pollutants as, 15
  in productivity measures, 115–16
  scope of, 175
  water as, 206, 224(45)
commodity lands, 213–14
Common Land, British, 77(14)
common property, 59–60
Common Varieties Act, 50(23)
commons
  and bureaucratic entrepreneurs, 68
  disguised, 69
  and environmental problems, 17, 59–62
  and freedom, 194
  public domain as, 118
  and regulation, 57, 60, 69, 118
  regulatory, 60, 69
  tragedy of, 60–62, 77(14)
Commonwealth Edison Co. v. Montana, 23(14)
Commonwealth of Massachusetts v. Andrus, 23(16)
community grazing, 62, 77(18), 210
compensation
  hypothetical, 89, 98
  for privatization, 99
  for range improvements, 64
  for takings, 97
competition, promotion of, 191
competitive equilibrium, 87, 105(8)
complete right, 62, 101
compromise, 31–32, 46, 48, 186
computer models, 78(23)
Connecticut, viii, 31
Conrad, Joseph, 172
consciousness, 158
consequences, judging, 137
consequentialism, 73

consistency
  of ends, 142
  of preferences, 196–97
consumer interests, 191, 193, 195
consumer preference
  and advertising, 172
  and citizen preference, 192–93, 196–97
  over consumption plans, 84
  and desires, 82
  and free market, 69–71
  and indifference curves, 92
  and preservation, 171
  and productivity, 82
  ranking, 84, 96, 193
  rationality of, 167–68
consumer price index, 6
consumer sovereignty
  and bettering desires, 202–3
  and environmental values, 208
  and individuality, 173
  and public land policy, 212
consumer surplus
  aggregate, 91
  individual, 90
  see also consumer surplus measures
consumer surplus measures
  adequacy of, 97
  compensating variation (CV), 90
  divergence of, 92
  equivalent variation (EV), 90
  inconsistency of, 94
consumption
  bundle, 69, 82, 84, 191
  gifts as, 183–84
  plan, 84
  and production, 115
Continental Congress, 32, 49(2), 49(3)
contingent valuation, 129(11), 224(51)
contracting-out, 13, 217–19, 226(82),
    227(85)
Convention for the Protection of Migratory
    Birds, 43
Coos Bay Wagon Road, 54(93)
cost shifting
  in collective management, 57, 69, 181
  in commons, 61–62
  in firms, 182
  by spillover, 173
  by USFS, 206
costs
  project, 95–97
  unavoidable, 59
Cotter Corporation, 49(8)
Council of Economic Advisors, 8
County Movement, 11, 27(69), 27(67)

covenants
  and future contingencies, 129(18)
  inflexibility of, 114
  and market failure, 113
  under privatization, 102, 218
Crawford, Stanley, 211
credit sales, 32, 49(4)
Crown lands, 36
Crusoe, Robinson, 83
cui-ui, 9, 10
cultural values
  and County Movement, 11
  and federal power, 4
  and federal subsidies, 115, 213
  and free market, 213, 217
  and historic preservation, 115, 130(19)
  and logging, 209, 215
  and marketization, 209
  and ranching, 115
  and water rights, 210–11
Cumberland Gap National Historic Park, 220
cv, 90
CV, 91
CV; see consumer surplus measures
cyanide leaching, 84

Dahlman, Carl, 105(9)
Dark Canyon, 220
Davis Canyon, 224(50)
deficit
  federal; see federal deficit
  timber sales; see federal timber sales
deforestation, 38, 57, 59, 76(6)
Delicate Arch, 170
$\Delta w$, 99
$\Delta W$, 99
democracy
  of market, 190, 195
  and public land policy, 201, 203
Demsetz, Harold, 161–63
Dennis, William, 188, 190, 195
Denver (CO), 210, 225(55)
Department of Agriculture (USDA), 13, 38,
    39, 118
Department of Energy (DOE), 224(50)
Department of the Interior (DOI)
  BLM, 43
  FWS, 43
  GLO, 39, 44
  GS, 44
  NPS, 41
  Office of Policy Analysis, 8
depletion, range, 119
Descartes, René, 8
desert bighorn sheep, 89, 118

Desert Lands Act, 49(13), 26(54)
desert tortoise, 56
De Sica, Vittorio, 98
desires
    and advertising, 165
    autonomous, 165
    better satisfying, 82, 109, 127, 146–47, 202
    bettering, 157, 164–66, 202–4, 208
    for collective action, 191
    criticizing, 165–68, 196
    and economic values, 132
    and happiness, 146, 177(23)
    harmful, 165
    inconsistent, 165
    and individual welfare, 136, 145, 149–50
    in preference utilitarianism, 145–46
    and productivity, 82, 109
    transformation of, 202
    unworthy, 165
    and utility, 146
determinism, 179, 198(2)
Diamond International Corporation, 205
discount rate, vii, 106(23), 123
Disney Enterprises; see Mineral King
disposal era, 4, 32–37, 48, 57–59
District of Columbia, 32
DOE; see Department of Energy
DOI; see Department of the Interior
Dolores River, 90
dominant use, 43
Dorgan, William, 199(20)
Douglas fir, 70, 217
Douglas, Associate Justice William, 68, 184
Dowdle, Barney, 22(5), 76(5), 77(15), 113
droit du seigneur, 162
duck stamp program, 43
Ducks Unlimited, 65
duty, and happiness, 186
Dvorak, Antonin, 143

easements, 53(78), 113
    see also covenants
economics
    and equity, 58–59, 159
    and scarcity, 69–70
    and science, 133
    and value judgments, 133
    von Mises on, 142
Edelson, Nathan, 169
Edgeworth box diagram, 94
efficiency, economic, ix, 48
    and consent, 177(9)
    as productivity, 82
    and welfare, 177(9)
    see also productivity

EIS; see environmental impact statement
elitism
    of criticizing desires, 166
    of environmentalists, 12, 17, 169
    in public land management, 169
elk, 64
eminent domain, 23(13), 102
emission
    standards, 15
    taxes, 79(47), 191
    TEAs, 15
end
    treating another as an, 141
    treating oneself as an, 142
endangered species
    cui-ui, 9–10
    and endangered ways of life, 209
    grizzly bear, ix
    and marketization, 206–7, 223(25)
    red cockaded woodpecker, 222(22)
    spotted owl, northern; see northern spotted
        owl
Endangered Species Act
    FWS administration of, 5
    and marketization, 206–7
    and non-federal lands, 5, 24(20)
    on "taking" endangered species, 5
ends, 142, 165
    see also desires
Energy Policy Act, 51(44)
Engdahl, David, 25(34)
England
    colonial land grants of, 31
    naval forest reserves, 38
Enlarged Homestead Act, 49(6)
entitlements, and respect for persons, 140,
        151
entrepreneurs
    bureaucratic, 68
    and consumer sovereignty, 174
    and transaction costs, 86
    and waste, 57–58
Environmental Defense Fund, 16
environmental impact statement (EIS), 46
Environmental Protection Agency (EPA),
    Clean Air Act administration, 6
    TEA experiment, 15
environmental values
    and efficient markets, 204–5, 213, 217
    and market failures, 205
    and property rights, 17, 173
    see also natural values
envy, 83
EPA; see Environmental Protection Agency
Epstein, Richard, 106(24)

equal footing doctrine, 25(34)
equity
    argument for parks, 18
    and economics, 58, 159
    and efficiency, 176(6)
    and expected utility, 59
    and Homestead Act, 59
    and hypothetical compensation, 98
    as political problem, 58, 159
    and privatization, 160–61
    and productivity, 74
    and property rights, 72, 159
    and rafting permits, 108(37)
    and satisfying desires, 157
    standards of, 152(3)
    and utility, 144
estray law, 23(12)
*ev*, 91
*EV*, 91
EV; *see* consumer surplus measures
excellence, 165
exchange
    free, 19, 100
    utility of, 69–70
existence value, 177(8), 222(22), 224(51)
expected utility
    of advocacy, 181
    and equity, 59
    and time preference, 124
experience machine, 150, 154(34)
externalities; *see* spillovers

fairness; *see* equity
false targets, 144, 158, 185
Fantine, 159
feasible plan, 84
federal deficit, 14
federal grazing fees
    pricing, 62, 111, 119, 128(4), 213, 216
    and ranch viability, 30(101), 64, 216
    and range management costs, 12
federal grazing permits
    incomplete rights conferred by, 63
    non-transferability of, 64, 78(25)
    non-use permit, 64
    obtaining, 64, 111
    as private property, 11, 12, 27(65), 34, 62
    and property taxes, 119
    renewal preference, 64
    security of, 64, 119
    value of, 62, 77(20)
federal judges, accountability of, 68, 188
federal land management
    accountability in, 66
    constraints on, 35, 48, 63–64

contentious nature of, ix, 9, 47, 175
    costs of, 66
    economic return, 12, 16, 105(4), 114, 205–6
    local influence on, 35, 122, 214, 225(66)
    and market failure, 128(6)
    planning, 68
    productivity of, 114
    as socialism, 3, 13, 48
    *see also* federal land policy; BLM; FWS;
        NPS; USFS
federal land management agencies; *see* BLM;
        FWS; NPS; USFS
federal land policy
    agency influence on, 47, 52(60), 68
    as compromise, 48
    and equity, 18, 59, 160
    investments in, 48
    marketization of, 15–17, 156, 160,
        203–10
    and national heritage, 115, 213, 220
    preemption of, 34
    and prices, 111
    public participation, 45, 46
    revenue sharing, 51(46)
    subsidies, 204
    transaction cost justification of, 111–12
    and transaction costs, 111–12
    *see also* federal land management, BLM;
        FWS; NPS; USFS
Federal Land Policy and Management Act
        (FLPMA)
    Allotment Management Plans, 62, 77(19)
    BLM authority, 51(41), 63, 78(24)
    citizen advisory councils, 54(104)
    compensation for range improvements,
        78(27)
    and County Movement, 27(67)
    on economic return, 29(98)
    Grazing Advisory Boards, 78(33)
    grazing permit renewal, 78(27)
    grazing permits, 78(24)
    grazing regulation, 62
    land exchanges, 78(24)
    land sales, 78(24)
    land use plans, 27(67), 54(104), 62
    land withdrawals, 78(24)
    multiple use, 23(8), 44, 54(96)
    public participation, 54(104)
    Resource Management Plans, 62, 77(21)
    retention clause, 22(6)
    wilderness review, 47, 55(114)
federal lands
    acquisition of, 31, 33, 36, 38
    anomaly of, 3, 31
    area of, 3, 4, 22(3)

federal lands (*Cont.*)
  capital value of, 14
  disposal of, 4, 32–36
  local and state regulation of, 5
  local and state taxation of, 5
  as political compromise, 32
  private use of, 3, 34–35, 102, 218
  reservation of, 4, 36
  resources of, 3
  retention of, 36–37
  by state, 22(7)
  zoning of, 37, 213
  *see also* BLM lands; National Forests;
    National Parks; National Wildlife
    Refuges
federal mineral rights, 22(3), 68
federal payments in lieu of taxes, 23(14)
federal timber sales
  below-cost, 7, 40, 52(59), 81, 105(4), 114,
    221(10)
  costs of, 40, 114, 205–6
  and endangered species, 223(24)
  and exports, 40, 52(59)
  O&C, 44
  perverse incentives of, 206
  Tongass, 52(59), 194, 200(33)
  trends, 6, 24(24), 40, 52(58)
  and wilderness review, 68
federal water policy, marketization of,
    224(45)
federal water projects, 5, 9
federal water rights, implied, 9
first fundamental theorem of welfare
    economics, 89, 105(8)
  and argument from productivity, 84
  and consumer preference, 171
  and firms, 182
  and ideal markets, 110
  and prices, 115, 121
  and public goods, 129(9)
  and reality, 122
  and self-interest, 183
  and spillovers, 84
Fish and Wildlife Service (FWS), 4, 5, 43
Fisheries Management Councils, 15
Fishery Conservation and Management Act,
    29(92)
fishing and
  FWS, 43
  ITQs, 15
  logging, 85, 216, 226(74)
  privatization, 66
  water diversions, 9–10
  Wilderness, 25(33)
Florida, 34, 43

FLPMA; *see* Federal Land Policy and
    Management Act
Forbes grant, 34
Forest Reserve Amendment, 38
forest reserves, 38
  and commons, 59–60
  renamed National Forests, 39
  statutory purpose, 39
Forest Roads and Trails Act, 206
Forest Service (USFS), 4, 37–41
  budget, 38
  grazing program, 6, 44, 64, 220
  history, 39–40
  multiple-use management, 4, 40, 64, 81,
    114, 220
  National Recreation Strategy, 13, 28(80),
    219, 226(83)
  official name, 37
  professionalism, 39
  as socialist enterprise, 13
  timber program; *see* federal timber sales
  *see also* National Forests
Forest Service Organic Act, 51(40)
Foss, Phillip, 8, 214
France, Tom, 225(66)
Francis, John, 129(18)
fraud, in disposal era, 33, 36
free market
  and autonomy, 19, 195
  and cultural heritage, 171
  democracy of, 190, 195
  disutility of regulation, 15, 58, 76(10), 168
  and environmental values, 205
  environmentalism, 15–16, 29(93), 222(14)
  ideology of, 174
  and natural heritage, 171
  and preference utilitarianism, 76(11),
    153(8), 156, 179
  and productivity, 17, 69–71, 85–86
  vs. socialism, 175
  unpatterned allocation by, 204
  utility of, 58, 76(11), 131(51)
free rider problem, 112, 160, 176(8), 222(22)
freedom
  restricting, 151, 165–68
  use of, 156, 164–65, 168–72, 176
  utility of, 76(11), 141, 155(45), 196
  *see also* autonomy; coercion
Friedman, Milton, 176(8)
fuel minerals, 36, 50(23)
future benefits
  argument from, 110, 123, 147
  discounting of, 106(23), 110, 123, 173
  and future persons, 126
  and future preferences, 126

future benefits (*Cont.*)
  present value of, 123
  reckoning, 125
future persons
  duty to, 131(51)
  identity of, 131(51)
  representation of, 58, 67
FWS; *see* Fish and Wildlife Service

gain
  individual, 90, 97
  net, 88
  personal, 184
  social, 97
gains from trade, 85
Gardner, B. Delworth, 76(13), 111–13,
    128(2), 128(6), 133, 152(3), 215
Gates, Paul, 32, 76(6)
*Geer* v. *Connecticut*, 24(17)
General Land Office (GLO), 39, 44
General Mining Law, 34
  BLM administration of, 5
  and Locke, 50(21)
  and mineral leasing, 45
  scope of, 50(23)
General Revision Act, 38, 50(20)
General Swamp Land Act, 36
Georgia Pacific, 70
gifts
  as consumption, 183–84
  efficiency of cash, 159
  and wealth change, 107(27)
Gila National Forest, 12
Gilbert, Bil, 211–12, 225(55)
Glacier National Park, 41
Glahe, Fred, 167–68, 177(23)
Glen Canyon, ix, 7, 194
Glen Canyon Dam, 194
GLO; *see* General Land Office
"God Bless America," 22(2)
good
  individual; *see* individual good
  of one's own, 144–45
  and right, 135
  social; *see* social good
good, economic
  as bundles of services, 196
  inferior, 93
  superior, 93
Gorbachev, Soviet Premier Mikhail, 9
Gore Range Eagles Nest Primitive Area, 68
Graduation Act, 33, 49(5), 49(13)
Grand Canyon
  air quality at, 86, 105(11), 212
  and consumer sovereignty, 166, 171

motors in, 91
  proposed dams in, vii
  rafting permits, 103, 108(37)
  rafting regulation, 169
  Theodore Roosevelt on, 171
Grand Canyon National Park, 41
gravel, mining of, 50(23)
grazing
  allotment, 34
  district, 34, 36, 44, 59, 60
  *see also* federal grazing permits; federal
    grazing fees; BLM, USFS
Grazing Advisory Boards, 44, 67
Grazing Service (GS), 44
Great Basin, 3, 33, 120
Great Basin National Park, 37, 212
Great Plains, 33, 43, 119
Green River, 42
Gregg, Frank, 8, 11
grizzly bear, ix, 112, 206
growth curve, biological, 60
GS; *see* Grazing Service
Guadalupe Mountains National Park,
    25(32)
Gulf Oil Corporation, 23(15)
Guthrie, Woody, 2, 3, 22(3)

Hagenstein, Perry, 31, 212
Hamilton, Alexander, 32, 33
Hanke, Steve, 8, 109, 152(7)
happiness
  and desire satisfaction, 146, 177(23)
  and duty, 186
  interpersonal comparison of, 147
  intrapersonal comparison of, 147
  measurement of, 147
  paradox of, 144
  pursuit of, 185
  quality of, 149, 154(38)
  in roles, 185–6
  and wealth, 134
Hardin, Garrett, 69, 77(14)
hardrock mineral; *see* mining claims;
    locatable mineral
Hare, Richard, 138
Harrison, President Benjamin, 38
Hartford (CT), viii
Hatch, Senator Orrin, 26(35)
Hawk Inn and Mountain Resort, 176(7)
Hayek, Friedrich, 58, 63, 76(9), 76(10),
    76(11), 78(23), 131(51), 152(8), 166,
    175, 195–96, 203
Hayes, Jim, 75(4)
Hendry, Jim, 226(72)
Hensley settlement, 220

heritage
  cultural, 115, 156, 213
  national, 115
  natural, 156, 192, 194
Hetch Hetchy controversy; *see* Yosemite
    National Park
Hickel, Interior Secretary Walter, 187,
    198(18)
high quality forestry, 217
Hobbes, Thomas, 9, 72, 107(27), 183
Holmes, Sherlock, 143, 154(27)
Holy Cross Reserve, 23(12)
Homestead Act
  acreage limitation of, 32, 33, 49(6)
  and equity, 59
  reservation of coal, 22(3)
Hook, David, 12
horses, wild, ix, 5, 24(19), 101
Hume, David, 26(52), 138
*Hunt* v. *United States*, 24(18)
hunting
  and BLM land, 63–64, 114, 215
  and marketization, 222(21)
  and National Parks, 6, 25(32)
  in National Wildlife Refuges, 43
  and privatization, 66
  in Wilderness Areas, 25(33)
hypothetical market, 129(11)

$I \rightarrow II$, 82
Ickes, Interior Secretary Harold, 44
Idaho, 22(7), 222(21)
ideal market, 84–85
  approximating, 113
  and marketization, 156, 206
  optimality in, 17, 111
  and privatization, 171
  self-interest in, 183
ideology of
  free market, 174–75
  professionals, 188
ignorance
  problem of, 78(23), 203
  refuge of, 104
impartiality, 72
imperative
  Categorical, 139, 141
  conditional, 134
Imperial Valley, 34
improvement standards
  aggregate consumer surplus, 91
  defensibility of, 88
  Kaldor criterion, 89
  net benefits, 96
  net gain, 88

Pareto criterion, 83
  and preference utilitarianism, 147
  and privatization, 192
  and productivity measures, 109
  Scitovsky criterion, 89
  and value judgments, 133
  wealth, 99
inaction, legislative, 53(80)
incentives, bureaucratic, 67, 112, 205
income
  effect, 92–93, 96
  guaranteed, 76(10)
  redistribution, 159–60, 176(6), 190–91
incremental privatization, 11
indifference curve, 92
individual demand curve, 96
individual good
  and consciousness, 158
  and desire satisfaction, 74, 136, 157, 165,
    167–68, 176, 191
  and happiness, 136, 165, 168
  and preference, 19, 70
  and valuation, 136
  *see also* desires; interests
individual transferable quota (ITQ), 15
individual welfare; *see* individual good
inequity, utility of, 58, 76(9)
inferior good, 93
inflation, 123
inholdings
  access to, 49(8)
  condemnation of, 5, 23(13)
  regulation of, 6
integrity of persons, 20, 74, 140
  *see also* autonomy; respect for persons
interest, public; *see* public interest
interest, rate of, 123–24
interests
  citizen; *see* citizen interests
  consumer; *see* consumer interests
  and desires, 156, 166–70, 190
  ideological, 187
  of non-humans, viii, 145, 148, 158, 187
  notions of, 75, 156
  personal, 187
  and rational choice, 167
  and rights, 103
  and roles, 187
  *see also* individual good; desires
Interstate 84, viii
interstate highway system, privatization of,
    13
invisible hand, 139, 153(12)
ITQ; *see* individual transferable
    quota

*Izaac Walton League of America* v. *St. Clair*, 23(13)

Japan, 40, 52(59)
Jefferson, 32, 33
Jesus, 19, 73, 172
Jobes, Patrick, 209
John Paul II, Pope, 178(42)
Judas, 19
juniper, 61
*Just* v. *Marinett Co.*, 198(10)

Kaibab National Forest, 24(18)
Kaldor criterion, 89
  and consumer surplus, 106(19)
  inconsistency of, 89, 105(15)
Kaldor improvement; *see* Kaldor criterion
Kampgrounds of America, Inc. (KOA), 219
Kant, Immanuel, 26(52), 73, 135, 136,
    139–43, 149, 162
Kantianism, 20, 134, 151–52, 156, 196, 201
Khrushchev, Soviet Premier Nikita, 13
Kings Canyon National Park, 41
Klein, Joe, 15
*Kleppe* v. *New Mexico*, 24(19)
Knetsch, Jack, 131(50), 132
Knutson–Vandenberg Act, 206
KOA; *see* Kampgrounds of America, Inc.
Krutilla, John, 81
Ku Klux Klan, 202

Lahontan Reservoir, 9
Lahontan Valley, 9, 10
Lake Powell, 194
Land Act
  of 1796, 33, 49(4)
  of 1800, 49(12)
  of 1804, 49(12)
  of 1820, 49(12)
land community, 216, 226(75)
land grant colleges, 35
land grants
  military, 35
  to Native Alaskans, 22(3), 54(92)
  railroad, 35
  Spanish, 34
  to states, 35, 36
Land Ordinance, 32
land treatments, 7, 117
*LaRue* v. *Udall*, 25(29)
Las Cruces (NM), 211
Las Vegas (NV), 127, 210, 225(55)
leasing
  mineral; *see* mineral leasing; Mineral
    Leasing Act

of public lands, 3, 41, 207, 214, 218–19
Lee, Dwight, 167–68, 177(23)
legislators
  accountability of, 67, 188–89
  self-interest of, 67
Leopold, Aldo, 216, 226(75)
Libecap, Gary, 117–22, 212
libertarianism, 141–43
  *see also* coercion; freedom
liberty; *see* freedom
life
  plan of, 150, 165–66
  as property, 107(28)
  value of, 97
*Light* v. *United States*, 23(12)
Lincoln Memorial, 212
Linowes Commission; *see* President's
    Commission on Privatization
livestock
  cattle, ix, 23(12), 34, 53(91), 56, 60–62, 64,
    89, 114, 118, 120, 122, 215, 217,
    225(55), 225(66)
  federal share of production, 215
  sheep, 34, 103, 115, 122, 225(55)
  *see also* BLM; federal grazing permits;
    USFS
Locke, John, 34, 38, 50(21), 103, 164, 177(14)
Locke's proviso, 38, 164
logging
  cut-and-run, 36, 50(20), 76(5)
  on federal lands; *see* federal timber
    sales
  on private lands, 39, 58, 209–10
Los Angeles (CA), 210
Los Padres National Forest, 23(15)
loss; *see* gain
Louisiana Pacific Corporation, 56
*Lucas* v. *South Carolina*, 198(10)
Lueck, Dean, 30(105), 83, 87, 102, 103,
    106(25)
Lufkin, Joseph, 154(33)
lumber, engineered, 217

Madany, Michael, 131(41)
Maine, 36
Manzanar (CA), 193
marginal rate of substitution, 105(15)
marginal utility, diminishing, 144
marijuana, 103
Mariposa Grove, 53(66), 41
market
  free; *see* free market
  ideal; *see* ideal market
  perfect; *see* perfect market
market demand curve, 96

market failures
  correction of, 15, 113, 206
  and environmental problems, 205
  and marketization, 206
  and public lands, 112, 128(6), 205–6
  *see also* public goods; spillovers;
    transaction costs
marketing, as production, 172
marketization
  and citizen interests, 209
  and consumer sovereignty, 208
  and endangered species, 222(22)
  and environmentalists, 204, 221(10)
  and forest management plans, 207
  and ideal markets, 156, 206
  and market failure, 206, 222(22)
  and non-game species, 223(25)
  and off-road vehicles, 207
  and preservation, 156
  and privatization, 15–17, 160, 208
  and public goods, 206
  and public ownership, 223(33)
  and public participation, 207, 209
  and recreation fees, 206, 222(21)
  and vacation homesites, 207
Marlboro cigarettes, 172
Marsh, George Perkins, 38
Martin, Dolores, 208
Martin, William, 198(15)
Maryland, 31–32, 49(2)
Mason, Larry, 24(20), 226(73), 226(74)
Massachusetts, 5, 31, 36
*Massachusetts* v. *Andrus*, 24(16)
Mather, Stephen, 42
Maui, 225(55)
maximum sustainable yield (MSY), 60
maximum willingness-to-pay (MWTP), 90
  in advance, 107(27)
  determination of, 95
  and mWTA, 93, 106(20), 208
MCA; *see* Music Corporation of America
*McCulloch* v. *Maryland*, 23(14)
McKenzie, Richard, 167–68
*McMichael* v. *United States*, 25(30)
means
  treating another simply as a, 141
  waste of, 142
Michigan, 51(48)
Migratory Bird Conservation Act, 43
Migratory Bird Hunting and Conservation
    Act, 53(86)
Military Reservations, 35
Mill, John Stuart, 79(49), 138–39, 141, 147,
    148–50, 153(18), 154(38), 154(42),
    155(44), 155(45), 175, 178(40), 185

Mineral King, ix, 116, 130(21), 207
mineral leasing, 36, 45, 63
Mineral Leasing Act
  fuel minerals, 50(23)
  leasing provisions, 45
  and revenue sharing, 23(14)
mineral rights, reservation of, 22(3), 36, 45,
    68
Minerals Management Service, 54(94),
    54(95)
minimum willingness-to-accept (mWTA), 90
  determination of, 95
  and MWTP, 93, 106(20), 208
mining claims
  abandonment of, 5
  locatable mineral, 34
  patenting, 34
  unpatented, 50(24)
  valuable discovery, 34, 50(22)
Minnesota, 81
Mises, Ludwig von, vii, 142, 172–75, 195
Mississippi River, 31
Mohave Desert, 45, 56
Monadnock Building, 170
monopoly, 15, 191
  profits, 70
Montana, ix, 23(7), 23(14), 43
Morrill Act, 35
motive, and right action, 73, 138–39
Mt. Rainier National Park, 41
MSY; *see* maximum sustainable yield
Muir, John, 37, 42, 184, 185
multiple use
  difficulty of, 214
  environmentalists on, 40, 216
  of federal lands, 4, 37, 40, 44, 62, 64, 81,
    102, 114, 214–17
  to internalize externalities, 18
  of private lands, 113
  and privatization, 102
  statutory definition, 40
  and timber sales, 81
  and zoning, 67, 214
Multiple Use and Sustained Yield Act
    (MUSYA), 40, 52(60), 221(10)
Munger, Michael, 199(20)
Music Corporation of America (MCA), 219
MUSYA, 52(61)
mWTA; *see* minimum willingness-to-accept
MWTP; *see* maximum willingness-to-pay
MX missile, 5

Nagel, Thomas, 143
National Audubon Society, 7, 10, 16, 172,
    223(37)

National Bison Range, 43
National Commodity Use System
    (proposed), 12, 28(74)
national debt, 4, 8, 14, 32
National Environmenal Policy Act (NEPA),
    46–47
National Forest Management Act (NFMA)
    annual allowable cut, 24(23)
    multiple use, 23(8)
    NDEF, 41, 52(63)
    public participation, 54(104)
    Renewable Resource Assessments, 29(99),
        54(104)
National Forests, 4, 37–41
    annual allowable cut, 6
    area of, 37
    campground management, 13, 219
    grazing in, 44
    leasing of, 218
    management objectives, 40
    management plans, 221(10)
    marketization of, 206–9, 218
    Pinchot on, 39
    pressures to log, 40
    purposes, 37
    recreational use of, 39, 52(58)
    roading of, 40, 114, 206, 218
    strip mining, 51(44)
    timber sales, 81, 52(58), 105(4)
    and trade deficit, 40
    Wilderness in, 47
    zoning of, 208
    see also federal timber sales; Forest
        Service; NFMA; multiple use
National Grasslands, 38
National Inholders Association, 207
National Monuments, 6, 41
National Park Service (NPS), 4, 41–42, 45
National Park Service Organic Act, 53(76)
National Park System, 41, 212
National Park Users Association, 28(72)
National Parks, 4, 41–42
    additional, 212
    air pollution in, 6, 24(21), 86, 105(11), 112,
        212
    concessionaires, 12, 218
    and consumer sovereignty, 212, 224(50)
    establishment of, 41–42, 184
    and free rider problem, 112, 160, 176(8)
    hunting in, 6, 25(32)
    inholdings, 5, 6, 23(13)
    justification of, 18, 160, 170, 176(8), 204
    as predator refuges, 5
    and privatization, 21
    recreation pressures on, 42

statutory purpose of, 42
National Rangeland Grazing System Act
    (proposed), 28(71)
National Rifle Association, 6
National Wildlife Refuge Administration
    Act, 53(84)
National Wildlife Refuge System, 43
National Wildlife Refuges, 4, 43
    acquired and leased lands, 53(78)
    oil and gas leases in, 53(79)
    see also ANWR
Native Americans
    Alaskan, 22(3), 54(92)
    and commerce clause, 24(17)
    conquest of, 34
    Paiute, 9–10
    reservations of, 9–10, 23(7), 34
natural gas, federal share, 6
natural heritage; see heritage, natural
Natural Resources Defense Council, 204
natural values
    and efficient markets, 171, 204–5, 213, 217
    and market failure, 205
    and property rights, 17, 173
Nature Conservancy, 192, 226(77)
Naval Petroleum Reserve, 36
NDEF; see non-declining even flow
negative campaign, 180
negative rights, 161
neighborhood effects; see spillovers
Nelson, Robert, 3, 11, 14, 64, 129(18), 209,
    213–14
NEPA; see National Environmental Policy
    Act
net benefits; see aggregate net benefit
Nevada, ix, 4, 5, 9, 26(35), 37, 50(24), 53(91),
    212
New Federalism, 5
New Haven (CT), 199(28)
New Mexico, 11, 22(7), 24(19), 118, 210–11
New York, 14, 205, 222(12)
New York (NY), 14
Newton, Wayne, 225(55)
NFMA; see National Forest Management Act
Nine Mile Canyon, 30(103)
Niskanen, William, 8, 201, 222(16)
Nollan v. California Coastal Commission,
    198(10)
non-declining even flow (NDEF), 41
North Cascades, 220
North, Colonel Oliver, 187
Northern Rockies National Wildlife
    Federation, 225(66)
northern spotted owl
    as endangered species, 24(20), 223(24)

northern spotted owl (*Cont.*)
  habitat, 216, 226(73)
  as indicator species, 217
  and logging, 209, 217, 223(24)
  and marketization, 207, 222(22)
*Northern Spotted Owl* v. *Hodel*, 222(24)
Northwest, old, 31
Nozick, Robert, 150, 154(34)
NPS; *see* National Park Service

O&C lands, 44, 54(93)
OCS; *see* outer continental shelf
Office of Management and Budget, 5
Office of Surface Mining (OSM), 51(44)
off-road vehicles
  all-terrain vehicles (ATVs), 217
  and marketization, 207
  in Mohave Desert, 56
  and National Forest management, 25(30),
    35
  and Wilderness Areas, 6
Ohio, 35, 50(32)
Ohio River, 31
oil
  federal share, 6
  lands, 45
  shale, 5
Olympic National Park, 185, 212
O'Neill, Onora, 142
opportunity cost
  in forest management, 206
  and private resources, 208
  of ranching, 62
  of Wilderness, 69
optimality
  Pareto, 83–86
  problem of second best, 113
  and relative superiority, 87, 112
option value, 213, 222(22)
Oregon, 22(7), 44, 54(93), 221(10)
OSM; *see* Office of Surface Mining
O'Toole, Randal, 29(88), 205–10, 218,
    222(21), 222(22), 223(25), 223(33)
"ought" vs. "is," 73, 74
outer continental shelf (OCS)
  mineral leasing, 5, 44, 54(94)
  ownership, 22(3)
Outer Continental Shelf Lands Act, 22(3)
overgrazing
  of commons, 60–62, 118
  effects of, 61
  and federal grazing fees, 204
  of federal range, 44, 65, 118–22, 216,
    225(71), 226(72)
  of private range, 119–20, 122, 130(23)

ownership
  and autonomy, 163
  as bundle of use rights, 72, 101
  divided, 163
  full, 164
  *see also* property rights
Oxfam, 174

Pacific Lumber Company, 205, 221(11)
Paiute Indians, 9
paradox of happiness, 144
*parciante*, 210
Pareto efficient; *see* Pareto optimal
Pareto improvement, 83–84, 86, 87–88, 89,
    98, 103, 109, 115, 147
Pareto optimal, 83
Pareto optimality, 84–87, 176(6)
*Parker* v. *United States*, 68, 78(39)
Parks, National; *see* National Parks
Partridge, Ernest, 158
Parunuweap Canyon, 95, 97
passenger pigeon, 59
paternalism, 75, 166–70
Pelican Island, 43
Pendley, William Perry, 226(76)
Pennsylvania, 38
perfect market; *see* ideal market
*Perkins* v. *Bergland*, 25(28)
persons; *see* autonomy; future persons;
    integrity of persons; respect for persons
Phoenix (AZ), 210, 225(55)
pig, problem of contented, 147–50, 154(42),
    158
Pinchot, Gifford, 39, 42, 52(56), 52(60)
*pion*, 210
plan
  consumption, 84
  feasible, 84
  land-use; *see* FLPMA
  of life, 166
  production, 84
  resource-release, 84
pleasure; *see* happiness
Plum Creek Timber Company, 209
political rights, 191
*Pollard* v. *Hagen*, 23(7)
Pope, Carl, 222(14)
Posner, Richard, 56, 99–102, 106(26),
    106(27), 107(29), 108(30), 134–35, 145,
    184
Powell, John Wesley, 204, 210
preemption
  of federal land policy, 34–35
  prospective, 50(20)
  rights, 34, 102–3

preference
  alteration, 186
  citizen; *see* citizen
  consumer; *see* consumer preference
  and desire, 146
  and happiness, 168, 185
  informed, 150
  and prescription, 197
  and preservation, 171
  and productivity, 82
  revelation of, 71, 192–93
  and willingness-to-pay, 193
preference ranking, consumer; *see* consumer
    preference
preference utilitarianism, 145–47
  incoherence of, 193
  and preference change, 146
  and privatization, 191
  and productivity, 135, 156, 161
President's Commission on Privatization, 14,
    15
prevention of significant deterioration, 6
prices
  distortion of, 117
  market, 84–85, 111
  market-clearing, 85
prior appropriation doctrine, 9
prisoner's dilemma, 60, 61, 62, 65, 69, 77(17)
privatization, 13
privatizing public lands, ix, 3, 7
  argument from integrity of persons for, 74
  argument from productivity for, 71
  and citizen preferences, 193
  and consumer sovereignty, 208
  costs of, 66, 74, 110, 124
  current disposal policy, 211
  equity argument for, 59
  fraud in, 59, 76(13)
  goal of, 21, 106(25)
  and Locke, 164
  and national debt, 14
  net benefit of, 66, 110, 123
  present value of, 123
  process of, 21, 59
  rangeland, 117
  in Reagan era, 8
  redundancy of, 114
  and Sagebrush Rebellion, 7
  utility of, 183
  and wealth maximization, 100–3
  Wilderness Areas, 7, 101, 108(31), 223(37)
probability, 167
production, 69
  and consumption, 115
  plan, 84

productivity, 82
  argument from, 17, 57, 72–73, 87
  and autonomy, 19
  concept of, 18, 82, 104
  and desires, 88
  and equity, 18
  of exchange, 70
  in ideal markets, 18, 84–85
  managing for, 211
  meaning of, 74
  measures; *see* productivity measures
  and prices, 111
  of privatization, 18, 104, 161
  of production, 70
  of rangeland, 60, 118, 120
  in real markets, 18, 85–86
  as social goal, 191
  standards; *see* improvement standards
  and value judgments, 133
  and willingness-to-pay, 70
productivity measures, 109
  likeness to ideal, 110–15
  net output, 115–17
  value of net output, 117–18
products, individuation of, 116
Professional River Outfitters Association, 65,
    169
professionalism, 188–89
property; *see* property rights; ownership; use
    rights
property rights
  advantages of, 65
  attenuation of, 182
  and autonomy, 156, 163, 196
  complete, 62
  conflicting, 72
  distribution of, 159
  efficiency argument for, 157–63
  environmental utility of, 59, 173
  incompleteness of, 72
  and individual welfare, 151, 156
  and land stewardship, 173
  Locke's justification of, 50(21), 164
  and opportunity costs, 208
  productivity of, 72
  and property taxes, 223(37)
  and respect for persons, 151, 162–63, 179
  secure, 62–63
  social utility of, 63, 70, 76(11)
  transferability of, 86, 164
  transferable, 62
Providence (RI), viii
public domain, 4, 44, 60
public education, 178(40)
public goods, 129(9)

public goods (*Cont.*)
  aspect of wilderness, 222(22)
  financing, 129(12), 206
public interest, 67, 166, 182, 190, 193
public land states, 35, 50(32)
public lands
  justification of, 151–52, 170, 176, 202
  *see also* federal lands
public participation, 45–46
  impact of, 67
  and individual welfare, 203
  and marketization, 207, 209
  and revealed preference, 71
  value to agencies, 68
Public Range Improvement Act, 128(4)
public resources
  allocation of, 170
  productivity of, 70
public trust, 203, 221(6), 224(47)
public values, 199(30)
purchaser credits, 206
Pyramid Lake, 9, 10
Pyramid Lake Reservation, 9, 10

"rain follows the plow," 32, 122
ranching
  economics of, 30(101), 78(28), 198(15)
  and federal subsidies, 209
  and wealth-maximization, 184
range
  condition, 118–22, 130(23)
  condition index, 119, 121, 131(44)
  ecology, 60–61, 122
  improvements, 7, 64, 120
RARE I, 47
RARE II, 47
rational agency, 142–43
  as a good, 143
  respecting, 151
  as source of value, 139
rational choice, 142, 167, 169–70
rational ignorance, 66, 181, 198(20)
rationality
  concepts of, 142–43, 167–68
  of desires, 192
  economic, 201, 204, 215, 220, 221(10)
  of ends, 142
  of individual preference, 79(44)
  of social preference, 79(44)
Reagan, President Ronald, 8, 198(10)
Reagan Administration
  Asset Management Program, 8, 11
  and government responsibilities, 13
  OCS leasing policy, 5, 23(16)
  privatization advocates in, 8

  and Sagebrush Rebellion, 7
Reclamation Act, 34, 49(13), 50(28)
Reclamation Reform Act, 35
recreation lands, 213–14
recreational ranchettes, 64–65, 127
red-cockaded woodpecker, 222(22)
redwoods, 2, 3, 19, 41, 70, 194
reforestation, 40, 70, 206
relict areas, 120, 131(41)
Renewable Resource Assessments, 16,
  54(104)
residence requirements of disposal
  legislation, 33
Resource Management Plan (RMP), 62
resource management plans, 45
resource release plan, 84
resources
  allocation of, 82
  economic notion of, 82, 88
  efficient allocation of, 48
  waste of; *see* waste
respect for persons
  Categorical Imperative (RP), 139
  and collective action, 201
  content of, 141, 151
  and respect for self, 142
  *see also* autonomy; integrity of
    persons
responsibility; *see* accountability
revenue sharing, 23(14), 54(95)
Rich County, 120
Richardson, Henry, 171
right
  and good, 73, 135, 138
  and motive, 80(51), 138–39
rights
  complete, 62
  and interests, 103
  negative, 141, 143, 151
  of non-humans, viii
  political, 191
  positive, 142, 151
  property; *see* property rights
  rationalizations of, 196
  and respect for persons, 140–41
  secure, 62–63
  transferable, 62
  use; *see* use rights
  utilitarian basis of, 140, 153(16), 161
RMP; *see* Resource Management Plan
Rocky Mountain National Park, 41
roles
  demands of, 185–86
  and happiness, 185
  of legislator, 189

Roosevelt, President Theodore, 39, 41, 43, 45, 53(73), 171
Roslyn (WA), 209, 224(43)
royalty, 45, 184
RP; *see* respect for persons

sagebrush, big, 61, 121
Sagebrush Rebellion, 7, 225(55)
  and County Movement, 11
  and equal footing doctrine, 25(34), 36
Sagoff, 130(20), 177(9), 191–94, 199(30), 201, 224(38)
St. George (UT), 95–96
salmon, and logging, 216, 226(74)
Salmon River, 222(21)
San Bernardino National Forest, 194
San Francisco (CA), 42
San Isabel National Forest, 220
San Juan Resource Area, 66
sand, mining of, 50(23)
Santa Fe (NM), 211
Sargent, John Singer, 170
satisfaction; *see* happiness
Save the Redwoods League, 192
Sax, Joseph, 156, 191–94, 198(7), 199(26), 201, 212
Scanlon, Thomas, 153(16)
scarcity, 69, 157
school lands, 32, 49(8), 50(32)
Schurz, Interior Secretary Carl, 38, 39
science, and values, 133
Scitovsky criterion, 89
scrip, 21, 35
SCS; *see* Soil Conservation Service
seat belt laws, 75, 167–68
*Seattle Audubon Society* v. *Evans*, 223(24)
second best, problem of, 113
second fundamental theorem of welfare economics, 176(6)
section, township, 32
secure right, 62–63
self-interest
  assumption of, 69, 72, 179
  of bureaucrats, 67
  in collective management, 186
  constraint of, 70, 72, 181, 183
  of federal judges, 68
  of federal land managers, 63
  of federal land users, 67
  and happiness, 185
  in ideal markets, 84
  and personal interests, 189
  in prisoner's dilemma, 61
  and productivity, 72–73
  and public interest, 186

senses of, 183–84
  of voters, 66
sequoia; *see* redwoods
Sequoia National Forest, 130(21)
Sequoia National Park, 41, 116, 130(21), 194, 207
sheep; *see* livestock
Sheldon National Wildlife Refuge, 53(91)
Sheridan (WY), 225(66)
Sidgwick, Henry, 146
Sierra Club
  on economic rationality, 221(10)
  on federal grazing fees, 16
  and free market environmentalism, 222(14)
  and Grand Canyon dams, vii
  on high-quality forestry, 226(78)
  as interest group, 65
  on multiple use, 104(3)
  on recreation fees, 29(94)
*Sierra Club* v. *Hickel*, 130(21)
*Sierra Club* v. *Morton*, 130(21)
Sierra Nevada mountains, vii, 9
Simmons, Randy, 187–88, 190, 195
"simple gifts," 150, 155(49)
Simpson, Senator Alan, 226(71)
Singer, Peter, 154(28)
Sisk, John, 104(2)
slavery
  of addictions, 169
  buying freedom from, 162
  consent to, 175
  and consumer interests, 192
  consumerism as, 176, 178(42)
  and slave wages, 196
"slow elk," 64, 114
Smith, Adam, 153(12)
Smith, Vernon, 21
social good
  irreducible, 145, 158
  reduction to individual good, 70, 74, 136, 143
social preference, 79(44), 199(30)
Social Security System, 59, 76(12)
social welfare; *see* social good
socialism
  and capitalism, 175
  costs of, 77(15)
  and environmental regulation, 15
  federal land management as, 3, 13, 48
Socrates, 147
softwood inventory, federal share of, 6
Soil and Conservation Service (SCS), 119
South Bronx (NY), 170

Southeast Alaska Conservation Council,
    104(2)
Southeast Utah Association of Local
    Governments, 226(82)
Southern Oregon Resources Alliance,
    108(32)
sovereignty, federal, 5
Spain, 34
Spanish-American War, 35
*Spann* v. *City of Dallas*, 79(46)
Spire Point, 220
speculation, 33, 50(20), 58
spillovers
    bargaining to contain, 85
    containment by merging, 18, 79(45)
    and cost-shifting, 173
    and ideal markets, 84
    inevitability of, 71
    and multiple use, 18
    and optimality, 113
    and Pareto improvements, 147
    and privatization, 47
    and property rights, 162
split estate lands, 22(3), 51(44)
Stanley, Henry M., 221(8)
state cessions, 32, 49(3)
*State of Utah* v. *Andrus*, 49(8)
status, 184–85
Stillwater National Wildlife Refuge, 10
Stock Raising Homestead Act, 22(3), 49(6)
strip mining, 51(44), 71
Stroup, Richard, 8, 30(104), 66–68, 76(12),
    78(34), 78(35), 79(44), 79(45), 113, 115,
    152(7), 166, 173, 178(28), 179–84, 186,
    190, 198(6), 205
subjectivism, 134, 152(5), 178(35)
Submerged Lands Act, 22(3)
subsidies, non-cash, 35
Sullivan, Louis, 171
superior good, 93
Superior National Forest, 81
Surface Mining Control and Reclamation
    Act, 51(44)
sustained yield, 39–40, 60–61
Symms, Senator Steven, 28(83)
synthetic fuels program, 5

Taft, President William, 45
takings, 23(13), 51(44), 182, 198(10)
tax refund checkoffs, 129(13)
taxes
    cost shifting via, 14, 87, 180
    federal immunity from, 5
    and federal lands, 14, 66, 160, 166, 169
    income redistribution via, 159

    payments in lieu of, 23(14), 54(95)
    property, 87, 119, 160, 170, 193, 223(37)
    severance, 23(14)
Taylor Grazing Act
    compensation provisions, 119
    and grazing commons, 118
    grazing permits vs. private property, 77(20)
    GS authorization, 44
    and preemption of federal grazing policy,
        34
    on range improvements, 78(27)
TEA; *see* transferable emission
        allowance
Teresa, Mother, 184
Texas, 50(32), 118, 226(77)
theft
    of forage, 65
    and net gain, 98
    of timber, 38
    as transfer activity, 182
    and wealth change, 107(27)
"This land is your land," 3, 21(1), 22(2)
Thoreau, Henry, 174, 175
Timber and Stone Act, 51(39)
timber barons, ethos of, 38
timber famine, 38–39
timber sales; *see* federal timber sales
time preference, 123, 131(50)
Tolstoy, Leo, 153(13)
Tongass National Forest, 52(59), 104(2), 194
Tongass Timber Reform Act, 52(59), 200(33)
township, 32
transaction cost barriers
    and citizen interests, 191
    and consumer preference, 171
    and government intervention, 86
    and land stewardship, 173
    and multiple use, 161
    and parks, 18, 176(8)
    and privatization, 72, 101, 108(31), 159,
        160–61
    and productivity, 18
    and public goods, 86, 160
    and spillovers, 161
    and wealth maximization, 101, 108(30)
transaction costs, 86
transfer activity
    in private sector, 182–83
    in public sector, 180–81, 198(6)
transferability, of rights, 62
    in federal grazing program, 63–65
    social restrictions on, 86
transferable emission allowance (TEA), 15
transferable right, 62
transitivity, 88

travel costs, vii, 96
Truckee Canal, 9
Truckee–Carson Pyramid Lake Water Rights
　　Settlement Act, 27(59)
Truckee River, 9, 10
Tucker, William, 223(37)

uncertainty, 123
Underwood, Dennis, 224(45)
Union Pacific Railroad, 68
United Four Wheel Drive Associations, 12
U.S. Constitution
　commerce clause, 24(17)
　enumerated powers, 25(34)
　property clause, 6, 25(34)
　supremacy clause, 11, 23(14)
　takings clause, 23(13)
U.S. Olympic Committee, 129(13)
*United States* v. *Brown*, 25(32)
*United States* v. *California*, 22(3)
*United States* v. *Coleman*, 50(22), 199(31)
*United States* v. *Fuller*, 77(20)
*United States* v. *Locke*, 23(9)
*United States* v. *Midwest Oil Co.*, 53(80),
　　54(101)
*United States* v. *Union Pacific R.R. Co.*, 68,
　　78(36), 184
Unlawful Enclosures Act, 77(16)
USDA; *see* Department of Agriculture
use rights
　complete, 62
　to federal lands, 62–66, 102–3, 157, 161
　and Locke, 164
　ownership as bundle of, 72, 101
　secure, 62–63
　transferable, 62
USFS; *see* Forest Service
Utah, 5, 22(7), 25(34), 26(35), 30, 47, 49(8),
　　66, 95, 115, 120, 131(41), 170, 220
Utah Wilderness Coalition, 47, 55(116)
utilitarianism, 135–36
　act, 135, 137–38
　and argument from productivity, 135, 156
　classical; *see* classical utilitarianism
　and desert, 138
　and dignity, 149
　and motives, 138
　preference; *see* preference utilitarianism
　and rational agency, 145
　and respect for persons, 140
　and rights, 141
　rule, 136–38, 153(8), 156
　and self-concern, 139
　and virtue, 139, 186
utility, 135–36

function, 144
interpersonal comparison of, 147–48,
　　154(35)
monster, 108(29)
*see also* happiness

Vale, Thomas, 120
valid existing rights (VER), 51(44), 223(27)
value
　economic, 132
　and individual preference, 69
　judgments, 133
　of life, 93, 97
　objective, 134, 152(5)
　present, 123
　subjective, 134, 152(5)
　and valuation, 136
　*see also* individual good; social good
values; *see* citizen interests; cultural values;
　　natural values
*Van Brocklin* v. *Tennessee*, 23(14)
*Ventura County* v. *Gulf Oil Corp.*, 23(15)
VER; *see* valid existing rights
verificationism, 154(35)
Vermont, 74
virgin lands, Soviet, 13
Virgin River, 106(21)
virtue, 136, 186
visibility
　auction, 112, 129(11)
　and consumer sovereignty, 212
　in National Parks and Wilderness Areas, 6,
　　24(21), 86, 105(11), 112, 212
Voght, Hildamae, 25(33)
voters, 66, 181, 198(20)
Voyageurs National Park, 23(13)

Wald, Johanna, 204, 221(10)
Walt Disney Productions; *see* Mineral King
War of Independence, 4, 31, 32
Washington, 23(7), 220, 226(73)
Washington (DC), 4
Washington County (UT) Water
　　Conservancy District, 95, 97
waste
　in commons, 59
　in disposal era, 38, 57
　of freedom, 151
　government, 180
　by incomplete rights, 63
　by insecure rights, 64–65
　of means, 142
　by non-transferable rights, 64
　of one's life, 161, 175
　and productivity, 82

water, 5, 9–10, 210–11
*see also* water rights; federal water projects
water rights
adjudication of, 210, 224(47)
and grazing rights, 27(67)
implied federal, 9
junior, 210
prior appropriation doctrine, 9
senior, 210
Spanish, 210
state allocation of, 26(54)
transferability, 210, 224(45)
waterfowl habitat, federal acquisition of, 43
Watt, Interior Secretary James
on Grand Canyon, vii
and Sagebrush Rebellion, 7, 26(36)
wealth
and action, 184–85
and CV, 100
distribution of, 181
notions of, 184–85
Posner's notion of, 99–100
wealth change, 99, 185
wealth maximization, 99
and animals, 145
and range management, 121
rationalization of, 134–35
Weeks Forest Purchase Act, 38, 51(44)
Weinberger, Defense Secretary Casper, 187,
198(19)
welfare; *see* individual good
welfare economics, and welfare, 183
Wenatchee (WA), 226(73)
West Coast Alliance for Resources and
Environment, 215
West, Neil, 131(41)
West Virginia, 50(32)
Western Cattlemen's Association, 65
Weyerhauser Corporation, 58
White River National Forest, 68
Wild, Free-Roaming Horses and Burros Act,
24(19)
wilderness
and bettering desires, 171–72
as resource, 82
statutory definition, 46
Wilderness Act, 46
judicial interpretation, 68
and marketization, 206–7
mining provisions, 46, 223(27)
motor vehicle provisions, 6, 25(30)
and proposed Commodity Use System,
28(74)
Wilderness Areas
hunting and fishing in, 25(33)

justification of, 204
marketization of, 206–7
permitted uses of, 46
privatization of, 7, 101, 108(31), 223(37)
Wilderness designation
as locking up resources, 47
and release language, 212
Wilderness Preservation System, ix, 12,
46–47, 212
Wilderness Society, 70
wildlife
buffalo, 43, 59
burro, 5, 24(19), 101
cui-ui, 9–10
desert bighorn sheep, 89, 118
desert tortoise, 56
elk, 64
endangered; *see* endangered species
grizzly bear, ix, 112, 206
heron, 43
horse, ix, 5, 24(19), 101
management of, 5, 24(18), 24(19), 43
and marketization, 206–7, 222(22),
223(25)
ownership of, 5, 24(17)
passenger pigeon, 59
red-cockaded woodpecker, 222(22)
salmon, 43, 216
spotted owl; *see* northern spotted owl
waterfowl, 10, 43
wolf, 81
*see also* ANWR; fishing; hunting; National
Wildlife Refuges
Wildlife Refuges; *see* National Wildlife
Refuges
willingness-to-pay
and ability to pay, 19
and intensity of desire, 147, 192
and willingness to accept, 208, 223(38)
*see also* MWTP
Wind River Mountains, 220
Winnemucca Lake, 10
*Winters* v. *United States*, 27(55)
Wise Use movement
on below-cost timber sales, 221(10)
and economic rationality, 204
on environmentalists, 12, 169
funding, 17, 30(102)
on Wilderness, 12
wolf, 81
Worland (WY), 225(71)
Wounded Knee, 170
Wyoming, 22(7), 220, 225(66), 225(71)

*X*-future, 137

Yellowstone National Park, 41, 177(8),
    212
Yosemite National Park, 41
    Hetch Hetchy controversy, 42
    and MCA, 219
    Yosemite Valley cession, 41, 53(66)

zoning
    criteria for, 214
    historical, 171
    and multiple use, 67
    of public lands, 213
    and transfer activity, 182